# Literature and Moral Feeling

An influential body of recent work on moral psychology has stressed the interconnections among ethics, narrative, and empathy. Yet as Patrick Colm Hogan argues, this work is so vague in its use of the term "narrative" as to be almost substanceless, and this vagueness is in large part due to the neglect of literary study. Extending his previous work on universal story structures, Hogan argues that we can transform ill-defined intuitions about narrative and ethics into explicit and systematic accounts of the deep connections between moral attitudes and narratives. These connections are, in turn, inseparable from empathy, a concept that Hogan proceeds to clarify and defend against a number of widely read critiques. In the course of the book, Hogan develops and illustrates his arguments through analyses of global narratives, constructing illuminating ethical interpretations of literary works ranging from Shakespeare to Chinese drama and the Bhagavad Gita.

PATRICK COLM HOGAN, Board of Trustees Distinguished Professor in the English Department and the Cognitive Science Program at the University of Connecticut, is the author of more than twenty scholarly books, including *The Mind and Its Stories: Narrative Universals and Human Emotion* (Cambridge University Press, 2003) and *What Literature Teaches Us about Emotion* (Cambridge University Press, 2011).

# STUDIES IN EMOTION AND SOCIAL INTERACTION
## Second Series

Series Editors

Brian Parkinson
*University of Oxford*

Maya Tamir
*The Hebrew University of Jerusalem*

Daniel Dukes
*University of Fribourg*

*Titles published in the Second Series:*

*The Psychology of Facial Expression*, edited by James A. Russell and José Miguel Fernández-Dols

*Emotions, the Social Bond, and Human Reality: Part/Whole Analysis*, by Thomas J. Scheff

*Intersubjective Communication and Emotion in Early Ontogeny*, edited by Stein Bråten

*The Social Context of Nonverbal Behavior*, edited by Pierre Philippot, Robert S. Feldman, and Erik J. Coats

*Communicating Emotion: Social, Moral, and Cultural Processes*, by Sally Planalp

*Emotions across Languages and Cultures: Diversity and Universals*, by Anna Wierzbicka

*Feeling and Thinking: The Role of Affect in Social Cognition*, edited by Joseph P. Forgas

*Metaphor and Emotion: Language, Culture, and Body in Human Feeling*, by Zoltán Kövecses

*Gender and Emotion: Social Psychological Perspectives*, edited by Agneta H. Fischer

*Causes and Consequences of Feelings*, by Leonard Berkowitz

*Emotions and Beliefs: How Feelings Influence Thoughts*, edited by Nico H. Frijda, Antony S. R. Manstead, and Sacha Bem

*Identity and Emotion: Development through Self-Organization*, edited by Harke A. Bosma and E. Saskia Kunnen

*(Continued after the index)*

# Literature and Moral Feeling

*A Cognitive Poetics of Ethics, Narrative, and Empathy*

Patrick Colm Hogan
University of Connecticut

Shaftesbury Road, Cambridge CB2 8EA, United Kingdom

One Liberty Plaza, 20th Floor, New York, NY 10006, USA

477 Williamstown Road, Port Melbourne, VIC 3207, Australia

314–321, 3rd Floor, Plot 3, Splendor Forum, Jasola District Centre, New Delhi – 110025, India

103 Penang Road, #05–06/07, Visioncrest Commercial, Singapore 238467

Cambridge University Press is part of Cambridge University Press & Assessment, a department of the University of Cambridge.

We share the University's mission to contribute to society through the pursuit of education, learning and research at the highest international levels of excellence.

www.cambridge.org
Information on this title: www.cambridge.org/9781009169493

DOI: 10.1017/9781009169509

© Patrick Colm Hogan 2022

This publication is in copyright. Subject to statutory exception and to the provisions of relevant collective licensing agreements, no reproduction of any part may take place without the written permission of Cambridge University Press & Assessment.

First published 2022
First paperback edition 2024

*A catalogue record for this publication is available from the British Library*

Library of Congress Cataloging-in-Publication data
Names: Hogan, Patrick Colm, author.
Title: Literature and moral feeling : a cognitive poetics of ethics, narrative, and empathy / Patrick Colm Hogan, University of Connecticut.
Description: Cambridge ; New York, NY : Cambridge University Press, 2022. | Series: Studies in emotion and social interaction. Second series | Includes bibliographical references and index.
Identifiers: LCCN 2021055365 (print) | LCCN 2021055366 (ebook) | ISBN 9781009169516 (hardback) | ISBN 9781009169493 (paperback) | ISBN 9781009169509 (epub)
Subjects: LCSH: Literature and morals. | Narration (Rhetoric)–Moral and ethical aspects. | Ethics in literature. | Empathy in literature. | BISAC: PSYCHOLOGY / Cognitive Psychology & Cognition | LCGFT: Literary criticism.
Classification: LCC PN49 .H624 2022 (print) | LCC PN49 (ebook) | DDC 809/.93353–dc23/eng/20211222
LC record available at https://lccn.loc.gov/2021055365
LC ebook record available at https://lccn.loc.gov/2021055366

ISBN   978-1-009-16951-6   Hardback
ISBN   978-1-009-16949-3   Paperback

Cambridge University Press & Assessment has no responsibility for the persistence or accuracy of URLs for external or third-party internet websites referred to in this publication and does not guarantee that any content on such websites is, or will remain, accurate or appropriate.

To the memory of my mother-in-law, Kamalavati Pandit,
a moral exemplar

# Contents

| | |
|---|---:|
| *List of Figures* | *page* viii |
| *Acknowledgments* | ix |
| Introduction: What (Comparative) Literature Tells Us about Ethics | 1 |
| 1 Defining Ethics | 9 |
| 2 The Implied Ethics of *Julius Caesar* | 40 |
| 3 Narrative Universals, Emotion, and Ethics | 52 |
| 4 Ethics and Narrative Genre: Some Illustrative Cases | 89 |
| 5 Emotion and Empathy | 150 |
| 6 The Dynamics of Empathic Response: Simulation and Inference in *A Midsummer Night's Dream* | 182 |
| 7 Evaluating Empathy | 197 |
| 8 The Critical Empathy of *Angels in America* | 242 |
| Afterword: The Limits of Ethics: On Free Will and Blame | 260 |
| *References* | 272 |
| *Index* | 290 |

# Figures

| | | |
|---|---|---|
| 4.1 | A possible schematization of cross-cultural story genres | *page* 92 |
| 4.2 | A modified and simplified connectionist model of an anti-Semitic associative network | 145 |
| 4.3 | A modified and simplified connectionist model of the associations fostered by *Nosferatu* | 145 |
| 9.1 | Transcendental freedom (for person A as observer) | 268 |

# Acknowledgments

An earlier version of the *Nosferatu* analysis was delivered as a plenary address at the "Narration, Imagination, and Emotion in Moving Image Media" conference of the Center for Cognitive Studies of the Moving Image at Calvin College, Grand Rapids, Michigan, in July 2004. I am grateful to Carl Plantinga for inviting me to present this work. I am grateful to the participants for their comments and criticisms. It was subsequently published as "Narrative Universals, Nationalism, and Sacrificial Terror: From *Nosferatu* to Nazism" in *Film Studies: An International Review* 8 (2006): 93–105. I am grateful to the guest editors of that issue, Daniel Barratt and Jonathan Frome, for their very helpful suggestions for improving and clarifying the analysis, and to Manchester University Press for permission to reprint.

An earlier version of part of Chapter 3 was published as "Negativity Bias, Emotion Targets, and Emotion Systems" in *Behavioral and Brain Sciences* 37.3 (2014): 314–315. I am grateful to Paul Bloom for inviting my reflections on this topic; I am also grateful to Cambridge University Press for permission to reprint.

An earlier version of a different part of Chapter 3 and part of Chapter 4 was published as "Narrative Universals, Emotion, and Ethics" in *Poetics Today* 41.2 (2020): 187–204. I am grateful to Lisa Zunshine for inviting the essay and for leading me to think more seriously about the role of comparative literary study in ethics; I am also grateful to Duke University Press for permission to reprint.

An earlier version of part of Chapter 6 was circulated at a seminar for the 2020 annual convention of the Shakespeare Association of America. I am grateful to Bradley Irish for inviting me to the seminar and to the participants for their comments and suggestions.

An earlier version of part of Chapter 7 was presented at the 2018 Modern Language Association Convention in New York City. I am grateful to the other panelists – Paul Bloom and Joshua Landy – and to the moderator, Lalita Pandit Hogan, for their comments and criticisms.

I am grateful to Robert Sapolsky for comments on my brief treatment of neo-group selection and to Ruijia Wang for invaluable help with the Chinese in the Yuan plays.

Stephen Acerra, Emily Watton, and Janka Romero of Cambridge University Press have been kind and helpful throughout. Two anonymous referees gave valuable feedback on the manuscript. Finally, Brian Parkinson, Maya Tamir, and Daniel Dukes were generous and painstaking in their reading of and response to the manuscript; they saved me from numerous errors and missteps (needless to say, I remain responsible for any errors and missteps that remain).

# Introduction: What (Comparative) Literature Tells Us about Ethics

Ethics has been a central concern in literature since the earliest works treating the purposes of poetry and stories. Plato famously criticized poets for their inculcation of morally improper inclinations, advocating an extensive state censorship that would enable literature to contribute to the development of ethically upstanding citizens. Plato was not alone. Over the centuries, political and religious figures have sought to control what stories were written or read, in part for moral reasons. In a more liberal vein, the medieval Muslim literary theorists sought to explain the processes by which literary works could cultivate the Islamic virtues (see Cantarino 1975; Ibn Sinā 1974; Ibn Rushd 1966, 1986). The close relation between literature and ethics has not always been viewed as involving the guidance of literature by philosophers or theologians. Sometimes, writers did not privilege philosophy over literature but rather viewed the two as contributing more equally to a program of understanding ethics and behaving morally, and some gave literature a place of particular esteem. Thus, the ancient Sanskrit Nāṭya Śāstra (roughly, *Treatise on Drama*; n.d.) asserts that "drama teaches the path of virtue" (9) and that the study of drama is "conducive to righteousness" (2). More strikingly, Kǒngzǐ (Confucius) urged his followers to study the *Classic of Poetry* (*Shījīng*), explaining, "The Odes serve to stimulate the mind. They may be used for purposes of self-contemplation. They teach the art of sociability. They show how to regulate feelings of resentment. From them, you learn the more immediate duty of serving one's father and the remoter one of serving one's prince" (*Analects* 17.9). Confucian interpretations of poetry particularly emphasized moral themes (commonly through "moral" and "ethico-political allegory" [Cai 2018, 3, 8]). This integration of literature and ethics did not stop centuries ago. A prominent, recent example of interweaving moral philosophy with literary study may be found in Martha Nussbaum's influential explorations of literary works as repositories of nuanced ethical insight (e.g., see Nussbaum 2003).

As these instances already suggest, the study of literature and ethical theory may be concerned principally with literature (e.g., how to evaluate literary works morally) or ethics (e.g., how to think in more nuanced ways about ethical problems in real life). In the following pages, I focus primarily on topics in ethics. Of course, I hope to have something worthwhile to contribute to our understanding of the literary works I discuss – *Julius Caesar*, *A Midsummer Night's Dream*, and so on. But my principal goal is to advance our thought about topics in ethical theory, not about literature.

Whatever one's particular focus – literature or ethics – it is probably also clear already that we can take up two different tasks in examining literature and ethics. On the one hand, we might simply wish to explore what Plato or Kǒngzǐ had in mind in making claims about poetry and morals, or how these claims derived from or impacted the societies in which they were living, or how they reflect the sorts of normative, sociopolitical quandaries that arise in a range of complex societies. These are descriptive issues. In a descriptive approach, we are not setting out to say, for example, what is moral or immoral but merely what Plato thought about the topic, or what Athenians believed at his time, or what similar views thinkers in a range of societies have taken up and debated. As this implies, the alternative to a purely descriptive account is a normative account, considering whether we agree or disagree with Plato and what we would conclude is ethically proper in any given case.

This division – between descriptive ethics and normative ethics – is enormously important. It is certainly recognized in principle by ethicists. But writers often mix up the two and move from one to the other without carefully considering when this is or is not logically valid. This is not simply the result of intellectual carelessness. There are reasons for mixing descriptive and normative concerns that have to do with the nature of ethical reflection (as I will discuss in Chapter 1). However, this does not mean that the distinction is inconsequential. It does suggest that we might wish to consider the two together. But it actually makes maintaining the conceptual distinction even more imperative.

In keeping with these points, *Literature and Moral Feeling* is divided into two parts. The first part addresses descriptive ethics. It also includes occasional elements of normative ethics, insofar as these arise inevitably in a descriptive project; I have tried to mark these explicitly so that they do not distort the (nonnormative) analysis. The second part addresses normative ethics (necessarily with some elements of descriptive ethics). Needless to say, I do not aim to address everything that is covered by these two categories. That would require something more like an entire library rather than a single book. Instead, I focus on two issues that have particular significance in literature. Specifically, I take up and respond to recent, influential – but, I believe, often misdirected – arguments about two topics that are centrally important to literature. These are narrative and empathy. The mutual relevance of narrative and literature hardly requires argument. As to ethics, it has become increasingly common in recent years to link ethical thought and action with story formation. However, the basic terms of such analysis (e.g., "narrative") are often undefined, and the arguments equivocal. The second topic, empathy, bears specially on literature as it is most often the response authors cultivate in readers with respect to the protagonist of a work.[1] In other words, our engagement with a narrative is a function not only of the actions undertaken by a protagonist and the events that affect him or her, but also of just what that protagonist is feeling and our relation to his or her emotion(s). Even more than narrative, empathy has come to be a pivotal issue in recent discussions of ethics, ranging from its positive invocation in Joe Biden's campaign for the US presidency to its harsh criticism in some widely read works in philosophy and psychology. Once the terms have been clarified, narrative connects more obviously with descriptive ethics, whereas empathy regularly has normative implications. I therefore treat them in those contexts.

As suggested by the preceding references to Plato's aims, their relation to Greek concerns at the time, and cross-cultural patterns in ethical reflection, there are different levels at which we may conduct an analysis of either descriptive or normative ethics. Specifically, we might be concerned with the idiosyncratic, moral psychology of an individual. This is to some degree the case whenever we examine a literary work or philosophical argument by a single author. Beyond this, we may be interested in culturally or historically defined patterns in ethical ideas and attitudes. This too is a necessary part of almost any study of a text or set of texts, for we commonly require cultural and historical knowledge to make sense out of such texts. Finally, we might be interested in cross-cultural patterns, aspects of broadly human psychology, or social dynamics that recur in ethical thought and action across traditions. These too are necessary, for we can relate to other cultures, or even to other individuals within our own culture, due precisely to the existence of human commonalities that are specified or particularized in cultures, historical periods, and individuals.

Such cross-cultural commonalities define the most prominent and consequential level of analysis in the following pages, though again they are inseparable from their instantiation in culture, history, and individual

---

[1] The standard treatment of empathy and narrative is Suzanne Keen's extremely valuable *Empathy and the Novel* (2010). Though our projects are clearly related, Keen's focus is very different. She is concerned primarily with literature and readers' responses to literature, not with drawing on literary study to articulate descriptive and normative ethics. The complementary nature of the works, however, means that they can be read together with, I believe, particular benefit.

psychology. The isolation of cross-cultural patterns is made possible only through the systematic study of a range of literary traditions, thus through a (non-Eurocentric) comparative literature. Of course, the isolation of patterns does not constitute an explanation of them. Like much of my work, this project combines literary study with cognitive and affective science. Here, the principles of these fields of research and theorization provide the explanatory framework for the study of both literature and ethics. But this is not simply a unidirectional relationship. A fuller descriptive and explanatory account of literary, ethical imagination and evaluation should not only benefit from cognitive and affective science as they currently stand; it should advance cognitive and affective science as well. In both the literary and psychological projects, the present volume extends the treatment of story universals that I first developed in *The Mind and Its Stories* (2003).

More precisely, Chapter 1 takes up the task of defining ethics, considered as a set of psychological structures and processes. In other work, drawing on Murphy and Hoffman's account of the types of concept (2012, 166), I have argued that the three kinds of categorization process are highly consequential for our response to literature (see Hogan 2016, chap. 4). Specifically, we make use of rule-defined categorization, prototype-defined categorization, and exemplar-defined categorization. In some cases, approaches to ethics are distinguished by their virtually exclusive stress on one or another variety of categorization. For example, at least as commonly understood, Kant's ethical theory is rule-based. In contrast, consider the stress of some Muslim writers on following the path of the Prophet or the emphasis of writers such as Ibn Sinā on literary representations of "the actions of some persons whom others emulate and imitate by following their example in deed" (1974, 102–103). These are cases of exemplar-based moral reflection and response. Other writers refer to more than one variety of ethical discourse, but often only in passing, and with different implications about their nature and consequences. For example, Baker notes, "A community's morality ... may be disseminated as 'dos and don'ts' [thus, rules] or by stories of moral heroes and immoral villains [thus, exemplars]" (2019, 17). In my descriptive account of ethics, all three types of concept enter into our moral responses, which is to say, our moral thought, feeling, and behavior.

In connection with rule-based categorization, I argue that we have broad or fundamental ethical orientations that are guided by the setting of parameters within general principles. These parameters concern such issues as what sorts of action or condition fall under the scope of morality. For example, there appears to be a broad division between people who are principally concerned with ending unjustified pleasure and others whose primary moral worries bear on undeserved pain. I explore this level of ethics in Chapter 1. Chapter 2 develops and concretizes this relatively abstract treatment of ethical principles and parameters through a close examination of the ethical concerns underlying characters' judgments and behaviors in Shakespeare's *Julius Caesar*.

Chapter 3 moves to the level of ethical prototypes, which give needed specificity to the very general ethical orientations defined by principles and parameters. In ethical decision and behavior, we are concerned with sequences of actions and the motivations guiding these actions. In other words, we are concerned with stories. In this chapter, I argue that the prototypes at issue in specifying our ethical orientations are, most importantly, the universal story structures that I have sought to isolate in earlier works, such as *The Mind and Its Stories: Narrative Universals and Human Emotion* (2003). As the preceding title indicates, these narrative structures are inseparable from human emotion systems. In fact, I have argued that story universals are shaped by emotion–motivation systems and that those systems account for their universality. I have also argued in other work that these story genres are of crucial importance for the way we think about and respond to various worldly concerns, such as politics. Chapter 3 extends these arguments to ethics. (As to the remaining, exemplar level of categorization, each particular literary work is itself an exemplar – or a complex of exemplars – not a prototype. I therefore treat exemplars each time I consider a literary work. However, I do not explore exemplars in broad, theoretical terms.)

Just as the second chapter provides a literary development of the relatively abstract first chapter, so too Chapter 4 provides literary developments of the cross-cultural genres treated in Chapter 3. Specifically, this chapter considers literary cases of all the prominent cross-cultural genres, examining their implications for ethical evaluation and action. In this chapter, I treat some works by Shakespeare (due primarily to his familiarity to a wide range of readers).[2] However, to expand the cultural and historical scope of the discussion, I treat a number of earlier East and South Asian works, as well as several modern works from different regions. The longest section develops a particularly detailed interpretation of the sacrificial structure in F. W. Murnau's 1922 film, *Nosferatu*. I undertake a more extensive development of this analysis in order to illustrate more clearly the impact of story structure on moral response.

---

[2] Shakespeare has also received considerable attention for specifically ethical concerns in his plays. For valuable, wide-ranging treatments of Shakespeare and ethics, see Parvini (2018) and Zamir (2006).

Having focused on descriptive ethics to this point, with Chapter 5, I begin the section treating normative ethics, thus what ethical ideas and attitudes I believe should guide our moral evaluations and actions. I am not setting out to articulate anything along the lines of a detailed ethical theory. The purpose of this half of the book is simply to advocate a fairly general criterion for setting ethical parameters (thus defining ethical orientation) and adjudicating among contradictory ethical-narrative prototypes. To put it simply, that criterion is an effortful generalization of empathy. The particular stress on empathy derives from the basic definition of ethics, which I present in the first chapter, before treating the varieties of ethical concepts (i.e., rules, prototypes, and exemplars). Specifically, in that chapter, I contend that ethical decisions are decisions that conflict with what I call "egocentric self-interest." This does not mean that they substitute one form of egocentric self-interest for another (e.g., going to heaven versus committing some sin). It means that, in order to count as what I will later call a "moral choice," one's action must either lack self-interest or escape egocentrism. I argue that all actions are self-interested. (I later qualify this by reference to automatic actions, which we presumably do not wish to count as moral choices anyway.) That leaves only nonegocentric – which is to say, allocentric – options. But it would seem that the only sort of allocentric self-interest we might have is driven by empathy. (There are some other possibilities, such as doing something because God wants one to do it. But my suspicion is that these are either empathic, with the actor tacitly imagining that God will be disappointed, or egocentric, with the actor tacitly considering the otherworldly consequences of his or her action.) This necessarily makes empathy central to ethics, including normative ethics. As such, it makes our evaluation of empathy crucial to normative ethics.

To provide background for my description, explanation, and defense of empathy, in Chapter 5, I draw on current cognitive and affective science to outline an account of human emotion and empathy. I take it that the account I articulate is compatible with what research tells us about emotion and empathy. Nonetheless, it differs from common accounts of both in some consequential ways. For example, I do not view empathy as a narrowly defined concept that refers to sharing the same emotion as a target. Rather, I take it to be a scalar concept that refers, fundamentally, to experiencing the same emotional valence as a target (positive or negative). That positive or negative empathic feeling is based on one's own experiences, which may be more or less similar to those of the target. As the source of one's empathic response becomes more similar to that of one's target, one's empathic experience is likely to increasingly approximate the target's particular feelings (not only the valence of those feelings). In keeping with the pattern established in the first part of the book, the sixth chapter turns to a literary development of the theoretical points, presenting a close examination of *A Midsummer Night's Dream*.

Though the term "empathy" is relatively recent,[3] there has been a long history of valuing the ability to share a target's feelings. (On the importance of distinguishing "the history of the phenomenon" from that of "the term," see Matravers 2017, 2.) The point is by no means confined to the modern West. For example, in the *Analects*, Kǒngzǐ (Confucius) says, "My way [dào] is one thing." One of his disciples explains, "The way [dào] of Heaven [tiān] is loyalty [or devotion {zhōng, 忠}] and empathy [shù,恕]" (4: 15; translation altered from Legge). Zhang elaborates on the latter, writing that "the concept of empathy, shu, is a further extension of the idea of benevolence," with benevolence being the cardinal Confucian virtue. Zhang continues, "The term *shu* means 'to put oneself in the position of another and to look at the world from that perspective .... The character itself combines the graphs for the mind/heart with that meaning 'to be like'" (2003, 285).

Several influential writers, such as Paul Bloom and Jesse Prinz, have recently argued against empathy. In Chapter 7, I take up and seek to refute the main arguments of the anti-empathy writers. For the most part, my contention is that the arguments at issue actually suggest the need for more empathy, not less. Crucially, many of the arguments show the problems with spontaneous empathy. But the whole point of an ethical advocacy of empathy is that we should not rest content with spontaneous empathy but should undertake the effort to extend empathy (e.g., to members of out-groups). Chapter 8 develops these points further in connection with the close interpretation of a literary work. In this case, I have chosen to take a contemporary American play, Tony Kushner's widely admired, award-winning treatment of the AIDS crisis, *Angels in America*. This chapter also develops a concept of "critical empathy" designed to respond to some potential problems raised by critics of empathy.[4]

Since I devote half the book to advocating a particular ethical attitude, readers might reasonably conclude that I feel ethical evaluation is a very good thing. In fact, I tend to believe it is often (though not invariably) good when aimed at one's own actions but almost always a fairly bad thing when aimed at other people's actions. To make matters worse, we

---

[3] It is also ambiguous (see Batson 2009).

[4] Though my concept of critical empathy is different, the general principle is not unlike Jackson's view that "empathy ... should be incorporated into critical reflection" (2021, 113).

appear to have a greater inclination toward the latter than toward the former. In a brief afterword, I turn from descriptive and normative ethics to a third form of ethical study, metaethics (cf. Keown 2005, 21). There, I set out these qualifications, urging that ethical blame should be very narrowly restricted, principally because our attribution of free will should be narrowly restricted.

# CHAPTER 1

# Defining Ethics

Perhaps the fundamental distinction in any study of ethics is that between descriptive and normative ethics. Clearly, ethical evaluations always involve norms. However, a study of ethical evaluations – for example, an ethnographic account of the moral principles affirmed by a particular group – need not take any stand on the "true" value of the acts or conditions being evaluated. For example, when the Pope characterizes abortion as sinful, he is engaging in normative ethics. In contrast, when a historian is surveying the development of Catholic views on abortion, he or she is engaged in descriptive ethics (unless, of course, he or she goes beyond a historical analysis to take a stand on the issue).

This distinction is crucial to any treatment of ethics, and it is important that authors be clear about precisely what project they are engaged in. As I have already explained, the first half of the present volume addresses the descriptive task, while the second half takes up normative ethics. In the course of the first four chapters, then, I hope to identify some key features of ethical thought and feeling in general and, perhaps more importantly, to isolate patterns that differentiate distinct, often opposed, ways of thinking about ethics. Specifically, I hope to clarify, systematize, and explain what I take to be two levels of ethical thought and action. The first level, what I call "fundamental orientation," is very broadly defined by the setting of a few parameters in individual ethical response.[1] That is

---

[1] In speaking of principles and parameters, I am obviously drawing on some of Noam Chomsky's work and the mathematical models he took up to think about language variation. This work was brought into the study of ethics by Marc Hauser. My account therefore has some points of contact with those of Chomsky and Hauser. However, it is important to point out right from the start that my use of a principles and parameters framework is very different from that of either author. Most important, I am not positing innate ethical principles with associated sets of variables. Rather, I see ethical attitudes and values as arising from the interaction of a range of nonethical processes, some biologically innate, some developmental, some deriving from group dynamics, and so on. In this way, ethics is not, so to speak, a biological system. It is rather a set of evaluative responses and behaviors that we can categorize together but that are not a "natural kind" in the sense of phenomena that play a coherent causal role in evolution. (In contrast, various nonethical processes that contribute to ethics do form natural kinds

the focus of the current chapter (with further development and literary illustration in the following chapter). In the third and fourth chapters, I will turn to the greater specification of ethical response in prototype assimilation, specifically attending to the role of story prototypes in construing ethically relevant situations and organizing our ethical motivations and actions in those situations.

In both the case of fundamental orientation and the case of prototype assimilation, I am relying on and extending research and theorization in cognitive science, affective science, and narratology, as well as ethical theory. For the broad division between rules and prototypes, I am drawing on work in categorization, as ethical evaluation centrally involves ethical categorization. In particular, I take up research indicating that we organize categories in three ways (Murphy and Hoffman 2012, 166), as follows: (1) by rules with variables (alternatively, principles and parameters), (2) by approximation to weighted averages (prototypes; for an introduction to prototypes, see Rosch 2011), and (3) by particular cases (exemplars). In the sciences, we typically try to define categories strictly in terms of rules with variables. For example, a chemical element has a fixed number of protons, but isotopes of the element vary in the number of neutrons. In ordinary speech, we tend to rely more on average cases. To take the standard example, we tend to think of birds as, roughly, things like robins. Thus, some cases of birds are more "bird-like" or prototypical than others. For instance, we would consider a sparrow to be a "better" case of a bird than a chicken or a penguin. The prototype is a *weighted* average because the psychological processes that produce prototypes enhance the contrast with opposed categories. To take another standard example, lettuce is identified as a highly prototypical diet food (Kahneman and Miller 1986, 143). But lettuce's zero-calorie value clearly enhances the contrast between diet and non-diet foods. Diet foods have fewer calories than comparable non-diet foods, but they almost always have some calories; their average caloric value is not zero. Similarly, our prototypes for male and female tend to be more "masculine" and more "feminine" than average. Categorization by exemplars – similarity to a prominent, specific case – is very important, including for ethical study. As already noted, I will not discuss it as a theoretical topic here. However, all the literary works I consider are particular cases, thus operating as

in this sense; these nonethical processes would include theory of mind [ToM], affective empathy, particular causal inference, and others.) Moreover, I am skeptical about the ways in which Hauser – and, indeed, most evolutionary and empirical ethicists – gathers relevant data. For example, I do not trust the results of surveys bearing on trolley problems, as will be clear in what follows.

exemplars – or as composed of exemplars – insofar as they, in their specificity, have consequences for ethical response.

The varieties of categorization are crucial to this study because ethical response is, again, inseparable from categorization. I respond to a situation as an ethical dilemma only if I categorize it as such. This does not mean that I have to self-consciously think, "This is an ethical problem" or the like. It merely means that the situation has to activate networks of thought and emotion that are connected via ethical categories, which may be rule-based, prototype-based, or exemplar-based. To take a simple example, suppose Jones is engaged in video piracy. Someone convinces him that he may be caught, so he stops out of fear of unaffordable fines. Smith too is engaged in video piracy. Someone convinces him that this hurts the video artists. Smith feels guilty and stops. It seems clear that Jones's discontinuation of piracy does not involve categorization of piracy as immoral and is not an ethical response (though we would presumably say that the behavior is the same as would have resulted from an ethical response). In contrast, it seems clear that Smith's discontinuation is an ethical response. Moreover, I do not believe that this requires Smith to think anything explicitly ethical. The categorization operates as soon as he (tacitly) connects the piracy with its effects on people and feels guilty. In terms of the analysis developed later in this chapter, Smith's response relies on a fundamental (ethical) orientation toward avoiding harm to others if one has no (nonegocentric) justification for inflicting that harm.

## Some Complications of Descriptive Ethics

Again, this and the following three chapters treat descriptive ethics, focusing on some significant, literature-relevant consequences of categorization processes. However, as noted briefly in the introduction, there are difficulties with entirely segregating descriptive ethics from normative ethics. Specifically, I (like everyone) have my own preferences regarding ethical values, and I am necessarily concerned with the normative issues that are addressed by the ethical responses I am describing. These preferences turn up in two ways. First, and most obviously, they turn up in my explicit, self-conscious statements about, and arguments regarding, moral values that I advocate. These statements are part of the book's attention to normative ethics. These self-conscious attitudes might in principle distort my descriptive and explanatory account of ethics. But it does not seem terribly hard to segregate my explicit preferences from, say, claims that various sorts of ethical preference (including those I advocate and those I reject) may be understood in terms of narrative prototypes and dominant emotion systems. For example, my obvious leaning toward the ethics associated with romantic emplotment does not appear to inhibit my identification and analysis of other ethical attitudes, such as those associated with heroic emplotment.

The second way in which my own ethical values bear on the present study is more implicit, and thus potentially more troublesome. It concerns the definition of just what counts as ethical. It might seem at first that what counts descriptively as ethical is easy to ascertain – simply include whatever people use the term "ethical" or "unethical" to refer to. Unfortunately, things do not work out that neatly. The most obvious problem is that different languages use different words, and it is often difficult or impossible to find things that we would consider exact equivalents. The less obvious problem is that even people who use the same labels – such as "ethical" – differ in their understanding of the meaning and extension of those labels. (The meaning of a label – or lexical item – is the complex of concepts connected with it; the extension is the set of physical, mental, abstract, or other objects to which it may be used to refer.) It is, then, generally not possible to simply take what everyone refers to as "ethical" or "unethical" and treat the resulting collection as delimiting a unified social or psychological phenomenon.

One result of the preceding points is that writers commonly rely to some extent on their own moral attitudes in deciding even what is to count as ethics. To take a simple example, Jones might use the word "unethical" to cover cases of behavior that are harmless but violate what he admits are changeable social conventions. In contrast, Smith might use different terms – say, "ethical" and "conventional" – for acts that Jones labels "ethical." There are at least two ways of treating this contradiction. One might assume that for Jones, ethics is in reality much larger than it is for Smith. However, this risks overextending Jones's view of ethics, which may in practice be more discriminating than his speech indicates, and indeed it may be more discriminating than he is aware. The other way of treating the contradiction is to assume that Smith's more fine-grained division is shared by Jones, though obscured by the latter's imprecise terminology. This risks excessively limiting Jones's view of ethics, if it is in fact more capacious than that of Smith. My suspicion is that in cases of this sort, we are almost all likely to favor interpretations consistent with our own moral preferences.

So, it appears that, in practice, normative ethical preferences are likely to color our selection of what counts as ethics. Thus, such preferences are likely to affect our descriptive and explanatory projects. However, this is not a reason to reject the distinction. The distinction is deeply important. The likely interference of normative inclinations in descriptive programs actually gives us greater reason to try to hold the distinction in mind, making it as clear and explicit as possible at each point in our analysis, in order to limit confusion between the two as much as possible.

## Some Distinctions That Complicate Both Projects

There are, of course, other distinctions that are important to keep in mind when treating ethics. One of these is the difference between ethical deliberation and character development. Some ethical theories focus on how one should adjudicate ethical demands in particular cases. For example, how does a physician decide which of two people should receive the one remaining dose of a medication that both need? In connection with cases of this sort, it is usual to distinguish two broad types of moral decision as well – deontological or intrinsic and consequentialist. A deontological evaluation would begin from the premise that the ethically right decision has to do with the nature of the act itself. For example, a deontologist might argue that murder of innocent people is wrong, even if the murder would increase the well-being of many other people, prolonging their lives and increasing their happiness. In contrast, a consequentialist would focus on the likely results of each alternative. (There are also intermediate positions. For example, if I understand her correctly, Martha Nussbaum maintains that there is a core of intrinsic ethical rights, but the majority of ethical issues need to be evaluated in relation to the consequences of actions [see 2016, 173–174].)

But, again, our ethical concerns are not solely a matter of specific deliberative choice. Often, our ethical responses to situations are automatic, a matter of responding spontaneously and unreflectively. Robert Sapolsky refers to cases of people risking their life to save someone in an emergency (e.g., a child who has fallen on the subway tracks). When interviewed later, these rescuers regularly say they did not make a self-conscious decision to help but just acted spontaneously (see Sapolsky 2017, 566). This sort of behavior presumably results in part from innate propensities (e.g., spontaneous empathy). But it also results in part from more individual dispositions that derive from upbringing; in Sapolsky's words, an "act of implicit automaticity" is "the product of a childhood in which doing the right thing was ingrained as an automatic, moral imperative" (2017, 593). We often refer to an individual's interconnected innate and acquired dispositions as "character." A good deal of what we think of as ethics is a matter of the development of character. For example, among other matters, Foucault sets out to examine the history of responses to questions such as "What are the means by which we can change ourselves in order to become ethical subjects?" (1997, 265). In doing this, he is not addressing ethical deliberation but character. We see this also in his stress on care of the self (though that may be more prudential than ethical).

In practical terms, focusing on character makes sense. As Sapolsky points out, "It's great if your frontal cortex lets you avoid temptation, allowing you to do the harder, better thing. But it's usually more effective if doing that better thing has become so automatic that it isn't hard" (2017, 671). However, I will be focusing on deliberative ethics. This is principally because, in ethical theorization, deliberation is necessarily more foundational than character. Of course, one's character develops in tandem with one's ability to engage in moral deliberation, and it develops prior to theoretical reflection regarding ethics. But that theoretically informed, critical reflection is necessary to determine just what sort of character development is ethical or unethical to begin with.[2] Thus, we need to engage in ethical deliberation, determining what sorts of action are good or bad, before we can engage in a program of training and educating children so that they will be morally good, which is to say, so that they will spontaneously act morally in particular cases. What counts as moral in those cases is defined by, precisely, ethical evaluation.

On the other hand, it is important to recognize that character development is often central to people's conception of ethics. This may be one reason for some divergences in what people consider to be ethical. In certain cases, the difference may not be precisely a matter of the acts themselves. It may be a matter of whether we trust the broader ethical orientation of the people involved. For example, Haidt tells a fictional story of a man who masturbates with a chicken carcass. He finds that at least some groups of US academics tend to say that the act is disgusting but not immoral, whereas (ordinary or "normal") people tend to say it is immoral (Haidt 2012, 111–112). Roughly the same point apparently applies to Haidt's other anecdotes. For example, one concerns a brother and a sister who have consensual sex once. The narrative fiction putatively covers all possible, practical contingencies, stipulating that they took foolproof contraceptive precautions, left no possibility of discovery, and so on. There are many possible reasons for the divergence between academics and nonacademic (normal) people in their responses to these anecdotes. Perhaps academics are more comfortable with the convention of stipulating that particular aspects of the story are certain, even though they would not be certain in real life.[3] But another possible reason is that US academics are confining their judgment to the specific, deliberative

---

[2] There are other, related possibilities beyond character, such as pride in "moral identity," "a source of moral motivation linking moral reasoning (our judgments about whether certain actions are right or wrong) to behavior" (Hardy and Carlo 2011, 495). These too rely on prior, deliberative judgments, as the preceding quotation indicates.

[3] This is a fatal problem with such famous "trolley" problems as the one in which test subjects are asked whether it would be moral to push a fat man onto the trolley tracks if you knew his body would stop the trolley and thereby save the lives of five people farther down the tracks. In real situations, you could never know such a thing.

choice, whereas nonacademics are implicitly taking into account whether they would trust the moral character of someone who engaged in such an act (e.g., whether they would implicitly assume that these incestuous siblings would more readily violate other, uncontroversial social norms as well). It may be that the responses of the two groups would be more similar if the research focused on our implicit moral trust of the siblings. (I say "implicit," as I imagine many of us would recoil from people who did this, even if we were to judge deliberatively that it does not in fact reflect negatively on their moral character.)

I suspect that most people would take the most important distinction in types of ethical response and reflection to be that between foundationalism and relativism. The former is the view that norms have an identifiable, objective basis, whereas the latter is the view that they are merely a matter of convention, stipulation, or preference. Within this general division, two further subcategories may appear particularly significant. Among foundationalists, we may distinguish theological from secular approaches. Theological foundationalists view moral norms as defined by God or some other transcendent, religious principle. Commonly, the issue of moral deliberation in this context is a matter of ascertaining divine will (e.g., through the interpretation of divinely revealed scripture).[4] Secular foundationalists appeal to some nonreligious absolute, such as the laws of reason; for example, in Kant's view, it is immoral to engage in actions that (roughly speaking) would prove contradictory (1981, 32) if their norm were willed as a general law. The most common form of relativism sees moral norms as varying by society or culture. Each of these approaches has some fairly obvious difficulties, which we can leave aside for the present.

For purposes of the current chapter, the key point is that these different methods of ascertaining what is ethical are likely to be consequential for describing ethical deliberation. In connection with this, I should comment on my own normative view here because it bears on the connection between descriptive and normative ethics, which is clearly important for a book that sets out to discuss both. I myself am certainly not a foundationalist. But I also bridle at the label "relativist," principally as I do not view the ethical customs of a given society as having presumptive validity even within that society. For example, like almost everyone I know, I believe that condemnation of homosexuality is wrong; I do not think that such condemnation is wrong in the United States but right in,

---

[4] In terms of the definition I will propose in what follows, the "allocentrism" of theological foundationalism is often limited to God or the equivalent (e.g., heaven [tiān, 天], in some ethical traditions of China), which then serves as the single, definitive source of all ethics.

say, Iran (see Walsh 2019). Rather, I see myself as holding a third view, different from foundationalism and relativism, a view that I believe is actually fairly widespread, and even defended in different versions, but that is rarely identified and labeled as such.

Specifically, I hold the same view on ethical norms as I do on aesthetic norms (as discussed in Hogan 2016). I do not believe that such norms have any objective existence making them right "in themselves." However, I do not believe that the crucial question is whether or not we can establish a foundation for norms. Rather, the key issue is whether we can make rational arguments in favor of one or another ethical position. I believe that we can do that. Specifically, we can do it through dialogue in which we seek to isolate common presuppositions and then reason over the implications of those shared presuppositions. The method for doing this is actually widespread in ethical theory. It involves considering specific cases, finding out whether we agree on those specific cases, seeking to draw out general principles, testing agreement on further cases consistent with those general principles, and so on.

For example, suppose Jones and Smith disagree about abortion. Jones asserts that the fetus is a human life and that the life or death of one person always outweighs lesser interests of others. Smith responds, "But I don't think you believe that. For example, suppose I needed a kidney to live. You have two kidneys. It would certainly be good of you to give one to me. But do you really think that the state would be justified in mandating that you have to give a kidney to me, since – by your principle – my continued existence would trump any interests you have in keeping your kidney, avoiding surgery, and so on?" Jones may in turn respond, "You are right about the kidney case. But that is because virtually anyone could provide a kidney. The state cannot single me out to make that sacrifice. In contrast, the mother is uniquely able to support the life of the fetus. (By the way, I grant that it should be legal for the mother to have the fetus removed and raised in an artificial uterus, if that were to be developed.)" "But it doesn't really help your case to say that the mother is unique. Suppose I have a vastly rare blood type and need a blood transfusion, and you are the only known person with that blood type. I suspect you still would not believe that the state could reasonably make it illegal for you to refuse to have your blood drawn." (A dialogue of this sort might continue until the parties come to an agreement or discover a fundamental difference in their ethical beliefs.)

One difference between the way I approach these issues and the way many others do is that I take there to be a set of cross-culturally available moral attitudes that are central to our moral thought and action. I am not alone in this view about cross-cultural moral attitudes. It is shared by, among others, some evolutionary ethicists and a number of writers in cognitive and affective science. For example, Jonathan Haidt (2012) suggests something along these lines in his "moral bases." In my account, these cross-cultural attitudes – derived ultimately from emotion systems and bound up with narrative prototypes – provide partial, implicit bases for rational dialogue on moral issues. The general operation of empathy, simulation, and other cognitive and affective processes contributes to the possibility of such dialogue as well. Note that we do not all share equal commitment to all cross-cultural moral attitudes. Thus, there are likely to be some issues – sometimes, many issues – on which two people are unable to find a common ground. For example, I will argue that the bonding of romantic love and the associated narrative prototype favor ethical norms supporting free individual choice and opposing social identity categorization. In contrast, heroic narratives – with their celebration of group pride – tend to purvey norms of in-group loyalty and obedience to social authority. People who particularly stress the former are likely to find it difficult to engage in productive dialogue with people who particularly stress the latter, and vice versa.

As to cultures, they clearly disagree to some extent on the precise norms – thus, the emotion systems and narrative prototypes – they emphasize. On the other hand, there is always some distance between the norms affirmed by a society or any individuals in that society and the norms they actually follow in their daily lives. As Justin Barrett (1999) has argued, there is often verbal conformity to "theological correctness," which is belied by actual practice. The point clearly bears on "moral correctness" as well. In consequence, it is not necessarily true that a difference between two societies' claims about ethics reflects differences in their real ethical attitudes and behaviors. Moreover, even when two cultures genuinely diverge in which moral attitudes they emphasize, the same sorts of ethical attitudes are likely to appear in both societies, even if they do not do so in the same proportions. In short, these recurring moral attitudes enable rational moral dialogue between some people, even in different cultures, while also inhibiting such dialogue between other people, even in the same society.

**So, What Is Ethics, Then?**

Given the distinctions just outlined – as well as others that we will be taking up later – the first proposal I would make is that we should not consider ethics to be a concept with strict necessary and sufficient conditions. We should, rather, understand it as a prototype concept. There are, in other words, concerns that are more centrally ethical than others. In defining ethics, we want to capture the most central cases. Where we leave off on more peripheral cases seems less important, though there will certainly be differences – personal, cultural, and other – in just how much one is inclined to include.

How, then, do we go about identifying core cases of this or any other prototype concept? It is often valuable to consider what sorts of primary contrast there are with a given idea. In the case of ethical decision, there is one clear and consistent contrast: acting out of self-interest. Moral behavior is difficult precisely because it so frequently conflicts with self-interest of some sort. As Schramme puts it, "Moral demands often oppose our own self-concerned desires," such that "morality and egoism are opposing forces acting on the agent" (2017, 204). Roughley and Schramme write similarly that "moral action ... is at least primarily a kind of action for other-regarding reasons" (2018, 6). Indeed, the entire point of having a moral code is to establish a norm that can overrule self-interested decisions and behaviors. If ethics converged with self-interest, we would not need ethics. Ethics would simply be what we did when acting selfishly, which we would do automatically. Or, rather, this would be the case if it converged with what we might call "egocentric self-interest."

I will use the term "self-interest" to refer to any motivation to pursue one's own well-being. I take it that all our behavior is in fact self-interested in this broad sense – though, of course, the "well-being" at issue may be short term, misguided in various ways, or even simply wrong about one's preferences. (To take a trivial example, for years I thought I liked jalfrezi and would order it in restaurants, only to recall upon its arrival that jalfrezi is something completely different from what I remembered; nonetheless, on each of these occasions, I was pursuing self-interest with my order.) I would call self-interest "egocentric" insofar as it is not contingent on the well-being of others. I may act out of largely – perhaps even entirely – "allocentric" self-interest if I am distressed by someone else's suffering and am myself relieved when that person's suffering is alleviated. Many authors refer to this as "altruism." That seems to me reasonable only if by "altruism" they mean behavior that provides one with no benefits beyond relief at the ending of another person's suffering (or, in other cases, satisfaction with his or her joy).[5] However, if one is using "altruism" in the strict, motivational sense – where the agent receives no benefit whatsoever – then this

---

[5] For example, Rottschaefer explains that he uses "altruism" interchangeably with "prosocial." He goes on to define "prosocial intentions and actions" as "those that have the benefit of another as their object" (1998, 86). Rottschaefer also explains that "a survey of studies shows that in adults, empathy ... is positively associated with prosocial behaviors" (1998, 93). For a thoughtful analysis of altruism, though one that bypasses this aspect of the issue, see Kitcher (2006).

characterization seems to me clearly wrong.⁶ If I help a suffering person, I do so because I care that he or she is suffering. Thus, I am gratified when his or her pain is allayed. I am not indifferent. It is only if I am indifferent to his or her misery that I could be said not to benefit from the action in any way. (I leave aside cases where I help the suffering person because I want to be rewarded by God or the like, since these are clearly not altruistic.) When we speak of a conflict or an opposition between ethics and self-interest, we are not generally speaking of allocentric self-interest, but of egocentric self-interest.

With this in mind, I give the following preliminary and partial characterization of ethics, or rather of ethical evaluation and related behaviors: A value judgment and associated action are more prototypically ethical to the extent that they oppose egocentric self-interest. If I am correct that all action is in fact self-interested, then an ethical judgment can have motivational force, and therefore can lead to action, only insofar as it is allocentrically self-interested. Thus, judgment and action are more prototypically ethical insofar as one's (self-interested) well-being is contingent on the well-being of others (thus, is allocentric).⁷ We have the highest degree of ethical prototypicality when egocentric well-being is fully contradicted by the ethical alternative, as when it leads one to sacrifice one's life.

Though my precise formulation is necessarily specific to my analysis and larger project, this definition is broadly in keeping with the observations of many other writers. For example, Haidt's definition reads as follows: "Moral systems are interlocking sets of values, virtues, norms, practices, identities, institutions, technologies, and evolved psychological mechanisms that work together to suppress or regulate self-interest and make cooperative societies possible" (2012, 314). Durkheim similarly writes, "What is moral is everything ... that forces man to ... regulate his actions by something other than ... his own egoism" (quoted in Haidt 2012, 314). Howard Brinton makes the related claim that "in all religions self-centeredness is the chief sin from which all other sins are derived" (1973, 71). The Golden Rule – the paradigmatic ethical principle in Christianity – adjures reversing egocentrism into allocentrism: "Therefore all things whatsoever ye would that men should do to you,

---

⁶ Another use of "altruism" makes sense here but seems irrelevant to our concerns with ethics, as it is nonmotivational. Specifically, De Waal points out that "'altruism' is defined in biology as behavior costly to the performer and beneficial to the recipient regardless of intentions or motives" (2006, 178).

⁷ I should note that this relation may be inverse rather than parallel. Indeed, that is typically the case regarding out-group members, as we will see. However, due to my own ethical preferences, I will most often stress empathic allocentrism.

do ye even so to them" (Matthew 7: 12, King James version).[8] The Confucian stress on shù (恕) or empathy involves the same idea. In a famous passage of the *Analects*, one of Kǒngzǐ's followers asks, "Is there one word which may serve as a rule of practice for all one's life?" Kǒngzǐ replies with the word "shù" (恕), explaining, "What you do not want done to yourself, do not do to others" (15.24, altered from Legge's translation; see also 4.15). The same idea is repeated in "The Great Learning" (*Dà Xué*, 大學, 13).[9] The general idea is consistent with Kant's assertion that one should "act in such a way that you treat humanity, whether in your own person or in the person of another, always at the same time as an end and never simply as a means" (1981, 36; treating someone simply as a means would presumably be a matter of using them to satisfy one's egocentric self-interests). It is also consistent with utilitarian consequentialism, which displaces egocentric self-interest with a calculus of general happiness (in which one's own well-being does count, but only as much as that of any other individual).

Note that this definition or characterization does not bias ethics toward any particular outcome. It is consistent with supporting the free choice of lovers, including choice that violates racial or other forms of segregation. But it is also consistent with supporting the self-sacrifice of soldiers, or the killing of unknown enemies, or the decision of lovers to separate in conformity with dominant racist prejudice. Personally, I favor universalism in ethics and find in-group preference highly immoral. As Patricia Greenspan writes, "The universal element of morality lies ... in its application to everyone, regardless of culture or some narrower set of personal affiliations" (2010, 244). But clearly many other people disagree. As Marilynn Brewer explains, "Research indicates that laypersons ... view ingroup favoritism as normative ... and that they reveal implicit preference for an ingroup member who discriminated in favor of fellow ingroup members over one who behaved in a fair, egalitarian way"

---

[8] See www.kingjamesbibleonline.org (accessed September 2, 2020).

[9] As I discuss in connection with Goldie's views, we usually need to alter our simulation of others' experiences and desires, taking account of differences between us. However, a risk of such "correction" is that it will rely on stereotypes or other false beliefs, thereby increasing rather than decreasing error. As Nickerson, Butler, and Carlin point out, "under certain conditions, people who project their own opinions to others may predict other people's opinions more accurately than those who do not" (2009). On the other hand, it also remains true that "models of others' knowledge that are based solely on one's own knowledge are likely to need some degree of adjustment on the basis of individuating information if they are to avoid being inaccurate in many particulars" (2009, 48).

(2017, 102).[10] Both the in-group favoritism and the universalism count as descriptively ethical by this definition, as neither is simply egocentric.

A further benefit of this formulation is that it both distinguishes and relates ethics and prudence, which is, I believe, appropriate. There is something almost moral about being prudent. Doing what is best for me in the future is clearly not the same sort of thing as doing what is best for someone else. However, "me in the future" is different from me now. To choose the prudent option, I must in a sense choose the well-being of someone who is, so to speak, "less me" than I am right now. Indeed, when I imagine myself in the future, I have to take up empathic processes to try to determine what I will feel in the future, much as I have to do with others (see Soutschek and colleagues 2016; Yong 2016). Of course, the difference is that if something harms me in the future, I will directly feel the harm; it will not merely be empathic at that future time. Thus, prudent decisions remain egocentric, but they are egocentric in a somewhat attenuated sense.

A possible objection to this characterization is that it to some extent excludes forms of behavior that many people would consider ethical, specifically conformity to precepts due to fear of punishment or desire for reward. It makes such behavior prudential, rather than ethical as such. But that seems right to me. At the very least, it seems relatively clear that it is more ethically praiseworthy to help one's neighbor out of fellow feeling than out of fear of postmortem torment. In the latter case, the judgment and action involve a form of egocentric self-interest, even if one that is (again) attenuated.

## Specifying a Fundamental Ethical Orientation

Up to this point, I have only set out a broad characterization of ethics and pointed to a few general parameters (e.g., deontological versus consequentialist) that, when set differently, may lead to different ethical orientations (which in turn will need to be further specified into more particular ethical ideas and attitudes, which I refer to as "prototypes"). Rephrasing the preceding conclusions, I might say that ethical norms are principles that one acts on for nonegocentric reasons, thus reasons other than direct benefit to oneself; more precisely, the actions benefit oneself only as a function of benefiting someone else. This definition is intended to mark a broad area constituting ethical thought in general. Thus, it encompasses a range of contradictory systems, including the entire

---

[10] This is consistent with de Waal's plausible suggestion that "morality likely evolved as a within-group phenomenon" (2006, 53).

spectrum of political attitudes. For example, it includes the Fascist morality of absolute devotion to the state, articulated by Mussolini and Gentile as a "conception of life" that is "ethical" (2012, 6; "etica" [1935, 2]) "in a world sustained by moral forces" (2012, 6; "forze morali" [1935, 2]); more exactly, "anti-individualistic, the Fascist conception of life stresses the importance of the State and accepts the individual only in so far as his interests coincide with those of the State" (2012, 7).

Clearly, then, this broad definition of ethics is too broad to lead to any particular ethical decisions, either spontaneously and intuitively (when we feel a particular action is moral or immoral) or through self-conscious deliberation (as in ethical theory). To get any sort of concrete ethical response, we need to specify the values of some key ethical concerns that vary across moral agents. I have referred to this as establishing a fundamental ethical orientation. It is probably the case that, for each of us, these variables are initially set through developmental experiences in childhood. Those developmental settings are probably enduring and are likely to be crucial to our spontaneous ethical response. However, we may also come to self-conscious conclusions about which settings are valid, as when we engage in ethical philosophy. The unselfconscious and self-conscious settings may be consistent or inconsistent with one another. In addition, both types of setting may vary with context. For example, we might spontaneously evaluate acts in terms of intrinsic morality but adopt an ethical theory that is consequentialist; in addition, our spontaneous evaluation might change in contexts where the harmful results of an action are unusually salient. Thus, there is considerable complexity in the actual operation of these principles and parameters. In this section, I will consider some of the more consequential variables that differentiate kinds of ethical orientation, conceptualizing these in terms of the parametric specification of ethical principles. However, to make clear the basic operation of such parameter setting, I will largely leave aside the complexities just mentioned.

I take three ethical parameters to be particularly consequential for defining types of ethical orientation. Again, ethical issues enter when there is a conflict between our individual well-being and that of others. However, an ethical preference for others' well-being does not tell us how to resolve several difficulties. The first is that other people's conditions of well-being will come into conflict with one another. Our ethical orientation must be able to determine which people should be the object of our ethical concern. Put differently, we need to set a parameter defining who receives our ethical consideration. I refer to this as the *scope parameter*. For example, nationalists confine ethical preference to the nation (and, within that group, Fascists confine it to the state). (There may be scope subvariables that hierarchize nonnational groups as well.) In contrast, ethical universalists set the scope parameter at humanity (or, in some cases, all sentient beings).

The scope parameter alone is insufficient to specify ethical response. Another concern is just what constitutes the "well-being" at issue. We tend to evaluate well-being relatively, not absolutely. This is indicated by the association between well-being and "downward comparison" (see Wills 1981), a feeling of (in this case) in-group dominance in status, wealth, or some other property or condition. It is also indicated by the preference of individuals for establishing in-group superiority over out-groups, even when the absolute level of concrete benefit to the in-group would be higher if the groups were equal (see Duckitt 1992, 68–69). Moreover, except in the case of universalism, the scope parameter identifies preferred and dispreferred groups – for example, the home nation and other nations, respectively, for a nationalistic scope. Once we have a particular set of targets for ethical preference, along with a set of targets defined as falling outside this preferred group, we may be supportive of the well-being of the preferred group or critical of the well-being of the dispreferred group. Specifically, our particular ethical judgments, and the encompassing systems of interlocking principles that they form, tend to stress either pleasure or pain, commonly seeking to confine one or the other to putatively "merited" cases. I refer to this as the *valence parameter*.

As just indicated, ethical preference is defined by reference to group membership – for example, national or racial group membership in the case of fascism. But that is not the same as merit. Whatever scope governs one's ethical orientation, there are some cases of unmerited pleasure and some cases of unmerited pain for members of all groups (though one is likely to be concerned with only some of these cases, depending on how one's valence parameter is set). One needs to determine precisely what constitutes merit. Merit is a function of conforming to a moral precept. Unmerited pain occurs when the target did conform to the relevant moral precept or when his or her violation is considered to be less severe than the punishment. Unmerited pleasure occurs when the target did not conform to the relevant moral precept (e.g., did not get married before having sexual relations) or did not engage in the more morally elevated, benevolent activities (e.g., religious practice or charitable giving) that would ethically justify reward. Thus, one needs a means of isolating what constitutes merit in these cases. I refer to this as the *method parameter*. As already suggested, methods are generally seen as falling into two broad groups: consequentialist (e.g., utilitarian), which evaluates ethical alternatives on the basis of (predicted) outcomes, and intrinsic or deontological (e.g., Kantian), which grades actions on (inferred) intrinsic worth.

In short, I will be stressing three parameters of allocentric judgment and behavior: first, the scope of the targets; second, the valence of the targets' experience; and third, the method for adjudicating among evaluative and behavioral alternatives. There may well be other important parameters. However, it seems clear that these three are highly consequential, even if they turn out to be three items on a longer list. I will consider them in turn.

Before going on to these, however, I should say something about the next level of ethical categorization – prototypes. Though we will not turn to prototypes until Chapter 3, it is important to briefly consider their place in ethical response. As work by Eleanor Rosch and others has demonstrated (see Rosch 2011 and references therein), human beings tend to categorize things and events, concrete and abstract, not by applying strict, rule-based, necessary, and sufficient conditions. Rather, in ordinary life, we tend to categorize by evaluating a target's similarity to some (roughly) average case of a category. Thus, scientists judge something to be a bird by reference to strict criteria, but in ordinary life, we basically judge things to be birds based on their similarity to robins. Likewise, when doing ethical theory, we may evaluate the morality of an act by reference to strict criteria, beginning from the self-conscious version of our ethical orientation. However, when reacting ethically to situations in real life, we are likely to rely on their assimilation to standard cases. In ethical response, the situations and responses at issue are not static things. They are, rather, dynamic sequences of events and (human) actions. The trajectories of such sequences are given in stories, and thus the prototypes that guide our ethical understanding, evaluation, and response in such cases are, most importantly, narrative prototypes.

This is not to say that fundamental orientations do not play a key role in our ethical response. Rather, they play precisely an orienting role, guiding our attention to certain aspects of a situation, tilting our emotions one way or the other, affecting just what narrative prototypes are activated (thus likely to further organize and specify our response), and so on. Indeed, the use of prototypes in ordinary categorization has been overstated in the psychological literature. Prototypes are crucial, but they interact with necessary and sufficient conditions. For example, in ordinary activity, being organic is a necessary condition for being a bird, as opposed to a bird toy or a painting of a bird. (We may speak loosely of these as being "birds," but obviously, if asked, we would all say that a painting of a bird is a painting, not an actual bird.) This sort of interaction between strict conditions and prototypes occurs in ethics as well.

*The Scope Parameter*

Again, the scope parameter sets the extent to which a non-self preference extends ethically. By the definition given above, simply in order to count as ethical, a motivation must be nonegocentric. As a general principle, we could say that acts become more paradigmatically ethical to the extent that they generalize beyond the self up to some ideal level, at which point ethicality begins to decline. A minimal extension of ethical obligation may be to one's immediate family. A broader extension might encompass one's nation, ethnic or racial category, or religion. A still broader category would include all humans. All sentient beings would go beyond even that. In the *Xiàojīng* (*Classic of Filial Piety*), this parameter is set to the family, or more precisely one's parents (see section 9 in de Bary and Bloom 1999, 328; see also the *Analects* 13.18). In Mussolini and Gentile's *The Doctrine of Fascism* (2012), the nation – more exactly, the state – is the definitive level for ethical decision. This means that in cases of conflict, one should base one's ethical decisions on the condition of the nation, not of one's individual family or of humanity as a whole. In contrast, setting the parameter to humanity as a whole would subordinate concerns of the nation.

It is probably obvious that in setting the scope parameter, I favor a very broad scope as morally definitive.[11] In the context of the present book, I will stress humanity as the morally definitive level of generalization. My argument in favor of this is based primarily on the fundamental characterization of ethics. Again, to count as ethical, a judgment and an action must derive their motivational force from the condition of some other person (or other appropriate target). Since the definition itself takes the ethical norm to be opposed to egocentric action, it seems clear that the most paradigmatic target of our ethical concern would be the one that is most fully removed from the egocentric interests of the ethical agent. Families involve more egocentric concerns than nations, which involve more egocentric concerns than humanity as a whole. It would thus seem that the logic of ethical nonegocentrism pushes toward more and more inclusive groups. This logic actually leads beyond species and therefore arguably extends to sentient beings as the proper level for setting the scope parameter. However, there are complications here (e.g., bearing on the similarity between the empathizer's experiences and those of the target, which presumably vary more radically

---

[11] Though this part of the book is devoted primarily to descriptive ethics, I believe it is valuable to inform the reader of my normative views on the parameters and to give a basic idea of my reasons for these views. I say this for two reasons. First, I serve as an illustration of the description, which is of course relevant to the descriptive part. Second, I will not be focusing on fundamental orientation – or even prototypes – in the normative part, so it is more fitting to sketch my normative views on these topics here.

across species than within species). Consequently, I will largely leave aside the issue of species preference.

Before going on, I should briefly respond to an objection that sometimes comes up in this context (see, e.g., Churchland 2019, 160). If I say that the scope of ethics is this broad, does that not commit me to the view that one should let one's child starve to death if it means providing food to two people in Africa? No, in fact, it does not mean this. First, the scope parameter does not mean that there are no social arrangements that bear on ethics. Social organization entails that I have some responsibilities and not others. For example, it may be that, on a certain day, I would do more good by visiting some lonely patients in the hospital rather than teaching my class on empathy, ethics, and narrative. It does not follow that I should abandon my class simply for that reason. Our ethical obligations are affected by social arrangements that allocate obligations, even in cases where that allocation is arbitrary. Clearly, given the organization of society, one has obligations to one's own children that one does not have to others' children. Moreover, socially defined obligations of some sort would bear on the ideal society. If we understand ethical action as the type of action everyone would undertake in an ethically ideal society, that gives further moral weight to fulfilling one's socially defined obligations (though of course in both real and ideal societies, there would be exceptions).

But what about foregoing nonobligatory benefits for one's children in order to benefit unknown people in another continent? In fact, this seems to me a plausible ethical choice, assuming one has already sacrificed one's own superfluous pleasures. (It hardly seems ethical to deny one's children, say, a vacation if one takes vacations oneself.) Of course, socially allocated obligations are not entirely clear, nor are they all equally obligatory. Providing food and shelter are strongly obligatory; providing a college education is intermediate; providing fashionable, prestigeful clothing has arguably no moral weight. Note that moral weight here needs to incorporate considerations of the child's sense of being cherished by his or her parents; it is not merely a matter of some sort of objective need. It does seem to me that giving money to keep someone from starving is indeed ethically preferable to spending money on a vacation. It is even arguable that it is ethically preferable to paying for one's child's college education (again, given the qualification that one has deprived oneself as far as ethically reasonable already), though I personally see educational support as having the stronger argument, given current social circumstances. However, given common social practices, we are likely to count such acts of charity to strangers as morally benevolent rather than as morally obligatory. In other words, even in cases where favoring others over one's own family seems ethically preferable, we are unlikely to judge the kin preference to be sinful; we are more likely to see the alternative as saintly. In any event, it is a preference that we can most often discuss rationally. Moreover, in my view, we generally overvalue kinship relations in this regard and should typically count more actions benefiting non-kin as obligatory rather than as merely benevolent.

These points may be captured by a slight complication of the theoretical apparatus I have been invoking. In addition to the larger parameters, which may be thought of as defining ethical systems, there are also more restricted variables that affect the particular ways in which the systems operate. So the scope parameter fixes the paradigmatic reference level for ethical adjudication generally. However, there are different ways in which this general adjudication could be worked out. For example, societies are typically set up in such a way as to assign different sorts of obligation to different people. In traditional Hindu ethical theory (see O'Flaherty 1978; Parekh 1989), for example, there is the range of "swadharmas," the particular dharmas or duties that apply to us individually, as well as the principles of sādhāraṇadharma or universal dharma, which apply to everyone. The swadharmas include one's particular obligations within the family. In almost all societies, there is some sort of special ethical obligation one has toward one's family. There is also often a special ethical obligation that derives from one's profession (e.g., doctors and lawyers have ethical obligations that bear on their professions and that do not bear on the profession of, say, a literature professor). Just how we set these subparametric variables will determine how we believe someone should act in particular cases of ethical conflict. For example, one's special, socially defined responsibility to one's family may lead one to having certain obligations to them over others even when one's fundamental ethical relation is to humanity as a whole. The scope parameter, then, does not reduce all ethical preference to a single level. However, it provides the broader context in which subparametric variables operate. For example, one's primary moral obligation may be to humanity, but in particular circumstances (e.g., saving people from some natural disaster), one's first obligation may be toward the segment of humanity that constitutes one's family, or some other group for which one has some socially defined responsibility.

*The Valence Parameter*

Our response to other people's emotions is focused principally on valence. Thus, it is primarily a matter of responding to their hedonic or aversive experiences. The point appears to hold both in general and for ethical response in particular. As indicated by the basic characterization of ethics as allocentric, what makes a given act ethical or unethical is necessarily its relation to other people or to other sentient beings. For example, stealing a necklace from a storefront display is immoral not because the vandals have been mean to windows or jewelry, but because their actions on windows and other items have consequences for people. Those consequences are presumably painful in this case. If we are considering a case of generosity, rather than vandalism, then the consequences would presumably be pleasurable for some other people. In principle, we could all have ethical concerns for both the pleasures and the pains of other people. Indeed, this strikes me as preeminently sensible. However, it seems that we tend to focus our ethical interests on one or the other, though the point does not appear to have been widely recognized. Specifically, our ethical response to other people tends to focus on the degree to which those people may be considered to merit some quality of experience. To put the point simply, some of us appear to be most concerned to restrict unmerited pleasure; others appear to be most concerned to restrict unmerited pain. In some cases, these orientations produce the same or nearly the same result. For example, moral judges of both persuasions would condemn the theft of jewelry. The anti-pleasure group would grudge the thief the unmerited enjoyment of the necklace. The anti-pain group would pity the shopkeeper for his or her undeserved loss of the investment. In other cases, however – for example, in moral assessments of consensual sexual indulgence – the orientations will diverge.

I imagine it will not come as a surprise to any reader that I am in the second group. My argument for this is twofold, concerning both the ethics of hedonic restriction (against unearned pleasure) and the ethics of relief (against undeserved pain), as we might call them. The ethics of relief is somewhat simpler, so I will begin with it. The desire to lessen or end someone else's pain is generally an empathic response. In some cases, it may be an egocentric response to one's own personal distress (e.g., when one cannot simply leave the situation). But most often it is empathic. As such, it is highly prototypical for ethical allocentrism.

The ethics of hedonic restriction, on the other hand, seems to be routinely connected with egocentric motives, most obviously envy (for unmerited wealth or social status), jealousy (for unmerited love), or disgust (for unmerited physical enjoyments, especially sexual, but also gustatory). Indeed, in the case of moral condemnations of pleasure, it seems to me often very difficult to separate a nonegocentric component from a person's own feelings of deprivation and resentment. For example, I am often unhappy when literary "theorists" receive great adulation for analyses that I believe are muddled and lead to badly mistaken conclusions. This is in part an ethical attitude, and I do not wish to deny that there are ethical issues bearing on elevation in social prestige, which typically goes along with increased wealth and power as well. However, it does not take a psychoanalyst to figure out that my animus against such celebrated figures is inseparable from my feeling that my own (lucid and insightful?) analyses are (woefully?) underappreciated. Moreover, insofar as these concerns can reasonably be judged to have genuine ethical force, it seems that such force is largely a matter of harm anyway – the harm done to theorists who do not receive the advancement needed to continue their work, the harm to other academics who are deprived of the possible insights, and so on.

But, of course, as with the other parameters, this is not even close to a definitive argument. It is merely an indication of why we might reasonably prefer an ethics that seeks to limit harm over an ethics that focuses on limiting pleasure. I believe this is also consistent with the general asymmetry between pleasure (to which we readily habituate, so that the initial experience stops being pleasurable) and pain (to which it is much more difficult to habituate), as well as that between opportunities and threats.

*The Method Parameter*

The most complicated of the three parameters, at least in my own reflections and attitudes, is that of method. Indeed, in this case, the necessity of subparametric variables becomes abundantly clear. The first parameter setting is one in which one defers to a moral authority or, alternatively, assumes the individual's ability to make moral judgments and infer moral precepts himself or herself – roughly, ethical heteronomy versus ethical autonomy. For example, someone with the former ethical orientation may take morality to be defined by the prescriptions of a sacred text. Of course, things do not stop there. Subparametric variables include new versions of heteronomy versus autonomy. For example, in interpreting the sacred text and in applying it in particular situations, one may defer to canonical commentaries or engage in interpretive effort oneself. I will largely ignore this parameter, as I am interested in autonomous moral responses. This in in part due to my own ethical preferences. But it is principally due to what I see as a general human propensity to assume moral autonomy in intuitive moral responses. We may assert adherence to an exogenous moral code, and indeed that moral code may make some difference, particularly in our self-conscious judgments. But it seems that our (tacitly autonomist) spontaneous judgments are primary and that we interpret our external moral laws in such a way as to make them fit our intuitions, rather than abandoning the latter when they do not fit the external system. Notorious cases include the convoluted justifications of aggression by Christians (i.e., followers of Jesus, who advised turning the other cheek [see Matthew 5:39], not, say, dropping cluster bombs). (See Haidt 2012, chap. 2 for empirical research supporting this view.)

Setting aside autonomy/heteronomy, then, the main issue in method (as I am using the term here) is the degree to which one conceives of acts as intrinsically ethical or unethical and the degree to which one conceives of ethicality as a function, not of the acts themselves, but of the outcome of the acts. To complicate matters, not everything falls neatly into one of these categories. There are also mixed cases, such as Nussbaum's advocacy of a core of rights (which define intrinsic moral values) integrated with a wide-ranging consequentialism (2016, 173–174). A particularly important mixed case is the ethics of care. In that case, the parameter is set to "intrinsic" for the core value of care about particular persons in a given situation, but the response following the cultivation of such care is consequentialist (at least in the cases I am familiar with).[12] Alternatively, one could say that almost all approaches are mixed, assuming some intrinsic value or values and supplementing those with attention to consequences. For example, utilitarians mandate utility maximization as their intrinsic good, leaving all the rest to consequences. Indeed, even Kant would seem to rely on some sense of consequences. For example, how can one possibly attend to treating someone as an end or as a means without considering the consequences of one's acts? Moreover, Kantian universalization explicitly relies on hypothetical consequences.

One reason this is a difficult parameter to discuss is that, I suspect, people's preferences in this case are less clear and less stable than in the cases of scope and valence. In other words, I imagine that we are all inclined to accept some intrinsic values and some consequentialist concerns, but not always consistently. Nonetheless, for ease of exposition, I will treat these alternatives as if they were as clearly separated in practice as they are in concept.

There are many arguments for and against both approaches. For example, as to deontology, few people are willing to agree with Kant that one is morally obligated to tell the truth about the hiding place of an innocent man who is being sought by a murderer (see "On a Supposed

---

[12] Care ethicists are often opposed to being characterized in terms of these two categories. I believe that this is a mistake and results in explanations of care ethics sometimes having a paradoxical quality. For example, in his valuable treatment of care ethics and empathy, Hamington asserts that "care does not take a preemptive formulaic approach to right action." But, in the immediately following sentence, he also asserts that "the care giver must be attentive and responsive to the other"; the "must" here is clearly moral and defines a preemptive formula for right action. He goes on to explain that "the moral concern is for the other" (2017, 265), which clearly implies an intrinsic value.

Right to Lie" in *Grounding* 1981, 63–67).[13] Note that this view is not a unique result of Kant's specific deontology. Someone committed to divine determination of moral value might find textual support for the view that lying (or bearing false witness) is morally wrong without exception. It is arguably the sort of problem that is likely to arise in relation to a range of intrinsic ethical orientations.

On the other hand, cases like the murderer seeking a victim – where the (evil) consequences are apparently quite clear – are not common, and that poses problems for consequentialism. Most often, the ramifications of an act are too complex and diffuse to make sense of beforehand. For example, the Nazi regime in Germany was obviously morally repulsive. It was also engaged in invading other nations. Going to war against Nazi Germany seems to be the one case of war that even the strictest pacificsts tend to agree was apparently necessary. In this case, the standard argument would be that at the time when the United States decided to enter the war, it seemed likely that this entry into the war was necessary on consequentialist grounds. Moreover, despite the incredible complexity of war, it appears retrospectively that such a consequentialist assessment was correct. However, we do not in fact know what would have happened if the United States had not entered the war but had undertaken some nonviolent (or at least less violent) alternative. For example, Robert Paxton (2005) notes that the Nazi "policy of expulsion" of Jews gave way to "a policy of total extermination," and that change needs to be accounted for. He goes on to explain that "a recent plausible theory locates" the change in December 1941, in Hitler's "reaction to the entry of the United States into the war and its transformation into a truly worldwide conflict. Hitler would thus be fulfilling the threat he made in a speech on January 30, 1939—that if the war became worldwide, the Jews were to blame and would pay (Hitler believed Jews controlled American policy)." I do not know enough to have a worthwhile opinion on this theory. The point is that something like this could turn out to be true, thereby potentially undermining even the most apparently uncontroversial consequentialist inferences.

Here, we might recall Gandhi's advocacy of nonviolence in resisting Nazism (see Kling 1991). Gandhi is often criticized or simply dismissed as naïve for this view. But, even on the face of it, one has to admit that the military response to Hitler, though successful in ending Nazism eventually, hardly prevented atrocities. Put crudely, the military approach succeeded only after millions upon millions had been killed.

---

[13] Varden has argued that Kant's claim has been seriously misunderstood. I adopt the common interpretation of Kant's view here because it poses an apparently greater challenge to the universalism I am advocating.

It is not necessarily obvious that a Gandhian approach would have led to more deaths. Of course, the idea is that the Nazis would never have stopped exterminating people and simply would have added the nonviolent protesters to the (ever-lengthening) list of victims. But, as Kling points out, there was a famous case of nonviolent resistance in Berlin in 1943. Jewish men married to non-Jewish women were arrested and imprisoned for deportation. But 6,000 women went to Rosenstrasse, where the men were housed, and refused to leave. They did not have grenades and machine guns. They did not throw bombs. But the Nazis eventually backed down and released the men. (Margarethe von Trotta made a fine film of the incident in 2003.) This at least appears to suggest that the outcomes of a nonviolent response to Nazism may have had a reasonable chance of success, possibly even at much less cost than resulted from the military option (a point suggested by Paxton 2005 as well; see Sinclair 2017).

Moreover, in such political cases as the decision of a government to enter a war (as opposed to an individual's personal decision about a private matter), our understanding of consequences is rendered even more uncertain and distorted by the interests of the political leaders and conflicting groups involved. Consider, for example, a standard case of "humanitarian [military] intervention" – the NATO attack on Serbia. Extensive Serbian atrocities are widely cited as evidence that "humanitarian intervention" was needed in that case. ("Intervention" in this context means military action, not diplomacy or other nonviolent forms of response.) However, as Chomsky (2002) has shown, for the most part, the Serbian atrocities cited retrospectively in justification of NATO bombing did not precede that bombing. Rather, the atrocities in question were provoked by the NATO attacks, as NATO leaders actually predicted beforehand. (Unsurprisingly, all sides had committed atrocities earlier, but that hardly supported bombing Serbia specifically.)

The preceding examples suggest that there are problems with both deontological and consequentialist approaches. My preference is to set the parameter to "deontology." As a default position, I believe that the ethical status of the act should be decisive. Or, rather, I believe that acting according to the deontological default is always ethically "safe" and thus not blameworthy. However, there is a subparametric variable here that allows one to override the default for consequentialist reasons. The strength of a case for a consequentialist override is a function of three variables: (1) the degree to which the act in question is unethical; (2) the degree of certainty of the relevant consequences of that act; and (3) the degree to which these consequences would violate ethical desiderata. The consequences in the last case need to be understood broadly, encompassing not only the direct consequences for the people involved, but also such concerns as the impact of having one's action stand as a model for other people (e.g., encouraging others to commit similar [unethical] acts in perhaps very different circumstances). The case for overriding the deontological default (e.g., telling the truth) becomes stronger to the degree to which the outcomes of all possible actions (e.g., lying and telling the truth) seem particularly clear; the outcomes of the default deviate greatly from ethical desiderata; and the intrinsically immoral act (e.g., lying to the murderer) deviates only minimally from the ethical desiderata.

For example, consider Kant's case in relation to these variables, and to my preferred settings of parameters, with intrinsic moral value defined by treating others as ends and not simply as means. Lying in this case would involve not treating the murderer as an end in himself on this occasion, which is unethical, but less unethical than causing someone's death (thereby ending the possibility of anyone ever treating him or her as an end). The likely consequences of both the truth and the lie are fairly clear. For example, it seems unlikely that such a lie would serve to encourage lying more generally. In contrast, the nearly certain outcome of telling the truth would be the murder of an innocent person.

Before going on, it is worth turning briefly to a type of case sometimes brought up in this context. A group of people is hiding from the Nazis. A baby in the group starts to cry. If he or she continues, it is virtually certain that the group will be discovered and then sent to a concentration camp where they will eventually die, after the excruciating experience of the camp itself. The baby will presumably be killed as soon as the group is discovered. For some writers, the ethical point of the anecdote is that there is an ethical obligation to suffocate the child to prevent the group's discovery. For example, this is the conclusion suggested by Paul Bloom's contention that the advocacy of empathy is ethically misguided because empathy is (among other things) innumerate (see 2016, 32–36).

The account suggested by Bloom's arguments, I believe, oversimplifies ethical issues such as this by treating them as if they are a matter of ethical criteria being or not being sensitive to numbers. By the preceding parameters and variables, this case should involve the following considerations. First, the act of killing the baby is an extreme violation of the principle of treating others as ends and not simply as means. Indeed, it is as extreme a single case as we can imagine since it involves the ultimate harm (death) doled out to a completely innocent person (a baby). Second, despite the instructions given with the example, it is never entirely certain in practice that the crying of the baby would lead to the other innocent people being found and killed; moreover, it is similarly unclear that killing the baby would prevent them from being found and killed. Third, any time we justify committing heinously immoral acts in some relatively public context, we risk establishing a precedent for the commission of other, similar acts in the future. It is true that the likely fate of the others (and even of the baby), were they discovered, could weigh in favor of overriding the default of nonharming. But every other morally germane aspect of the situation weighs in favor of maintaining the deontological default, thus against murdering the child. (Of course, this might change in specific circumstances.)

Part of the problem with this and other cases of moral reflection in ethical deliberation concerns the nature of thought experiments in ethics, which tend to stipulate certainties inappropriately. Ethical thought experiments typically follow the general experimental principle of seeking to control variables. This includes controlling for outcomes. For instance, in a famous trolley dilemma, we are told that a trolley is rushing toward four people trapped on the tracks. We are also told that if we push a fat man onto the trolley tracks, he will be killed, but the trolley will be stopped, thus preventing the deaths of the four other people farther down the tracks. To my mind, the key point about this ethical (pseudo-)dilemma is that the whole scenario is wildly implausible. The man would presumably resist being pushed; he might fall only partially on the tracks; and even if he falls fully on the tracks, how can we possibly know with adequate certainty that his body will stop the trolley?

This problem with thought experiments is particularly crucial for evaluating how one should set the method parameter. The nature of thought experiments tends to bias them toward consequentialism. I fear that this may be a problem with literature as well. For example, literature (including films and television programs) about torture often shows us that the suspect really did plant a bomb, really does know where it is and how to defuse it, and so on. It gives us certainty about these issues that no police force is likely to have (in addition to ignoring the tendency of such harmful acts as torture to proliferate once allowed). In contrast, it is usually a central feature of our moral decisions that they are made in conditions of uncertainty.

But, of course, to adopt a deontological orientation, we need to determine what makes an act intrinsically ethical or unethical. Here, I to a great extent agree with Kant, if Kant revised his view in light of the preceding discussion. First, I would say that an excellent rule of thumb is – as stipulated in the preceding examples – to "act in such a way that you treat humanity, whether in your own person or in the person of another, always at the same time as an end and never simply as a means" (1981, 36). This tells us that we should always try to empathize with others and constrain our behavior toward them by reference to their interests, particularly their physical or emotional pain, which we should always seek to minimize (given the "ethics of relief" setting of the valence parameter).

(In addition, given our uncertainties and fallibility, we need to add to this empathy a degree of self-criticism, as I will discuss in Chapter 7.)

Kant's categorical imperative is also relevant here, primarily in indicating that we should not exempt ourselves from general moral principles, as we are very much inclined to do. But it is not relevant in the criterial way that Kant imagined. Kant believed that we could infer moral precepts by universalizing the maxim that covers our behavior in any given situation. But, as a way of deciding what is ethical or unethical, this is notoriously faulty. Most crucially, it sets aside "the problem of relevant act descriptions" (see Nell 1975, chap. 2), which is exactly what the method parameter should address. The case of the murderer leads to one ethical decision when construed as "lying versus telling the truth" but another when construed as "assisting versus impeding the murder of an innocent person." I actually agree with Kant that lying is morally wrong even in this case. Where I disagree with Kant is that I see this as a case of moral conflict. In cases of moral conflict, I give greater weight to the less harmful option. In this case, I favor "impeding the murder of an innocent person" over "telling the truth," principally because the death of innocents is more important ethically than the communication of misinformation.

## A Brief Note on Blame: Character versus Action

I am of two minds as to whether to identify a fourth parameter, which identifies the primary target of ethical evaluation. Personally, I am a firm believer that acts are good or bad, not people. Moreover, I have also argued that our ethical theory must be based on the evaluation of at least some set of behaviors, as otherwise we have no way of distinguishing good from bad characters. But it does appear to be the case that many people think of ethical response and judgment as applying primarily to persons.[14] Indeed, as already noted, I suspect that a distinction along these lines is one reason for differences Haidt found in responses to his anecdote about a man masturbating with a chicken carcass (2012, 111 112) or the one about consensual incest. I suspect that many of the people who saw these behaviors as morally neutral were considering the act (in addition to confining ethics to issues of undeserved pain).

---

[14] This does not contradict the argument just mentioned because even agent-focused ethical response would need to be grounded in a sense that a (good or bad) person is, precisely, a person inclined to engage in particular sorts of (moral or immoral) acts. The difference between agent-focused and action-focused is not a matter of which is theoretically definitive. It is, rather, a matter of what one cares about ethically – what the target of one's emotion is and what one sees oneself as responding to.

In contrast, many of the people who judged the behaviors immoral might have been responding to a sense that the people involved had a bad character.

I do believe that these alternatives (agent-focused evaluation versus action-focused evaluation) are among the most important and fundamental ethical divisions. In that sense, they may be said to define possible parametric values for a fundamental ethical orientation. However, I have not included this as a fundamental parameter per se because I am inclined to view differences on this axis as deriving from other ideas and attitudes. Specifically, I am inclined to infer that we may differ in the degree to which we explain behaviors generally by reference to free choice along with dispositions (e.g., personality traits) versus the degree to which we explain such behaviors by reference to circumstances. It seems likely that an explanatory preference here would orient us toward an evaluative target. Thus, I am inclined to explain an agent-focused evaluative orientation by reference to a preference for dispositional (thus agent-focused) explanations of behavior. Similarly, a preference for situational explanations would seem more consistent with an action-focused evaluative orientation. This is not a specifically ethical parameter as it bears on explanatory preferences that go well beyond ethically relevant actions.

## Conclusion

There is a fundamental distinction between a descriptive study of ethics and a normative study of ethics. Descriptive ethical study investigates what ethical beliefs and attitudes may be found in or across different societies, historical periods, or individual people. It may stress the particularity of some local system, as would be the case with ethnography. However, it may also stress recurring patterns (as in Chapter 4 of the present volume). In contrast, normative ethical study treats what genuinely is ethical or unethical, rather than what people think is such. Ethical differences – for example, that between a focus on moral character and a focus on ethical deliberation – complicate both forms of study. Nonetheless, it is possible to isolate a coherent basic characterization of ethics that will allow discussion of both descriptive and normative topics.

Descriptive ethics proceeds by way of the usual methods of empirical study, conceptual analysis, and explanation through cognitive, affective, historical, or other relevant structures and processes. (The following chapters will stress cognitive and affective science.) Normative ethics cannot be established by empirical study. However, it is possible to rationally debate normative ethics, thus avoiding the apparent arbitrariness of relativism, without assuming some absolute foundation for morality. Such rational debate involves isolating shared ethical responses and

## Conclusion

then identifying and testing principles relative to those responses. There are, however, problems with this method. They include, among others, the artificial and unrealistic nature of the moral cases that ethicists typically consider, as well as the limited overlap in people's fundamental moral orientations even in a single society.

But just how might we define ethics as an area of study? Our actions require motivation and thus emotion. These motivations are always self-interested in that they bear on our achievement of goals defined by emotion systems. Those goals, however, may be either egocentric or allocentric. In other words, they may be contingent upon one's own condition or someone else's condition. Ethics is fundamentally an attempt to limit egocentric motivation and action. Thus, ethical evaluation and action are prototypically allocentric. In other words, they are responses to the emotion-defined goals of other people and thus, broadly speaking, their happiness. This leads to my views, developed in subsequent chapters, concerning the ethical centrality of empathy.[15] This basic characterization of ethics has the salutary consequence that it relates prudence to ethics. Specifically, prudence is closely related to ethics as it involves a form of empathy with a person who is between self and Other – oneself in the future (as opposed to oneself right now).

In considering people's ethical attitudes, three parameters appear to be particularly important. The first is the scope parameter. This governs just what set of targets (e.g., people) are viewed as the proper objects of ethical deference. There seem to be two widespread tendencies here. Some people are inclined to see ethical obligation as strongest regarding groups that are closer to oneself. For example, in this view, one's obligations to one's family are greater than those to one's nation, which are in turn greater than those to humanity. The other tendency goes in the opposite direction, with one's obligations to humanity being greatest. However, in practice these groups often differ less than one might expect since social arrangements assign obligations in ways that do not necessarily track general obligations (e.g., even the most ardent universalist is likely to recognize that social practices commit him or her to providing special care for his or her own children). Theoretically, we may refer to these more specific qualifications on the general ethical orientations as subparametric variables.

A second parameter is valence. We tend to focus our ethical attention on either pleasure or pain and on the degree to which people merit or do

---

[15] It is worth noting that the idea is suggested by several lines of research. For example, as Zaki and Ochsner emphasize, one important evolutionary function of empathy is enabling cooperative activity (see 2012, 207). In connection with this, Tomasello's (2016) linking of ethics with cooperation suggests the centrality of empathy to ethics.

not merit their experiences of pleasure or pain. While it is in principle possible to attend to both, as a matter of fact it appears that most people are particularly concerned with one or the other. Thus, we find two broad types of ethical orientation – ethics of hedonic restriction (in which one condemns unmerited pleasure) and ethics of relief (in which one condemns unmerited pain).

The third parameter is that of method.[16] This concerns the manner in which one determines what is ethical or unethical. The two main alternatives here are intrinsic (or deontological) and consequentialist. The former evaluates acts as intrinsically ethical or unethical, whereas the latter relies on a calculus of consequences. In fact, it seems that both are in some ways intrinsic and in some degree consequentialist. On one hand, the deontological view that Jones does not treat Doe as an end if he plunges a knife into Doe relies on the fact that doing so will cause Doe pain and very likely lead to his death. On the other hand, a consequentialist calculation of an act's consequences for producing or curtailing happiness clearly presumes that happiness has intrinsic value (as it is not a means to something else). The difference between the two methods is in part a matter of which consequences one takes into account. In the deontological case, the consequences are not confined to the case at hand but are generalized to the behavior of all moral agents in an ethically ideal society. In a pure deontological ethics, the important consequences are hypothetical, bearing on what would happen if everyone behaved ethically. In other words, they concern an ethical ideal. Pure consequentialism, in contrast, concerns what is likely to occur in actual, often very nonideal circumstances. A reasonable alternative for this parameter might be that we should generally set it to the "intrinsic" value of an act. But (as a subparametric variable) we may override that intrinsic value in cases where the intrinsic immorality of the act is low, the relevant consequences of all alternatives appear clear, and the likely consequences of the intrinsically ethical act are highly morally objectionable (e.g., when telling the truth would lead to the death of an innocent person.)

A further, important orientational difference is that between agent focus and action focus. An agent-focused ethical orientation concentrates moral evaluation on the person. An action-focused orientation, in contrast, concentrates on the behavior. This is as fundamental and

---

[16] Since this is not a book devoted to articulating a complete system of ethics, there are necessarily many aspects of ethical deliberation that I cannot discuss. However, it is important to note again that I am not claiming these are the only parameters that operate in defining ethical systems. Even more clearly, my brief references to subparametric variables are nothing more than a gesture in the direction of an actual account of such variables.

consequential a parametric division as the others. However, it seems likely to derive from explanatory preferences, favoring personal dispositions or circumstances. Thus, I have not counted it as an ethical parameter per se.

Finally, it is important to add that the setting of parameters is not fixed immutably. It certainly appears as if we all have inclinations toward one or another valence, scope, method, and evaluative target. However, it also appears to be the case that we may change these orientations in different circumstances, with some of us being more or less likely to change than others. One important context for change is self-conscious ethical deliberation. When we reflect on our ethical orientation, we may change it significantly.

# CHAPTER 2

# The Implied Ethics of *Julius Caesar*

Literary works are often pervaded by tacit ethical concerns. In that way, they are like life. We can consider life from an ethical perspective, or not. When we do think about life or literature in relation to ethics, we construe actions, events, and conditions differently than when we think of it metaphysically, or medically, or historically. In this chapter, I set out to think about Shakespeare's *Julius Caesar* as manifesting a set of tacit ethical concerns on Shakespeare's part. Specifically, I see the play as in some measure illustrating a number of the points about ethics sketched in Chapter 1. At this same time, the play not only illustrates but extends and complicates some of the claims articulated in that chapter.

I should stress at the outset that I am not saying Shakespeare was aware of the ethical concerns that manifest themselves throughout his play. Indeed, he certainly was not, at least not in the way I am going to formulate them. But that does not mean his writing and response to what he had written were unaffected by those ethical concerns. Rather, I would suggest that his sensitivity to values and evaluations was so much a part of the way he thought about the world that it would have been difficult for him to be aware of any but a small, even rather superficial part of the play's ethics. Perhaps I am underestimating Shakespeare's capacities for self-reflection in saying this. But, in any case, the point is that there is no need for him to have considered the ethical topics self-consciously. Rather, he simply needed to develop his characters – their feelings, thoughts, and behaviors – in ways that allowed ethical considerations to enter, on their part and on the part of audience members.

### Ethics and Revolution

Before looking at the text of the play, however, I should say something about the story genre and some elements of the history that provide a (largely implicit) background to this particular story. Given that ethical prototyping is the subject of Chapter 3, it would have been ideal to consider a work that explored fundamental ethical orientation in a way that did not require us to refer to prototyping. However, the two are not so readily separable in practice, though they are clearly conceptually distinct. The story of *Julius Caesar*, though based on historical events, largely develops one part of the heroic story prototype, specifically the part that treats a usurpation of legitimate social authority, with its ethical valuing of respect for authority and its setting of the scope parameter either to the national in-group or to the state. This part of the prototype concerns the internal governance structure of the society, its illegitimate overthrow, and (in comic versions) its reestablishment.

One ethically consequential aspect of the heroic structure, one that seems particularly important for historical occurrences, is that it can in principle be used to tell diametrically opposed stories about the same events. In terms of the parameters set out in Chapter 1, it almost invariably celebrates in-group loyalty (thus, national scope) and evaluates acts intrinsically (e.g., overthrowing the socially sanctioned hierarchy is wrong, whatever its consequences for the welfare of the people). In addition, it often denigrates the enjoyment of social status that deviates from traditional stratification (thus, hedonic restriction in valence). However, depending on which camp one favors and thus views as legitimate, it can be used to represent virtually any side as embodying the ethical norm. For example, the story of a popular revolution against a monarch may be told as a restoration of popular sovereignty, long denied through the usurpation of government by an aristocratic elite; alternatively, it may be told as a brutal assertion of mobocracy against the divinely elected order of hereditary rule. Historically, of course, the socially favored view is the one that tends to dominate this sort of emplotment in any given society.

What about *Julius Caesar*, then? It is a commonplace of criticism on the play that it is very difficult to determine just where Shakespeare stands on the legitimacy of any side in the play: Julius Caesar, Cassius and Brutus, or Mark Antony and Octavius Caesar. Perhaps the most common view – which I share (see Hogan 2013, 58–61) – is that Shakespeare's attitude is, to coin a phrase, "A plague o' both your houses" (*Romeo and Juliet* III.i.92). Shakespeare continually teases us with hints about the moral status of his characters, only to undermine those hints soon after. Specifically, the play begins by suggesting that Julius Caesar has illegitimately usurped the position of Pompey (without really taking a stand on the legitimacy of Pompey's own position). Brutus and Cassius then illegitimately usurp Julius Ceasar's position. Mark Antony and Octavius Caesar then continue the pattern by illegitimately usurping Brutus and Cassius. We have to await *Antony and Cleopatra* to see Octavius Caesar illegitimately usurp Mark Antony, but the history of Rome allows us to infer this from the end of *Julius Caesar*.

Does this mean that there is no legitimate leadership – thus, no real ethical norm – in Shakespeare's play, perhaps indicating that all governance is illegitimate and all moral choices are false? I do not think so. To get a sense of the appropriate relations of social organization, we need to consider some unstated implications of the play. Specifically, I believe Hadfield is right in his emphasis on the nature of the Roman Republic, in contrast with the monarchies that preceded and followed it. As he explains, the Roman Republic was "a stable form of state that treated all citizens relatively equally, trusting the senators who met in the Capitol building to determine how the city should be governed in consultation with other officials such as the tribunes (elected by the plebeians to represent them)" (Hadfield 2007, 5). The Republic "was famous—particularly in 16th-century England—as a model form of proto-democratic government" (2007, 283). This was preceded by a monarchy, which ended when Brutus's ancestor led an uprising against the criminal ruler, Tarquinus Superbus (whose rape of the virtuous Lucrece is recounted in Shakespeare's narrative poem). This ending of the Roman monarchy can presumably be identified as the heroic overcoming of a sort of usurpation and the restoration of authority to the citizens. The string of events recounted in *Julius Caesar* shows us the tragic reversal of this sequence, thus the usurpation of legitimate authority.

In Shakespeare's imagination, the usurpation is more complex and extended than is usually the case. The comments of Murellus and Flavius at the start of the play (I.i) suggest that the usurpation begins with Caesar's crossing of the Rubicon. But it continues, rather than being ended, through the murder of Julius Caesar by the conspirators, prominently including the descendant and namesake of the Brutus who led the earlier, Republican uprising. This historical precedent is crucial, for that earlier action – broadly, the uprising against Tarquin – defines an ethical exemplar, a morally esteemed case that may be invoked as a model for subsequent moral action. Moreover, this earlier Brutus stands as a personal exemplar, tacitly serving as a model for the Roman people to oppose and prevent the demise of legal (and ethical) social authority. But it is never entirely clear that the situations are appropriately paired, with Caesar taking up the role of Tarquin. Perhaps the acts of the conspirators are more in keeping with more usual usurpations. One issue here is the motivation of the characters. All the characters justify their acts morally. But Shakespeare repeatedly indicates that these justifications are false: mere hypocritical rationalizations.

In *Julius Caesar*, and in many other works, Shakespeare presents us with what we may call a "critical ethics." In this case, critical ethics involves a representation of putatively moral judgment and action, in which socially esteemed characters turn out to be highly egocentric while claiming some lofty allocentrism (with regard to the scope parameter); where such characters pretend to care about the suffering of some larger group, but are in fact envious of the privileges of others (the valence parameter); and where they engage in versions of the very acts they identify as intrinsically or consequentially immoral (the method parameter). As this suggests, such characters often pervert moral argument, using sophistical techniques to convince others rather than trying to reach valid moral conclusions. More generally, critical ethics is an attempt to deal with the problem that moral judgment appears to rationalize a great many immoral acts and to motivate very few moral ones. (We will consider this problem in the Afterword.) I take Shakespeare's view to be critical, rather than merely cynical, as the presupposition throughout is that genuine ethical dialogue, judgment, and action are indeed possible, though unfortunately rare.

This assassination clearly would not have happened without Caesar's own conflict with Pompey. The conspiracy and assassination, in turn, provide Octavius and Mark Antony with an opportunity and an excuse to kill off their political enemies, and then eventually for Octavius to establish the Roman Empire. However, even this view of legitimate authority is tempered by the fact that the ordinary people appear to be untrustworthy and cruel (as do the elite). They contribute to the end of the Republic as much as anyone. As we will see (in later chapters of this book), this is in part due to inhibitions on empathy, which are commonly related to out-grouping.

## Shakespeare's Words

We may now turn to Shakespeare's text, looking at some details of his implicit, critical ethics. The first scene presents us with two tribunes, "elected representatives of the commoners" (Hadfield 2007, 42). Shakespeare stages a conflict between the tribunes and some working people ("petit bourgeois craftspeople," in Marxist terminology). The tribunes criticize the people for failing to obey sumptuary laws. The people respond with verbal wit that simply confuses their social superiors, who are cognitively rather less supple. In part, this linguistic cleverness serves to provide humor and to establish the intellectual capacities of the ordinary folk. (This is important insofar as it suggests that they are capable of greater intellectual discrimination than they exhibit in their political attitudes over the course of the play.) But the precise nature of the wordplay is also important. The cobbler jokes that he is "a mender of bad soles" (I.i.14). Thus, he can "mend" the tribune (I.i.17). At one level, he is merely saying that he can repair the tribune's shoes (perhaps a greater service than what the tribune provides for the cobbler). But the exchange also suggests that there might be some fault in the tribunes' souls (and not merely their soles). The point is perhaps not so much to suggest that the cobbler is morally superior as it is to suggest that the tribune's indignation over a possible violation of a dress code is pseudo-moral, the elevation of a convention to the level of a moral precept. It thereby suggests the question of just what should constitute an ethical issue. For an ethics that is deeply bound up with group identity and social hierarchy (thus with in-group pride and respect for authority), dressing in accordance with such identity and hierarchy can indeed count as moral or immoral (just as dressing "obscenely" is a moral issue for an ethics closely connected with sexuality and disgust).

Things change, however, when we learn that the tribunes are chiding the people for their support of Caesar. Previously, they were happy to cheer Pompey (who "was associated with the defense of the Republic"; Hadfield 2007, 44). But now they celebrate Caesar for his prosecution of a civil war that threatened the very existence of the Republic. One of the most striking points they make is that the captives Caesar parades through Rome in humiliating subjection are themselves Romans (I.i.31–33). The criticism here is threefold. First, there is a prudential point – that the people are acting against their own long-term interests by celebrating Caesar, who is likely to prove an instrument of their disenfranchisement. Again, this is semi-moral in that concerns about one's future self are less fully egocentric than concerns about oneself right now. The second and third criticisms concern disloyalty. One is a matter of fundamental orientation bearing on the scope variable. The people have failed to maintain the appropriate level of in-group loyalty to other Romans. They are exalting a military leader who has fought a civil war against his own nation and has killed, imprisoned, and humiliated Romans. The final criticism addresses a violation of social hierarchy at the prototype level, relating to the heroic prototype. Specifically, the people are disloyal to an individual – Pompey – and thereby may be understood as showing inadequate respect for social hierarchy. In a development that subsequently appears to verify their prudential forebodings and their moral objections, the tribunes are severely punished for opposing popular adulation of Caesar (I.ii.287–288).

An apparent confirmation of the threat posed by Caesar and of the imprudence of ordinary people comes when Mark Antony offers Caesar a crown and the crowd calls out in an expression construed by Brutus as "applauses .../For some new honors that are heaped on Caesar" (I.ii.135–136). However, it turns out that things are not so simple (unsurprisingly, given Shakespeare's usual practices). First, Caesar refuses the crown. Second, the multitude apparently cheers, not the offer of a monarchy, but Caesar's refusal. There are also some small acts of Caesar's that suggest his character may not be without admirable qualities and thus that the judgments of the tribunes may have been unfair. For example, in contrast with the deceit of the conspirators, Caesar will not send a lie to the senate (II.ii.65). When faced with a petition bearing on his own well-being, he insists, "What touches us ourself shall be last served" (III.i.8). There is also something to be said for Caesar's insistence that he will not succumb to flattery; he will not reject what he takes to be fundamental principles in order to favor an importunate companion (see III.i.35–39). In contrast, the conspirators seem to condemn him for not facilitating nepotism. Note that nepotism is either an ethical violation in being egocentric or a violation of national obligations by setting the scope parameter to privilege family above the nation or the state. Moreover, this refusal of nepotism does not mean that Caesar falls short in his ethical response to close personal relations. For example, Caesar also appears to have the most companionate relationship with his wife.

Of course, Shakespeare makes it clear that Caesar is no idealized, moral exemplar. Indeed, the absence of general moral exemplars is characteristic of a critical ethics (though characters may still be exemplary in a particular relationship or act, as with the earlier Brutus). We see the criticisms of Caesar not only in the references to Pompey, but also in various observations by other characters. For example, Cassius comments that Caesar has come to be viewed as "a god" (I.ii.118). Henry Burton points out: "The Roman worship of rulers began with Julius Caesar. Divine honors were paid to him during his lifetime" (1912, 81). Cassius is surely correct that the apotheosis of a leader does not bode well for the continuation of a Republic. This is a profoundly sinful – even Satanic – development for a Christian audience of Shakespeare's time and a reminder of the usurpation of the Republic that followed soon after the events of the play.

But, here too, there are complications. It is immediately clear that Cassius envies Caesar his popular elevation. In effect, Cassius claims that he is more deserving than Caesar, suggesting the resentment of (putatively) unmerited enjoyment, in this case the enjoyment of status. In connection with this, Cassius does not address Caesar's military successes; his own later performance on the battlefield may suggest that Cassius does not merit the esteem in this area that is the first source of Caesar's stature. Rather, he claims to be superior to Caesar on the basis of an anecdote about a swimming contest in which the two of them engaged (I.ii.102–120). He does appeal to the importance of preserving the Republic, but this seems to be little more than a rationalization of his egocentric self-interest. In short, he poses the issue of *what to do about Caesar* as if it were an ethical dilemma. It may be such a dilemma, but that moral issue has virtually nothing to do with his actual emotional response to Caesar, and thus his motives for the assassination. Moreover, he violates basic principles of rational moral dialogue in trying to convince Brutus to join the conspiracy. This occurs most obviously when he deceives Brutus about popular attitudes by sending him messages as if they came from a range of concerned citizens (I.ii.317–322).

Initially, Brutus's case seems more straightforward. He explains that he is concerned with "the general good" (I.ii.87), thus allocentric rather than egocentric benefits. Moreover, at the end of the play, Mark Antony echoes this assessment, and he does so with no evident possibility of gain for himself, as Brutus is dead. Specifically, he judges that Cassius and the others "[d]id that they did in envy of great Caesar" (V.v.69). But Brutus alone was concerned with the "common good" (V.v.71). However, when Brutus states his commitment to "the general good" (I.ii.87), he immediately rephrases his commitment as one to "honor" (I.ii.88). Of course, it is honorable to be devoted to the well-being of others. But "honor" is ambiguous and may refer not to the moral value of the act itself but to the respect and admiration one receives from others once the act is broadcast. Indeed, Brutus himself uses the word in this sense in his funeral oration treating the assassination of Caesar. Specifically, he states that he did "honor" Caesar "for his valor" (III.ii.27–28).

The "public esteem" – thus egocentric – interpretation of Brutus's motivation becomes more plausible as Brutus explains his motivation more explicitly, stating that "I love/The name of honor more than I fear death" (I.ii.90–91). The conjunction with death makes it fairly clear that Brutus cherishes the good opinion of Rome, for it is that good opinion that will lead to his outliving his own death through popular celebratory remembrance of his (honored) name. This is further reinforced by Brutus's concern with his ancestor, whose Republican militancy did lead to long-enduring admiration, which is invoked by Cassius in his (successful) attempt to recruit Brutus to the conspiracy. Similarly, when Brutus opposes killing others, beyond Caesar, this may appear to be a moral choice. However, here too Brutus stresses opinion. He begins by stating that such a "course will seem too bloody" (II.i.162) and worries about what they "shall be called" – either "purgers" (which would be good, evidently) or "murderers" (II.i.180). The focus on reputation and esteem appears confirmed when, following the murder, both Cassius and Brutus conjecture that they will be immortalized by reputation for the deed. Brutus makes the particular point that they will be preserved in plays, as if he were imagining Shakespeare and this very play itself – though a version of this play that would be straightforwardly commendatory of Brutus, with none of the ambiguity of motive, thus without this very prediction.

So here again Shakespeare appears to suggest that the invocation of moral ideals is little more than a rationalization of cruel actions driven by egocentric motives – in this case, prominently envy and pride (including the desire for public esteem). Moreover, the act thus rationalized – murder – is perhaps the paradigm for guilt, the exemplary case of causing someone else (blameworthy) harm. Or, rather, it is such a paradigm only in those cases where we are inclined to empathize with the relevant target, what is sometimes called having a *parallel interpersonal stance* toward the target. (We will consider interpersonal stance more fully in Chapter 5.) Thus, the fundamental, practical task of the conspirators – beyond deceiving themselves and one another about their actual motives – is to cultivate antipathy (a nonparallel and therefore nonempathic interpersonal stance) toward Caesar. This does point to a difference between Brutus and the others. Their envy carries with it a partial stifling of empathy for Caesar. Brutus's desire for esteem does not. Cassius still needs to do some emotional work to secrete the needed spite. Shakespeare recognizes that we may murder in a moment due to burning anger or tremulous fear. But the cold calculation of an assassination plot might be initiated and sustained more effectively by disgust, which leads us to dehumanize the target and seek to purge it from the body of society, rendering a toxic place healthful by the eradication of this human pathogen. Thus, we find Cassius drawing on images of repulsive refuse to sustain his and Casca's commitment to the homicidal cause: "What trash is Rome,/What rubbish and what offal, when it serves/For the base matter to illuminate/So vile a thing as Caesar" (I.iii.108–111).

Even so, Brutus has a much tougher job since he must stifle empathy that is otherwise unaffected by (pseudo-)moral attitudes. Indeed, he claims to love Caesar (I.ii.84, III.i.183, III.ii.13–46), and – other than the rather contradictory fact that he killed Caesar – nothing seems to indicate unequivocally that this is wrong. It is clear that Caesar loved Brutus and thought Brutus reciprocated that affection. Cassius testifies to Caesar's feelings (I.ii.315), and we see these feelings movingly displayed in one of the most famous moments in the play – when a despondent Caesar sees that his dear friend too has the dagger out to murder him, then utters the renowned question, "*Et tu, Brutè?*" (III.i.77). Moreover, Cassius suggests the problems we have been considering when he implicitly criticizes Brutus for disloyalty to his friend (I.ii.316–317).

But just what does Brutus do to effect and rationalize this betrayal, so that he thinks that he is doing something moral? In part, he simply imagines Caesar's own future actions concretely, as if they were already facts. As writers realize implicitly, such concrete particularization can be highly effective in fostering or altering emotions. In connection with this, he draws on a dehumanizing model that fosters the empathy-stifling emotions of fear and disgust. Thus, he analogizes Caesar without a crown to "a serpent's egg/Which, hatched, would, as his kind, grow mischievous" (II.i.32–33). The hatching metaphorizes Caesar's crowning, making it inevitable, should the egg survive, unmolested. The "kind" is the outgroup Brutus imagines Caesar to be a part of, which is a subhuman – indeed, demonic – out-group. Brutus views Caesar as directly comparable to a dangerous serpent and thus akin to the repulsive source of all moral perfidy – Satan, who took the form of the serpent to engineer the Fall of humanity. In consequence, he concludes that the only reasonable way to respond to this Caesar-serpent is to "kill him in the shell" (II.i.34). (Admittedly, the Judeo-Christian associations of the serpent would be unlikely to have figured in the thoughts of the historical Brutus. But, in Shakespeare's play, we need to take account of the associations of the author and audience more than those of the historical person who was the model for the character.)

Brutus and Cassius both also embolden themselves and others by appeal to masculine gender norms. These are relevant to the present book in part because empathy, to use the current idiom, is ideologically "gendered," marked as feminine. In contrast, the pursuit of violent retribution, based on pride in honor, is a particularly masculine prerogative. Thus, when Cassius laments the apparent lack of a martial response to Caesar's elevation above his peers, he characterizes his fellow Romans' response as a matter of being "governed with our mothers' spirits" (I.iii.83). Similarly, Brutus asserts that those companions who do not join in the brave and manly act of killing Caesar – brave and manly because it involves some dozen armed assailants attacking an unarmed old man – have only "[t]he melting spirits of women" (II.i.122).

Perhaps more interestingly, Brutus takes up the faults that he finds easiest to imagine and condemn – that is, the faults that he himself is exhibiting – and imputes them to Caesar. This sort of behavior is, of course, deeply hypocritical but extremely common, not only in fiction but in the real world as well (a point suggested by the psychoanalytic identification of an entire defense mechanism of this sort – projection; see Laplanche and Pontalis 1973, 349–356). In this case, and many others, it has two functions. First, and most obviously, such hypocritical blaming enables antipathy, rationalizing the abridgment of empathy. Second, it helps to conceal the hypocrite's motives from himself and from others. After all, someone who is so committed to the defense of such-and-such a principle would appear to be the last person to violate that very principle, whatever his or her other faults might be.

When Brutus reflects initially on why the response to Caesar "must be ... his death" (II.i.10), the first charge he lays against Caesar is that he "disjoins/Remorse from power" (II.i.18–19) or, rather, will do so when crowned. Brutus immediately admits that he has never witnessed this inclination in Caesar. Nonetheless, he feels sure that he will disjoin "remorse" or compassion (as annotated by Hadfield 2007, 91) from cruel acts. In the course of the play, there is really just one moment that stands out as a dissociation of compassion from action – Brutus's own gouging of his dear friend's flesh, despite the old man's clear hope that he would be comforted (if not actually saved) by Brutus. Moreover, in the retrospective sense of "remorse," where it refers to a guilty regret, we find that Brutus is alarmingly lacking in remorse after the murder when he makes a callous joke about doing Caesar a favor (III.i.103–105) and then bizarrely urges the conspirators, "let us bathe our hands in Caesar's blood" (III.i.106).

After Brutus conjectures that Caesar will disjoin remorse from power, he turns to just what will lead to this consequence. Audience members familiar with the subsequent development of the play will not be surprised to find that Brutus here introduces the theme of ambition (II.i.22). Ambition is, of course, the very crime that Brutus later claims has justified the execution of Caesar (III.ii.26). Audience members often find this a curiously mild accusation, given the extremity of the punishment. Of course, Brutus has in mind a particular sort of ambition – to be the ruler of the Roman state. This does not appear to be anything that Brutus strives to achieve. Does that mean that Brutus is not guilty of this sin and that he has chosen a more objective accusation? I do not believe so. The sins of Caesar and Brutus are not identical. They are, rather, variations on a theme. Casca reports that Caesar's epileptic fit is apparently precipitated by his sense that the crowd "was glad he refused the crown" (I.ii.266). In part, Caesar aspires to power. But he also aspires to popular adulation. It is here that his ambition mirrors that of Brutus – specifically, Brutus's desire to be honored by the people. Thus, Brutus's blame of Caesar recalls Brutus's own faults. In sum, his invocation of ethical principles serves the end of rationalizing egocentrically motivated empathy suppression and harm.[1]

I do not wish to leave the impression that Mark Antony and Octavius are in any way morally superior to Brutus and Cassius. Antony understandably deceives the conspirators, which is certainly forgivable in the circumstances. One can even sympathize with his pursuit of "revenge"

---

[1] *Julius Caesar* has been the object of ethical analysis in recent years. However, that work is focused very differently from the present analysis. For example, Grady refers to Brutus's "admirably Stoic sense of ethics, his self-control, his moral scruples and practice of introspection" (2010, 18). Despite (or perhaps in part because of) these disagreements, Grady's analysis provides insights into moral deliberation in the play, insights that treat aspects of the play's ethics that I have not considered. A treatment closer in spirit to my own may be found in Feather (2010). This is due to her emphasis on some of the contradictory aspects of Brutus's character as well as her treatment (in different terms) of egocentric and allocentric motives. However, she focuses on Brutus's suicide, which makes her analysis (valuably) different from that presented here.

(III.i.272), despite the gross excess of violence and other evils that almost invariably accompany the pursuit of revenge. But it is worrisome that Antony not only predicts but also seems to call for a "curse" to "light upon the limbs of men" comprising "fierce civil strife" that will leave "[a]ll pity choked with custom of fell deeds" (III.i.264–265, 271). The prediction is partially borne out by the mob's call for "Revenge!" (III.ii.201), leading to the deaths of innocents (e.g., Cinna the Poet [III.iii]). Moreover, Antony's subsequent behavior is more a matter of political manipulation than grief and anger over the murder of his friend, not to mention ethical deliberation. One hardly knows what to make of his famous speech – a putatively moral argument – in which he claims to identify which rent in the fabric of Caesar's cloak was cut by Cassius, Casca, or Brutus (III.ii.171–173), something he could not possibly know. He then goes on to claim that Pompey's statue bled, despite the implausibility of the idea that a statue would bleed, but more importantly despite the fact that Pompey and Caesar were at war when Pompey was assassinated; Pompey would therefore be unlikely to waste his postmortem supernatural energies on conveying distress over Caesar's end. But this is straightforward deceit, with little ethical complexity. There is also little to be learned from the triumvirs' negotiations on who should be executed (IV.i), which also have no relation to genuine ethical thought or feeling.

Much of the remainder of the play either repeats ethical concerns that we have already isolated or takes up moral points in a way that does not inspire further reflection. Even so, one case is worth mentioning – the conflict between Cassius and Brutus. Recall that the immediate occasion for the murder of Caesar was Caesar's refusal to yield to the appeal of the conspirators that he rescind a punishment. Caesar claims that it is a matter of principle, not a mere whim to be altered due to flattery. The conflict between Cassius and Brutus begins when Brutus refuses to rescind a punishment. This again suggests hypocrisy on Brutus's part; if he believed Caesar was wrong to act as he did, then he (Brutus) should not repeat Caesar's action. More strikingly, the case at issue between Brutus and Casssius concerned bribery. Brutus goes on to accuse Cassius of illegitimately collecting funds, and he protests that he himself could not stoop to such "vile [therefore disgusting] means" (IV.iii.72). Finally, he accuses Cassius of having refused to send Brutus funds. In short, Brutus refuses to accept bribes, but he covets the bribes received by Cassius. This suggests that he is not so much committed to the ethically proper act as to keeping his reputation unsullied. It seems that he is quite content to use ill-gotten coins, as long as only Cassius's reputation – and not his own – is at risk in the ill-getting.

# Conclusion

Literary texts – like other forms of expression or action – may manifest ethical attitudes, norms, and evaluations of which the author is not self-consciously aware but that still guide his or her storytelling. In addition to manifesting a work's broad, ethical orientation, the implicit ethics of a work are often closely connected with its story genre – thus, its ethical prototype – such as the heroic usurpation (or restoration) story of *Julius Caesar*. The ethical views represented in a work may have a broadly trusting attitude toward the hero's ethical self-presentation or may take a more skeptical view of the characters. I refer to the latter as a "critical ethics." Critical ethics stresses the dissociation of a character's rhetoric from his or her actual motivation. By the definition of "ethics" set out above, both genuine ethical response and ethical dissembling appear to be a matter of allocentric self-interest only. Shakespeare's play, however, suggests that the assertion of allocentrism typically serves only to occlude egocentrism.

Beyond this attention to hypocrisy, the precise ethical evaluations present in the play are often not straightforward. This is in part because Shakespeare develops the heroic story in such a way that it never becomes entirely clear which act of which group is an illegitimate usurpation and which is a legitimate restoration of the proper social order. Such ambiguity regarding the events is consonant with the critical ethics of the characterization. Still, it does seem fairly clear that the various speeches and actions point toward a common setting of the scope parameter to nation or state and of the valence parameter to unmerited pleasure. Note that these do not define Shakespeare's ethical orientation, but the orientations of his main characters. Indeed, the play seems to indicate that Shakespeare's own parameter settings were more broadly human and attentive to undeserved pain. In keeping with its attention to hypocrisy, the play itself (thus, Shakespeare's orientation) is arguably agent-focused, stressing characters rather than acts themselves. The play's method parameter fixes the republican social order as an intrinsic good. The characters, in contrast, appear to be consequentialist regarding the establishment of their preferred social order. This conflict between the ethical orientations of the characters and that of the author is connected in this case with the heroic genre, which Shakespeare almost invariably treated critically (see Hogan 2013, chap. 3). This leads us once again to the topic of story prototypes and their associated particularizations of ethical orientations.

CHAPTER 3

# Narrative Universals, Emotion, and Ethics

As noted briefly in Chapter 1, it is important to distinguish between our spontaneous ethical intuitions and our self-reflective ethical deliberations. There are, of course, connections between the two, and they influence one another, with the intuitive influencing the deliberative rather more often than the reverse. Even so, they remain different ways of thinking about and responding to ethical issues. Despite their interaction, they are not the same and often are not even mutually consistent. This is part of the reason for our complex and often inconsistent responses to ethical issues.

The discussion of principles and parameters in Chapter 1 concerned both. However, unselfconscious parameter setting is typically less stable than deliberative decision (i.e., our spontaneous parameter settings are more likely to change from case to case, as the configuration of our perceptions, simulations, memories, and other psychological properties changes).[1] In consequence, enduring principles and parameter settings seem less determinative of our spontaneous responses than of our deliberations; the former appear to have more proximate sources. Like Jonathan Haidt, I see those sources in emotion and narrative, though our accounts are otherwise very different. In this chapter, I will be concerned to clarify the relation between spontaneous ethical response and narrative, with narrative understood in close relation with emotion. Ultimately, I will approach spontaneous ethics through the identification

---

[1] By "spontaneous ethical response," I am referring roughly to what is sometimes called "conscience." I have avoided the term due to its ambiguity and the various, often strong views people have about conscience. For example, Churchland gives the following definition: "Conscience is an individual's judgment about what is morally right or wrong, typically, but not always, reflecting some standard of a group to which the individual feels attached. The verdict of conscience is not solely cognitive, moreover, but has two interdependent elements: feelings that urge us in a general direction, and judgment that shapes the urge into a specific action" (2019, 5). This suggests some of the problems with the notion of conscience. Churchland first defines it as a judgment but then says that it is a set of feelings shaped by a judgment; she both connects it with and disconnects it from social norms. I suspect these difficulties stem from trying to capture the ambiguity of the term in ordinary usage.

of narrative universals, with the goal of isolating patterns in ethical universals as well.

When I mention ethical and narrative universals, people almost invariably infer that I am setting out to establish norms for everyone. Again, normative issues do enter into the present study. These enter as preferences, albeit preferences for which I believe one can engage in rational argument. I do not take them to be somehow objective facts. In contrast, arguments about ethical universals (as I am using the phrase here) involve claims about facts, not preferences. (Of course, my arguments may lead to false conclusions; that is part of what is involved in making claims about facts. The assertion that there are facts does not entail that I am dogmatically right. Rather, it entails exactly that I could be wrong.) Thus, ethical universals, in this context, do not tell us what "really is" good or bad. They just tell us what patterns in ethical response occur across genetically and areally distinct cultures. This does not at all mean that people have the same ethical attitudes – either across societies or within any given society. It means only that they share a core set of ethical alternatives. In discussing universals, one point I keep trying to make is that there is a great deal of diversity in the ethical views of people in a particular society at a particular time. That diversity exhibits patterns, and, to a surprising degree, the same sorts of pattern recur in various societies, though not necessarily in similar proportions. Patricia Greenspan makes a similar point when she writes that "social influence introduces variations" on universal patterns. In consequence, "competing emotional mechanisms" – bearing on, say, guilt – "might be mixed or balanced differently in different cultures or even by different personality types" (2010, 544). I would add that there are many sorts of variation, not merely those of culture or personality. Speaking about emotion, rather than ethics, Kelly writes aptly that research "reveal[s] a pattern of local variations on themes that are themselves universal" (2011, 64). The phrase could be applied to ethical response, narrative structure, and many other topics.

For instance, when some of us think about war and peace, we think of hippies slipping the stems of daisies into the barrels of police rifles and then sharing a vegetarian feast of bean curd and Alice B. Toklas brownies, maybe followed by the practical celebration of free love. So perhaps not everyone eats brownies or has rifles, but the pattern was not all that different in ancient India. There, the hippies were Tantricists (e.g., see "Black Blankets" in Jayánta 2005); the vegetarian peaceniks were the advocates of *sādhāraṇadharma* (universal dharma), with its focus on *ahiṃsā* or nonviolence, which included vegetarianism. In contrast, the grim-faced soldiers were supported by doctrines of *varṇadharma* or caste dharma, specifically *kṣatriyadharma*, the duty of the warrior caste (on dharma theory, see O'Flaherty 1978). Of course, the situations, practices, and ideas are not identical between San Francisco in 1968 and Kashmir in the tenth century (when Jayánta was writing). But the situations, practices, and ideas were not identical for any two people in San Francisco in 1968, or even for any one person at two different times.

More exactly, precepts and theories are not universal. However, patterns underlying dominant precepts – prominently, story prototypes and related emotion systems – are, or so I shall maintain. As Rogoff points out, "cultural differences are generally variations of themes of universal import with differing emphasis or value placed on particular practices rather than all-or-none differences" (2003, 64). In keeping with this, before going on, I should differentiate what I am saying from one very common view. It is fairly standard now to say that there are some universal biological aspects of morality, along with wide cultural variation. I don't exactly believe either. I take it that there are many (largely) innate (but not specifically ethical) propensities (e.g., those defined by emotion systems) and that these interact with real-world experiences – including group dynamics and complex systems processes – to produce what we call "ethics." These processes converge toward a set of distinct ethical orientations that turn up in almost all societies (some very small societies are likely to be more internally uniform). Thus, many, perhaps most, cross-culturally recurring patterns – both ethical and nonethical – are not innate as such but the result of many factors that collectively lead to convergence.[2]

I should immediately add here that the specification and distribution of these cross-cultural, ethical orientations do vary from society to society (e.g., one society may strongly emphasize militarism and downplay empathy; another might do the reverse, though both tendencies turn up in both societies). Indeed, since ethical orientations are to a great extent mutually exclusive or contradictory, societies typically need to organize them in hierarchical ways in order to give preference to one or another of

---

[2] Alasdair MacIntyre offers a somewhat similar view when he argues that some ethical principles are logically necessary "because no group in which they were absent could fall under the concept of a society" (1998, 50); he instances the ethical criticism of lying. Other ethical principles, such as the valuing of fairness, are not logically necessary but follow with virtual certainty because "certain very widespread and elementary facts about human life and its environment are what they are" (50). Others will arise regularly, though with occasional exceptions, due to "fairly widespread human desires" (50). On the other hand, MacIntyre is conceiving of cross-cultural principles as almost entirely uniform across and within societies. (I mean uniform in their general acceptance, not in their specification.) In contrast, I am particularly interested in the range of ethical attitudes that characterize any given society and the degree to which those (partially contradictory) alternatives – for example, those connected with heroic and romantic story structures – recur in different societies, thus the ways in which universals underlie the *non*uniform ethics of most or all societies.

the incompatible alternatives. This is, of course, one place where ideology enters; specifically, the dominant ethical ideology in a society tends to be the ideology of the dominant class. (Note that a consequence of this is that a putatively liberal affirmation of the dominant norms in another society is generally an affirmation of normal domination in that society as well.) But the dominant views are never the only views. Commonly, the official or standard ethical views in a society occlude this internal diversity.

In the following pages, I sketch a nonnormative account of how we might understand ethical thought and action if we integrate cognitive and affective science with a study of narrative universals. In order to do this, I begin with Jonathan Haidt's (2012) influential account of morality, which (as already noted) stresses emotion and narrative. I believe Haidt is correct in this emphasis, but I diverge from him on the precise nature of the emotions and stories at issue. After orienting the current project by reference to Haidt and outlining my differences from him, I turn to some background on comparative literary study and the isolation of literary universals. This leads to a further development of the affective-narratological account of ethics introduced in connection with Haidt.

## On Political Morality

Currently, Haidt is perhaps the most influential theorist to stress the centrality of emotion and narrative for understanding ethics in relation to current cognitive and affective science. Though I do not agree with the ways in which Haidt (2012) develops these points, I very much agree with the basic idea and will develop that idea in what follows. However, Haidt's primary goals in the book are political. I have much more thoroughgoing disagreements with Haidt on political issues. I should therefore sketch some of these disagreements before going on.

Politically, one fundamental problem with Haidt's account is the way he characterizes the differences between the political left and the political right. My objections to Haidt's views are not motivated principally by his apparent sympathies for the political right. They are, rather, based on a view that Haidt's claims are empirically or logically mistaken (hence their relevance to the descriptive part of the present volume). Indeed, I would equally dispute some recent characterizations of the left versus right division that are favorable toward the former.

### *A Partial Digression on the Supposed Negativity Bias of Right-Wing Political Views*

As just indicated, psychological analyses sometimes favor the left, not the right. Though the results of such analyses favor "my side," I am regularly skeptical of those claims as well. Before discussing Haidt, it may be worthwhile to touch on a case of this sort. In a widely read and influential series of studies, John Hibbing and his colleagues have argued that right-wing politics is guided significantly by "negativity bias" (see Hibbing, Smith, and Alford 2014). Hibbing and his colleagues have certainly identified a plausible psychological factor contributing to differences in political orientation. However, there are two potential difficulties with their analysis. Both the liberal/conservative opposition and the nature of negativity are ambiguous.

First, as to the liberal/conservative opposition, this may refer to attitudes regarding change or it may refer to left-wing and right-wing policies. There is presumably some correlation between the two, but they are not equivalent. For instance, the All-India Progressive Writers Association advocated socialist and egalitarian policies along with the retention of many Indian cultural traditions (Coppola 1974, 40). Similarly, conservatives work to dismantle, not to conserve, the welfare state. There is a question, then, as to how negativity bears on conservatism in these different senses. Churchland makes the related but more general point that "[a] semantic problem is that though our customary labels liberal and conservative may capture something of whatever brain disposition it is that our genes underwrite, they probably do not begin to do justice to the actual nature of that brain disposition" (2019, 121). Second, there is an ambiguity in negativity. As the authors indicate, liberals are more likely to envision disastrous consequences from environmental decline, whereas conservatives are more likely to see disastrous consequences in mass immigration. In some cases, then, it seems that liberals have greater negativity bias.

The problem of negativity ambiguity is perhaps more straightforward. The authors note that liberals score higher on empathy than conservatives (Hirsh et al. 2010). Empathy is a form of emotion system activation – specifically, the activation of a system in parallel with that of some other person, predominantly for an aversive emotion (i.e., we empathize with a target's pain more readily than with his or her joy; see Royzman and Rozin 2006). This may suggest that the negativity bias is greater in conservatives for prudential considerations (e.g., possible employment competition) but greater in liberals for (nonprudential) empathic targets (e.g., future generations suffering depleted resources). The tendencies are related in that intensified prudential negativity is likely to reduce empathic sensitivity (Preston and de Waal 2002, 8). In this sense, prudential negativity bias would be prior and determinative, as Hibbing, Smith, and Alford (2014) suggest.

On the other hand, even this may be overly simple. Proneness to empathy varies with a number of factors, including in-group/out-group divisions (Ambady et al. 2006, 213) as defined by identity categories, such as nationality or race (for a fuller discussion of emotion and identity categories, see Hogan 2009; I will consider this relation in subsequent chapters). The presence and nature of such divisions commonly modulate the proneness of individuals toward empathy and explain at least some of the difference in empathy itself. For example, it may appear obvious that some people are inclined to experience strong motivational responses to identity divisions while others are not. But a priori, it seems equally possible that people vary primarily in which (not whether) identity divisions have strong motivational consequences for them. In this case, part of the conservative/liberal difference may be less a matter of psychological properties per se than of social context. For example, someone whose most important identity division is Hindu/non-Hindu may be liberal in the United States but conservative in India, where that identity division is more socially functional. The difference would not be in broad psychological propensities as such, but in the social significance of some particular manifestation of those propensities – here, a specific identity category.

Another important variable concerns precisely which emotion systems are involved (we will consider emotion systems in Chapter 5; see also Hogan, 2011, *What Literature*, chap. 2). Specifically, the key emotion systems for negativity bias would seem to be fear, disgust, and anger. Here, too, eliciting conditions for the emotion are important. We may distinguish broad, dispositional sensitivities from responses to specific targets – for example, general fearfulness versus fear of black men. Among other things, this may be valuable in clarifying the relation between different senses of *conservative* or *liberal*. Conservatism in the root sense – roughly, resistance to political change – may be associated with some dispositional sensitivity, most obviously fearfulness, which should be assuaged by what is familiar. In contrast, we would expect specific policy responses (associated with conservatism in the right-wing sense) to bear on responses to specific targets. For example, we would expect disgust arousal at homosexuality to be connected with opposition to gay marriage (see Nussbaum 2010); fear of crime to promote advocacy of strict policing (e.g., see Gardner 2008, 209–213); and anger system activation for crimes already committed to encourage victim seeking and thus advocacy of harsh punishment (on victim seeking, see Berkowitz 1993).

This division might also help to explain the partial correlation between the two senses of *conservatism*. At least in the case of fearfulness, the disposition tends to favor familiarity and to foster fear responses to particular targets (e.g., fearful persons are presumably more likely to be afraid of targets that are often depicted as being dangerous). The former would favor anti-change conservatism, whereas the latter would incline one toward right-wing conservatism. At the same time, the two sorts of conservatism should diverge at points where current policies are based on well-established empathic responses (which someone resistant to change would preserve) or on novel, nonempathic, prudentially based considerations (which right-wing conservatives should be more likely to pursue). On the other hand, the differentiation of emotion systems may lead us to wonder why various forms of aversive response tend to cluster together, forming liberal and conservative platforms, rather than remaining separated in insular policies (e.g., regarding gay marriage, policing, and so on), in keeping with the diversity of views on specific topics noted by Hibbing, Smith, and Alford (2014, 305).

With two small additions, we may begin to answer this final question. First, a strong negative response in any of these systems would tend to become motivationally dominant. Severe disgust at gay sexuality is likely to become a strong motivational force relative to, say, a weak emotional response to the possibility of crime. Second, social dynamics will tend to cluster policies into a limited number of complexes, often tending toward two (see the research on alliances summarized in Ball 2004, chap. 12). In this case, the clustering seems likely to have its own effects. In consequence, someone who feels strongly disgusted at gay marriage and mildly opposed to the death penalty is unlikely to find a political outlet that opposes gay marriage and also opposes the death penalty. The result may be the partial revision of the person's more peripheral political attitudes. For example, an anti–gay marriage voter might revise more weakly held opposition toward the death penalty, in line with a socially available political platform.[3]

In short, the cognitive and emotional profiles of both liberals and conservatives seem to be much more complex, and much more similar, than Hibbing, Smith, and Alford (2014) suggest. The principal exception to this may be in empathic scope. Yet even here, liberals are perhaps not more inclined to be empathically inclusive than simply to select different groups for exclusion.

## Haidt on Moral Foundations and the Limits of Liberalism

In comparison with Hibbing and his colleagues (2014), Haidt (2012) isolates a broader range of ethical tendencies, which he then compiles

---

[3] An account of this sort would appear to be consistent with, for example, the development of the current conservative movement in the United States, as explained by Lepore (2019, see especially chap. 15, 662–683), or the convergence of very different political tendencies in support of the (conservative) Bharatiya Janata Party in India (see Banerjee and Duflo 2019, 127–128).

into a tripartite political typology of liberal, libertarian, and conservative, though he focuses on the first and third. More precisely, Haidt isolates some half dozen complexes of processes that yield ethical evaluations. He refers to these as "moral foundations." For example, one set of moral evaluative processes concerns the infliction of harm; another concerns the restriction of liberty; a third concerns the desecration of purity. As I will discuss in a later section, I believe Haidt is broadly correct in isolating these different sorts of moral attitude (though, again, I will formulate the principles differently). However, I believe that he is seriously mistaken in his criticism of the left based on this analytic of moral views.

A central contention of Haidt's book is that "conservatives care about a broader range of moral values and issues than do liberals" (2012, 184). Note that this is a normative evaluation, despite the fact that Haidt largely presents himself as articulating a scientifically grounded, descriptive, and explanatory account of political viewpoints. Haidt is clearly suggesting that caring about a broader range is superior. Specifically, liberals are, in his view, too fixated on harm. In contrast, conservatives – rightly, in Haidt's view – recognize concerns of purity, liberty, loyalty, and so on. There are numerous problems with this claim, and with Haidt's development of the claim. We will consider a few of them.

The most obvious problem here is that the various categories overlap. In testing his moral foundations, Haidt focuses on, for example, cases of purity that do not involve harm. But it seems clear that, in a broad range of cases, purity concerns do involve issues of harm, or what we would imagine to be harm. One consequence of this is that we are likely to associate impurity with harm, even in cases where no harm is actually involved. Haidt believes that he has taken care of this problem through experimental design. That design basically involves presenting anecdotes to test subjects and stipulating that no harm has been done. But I do not believe our simulative processes work that way. Our explicit logical inferences can accommodate such stipulated absolutes. But our simulations would not be very functional in evolution if they could be completely constrained by what is, in effect, wishful thinking. For example, one of Haidt's anecdotes (which I touched on in Chapter 1) concerns an act of sibling incest. He stipulates that no one ever learned about it, no pregnancy resulted, and the siblings' emotional relation to the event was positive (2012, 45). But many people would simulate the sequence of events very differently, because in real life there would be the possibility of discovery, pregnancy, remorse, and so on. Similar points could be made about all the moral foundations and their associated anecdotes.

A second problem is that, despite the care with which he designed his surveys, Haidt seems to have captured stereotypes about liberals and conservatives – including stereotypes that they hold about themselves – rather than actual preferences and behaviors. For example, Haidt seems to discover that conservatives care more about the family as an ethical concern. But it seems likely that this has to do with the rhetorical emphasis of the right on "family values" and related ideas. Had he begun his surveys with reminders of Trump's separation of immigrant families, or with reference to gay and lesbian marriage and adoption, or even to paid family leave, he presumably would have come up with very different results, with liberals being more family-oriented than conservatives. Along the same lines, Haidt sees conservatives alone as caring about loyalty and authority. But the left simply values different objects of loyalty and types of authority. Left-wing activists routinely advocate loyalty under the name "solidarity." Liberals stress the authority of independent human rights organizations, climate scientists, and, more recently, epidemiologists discussing the coronavirus.

Similar points apply to his categorization of certain policy preferences. For instance, he claims that conservatives care about proportionality. In connection with this, he cites "three strikes and you're out" legislation (Haidt 2012, 213). But why is it proportional to say that someone with three convictions for nonviolent crimes should be considered unredeemable (see "Three Strikes" n.d.)? Alternatively, why is the call for zero tolerance made by many advocates of #MeToo and #TimesUp not a case of concern for proportionality (since proportionality in this context seems primarily a matter of severity of retribution)? Or why wouldn't we say that opposing "three strikes" laws shows a concern for proportionality, since many would contend that the laws themselves tend to punish disproportionately?

In some cases, it is difficult to ascertain precisely why Haidt characterizes attitudes the way he does. For example, one of the basic divisions in Haidt's schema of moral types is the widely invoked distinction between collectivist and individualist cultures. In fact, this seems to me a false division. It probably is the case that some cultures are on the whole more "collectivist" than "individualist," and vice versa, in some sense of these terms. But it seems clear that all societies – at least all large societies – have both orientations, even if they differ somewhat in proportions. The apparent differences are largely a matter of self-concept, or even "cultural clichés," in Renato Rosaldo's phrase (quoted in Pinker 1997, 368), what people think it is right to say about themselves. This view is consistent with my experience of my in-laws' society, India (a putatively collectivist culture despite, for example, a long tradition of highly individualist spirituality), and my own family's United States (putatively hyper-individualistic, but with a proud legacy of conformism, extending back at least to the time of de Tocqueville, and including its nationalistic war fevers, as well as its racial identifications and oppositions, all of which are broadly collectivist). Indeed, Haidt himself repeatedly indicates that the U.S. population has many of the moral views he elsewhere seems to view as non-Western. For example, he asks, "[W]hy do so many Westerners, even secular ones, continue to see choices about food and sex as being heavily loaded with moral significance?" (Haidt 2012, 15). And he does not exempt Americans when he writes that "self-interest is a weak predictor of policy preferences," as "people care about their *groups*" (100). It seems to me that common claims about cultural identities are directly parallel to claims about individual identities. They both suffer from a "correspondence bias" (alternatively, "fundamental attribution error") in attributing simple, guiding dispositions to their targets, ignoring the diversity and conflict within individuals and the effects of circumstantial factors (on correspondence bias, see Gilbert and Malone 1995; on fundamental attribution error, see Ross 1977).[4]

But let us suppose for the moment that some societies (e.g., India) are concerned with the community, whereas others (e.g., the United States) are not. How can Haidt reasonably judge wife beating (2012, 19) to be communal or, equivalently, sociocentric? (As Haidt explains it, a sociocentric culture "plac[es] the needs of groups and institutions first, and subordinat[es] the needs of individuals" [17]; individualistic cultures do the opposite.) What sort of community concern allows half of a community to terrorize the other half? What social benefits come from wife beating? Haidt appears to mock Western insensitivities to cultural differences when he refers to how an individualistic society might view taboos on widows as morally wrong – despite the fact that many Indian writers, such as Rabindranath Tagore and Ishwar Chandra Vidyasagar, have also viewed them as morally wrong after considering them thoughtfully in relation to Indian traditions and scriptures (e.g., see Tagore's stories "The

---

[4] This seems to me a problem with Henrich's (2020) influential and controversial book as well. Much of the research he cites seems to concern either of the following: (a) what people in a given society or context believe they are expected to say, or (b) what they think they believe, which may or may not reflect the way they would actually behave in a real case. Thus, I would say that his conclusions about the "WEIRD" quality of Westerners are largely mistaken. However, I will grant that the "cultural clichés" can be consequential. Specifically, they can lead to the establishment of laws and institutions that may in turn foster changes in people's behavior. However, those laws and institutions are often far less effective than one might expect, at least in cases where one might wish them to be effective; think, for example, of the repeated disenfranchisement of African Americans in the United States, despite apparent legal remedies. Indeed, the reason for this ineffectiveness is presumably that, despite such legislation, Westerners are in fact not very "WEIRD" (e.g., they are not all that egalitarian, despite common assertions to the contrary).

Living and the Dead" and "Skeleton" in Tagore 1991; Parekh 1989, 16, on Vidyasagar; and Sen 1991). Just how, one might reasonably ask, are widowhood practices (e.g., limits on what widows can eat) beneficial to society – as opposed to being beneficial to individual, egocentric patriarchs who do not wish to feed the widows in their homes? (On some widowhood restrictions in India, see Lamb 1999.) Why is it sociocentric to say that a widow should be forbidden sexual relations because they would "offend the spirit of her dead husband" (Haidt 2012, 20), given that the husband is (or was) presumably an individual? And why is it individualistic to say that women (who clearly form a group) should not be subordinated to men or that the same general restrictions should apply to both? Moreover, according to Haidt, (Western) liberalism works against group unity (2012, 215). But the main obstacles to unity in the United States today appear to be racism and sexism, which are at least more clearly characteristic of the right than of the left. One might also ask about what to do with the enthusiasm of some Westerners for socialism in this context.

Similar points apply to other standard cultural typologies. Consider, for example, the isolation of a set of "honor" cultures. Nussbaum points out, "There is something comical in the self-congratulatory idea that honor cultures are in another time or at least another place (such as, putatively, the Middle East), given the obsessive attention paid by Americans to competitive ranking in terms of status, money, and other qualities" (2016). Referring specifically to the idea of "honor killings," she goes on to point out that "a sense of manly honor and competitive injury is involved in many killings of women in many countries" (Nussbaum 2016, 20).

Related to these points, Haidt appears to regret Western paucity in the "sacred" experience of communal oneness, "where the self disappears and collective interests predominate" (2012, 262). I'm not entirely sure why Haidt may have a positive view of this. Its most famous instances would include such eminently immoral – and Western – unities as Nazi Nuremberg rallies, as depicted in, for example, Leni Riefenstahl's *Triumph of the Will*. In *The Handmaid's Tale*, Margaret Atwood (2017) presents a chilling case of this in the "particicution" – the participatory execution – of a man torn to pieces by a group of enraged handmaids acting as a unified, retributive force. We soon learn that the man thus dismembered was an opponent of the regime who had been falsely accused and convicted of rape.

Another problem with Haidt's analysis is that at least some of the differences he isolates may be a relatively insignificant matter of what we mean by "moral." Consider, again, another one of Haidt's moral assessment anecdotes in which a man masturbates using a chicken carcass. Most of us would probably agree that sex with a chicken carcass is disgusting. We might worry about bacteria from the decaying meat, bacteria spread at least to the man's genitals and hands. In connection with this, many people would probably have some questions about the person's character or worries about associating with him. Some people would call these "moral" issues; others would not. It is not clear what consequences might follow from such divergences in labeling.

Perhaps most importantly, Haidt often acts as if there is no place for rational debate on normative ethics. He seems to take it for granted that if some group believes q to be a moral issue, then q is a moral issue. In consequence, it would appear that there is no place for ethical philosophy. Sometimes, he acts as if every ethical philosophy is simply disproven by the existence of multiple "moral foundations." However, most moral philosophers are not contending that no one uses the words "moral" or "ethical" differently than they do. They all acknowledge divergence, at least tacitly. For example, Kant (or Mill) would have no reason to argue in favor of his idea of morality if he believed that everyone already used the word "moral" to refer to the categorical imperative (or, for Mill, maximization of utility). Their arguments are for a particular account of morality that is going to go against common presumptions in some respects; otherwise, those arguments would not be worth articulating.

Finally, Haidt is, I believe, mistaken in his claims about cultural difference. First of all, surveys of ordinary Americans, outside of academia, show ethical responses that are more in line with the responses of ordinary people elsewhere (e.g., in disapproving of sex with chicken carcasses; see Haidt 2012, 112). Second, Haidt's method of ascertaining what people think is overly limited. Most obviously, he tends to stress explicit ethical theory when discussing the West and implicit, popular ethical response when discussing everyone else (on this distinction, see Keown 2005, 27). Moreover, Haidt ignores the range of ethical theory in the West (e.g., philosophers of law who advocate shaming; see Nussbaum 2016, 197–203).

Most egregiously, Haidt simply bypasses, without mention, the complex and internally diverse traditions of explicit moral theory in China, India, and elsewhere. As to China, the punitive orientation of Chinese Legalism (Fǎ Jiā; see de Bary and Bloom 1999, 190–192) is directly opposed by the important strain of Rú Xué (Confucianism) represented by Mèngzǐ (Mencius) and indeed Kǒngzǐ (Confucius) himself, who spoke against a punitive model for society. For instance, in the *Lún Yǔ* (*Analects*), "The Master said, 'The way (dào) of political power mixed with punishment: the people will have no sense of shame. The way (dào) of morals and kindness mixed with ritual (lǐ): they will have a sense of shame, and a framework" (2.3, altered from the Legge translation). As I noted earlier, Kǒngzǐ stresses empathy (shù, 恕); again, Zhang explains, "The concept of empathy, shu, is a further extension of the idea of [the key Confucian virtue of] benevolence. The term *shu* means 'to put oneself in the position of another and to look at the world from that perspective'" (2003, 285). Kǒngzǐ did advocate a preference for one's kin, but this was opposed by Mòzǐ, with his philosophy of "universal love" (see Burton Watson, 1999).

Similarly, in Indian tradition, there are areas of ethics focused on one's duties to family (*kuladharma*), one's occupational duties (*jātidharma*), and so on. These include, for example, the violent dharma of soldiers (*kṣatriyadharma*). But there is also a set of ethical principles treating universal duties (*sādhāraṇadharma*), including *ahiṃsā*, or nonharming (see O'Flaherty 1978, 96). Moreover, there is recurring debate on the priorities of contradictory ethical obligations in Indian tradition. One such debate initiates the *Bhagavad Gītā*, as we will discuss in Chapter 4. In these and other cases, it may indeed be that one way of discussing ethics was the official view (e.g., a somewhat Legalistically inflected Confucianism in China, caste-based dharma in Hindu India). But there was much more to each tradition than this official position or dominant ideology.

### Ethics, Affects, and Stories

Despite these (and other) points of disagreement, I believe two central claims made by Haidt are both correct and underappreciated. First, Haidt (2012) begins with the view that ethical ideas do not have consequences for action due to their logic, empirical adequacy, parsimony, or other information-processing properties. (Haidt does not put the point this way, but I believe it is consistent with his views.) Rather, they have consequences for action due to the emotions that they inspire. For me, this is an almost trivial matter. Our information-processing systems produce ... information. In contrast, emotion/motivation systems produce ... motivations. Thus, we act on ethical ideas due to motivation or emotion systems. Without emotion, we do not act – morally, prudentially, impulsively, or in any other way.

Whether the claim is or is not theoretically banal, the key point – that one is not motivated by reasoning as such – does not appear to be widely recognized. It is, however, stressed by Haidt. On the other hand, I believe that Haidt's formulation of the idea is vague and almost certainly overstated. For example, he appears to allow little room for cognitive processes of emotion modulation. I do not want to overstate the possibilities for modulation. But we can and do engage in such processes. For instance, Haidt writes, "We do moral reasoning not to reconstruct the actual reasons why *we ourselves* came to a judgment; we reason to find the best possible reasons why *somebody else ought to join us* in our judgment" (2012, 52). However, we also reason to consider whether we should maintain or change our response – as suggested, for example, by empirical research cited by Haidt (2012, 81) that shows people make more reasoned ethical judgments when forced to pause before delivering their evaluation. Somewhat paradoxically, it at times appears from Haidt's argument that other people are more susceptible to being swayed by moral analysis and argument than we are ourselves. In part, this is related to Haidt's problematic account of reason. He rightly suggests that reason does not provide us with goals. However, he presents a strange account of reason when he says that "it was designed to seek justification, not truth" (86). It would seem that reason was "designed" (by evolution) to allow us to infer conditions in the world, including intentions in other minds, and to calculate means to achieve goals established by emotion systems, all of which necessarily involves at least a functional approximation to truth. Even deceiving others through rhetorical manipulation is contingent on getting most of our reasoning right (e.g., with regard to other people's degrees and kinds of gullibility).

Take, for example, the case of hypnotic suggestion reported by Haidt (2012). In that study, some test subjects were hypnotized to feel a flash of disgust upon seeing the word "often." This influenced their moral judgments, sometimes bizarrely. For example, one-third of the test subjects with the disgust flash judged a person as unethical for trying to arrange social events that the people attending those events would enjoy. This is indeed shocking and shows the extent to which we are likely to rationalize our emotional responses rather than modulating them. However, the same test also suggests that the majority of the test subjects presumably felt the disgust but did not judge the person's actions as immoral. In many cases, this was presumably due to cognitive modulation. In addition, given the way these motivations commonly work, I suspect that if they had been informed of the flash of disgust and its role in their emotional response, many of them – perhaps almost all of them – would have changed their moral assessment and even their emotional response (on correcting emotion-induced biases, see Berkowitz et al. 2000). Consider, for example, the famous study by Schachter and Singer (1962) in which test subjects were given an injection of adrenaline, but they were told that the injection was something else. If they were told they might experience such irrelevant side effects as numb feet, they experienced the effects of the adrenaline as emotional arousal (e.g., anger). If they were told that they would experience such side effects as an accelerated heart rate and hand tremors, they did not experience the side effects as emotional arousal. The resulting modulatory effect on test subjects' responses was at least in part a matter of reasoning – in this case, causal reasoning – which affected the test subjects themselves (thus was not confined to persuading others).[5]

More generally, Haidt's (2012) claims about emotion are rendered less comprehensible by the fact that he does not articulate a clear account of how emotions operate or what the components of an emotion episode are. Again, I completely agree that we do not act on logic or empirical data alone. We only act when emotion–motivation systems are activated. But this does not mean that the former do not affect the latter. In technical terms, reasoning may impact the *eliciting conditions* of my emotional response as well as certain details of the *actional outcomes*. To take a simple example, suppose I go to the zoo and approach the lion cage. I notice that the gate to the cage is open and the lion is walking toward that opening. My information processing tells me what could result from this. I feel terrible fear and run away. The information affects the way I envision the series of possible events; that imagination in turn constitutes the eliciting conditions for my emotional response. That response, then, leads to my behavior. I would not act without feeling fear, but the fear is inseparable from cognitive processing. Moreover, that processing may include modulation (e.g., if I suppress my inclination to run on the grounds that this would provoke a chase).

Once stated, the necessity of motivation for action seems clear. Nonetheless, emotion is generally underappreciated in discussions of ethics; thus, it is important to stress its centrality. On the other hand, as the preceding example also indicates, this does not mean that reasoning has no role or is only a matter of rationalizing prior emotional preferences. Haidt asks, "[D]o people feel revulsion and sympathy when they read accounts of torture, and then invent a story about universal rights to help justify their feelings?" (2012, 38). But the causal sequence is not so simple and univocal. Emotion systems do not simply activate on their own; they are not autonomous. Indeed, the phrasing of Haidt's query suggests the contingency of emotion elicitation on one's experience of

---

[5] As should be clear from my treatment of emotion in Chapter 5, I do not hold a view of emotion anything like that of Schachter and Singer (1962). The point here concerns only the misattribution of causes for one's emotion-related experience and how such misattribution comes about and may be altered. (For some problems with the Schachter and Singer account, but also on plausible consequences of causal attributions, see Reisenzein 1983.) In cases such as that reported by Haidt (2012), experiences of disgust are "interpreted [by the test subject] in terms of the available stimulus" (Toates 2014, 169; Toates is not referring to Haidt, but making a general observation). My point is simply that if one knows the actual source of an (apparently) emotional response (e.g., the word "often"), it seems that one would be much less likely to evaluate an irrelevant target by reference to that response.

current conditions and the extension of those conditions in simulation. He refers to "accounts of torture." One's revulsion, empathy, and care are inseparable from the details of those accounts, including, for example, the degree to which the suffering of, say, tortured prisoners is depicted or the degree to which they are presented as an out-group guilty of crimes (perhaps with the suffering of their victims highlighted).

Consider, again, the example of the lion. What appears to happen in a case of this sort is that I simulate a particular causal sequence in which the lion exits the cage, sees me, and has a hunger-motivated actional response. Thus, I have an initial situation that I understand and reimagine in terms of category prototypes (e.g., the cluster of properties and propensities connected with being a lion) and associated trajectories of action (e.g., what predators are likely to do in these circumstances). As this suggests, we have cognitive structures that select and organize aspects of the current situation to produce the simulations that constitute the eliciting conditions for our emotional response. In the case of a lion, the cognitive structures at issue are fairly simple and straightforward. In the sorts of social situations that face us with ethical dilemmas, the relevant cognitive structures are likely to be far more intricate and equivocal than those involved in the zoo scenario. Moreover, it may be that a number of such structures could potentially apply to any given situation, yielding different results. Thus, there is often considerable complexity and ambiguity in our moral reflections, along with considerable scope for variable memories and simulations, resulting in variable eliciting conditions for emotional response.

This leads me to the second central claim by Haidt that I believe is correct, important, and underappreciated. This is his contention that narrative is crucial for our emotional and ethical responses. Indeed, Haidt maintains that "grand narratives" are at the "core of each [moral] matrix" (2012, 330). If I understand Haidt correctly, a moral matrix is a combination and specification of a set of moral foundations, a combination and specification that forms "a complete, unified, and emotionally compelling worldview" (125) for the members of the relevant community. In my account, narrative prototypes form a crucial part of such general moral structures. The structures I have in mind are more akin to Haidt's foundations than to his matrices. But the general connection between our views should be evident. (I will fill in some of the details shortly.)

There is a difficulty here, however. Haidt has a very capacious concept of narrative, perhaps one that is too capacious. For example, he refers to the "conservative narrative that Obama was a liberal universalist, someone who could not be trusted to put the interests of his nation above the interests of the rest of the world" (2012, 190). Here, Haidt seems to be speaking simply of a prototype – that liberals are universalists rather than nationalists – defining a character disposition. It would involve a narrative only in a case where that disposition developed into a particular series of actions and events. Moreover, the simplicity of the prototype here does not help us to understand what narrative structures might be deployed in diffuse, practical circumstances or just how they might operate. Haidt gives other examples that initially appear a bit more apt, such as the liberal "narrative" that history has involved a struggle for justice and democracy and the conservative "narrative" that liberals established a welfare state with deleterious consequences. But here, too, it is not clear that the idea of narrative goes beyond the observation that liberals believe that some things happened historically and conservatives believe that other things happened historically.

There are (at least) three levels at which we might wish to consider the relevance of stories to emotion and ethics. The most general level is simply that of a causal sequence. Any story is an instance of a causal sequence (see Hogan 2022b). Conversely, when we understand the word "story" in the broadest sense, any articulation of a causal sequence constitutes a story – for example, "too much pressure built up in the radiator; as a result, it cracked." When treating people's emotional and ethical responses, it is of course crucial to take into account such causal sequences (e.g., "He jumped because he thought the roar was from a real lion, rather than a recording"). But this is obvious. Moreover, we do not seem to advance our understanding of emotion or ethics by referring to causal sequences as "narratives." Indeed, this label may even be slightly obfuscatory. If we mean "causes and consequences," we are probably better off saying that rather than saying "narratives."

The other two levels are more promising. At a level of intermediate generality, we have genres. Genres are recurring story structures. They are more specific than mere causal sequences; these include, for example, the common pattern of love stories. My account of ethics and narrative will focus on genres as, in part, guiding structures for our ethical understanding and evaluation of situations and events and our behavioral responses to those situations and events.

The final level is the fully articulated, particular sequence of conditions and events – what we ordinarily call a "story" or "narrative." For example, unlike the genre of "romantic tragedy," the particular story of Shakespeare's *Romeo and Juliet* has well-specified characters going through experiences and engaging in actions that broadly fit the genre but specify it and, in some respects, deviate from its prototypical form. As the preceding examples suggest, Haidt emphasizes the level of particular stories in his account of narrative, emotion, and ethics. We see this, for example, when he writes that the crucial "narratives are not necessarily true stories—they are simplified and selective reconstructions of the past, often connected to an idealized vision of the future" (Haidt 2012, 328). But even when he is relatively explicit (as here), he remains unclear about just how particular stories affect moral response, and how this process differs from the commonplace process of taking (simplified) causal sequences into account.

## Emotions and Genres

As already noted, my attention to these issues has been focused on the level of genre. Even when addressing particular stories, it is essential to consider how more general or abstract narrative structures may have guided our thought about a particular situation and our moral and emotional responses to it (e.g., by drawing our attention to certain aspects of the situation or by leading us to draw some causal inferences rather than others). In earlier work (see Hogan 2003, 2011), I have argued that some narrative structures are highly prominent, recurring significantly across a range of unrelated literary traditions. In keeping with this prominence, these structures are particularly likely to guide our thought and feeling not only in fiction, but also in such political areas as nationalism (see Hogan 2009). Moreover, I have argued that the organizational structure of such narratives is a function of a few emotion systems that define happiness goals. If this is correct, then it would seem that we may resolve both our quandaries about ethics – emotional and narrative – simultaneously.

More exactly, we may specify the relation between emotion and ethics in the following way. Emotions lead us to envision ideals, which embody the perfection of hedonic conditions or the elimination of aversive conditions eliciting the emotions. Put differently, ideals are the prototypical cases of conditions we would like to sustain in positive emotions or conditions we would like to achieve in a change from negative emotions. The ideal of romantic love, for example – thus, what we would wish to sustain – is mutual, secure attachment and attraction. The ideal opposed to physical disgust – thus, what we would wish to shift to – is cleanliness or purity. Connected with these points, narratives prototypically involve a protagonist pursuing some ideal goal (e.g., mutual, secure, affectionate, and sexual love). Specifically, it involves the pursuit of an ideal that we imagine will, if attained, result in happiness. Indeed, happiness itself has an ideal; that ideal is unmitigated and enduring, as signaled by the formulaic ending of fairy tale romances – "and they lived happily ever after."

This is all germane to our present concerns because we may understand ethical response as a function of motivational ideals. Our ethical norms bear on the same targets as these ideals (e.g., romantic union or national sovereignty, in the cases of romantic and heroic stories, respectively). Moreover, the ideality of our fancied goals incorporates our spontaneous moral response; if it did not, then the ideals would be troubled and ambivalent, not ideal. In addition, our pursuit of those ideals is prototypically elaborated through the (emotionally intensified) narrative sequences that we simulate around those ideals. More exactly, there are a few prominent emotions that we view as defining types of happiness; these include, for example, attachment and pride (both individual and in-group). There are, in addition, prominent narrative prototypes that recur with those emotions; these include romantic stories (which derive in part from attachment) and heroic stories (which derive in part from individual and in-group pride). Given that our ethical responses are motivational insofar as they are emotive (not merely abstract judgments), it seems clear that those responses are closely linked with emotional ideals. And, given the close relation between emotional ideals and narrative simulation, we might also expect our ethical responses to be at least in part conditioned by salient, emotion-defined narrative structures. In other words, given the motivational importance of happiness-defining emotions, the causal elaboration of those emotions in story genres, and the role of emotion-based ideals in goal pursuit, we might reasonably expect that our ethical thought and feeling would often be closely interconnected with those emotions, their ideals, and the associated narrative prototypes.

It is important to note immediately that our narrative capacities are necessarily flexible. We are not confined to a small number of narrative alternatives for construing particular causal relations. But we do tend to favor some alternatives over others. Here, as in other aspects of human cognition and emotion, there is a trade-off between particularity and generality and between accommodation and assimilation (in Piaget's terms; 1971, 4, 8n.3). We need to be able to recognize the uniqueness of events and conditions. But we also need to be able to respond quickly to threats and opportunities before being harmed by the former or missing out on the latter. In consequence, we need to be able to recognize and respond to idiosyncrasy, but we also benefit from categorization. Categorization is not confined to physical objects, such as chairs and cats. It includes story structures comprising event sequences, scenes, and character roles. In the case of narratives, as in the case of ordinary material objects, those categories are often based on prototypes or (roughly) standard cases, rather than necessary and sufficient conditions (on prototypes, see Rosch 2011). In this case, the prototypes at issue are varieties of story structures – themselves, again, derived from emotion systems.

This leads us to the issue of just what the relevant story prototypes and associated emotions might be. Clearly, narrative structures and emotions may become more or less salient and efficacious in particular historical or cultural contexts. However, our first concern might reasonably be to isolate the prototypes that are psychologically most powerful, independent of historical or cultural contingencies. One obvious way of determining this is by examining what prototypes recur across cultures. Prima facie, we have good reason to expect that the narrative structures that occur prominently across unrelated traditions – thus narrative universals – are particularly psychologically forceful. The reoccurrence of narrative structures in the major works of a wide range of literary traditions suggests that those structures have a particularly important place in the imaginative and affective lives of human beings generally. This seems to be especially likely if these narrative structures derive from the nature and operation of human emotion systems.

If we are going to draw on narrative universals in understanding ethical cognition and emotion, it follows that comparative literature is crucial for its possible contributions to the cognitive and affective science of ethics. However, it is not comparative literature as usually practiced. Specifically, comparative literature is commonly taken to refer to the study of different national literatures or to the study of literatures in different languages. These are, of course, valuable forms of study and should have an important place in work that is cognitive and comparative. However, when I refer to comparative literature, I will be concerned principally with more strictly segregated bodies of literature, which I will refer to as "traditions." By "tradition," I mean a body of literary works that are densely and strongly interrelated, historically and/or regionally ("genetically and areally," in the terminology of linguistics). In addition, the works of one tradition are, at most, only sparsely and weakly interrelated with those of a distinct tradition.

National literatures are, of course, more closely interconnected internally than externally. English literary works have more interconnections with English literary works than they have (on the whole) with German works. Nonetheless, the historical and regional connections between the two national literatures are extensive. Historically, both share the Greek and Latin classics as well as biblical narratives. Regionally, they are linked by translations and bilingual reading. In consequence, comparative literary research on English and German works would not constitute a comparative study of traditions in my sense. In contrast, work on early Persian and Chinese narratives would. Of course, there are complications here. The important point is simply that there are significant differences in what comparative literary study tells us, depending on whether it focuses on different national literatures within a tradition or spans different traditions.

But what, then, does comparative literature (in my cross-tradition sense) tell us about narrative? It tells us that there are some genres, some prototypical sequences of events, that are remarkably similar across distinct traditions. The most common genres cross-culturally appear to be heroic, romantic, and sacrificial (see Hogan 2003, 2011). Again, genres are formed around ideals generated by emotion systems, such as the ideal of enduring reciprocal attachment and attraction in romantic love. The ideals do not represent the narrative prototypes' ethical norms directly. However, the norms are implied by the individual behavior and social conditions needed to achieve those ideals, insofar as the ideals do not bear directly on characters' own egocentric well-being. For example, to a great extent, the norms for the romantic plot bear on the parents of the lovers and on other members of society who fail to accept the lovers' interests and preferences. The norms do bear on the lovers themselves, but only insofar as they act for each other's benefit, rather than their own. For example, fidelity and trustworthiness are important virtues in the romantic narrative.

More exactly, the heroic genre focuses on pride, shame, and anger – to some extent individual, but more importantly connected with an identity group. The associated narrative commonly involves the deposing of a legitimate leader and the defeat of a social in-group (e.g., the invasion of the home society by alien forces), thus the devastation of individual and in-group pride. The legitimate leader and the home society, following the common process whereby shame provokes anger, rally their forces and defeat the enemy, perhaps shaming them in turn. An emphasis on individual and social pride, along with a stress on in-group and out-group divisions, is often (as here) connected with a hierarchical and militaristic ethics – an ethics of loyalty, bravery, and related virtues; it also tends to be linked with punitive enforcement of ethical standards and to involve the (often metaphorical) assimilation of a range of ethical problems to military conflicts. The two parts of the heroic structure – the threat–defense sequence and the usurpation sequence – are related to two fundamental features of human social life. The first is, of course, the classing of people into in-groups and out-groups. The second is a closely related feature, "the hierarchical organization of groups," in the words of Richeson et al.; as they explain, there is reason to believe that "this type of social dominance is a universal organizing principle in human societies" (2007, 9).

There is, however, a common addendum to the heroic narrative, what I call the "epilogue of suffering." In this addition to the heroic story, the dead are mourned; in some cases, the heroes acknowledge their immoral acts and engage in socially restorative penance. The epilogue of suffering often challenges in-group versus out-group divisions; it stresses sympathetic grief and, in some cases, even suggests an ethics of nonviolence and empathy.

Somewhat related to the heroic genre, and perhaps the epilogue particularly, is the revenge genre. The revenge genre is most often highly ambivalent.[6] It involves a great harm done to the protagonist – typically a sexual betrayal or the murder of a loved one – and the protagonist's attempt to "repay" that harm. The genre is ambivalent in part because the repayment often involves the death of innocents and of course it does not lead to any positive good, such as the restoration of the murdered beloved. The ethics of the revenge narrative commonly condemn the initial criminal act severely and may celebrate the loyalty and selflessness of the revenger, even while condemning vigilantism and perhaps criticizing the ineffectiveness or corruption of the official criminal justice system. Put differently, the hero of a heroic story is regularly represented as a largely idealized in-group member for the targeted audience (i.e., an in-group member who fulfills the norms of the in-group). In contrast, the revenger is regularly represented as an in-group member or as ambiguous regarding in-group/out-group status (as in the case of Othello); either way, he or she is typically not idealized but represented as violating group norms, specifically in the area of social justice.

The revenge genre may be contrasted with the criminal investigation genre, in which the crime and punishment are taken care of by a neutral social representative. The relation between revenge and criminal investigation is well illustrated by Aeschylus's *Oresteia*. (For an illuminating discussion of the concluding play of that trilogy, which is most crucial here, see Nussbaum 2016, 1–5.) Despite key differences, the emotional ethics of the criminal investigation genre are often continuous with those of the revenge narrative. Thus, this genre may involve an *Oresteia*-like affirmation of the value of neutral, evenhanded judicial processes. But it may also rationalize a hyper-punitive regime of policing – in effect, victim seeking engaged in by the state, rather than by private individuals. Vitale rightly points out, "Today, we are awash in police dramas" that "portray the police as struggling to fight crime in a complex and at times morally contradictory environment. Even when police are portrayed as engaging in corrupt or brutal behavior, as in Dirty Harry or The Shield, it is

---

[6] This is not to say that everyone takes revenge to be problematic. The mob in *Julius Caesar* does not appear to do so. More significantly, the (nonfictional) French revolutionary Alexandre Rousselin idealized the goal of revenge, proclaiming, "Vengeance is the only source of liberty, the only goddess we ought to bring sacrifices to" (quoted in Arendt 1977, 101).

understood that their primary motivation is to get the bad guys" (2017). However, "[i]t is largely a liberal fantasy that the police exist to protect us from the bad guys." My only disagreement with Vitale is in the suggestion that this is a contemporary, American phenomenon. We see much the same pattern in, for example, the paradigmatic Judge Bao criminal investigation narratives of the Yuan, Ming, and Qing Dynasties in China or stories of Judge Di (see van Gulik 1976).

It is important to stress that this portrait of policing, and the "law and order" ethics with which it is associated, do not derive from an objective depiction of the real world. As Vitale argues, "the basic nature of the law and the police, since its earliest origins, is to be a tool for managing inequality and maintaining the status quo." Police do not even investigate a wide range of reported crimes, and "[m]ost crimes that are investigated are not solved."[7] In this way, the criminal investigation genre commonly has the same general ideological orientation as the heroic genre.[8]

In relation to (implied) ethics, the romantic prototype is perhaps most fully in contradiction with the heroic and criminal investigation structures. The romantic plot focuses on attachment bonding in combination with sexual desire. It prototypically involves two lovers whose union is prevented by society, commonly due to identity group oppositions, such as socioeconomic class. The story leads to the comic union of the lovers or the tragic victory of oppressive social norms. An emphasis on attachment appears to foster an empathic response. This is not surprising, given the developmental relation between empathy and attachment (e.g., see Stern and Cassidy 2017), our enhanced sensitivity to the pain of an attachment

---

[7] Among the ironies of the proviolence approach to justice is the danger it poses to police officers themselves. A common argument in favor of police violence is that police deserve protection against violent criminals. However, Vitale points out that "[o]ffenders who are committed to evading police are more likely to use deadly force precisely because they know the officer is armed .... An armed suspect is much less likely to shoot an unarmed officer" (2017).

[8] It is also important to point out that the genre tends to reinforce our (anger-related) tendency to see punishment as the only viable approach to deterrence. In fact, punishment often fails to deter crime, and it may even be counterproductive. Consider, for example, the current frenzy over illegal immigration. Part of that frenzy concerns a supposed relation between criminal drug trafficking and people crossing the border illegally from Mexico. As Vitale points out, the punitive approach leads these men and women to "rely on the criminal underworld of 'coyotes' who charge thousands of dollars to facilitate passage but often fail to deliver and in some cases kidnap, rape, and kill those who pay them. Migrants in these circumstances are more likely to be coerced into carrying drugs" (2017). More generally, as Bruce Waller explains, "[e]ven when aimed at an offending target, punitive or retributive responses are grossly inefficient, as behavioral research has long since established; in addition, the side effects (such as blocking inquiry into deeper systemic causes) result in even greater harm" (1986, 12).

object (see Bucchioni et al. 2015), and more generally the connection between attachment feelings for a person and a parallel interpersonal stance in his or her regard. In addition, the operation of social norms and identity categories to (tragically) separate the lovers tends to connect the genre with an ethical libertarianism and opposition to identity categorization; the integration of attachment bonding with sexual desire commonly removes that desire from ethical censure, sometimes even leading to the celebration of sexuality as ethically positive. We see an instance of the last point in the 1960s slogan "Make love, not war!," a brief phrase that implicitly invokes the large contrast between an ethics based on romantic narrative and an ethics based on heroic narrative.

In its treatment of sexuality, the romantic prototype is related to – but also contrasted with – a less prominent, cross-cultural genre, the seduction or sexual violation genre. The sexual violation plot is based on sexual desire and involves a seduction or rape, followed by the abandonment of the victim by the seducer or rapist. This may result in the eventual (highly ambivalent) union of the couple or the purgative death of one or both. (The union is typical of "problem comedies," such as Terence's *The Mother-in-Law* and Shakespeare's *All's Well That Ends Well*.) The sexual violation genre tends to represent sexuality as shameful and as a paradigm of immoral activity. The "comic" version of the sexual violation narrative (ending in marriage rather than death) may suggest the value of social conformity above individual happiness or even social justice. Alternatively, it can be recruited to criticize gender hierarchies in the author's society, as may be the case with Terence.

Whereas the sexual violation structure gives us desire without attachment, the family separation and reunion structure gives us attachment without desire. Specifically, this genre involves the isolation of children from parents or siblings from one another, with their eventual reunion, sometimes many years later. It tends to foster an ethical orientation of attachment-enhanced empathy and care, in keeping with parent–child relations. It can elevate familial obligations above other, more general human relations. However, it does not typically appear to do so in a way that is discriminatory. Indeed, family separation and reunion narratives commonly serve to humanize out-groups and undermine divisions based on identity categories. For example, it is the most important story prototype in Harriet Beecher Stowe's anti-slavery novel, *Uncle Tom's Cabin*, and in a number of Rabindranath Tagore's socially progressive short stories.

Finally, sacrificial stories take up sin and the purging of sin from society. The sin is often sexual, and the primary emotions are commonly disgust and shame (understood as a feeling that one is an object of other people's disgust or is intrinsically disgusting). The basic structure here begins with a communal transgression, often the result of temptation or seduction by an out-group member. This transgression results in punishment, commonly a collective punishment in which the whole society suffers some devastation. That devastation is often famine (thus stressing hunger, understandably in the context of its motivational contradiction with the emotion of disgust) or, less often, epidemic disease (which may itself be disgusting). The punishment continues until the guilty community makes a sacrifice. This is often an innocent scapegoat, though it is sometimes the guilty parties; I refer to these as the penitential (innocent victim) and purgative (guilty victim) versions, respectively. This sacrifice returns the society to its prelapsarian well-being. This genre seems more ethically malleable than the others in the sense that it may focus on different sorts of sin. However, in the penitential version, its ideal remains constant, for this ideal is the scapegoat who, sinless himself or herself, sacrifices all egocentric self-interest for the benefit of others, commonly others within a specific in-group. The purgative version is different in stressing, indeed demonizing, the culpability of the seductive out-group and in stigmatizing virtually any in-group contact with the out-group. In consequence, the purgative version tends to be connected with the most extreme forms of out-grouping (e.g., Nazism), in effect absolutizing an antipathetic (thus, anti-empathic) interpersonal stance toward such groups, which is in a sense a perverse form of idealization – of just the sort we find in the writings of fascists, who often insist that fascism is a specifically moral system (e.g., see Mussolini and Gentile 1935, 2–4; Mussolini and Gentile 2012, 5–10).

In sum, ethical responses are motivated by emotion systems, which imply ideals such as constancy in the case of attachment. Those ideals also partially define narrative trajectories that typify the varieties of human pursuit of happiness, in relation to both egocentric and allocentric self-interest. Some of these trajectories recur across cultures and time periods and are particularly consequential for the ways in which they lead us to organize and imagine our pursuit of ideals. Specifically, the heroic genre celebrates group loyalty and selfless courage for an in-group (often national or religious) in violent conflict with an out-group. However, part of the heroic narrative – the epilogue of suffering – challenges the value of heroic violence and identity group opposition, valuing self-criticism and acts of penance for harming others in the past. The purgative version of the sacrificial plot (focused on the out-group members who seduced the in-group members to sin) takes up identity group opposition and associated violence, intensified by disgust at the out-group and their intimacy with in-group members. The penitential (innocent scapegoat) version of the sacrificial plot stresses selfless devotion to the group. However, in this case, the devotion involves the nonconfrontational choice of self-sacrifice rather than a violent struggle that risks harm or death. The other sacrificial virtue, characteristic of both the penitential and purgative version, is purity, especially sexual purity. The romantic plot most clearly advocates the virtue of tolerance and the willingness to let other people – including one's own children – make their own life decisions. It also values a tolerant (sometimes even celebratory) attitude toward sexuality and a rejection of identity group divisions, as well as fidelity and trustworthiness. The family separation and reunion plot stresses the importance of care for those who are socially placed in one's charge. These are usually one's own children or aged parents. But sometimes they include others (e.g., foundlings) who are made one's responsibility by circumstances. The seduction or sexual violation genre may stress the virtue of female chastity or that of male familial responsibility, both typically by contrast with the misbehavior of the characters themselves. The revenge genre may acknowledge the virtue of loyalty (by the self-denying devotion of the revenger) but more frequently advocates the virtue of self-restraint in deference to social authority (by contrast with the revenger). Finally, the criminal investigation narrative tends to elevate the integrity of the ideal state representative (e.g., the judge in Chinese crime stories), as well as the importance of such a representative's breaking the law when putatively "necessary" to prevent worse violations by criminals.

The preceding arguments regarding ethics and story universals suggest two conclusions that are important to spell out a bit more fully before going on. First, these story prototypes represent the main ethical tendencies to be found in any large, complex society. (Very small societies may be more uniform, perhaps in idiosyncratic ways.) Those tendencies are likely to appear in different proportions and different hierarchies, thus with different degrees of motivational force or social consequence. They will also vary in their precise application (e.g., depending on just what properties are taken to define in-groups and out-groups at a given time and place). The various ethical features tend to cluster together in the way depicted in the story prototypes. This is due largely to the properties of the emotion–motivation systems involved (e.g., the relation between attachment and empathy [in romantic works] or that between shame and rage [in heroic works]). Although other configurations are possible and do occur, they are not as common or enduring. This is not a mere incidental feature of stories. Rather, it results from the fact that the cross-cultural story genres are the prototypical forms in which people simulate emotion system ideals (or, in some cases, anti ideals) and the pursuit of those ideals as life goals. (This, in turn, indicates why literature is particularly informative regarding such ethical alternatives and is particularly consequential for our ethical lives.)

The second important suggestion here is that individuals tend to favor particular genres as a sort of default, though that default may be displaced in particular circumstances. For example, I seem to take the romantic structure, family separation and reunion narrative, and the epilogue of suffering as paradigmatic of ethical problems and responses. In other words, other things being equal, I tend to think of moral dilemmas in terms of, for example, the conflict between lovers and domineering parents. Thus, when I think of ethics and race relations, I am likely to have tacitly in mind such issues as interracial marriage. More generally, I am more likely than others to interpret situations of conflict as parallel to the arbitrary, parental imposition of norms. In connection with this, I am inclined to respond to such situations with emotional sympathy for the "children," enhanced by the involvement of attachment feelings based on my own emotional memories. All this is, in addition, interconnected with my setting of ethical parameters, which orients me differently from someone who tacitly assimilates interracial relations to, say, heroic structures (involving enemy attack) or sacrificial structures (involving sinful impurity). Among other things, the romantic prototype is likely to be connected with setting the scope parameter at the level of humanity. In contrast, the heroic model would be associated with a scope parameter at the level of some narrower (putatively threatened) in-group.

As a final point, I should perhaps note that my inclinations are not purely individual or idiosyncratic. To some extent, my preferences identify me as a child of the 1960s, the counterculture, the Vietnam War, and the peace movement. But they also identify me as only one possibility within whatever we take the encompassing culture and historical period to be. The other possibilities for the culture and period are, once again, as diverse as the emotional ideals from which people everywhere generate goals in life, and in stories.

**Moral Foundations**

As the preceding comments indicate, I would not divide up ethical orientations in precisely the way Haidt does. Nonetheless, there is a broad correlation between Haidt's moral foundations and my narrative prototypes, in the sense that most of the foundations find primary expression in one or another genre. It is worth going through Haidt's (2012) list of moral foundations – care, liberty, loyalty, authority, sanctity, and fairness – one by one.

Haidt's foundation of care is most clearly connected with the familial structure (where it is linked with family bonds). But it is also implied in the guilt and associated empathy across in-group/out-group divisions, as developed in the epilogue of suffering of some heroic plots. Indeed, it turns up as an ancillary virtue in perhaps every genre. As such, I see concern about harm as present in a range of categories (in keeping with the broadly orienting role of the valence parameter); I would not confine it to the care foundation, as Haidt does.

Liberty is manifest in the romantic narrative. Or, rather, individual liberty is valued in the romantic structure, whereas in-group escape from out-group domination features prominently in the heroic plot. "Liberty" in the second sense, however, is probably best understood as a matter of in-group pride. Insofar as in-group pride enters into Haidt's scheme, it falls most obviously under the rubric of loyalty.

Loyalty appears crucially in the heroic plot, as does authority. Indeed, depending on how they are defined, we may wish to categorize them as two aspects of one moral orientation, rather than two orientations. On the other hand, different versions of the virtue of loyalty and the norm of authority appear in different prototypes with different values, including inversions of these values, at least that of authority. For example, the romantic valuing of liberty often comes at the cost of respect for authority. Moreover, the romantic structure commonly values fidelity as a sort of *nonhierarchical* loyalty of one lover to another – as when the beloved refuses to consummate her union with the rival in the Persian story of Layla and Majnoon, the Chinese story of Liáng Shānbó and Zhù Yīngtái, and, of course, the story of Romeo and Juliet.

Haidt's sanctity (formerly "purity") foundation appears positively in the penitential version of the sacrificial structure and indirectly, by way of contrast, in the purgative version and in the seduction narrative. In the case of female characters, this positive/negative division is often linked with the common patriarchal dichotomizations of women into Madonna and "whore" (e.g., see Darbha 2002, 77). On the other hand, some seduction/sexual assault narratives are more damning of the seducer or rapist than of his victim (rightly so, of course). In any case, the celebration of purity is clearly the moral response to disgust. The obvious alternative to the ethics of sexual disgust/purity is the "sex-positive" attitude associated with the romantic structure.[9]

Finally, there is fairness. Fairness seems to me somewhat different from the other "foundations." Fairness is really a sort of metaethical principle, requiring a mathematically appropriate social division of benefits and/or burdens or harms. In terms of the preceding analysis, it basically dictates

---

[9] Haidt (2012) here links the sanctity or purity foundation with the political right. However, it is important to note that this is far from inevitable. In the confirmation hearings for Brett Kavanaugh, for example, the left was far more likely to express disgust over reports of Kavanaugh's sexual behavior, whereas conservatives seemed hardly to bat an eye over these reports.

the following. First, there is a default social distribution of rewards that is proportionate to the contribution of each person to the production of goods being distributed (cf. Boyer 2018, 175). This has a limiting case for windfalls; when no one contributed to the production of goods, the distribution should be egalitarian. Second, this default distribution is almost certainly qualified by considerations of need and of past, current, and future capacity. Thus, we would not consider it fair to deprive a toddler of needed food because he or she did not take part in the farming, though I suspect that responses of this sort are not typically the result of calculation but of more spontaneous, ethical response (e.g., our feeling of compassion for a hungry toddler). Third, the distribution of rewards and punishments may be qualified by ethical principles, guided by broad, ethical orientations. For example, depending on the setting of their scope parameter, members of a given society might think it is entirely fair to distribute almost all available produce to citizens of their own nation, even though the farmwork was done entirely by, say, prisoners of war (thus, national out-group members).[10] However, it does not have a clear connection with a specific narrative structure.

In short, fairness is "foundational" (as Haidt indicates). However, I take it to operate as a second-order principle in the sense that it governs the distribution of rewards and punishments for a range of ethical activities (e.g., for judging crimes, prosecuting war, and distributing food). It remains a function of ethical orientation (thus, our fundamental principles with their parameter settings), along with variations in empathic response. However, it may not typically operate through narrative prototypes (perhaps in part due to its basically mathematical properties), though of course it may combine with any narrative structure in specific cases.

**Narrative, Politics, and Evolution**

It is important to make two further points here before going on to discuss some literary examples. The first point concerns politics. I have already indicated my differences from Haidt (2012) on his account of the political left and right. However, I do not entirely disagree with his treatment of the broad ethical preferences of liberals and conservatives. Indeed, in my account, too, different emotional emphases and forms of emplotment are often connected with broadly liberal or conservative orientations (see Hogan 2009). For example, romantic emplotments tend toward liberalism

---

[10] For some complications of the way evaluations of fairness may develop, as well as the different ways in which they may be applied – sometimes with opposed consequences – see Boyer (2018, 196–200).

and heroic emplotments tend to be conservative (in the right-wing sense). However, different circumstances may evoke different emplotments for any given political orientation. For example, recent events surrounding sexual harassment connect some kinds of left-liberalism with disgust, and with a version of the "purgative" form of sacrificial emplotment. Indeed, insofar as there is such a phenomenon as "cancel culture," it is a good example. In part, the idea of "cancel culture" is an ideological tool operating to tar left-wing social criticism with the false identification of progressivism with authoritarianism. However, there is a real (if often overstated) tendency on part of the left to shame people accused of illiberal attitudes, such as sexism, racism, homophobia, or transphobia, and to insist that those people's public presentations be canceled, that they be denied awards, and in some instances that they lose their jobs. This is a clear case of a left-wing, purgative response to disgust.

Thus, liberals and conservatives do not simply batten on a single emotion and narrative structure. We all are likely to operate with a range of emotional concerns and narrative models. Differences – between liberals and conservatives, but also within liberalism or conservatism – are in part a matter of the degree to which we favor one narrative prototype over another. But they are also a matter of the contexts in which we invoke one or another (e.g., precisely when we appeal to disgust and sacrificial emplotment). Moreover, in any given case, liberals and conservatives (or people with other political orientations) might adopt the same genre but map the genre onto historical agents and events differently (I might emplot an event as an illegitimate usurpation while you emplot it as a restoration of legitimate government). Finally, there is no simple liberal or conservative uniformity in either case. Thus, ethical emplotment in part parallels but in part complicates such categories as "liberal" and "conservative."

The second point concerns evolution. It is common now to say that human ethics evolved, just as human capacities for simulation or for theory of mind evolved. The first thing to say about this is that, if true, it refers to ethics not as a set of objective values but as a set of practices motivated by principles that are taken to be objective values – or, alternatively, ethics as a set of practices that we may rationalize by reference to principles that we take to be objective values. Formulated in this way, however, the idea of the evolution of ethics might begin to seem questionable. It does not seem to be the case that we are in general motivated by genuine adherence to ethical principles. But if we merely rationalize actions that are motivated differently, then it is not clear why the rationalizations would have evolved in the biological sense. (In a loose, ordinary language sense, they certainly "evolved" historically, but that is very different.)

Of course, one might say that societies would never survive if we all acted with unmitigated egocentrism, lacking care, loyalty, and so on. That is true. But it seems that evolution has taken care of all that with the emotion systems, the processes of spontaneous and effortful empathy, and the capacity for simulation, as well as the possibility of emotion modulation – all of which evolved by way of serving a number of functions, most of which we would not be inclined to call "ethical." Haidt wishes to explain his moral foundations as specific, ethical adaptations. In contrast, I believe that the most plausible and parsimonious account of ethics relies on nothing more than ordinary cognitive architecture, prominently our feeling of empathy.

Consider the case of guilt, defined by Patricia Greenspan as "a distinctively human emotion involving empathy with a victim of one's own harmful behavior" (2010, 544; actually, de Waal's research suggests that it is not distinctively human, but that does not affect the present argument; for a graphic summary of his views, see de Waal 2006, 180). This seems to me to isolate the moral emotion very well.[11] Surely, if anything evolved as a specifically moral adaptation, it was guilt. But what constitutes guilt in this sense? As to eliciting conditions, there is suffering on the part of the target; there is empathy; and there is a sense of one's own causal contribution to the target's suffering. As to actional outcomes, there is an inclination to avoid such action in the future and a more immediate impulse to assuage the target's pain and indeed to go beyond mere normalization through some sort of reparation. (In Chapter 5, I will outline the nature of emotion episodes. However, I believe that the ideas of "eliciting conditions" and "actional outcomes" are intuitive enough to invoke before we turn to that analysis.)

As to function, empathy evolved for a wide range of reasons. For example, it is crucial to various forms of learning (as when, especially as children, we learn what to fear and thus what to avoid as threats). It is also crucial to social life, though not only what we might consider to be

---

[11] Rottschaefer similarly writes that guilt occurs following "the assessment by the empathizer that she herself is the source of the person's distress" (1998, 87). Rottschaefer, however, does not suggest that guilt is confined to this context. He is most likely correct about our use of the word "guilt." However, my point here is not that Greenspan's definition covers the entire range of ordinary language usage. My claim, rather, is that this is one distinct way in which our emotion systems operate, with descriptive and explanatory consequences. It is certainly part of our ordinary language concept. But ordinary language concepts cannot simply be taken over without qualification as if they were already scientifically adapted to the systematic description and explanation of natural phenomena. Thus, my use of the word "guilt," like Greenspan's definition, is narrower than the ordinary language use. My contention is that the narrowing is guided by the nature of the phenomena at issue.

moral aspects of social life. The sense of causal attribution is necessary for a wide range of adaptive functions. This clearly includes causal attribution to ourselves. Here, too, the process is crucial to our learning. We can only learn from our mistakes if we distinguish what we are responsible for. As to our feelings of regret, we will only be motivated to learn from our mistakes if the associated emotion is negative. Note that this process is not confined to learning from moral errors. It is, rather, a matter of learning from practical failures.

The impulse to assuage the target's pain may be a matter of adaptation for kin selection. In that account, we are generally more likely to come face-to-face with the suffering of kin than non-kin. Moreover, our attachment to kin intensifies our empathic care. (As Patricia Churchland puts it, "I am a mammal, and like other mammals, I have a social brain. I am wired to care, especially about those I am attached to"; 2019, 2–3.) By this account, empathic care for non-kin is simply the result of the empathic mechanism operating more widely than the strict adaptive function. In keeping with this, Churchland asks at one point, "Attachment begets caring; caring begets conscience?" (2019, 49).

Another explanation of compassionate helping broadens the function to a more encompassing in-group, reasoning that the cooperative success of a society is adaptive for its members. The in-group biased "parochial altruism" (Sapolsky 2017, 364) might arise through "neo-group selection" processes (see 362–364), enhanced by "ethnocentrism, religious intolerance, race-based politics, and so on" (399). Here, too, the mechanism overshoots the mark, leading us to empathize with out-group members in the unusual case where we witness their suffering and are not in the grip of an emotion (e.g., anger) that fosters antipathy. (This can occur with victors after the defeat of an enemy, as represented in the epilogue of suffering.) I suspect that the reparatory impulse serves to diminish the anger of others and is therefore also not specifically ethical.

So it seems that the various components of the feeling of guilt arise for the usual "selfish" reasons (even if the precise way selfishness operates has to be slightly redeveloped if we include neo-group selection).[12] Thus, there

---

[12] It would seem that group selection has to result from selective advantages for individuals passing on their genes (since only individuals do this), but that only occurs in the context of consequences for the group since group conditions affect individuals passing on their genes. To take Sapolsky's example (2017, 398), it would seem that increasing aggressiveness of chickens benefits the individual aggressors until a certain threshold is passed and the increased aggressiveness harms the group, thereby harming the individuals. At this point, other, less aggressive groups of chickens would reproduce more rapidly, perhaps overrunning the first, overly aggressive group. Chickens that had, for example, some sort of genetic mechanism that limited the spread of aggressiveness (e.g., a trait that sometimes inhibited relevant gene expression) would be the

does not seem to be any reason to believe that ethics evolved as a distinct system or as anything that we would generally characterize as ethical. Rather, a wide range of mental structures and processes evolved, for a wide range of reasons, and some of them are likely to play a role in activities we consider ethical, just as they may play a role in sports or fashion (without thereby constituting an evolved sports or fashion system).

Of course, there is still the issue of why different societies in different traditions regularly identify some set of behaviors as, roughly, ethical. How does it come about that we group various behaviors together in this way? Moreover, why do we engage in moral reasoning?

These points are significant. But I see no reason to view the category of ethics or the processes of moral reasoning as specifically moral adaptations. First, there is no need to believe that moral deliberation, as such, is genetically guided. Rather, it arises cross-culturally because our genetic predispositions and social circumstances result in different societies facing similar problems. The problems arise from the fact that our empathy, though biased toward family and in-group, is not rigidly restricted. Indeed, it can be promiscuous. We can face an enemy across the battlefield or an oppressed group in our own society and experience care about their condition. This is not what dominant groups in any society desire. Putting the point less intentionalistically, groups cannot become dominant in a society or across societies if there is very much intergroup empathy and care. The stability of a social hierarchy relies in part on the manipulation of our attitude toward other people – our "interpersonal stance," as I have been calling it (I draw the phrase from Frijda and Scherer 2009, 10) – the cultivation of specific types and degrees of empathy or antipathy. An antipathetic interpersonal stance aimed at enemies or oppressed groups is not inevitable. It needs to be cultivated.

My conclusion, then, is that attitudes, judgments, and behaviors that we might decide (in, say, ethical theory) to identify and class together as ethical responses resulted from the interaction of adaptations and social dynamics that are in themselves ethically neutral. Explicitly formulated ethical reflection developed through social adaptations (or "memes"),[13]

---

best adapted in the long run. In a case of this sort, the well-being of the group would figure centrally in the evolutionary sequence. But the (restricted) aggressiveness would still be passed on individually, and it would still be "selfish." It is just that the precise nature of the "selfish" genes would be honed in an environment that included groups (just as other cases of genetic "selfishness" would be honed in environments that included particular physical features, such as aridity or high temperatures).

[13] I should perhaps clarify here that I am not advocating any theory of memes, just the general (and, I would think, uncontroversial) idea that some social practices can arise and be passed on socially – without genetic alteration – because they have the same general sort of reproduction-enhancing effects as adaptive genetic mutations. In

not biological ones. Moreover, it developed primarily as a way of modulating emotion in deliberation. Crucially, societies often need to disable their citizens' tendency to empathize with and care for out-group members, thereby facilitating war, oppression, and other forms of harm. Earlier, I criticized Haidt's notion that reasoning was designed to rationalize and persuade, not to identify the truth. Haidt seems clearly wrong insofar as he would claim this about reasoning generally. But rationalization and persuasion are certainly common in moral reasoning (see Haidt 2012, 59). Of course, this is not a matter of self-conscious design. Social adaptations work like biological adaptations. Small changes produce some selective advantages, which accumulate, sometimes leading to larger reconfigurations. In social adaptations, some of the small changes are likely to be self-consciously chosen, whether in techniques of control by dominant groups or strategies of resistance by dominated groups. But generally, they are not reflectively manipulated, and the trajectory of the process as a whole is certainly not guided by any intention. Rather, ethical developments proceed mechanically with periods of equilibrium serving most often to stabilize hierarchical structures. These are some of the reasons why Pinker is right to say that we have "too much morality" (2011, 622), and why ethical deliberation is so likely to result in self-righteous propagation of atrocities. (We will return to this problem in the Afterword.)

However, construing the origins of ethical thought in this way (through what Paul Ricoeur [1997] would have called a "hermeneutics of suspicion") does not mean that we must rest content with ethical principles serving oppressive purposes. Here, as usual, mechanism and function do not coincide; the precise, causal processes that are at work in adaptations are never more than an approximation to the benefits we identify for them. For example, humans feel disgust at the idea of sex with someone they grew up with. That is a mechanism that approximates the function of incest avoidance. It is only an approximation because sometimes we grow up with people who are not related and sometimes we do not grow up with people who are related.

In keeping with these points, we are able to invoke ethical deliberation in ways that expand, rather than limit, empathy and care, thus ways that oppose oppressive and harmful policies and practices. As Foucault put it, ethics – or "justice," in this case – is an idea that "has been ... put to work in different types of societies as an instrument of a certain political and

---

addition, I am assuming the methodological value of simplicity or Occam's razor, such that we should not posit genetic changes if the phenomena at issue are adequately explained by social factors that we would have to accept anyway.

economic power or as a weapon against that power" (Chomsky and Foucault 2006, 54).[14] Moreover, as Buchanan (2020) has argued, we humans can to some extent create our own social environments in such a way as to systematically foster our inclusive, egalitarian inclinations while inhibiting our partial and discriminatory tendencies. (Though Buchanan does presuppose an evolved moral mind, his basic arguments and conclusions do not, I believe, rest on that presupposition.)

## Conclusion

Ethical responses are motivated by emotion systems, which imply ideals such as constancy in the case of attachment. Those ideals also partially define narrative trajectories that typify the varieties of human pursuit of happiness, in relation to both egocentric and allocentric self-interest. Some of these trajectories recur across cultures and time periods and are particularly consequential for the ways in which they lead us to organize and imagine our pursuit of ideals. Indeed, universal story prototypes encompass default ethical orientations not only for the individuals involved, but also for the larger society. Those defaults derive from the ideals associated with the underlying emotion systems. For example, with regard to social authority, the romantic plot includes a libertarian preference for individual choice (at least for attachment-based love) in cases of conflict.

The ideals of the prominent, cross-cultural genres find rough parallels in Haidt's (2012) moral foundations, though there are differences in the details of the ideals and precisely how they operate. The one exception to this is fairness, which appears to be a broader, "metaethical" concern. Specifically, it favors a proportionate distribution of rewards and punishments, modified by empathic response and the principles and

---

[14] On the other hand, Foucault limited justice to this rhetorical function, claiming that it "in effect has been invented" as such an instrument as well (Chomsky and Foucault 2006, 54). Moreover, despite his later attention to "care of the self," (see Foucault 1988), Foucault would almost certainly have been unsympathetic with the preceding references to empathy and care (the shared use of the word "care" does not mean that we are using the word in at all similar senses). Indeed, on the points where they disagree, I share the perspective developed by Chomsky in this dispute. After all, Chomsky would not deny that "justice" is commonly invoked in the oppressive ways Foucault indicates. In fact, much of Chomsky's political writings involve demonstrating the falsity of such invocations. I should note that the insights of both writers could be developed and clarified by reference to an analysis of power that draws on affective science. That goes beyond the scope of the present volume, but I refer the interested reader to Parkinson's illuminating treatment of emotion and power (2019, chap. 8).

# Conclusion 87

parameters governing fundamental ethical orientations. Thus, it does not appear to be linked with a particular narrative genre. Indeed, it seems likely that the fairness default, modified by fundamental ethical orientation, is further specified by each sort of emplotment. Thus, we are inclined to consider certain distributions of reward and punishment as fair in a heroic context and others in a criminal investigation context. For example, it seems likely that following 9/11, most Americans thought certain sorts of international military action were "fair" because, in national discourse, the 9/11 attacks were emplotted as a heroic war story (see Hogan 2009, chap. 5). It also seems likely that judgments of fairness (e.g., regarding the right to a trial) would have been at least somewhat different if those attacks had been construed in terms of a criminal investigation story.

On the other hand, none of this is deterministic. The default biases of general structures may be resisted through details of emplotment. Moreover, the same situation may be emplotted in different ways and integrated with different emotions, producing different ethical responses. This variability of emplotment is found across individuals in any given society, and even within individuals who are often ambivalent about ethical issues, thus changeable in their judgments and behaviors. As elsewhere in human psychology, the operative emotional and cognitive structures and processes involve tendencies, but these tendencies are both multiple (allowing for alternatives) and flexible (allowing for variability in implementation). Further study in cognitive science and comparative literature should enhance our understanding of both the broad tendencies and the nuanced variability of those structures and processes. In consequence, these disciplines should contribute to this common intellectual project at the intersection of affective science, narratology, and ethical theory.

Finally, we need to understand ethics in relation to evolution. However, that does not mean that we should see ethics as having evolved as such. Indeed, it is not clear that such a view would make much sense. Most obviously, there is no clear way to make sense of the idea that biology supplies actual norms. Rather, it seems likely that a wide range of psychological capacities and inclinations (e.g., affective empathy) evolved. If we wish to do so, we may categorize some of those together as ethical, valuing them socially or individually, and elaborating on them theoretically or doctrinally. Certainly, given the interrelation of these capacities and inclinations and their potential social functions, it is unsurprising that a wide range of societies have done just this. For reasons having to do with social dynamics, the dominant forms of ethical doctrine in any given society are likely to serve dominant groups (or groups seeking social dominance) in that society. The point is perhaps most obvious in the case of national invocations of the heroic prototype. But the ethical operation of narrative prototypes may be egalitarian as well. Moreover, all alternatives are, again, open to challenge – necessarily so, given the range of mutually incompatible ethical ideals associated with the various emotion ideals and story genres.

# CHAPTER 4

# Ethics and Narrative Genre: Some Illustrative Cases

In Chapter 1, I outlined a three-level account of ethical psychology, guided by different types of categorization process. Our fundamental ethical orientation would appear to be well captured by a model of principles and parameters in which we set broad ethical inclinations bearing on the scope of ethical concern, valence addressed by ethical regulation, and method used to generate ethical evaluation – as well as the precise target of evaluative concern (actions or character), though this seems to be set indirectly by causal considerations. However, this broad orientation does not define adequate responses to specific cases. We respond to actual situations through processes that prominently include prototype assimilation. By "prototype assimilation," I mean taking up standard story structures and using them to guide the construal and simulative elaboration of our more or less fragmentary experiences. (The third level takes up exemplars, which, again, enter through the specific works I consider.)

I explained the structure of the most consequential, cross-cultural story prototypes in Chapter 3. The purpose of the present chapter is to illustrate the operation of those genres in our ethical thought and action. I will begin with some disclaimers, trying to forestall a few possible misunderstandings. I will then turn to the genres, considering literary instances, or exemplars, of the heroic, revenge, criminal investigation, romantic, seduction, family separation, and sacrificial structures in sequence.

## Some Disclaimers

First of all, I should stress again that emplotment and ethical response do not have a constant, unidirectional relation. For example, it is not the case that we simply begin by being ethically neutral, then emplot a series of events in a genre, and then have an ethical reaction. Rather, in experiencing and considering events, we have various, complex emotional and cognitive responses. These include the partial activation (or "priming") of some genre prototypes or parts of such prototypes. The partially activated genres direct our attention or lead us to construe events in some ways rather than others. The unfolding of the events may converge with those construals, or it may diverge, thereby inhibiting the previously activated genre prototypes, perhaps partially activating others, and so on. In short, the process is complex and interactive.

Moreover, the process is in part governed by the events themselves and in part by fairly constant elements of cognition and emotion – that is, cognitive and emotional processes that are fairly constant across cultures, across individuals, and across circumstances. But there are also variations. Specifically, individual readers approach situations and operate with cognitive structures (including genre prototypes) that are in part idiosyncratic. That idiosyncrasy is itself in part dispositional (thus a matter of enduring tendencies on the part of the individual) and in part circumstantial (thus a matter of inclinations that change depending on the person's current condition). A portion of the dispositional and circumstantial idiosyncrasies will form cultural or subcultural patterns (thus exhibiting a degree of uniformity for a particular population). However, others will be more narrowly individual or will vary with categories other than culture (e.g., degree of attachment security or tendency to produce vivid mental imagery).

One consequence of this is that individual responses will vary. Another is that there are likely to be some broad tendencies by culture or other category (e.g., attachment type). Of course, there are also likely to be some similarities due to the genre prototypes or the individual works. For example, it should be the case that a higher percentage of readers sympathize with the lovers in a romantic plot than sympathize with the seducer in a seduction plot. But it does not follow by any means that all readers will sympathize with the former and no readers will sympathize with the latter. Similarly, one would expect readers of a heroic work to generally be more sympathetic with the nation of the heroes than with that of the enemy. However, one would expect that tendency to be lessened or even reversed in cases where the reader shared a prominent identity category with the enemy (as when, say, an Irish reader peruses a work in which English heroes battle Irish enemies).

It is important to note this because my claims here seem often to be misunderstood. For example, when I give talks on these topics, I am frequently faced with the question of how I can explain differences in literary response. It seems clear to me, however, that there is no special problem about the mere fact of different responses since any psychological account is almost certain to include those from the outset.

The point extends from general readers to those crucial readers who are authors and who therefore not only interpret stories but also make them. Though the genre prototypes tend to be connected with particular ethical ideals, those ideals are not absolute and determinative. Authors modulate the usual ethical attitudes of the genres they are drawing on, sometimes effectively subverting those attitudes. Indeed, it seems that many of the particular stories we consider to be "art" treat the prototypes and their ideals critically (e.g., to some degree challenging the nationalism of heroic works). We will consider some examples of this below.

In discussing the universal genres, I will organize them into three loosely defined groups. The first includes the heroic, revenge, and criminal investigation genres. These may be understood as stressing ethical values of social hierarchy and conformity to social rules related to egoistic and social emotions, such as personal pride and national pride. The second group comprises the romantic, seduction, and familial genres. Their ethical concerns are concentrated on individual, affiliative relations as these are connected with attachment bonding and sexual desire. The third group has only a single genre at the moment – the sacrificial. It addresses the moral contraries of extreme egocentrism in contributing to the devastation of the in-group (the purgative version) and extreme allocentrism in self-sacrifice for the redemption of the in-group (the penitential version); these are connected with such emotions as shame and wonder.

Given this tripartite division, it is possible to isolate a further pattern across these genres. The heroic and romantic genres incorporate morally contradictory – roughly, egocentric and allocentric – emotions. These include personal and group-based pride or anger in the heroic genre, and lust and attachment in the romantic genre. Moreover, both genres commonly redeem or elevate the morally problematic (egocentric) emotion by its integration with the morally laudable (allocentric) emotion. Revenge and seduction define a second set, in this case joined with the purgative version of the sacrificial genre. Works in these genres stress only the morally objectionable (egocentric) emotions (e.g., the seduction plot focuses on lust, unqualified by attachment feelings); moreover, those emotions cannot be redeemed, but they – and/or the people motivated by them – need to be eliminated, which is to say, purged. A final set includes criminal investigation, family separation, and penitential sacrifice. This group is characterized by an emphasis on the morally preferable (allocentric) emotion (e.g., attachment without lust in the familial separation and reunion genre).

These parallels suggest the existence of a further genre, treating the spiritual issues taken up by the sacrificial narratives but parallel with the heroic and romantic genres, something along the lines of a story treating individual salvation or enlightenment (see Figure 4.1). The last does seem to appear in a range of traditions. I will touch on this structure below. However, my discussion of it is very preliminary, as it really requires

**Moral Status of the Selected Emotions**

|  | Combined | Negative | Positive |
|---|---|---|---|
| **Dominant Emotions** | | | |
| Ego Anger/ Group Anger | Heroic Triumph | Revenge | Criminal Investigation |
| Lust/ Attachment | Romantic Union | Seduction | Familial Separation |
| Ambition/ Reverence | [Salvation/ Enlightenment] | Purgative Sacrifice | Penitential Sacrifice |

Figure 4.1 A possible schematization of cross-cultural story genres.

separate treatment, with the isolation of a range of cases and an account of its emotional sources.

I have already outlined the main features of these cross-cultural genres (excepting the tentatively added salvation or enlightenment genre). Even so, I will begin the following sections with a brief summary of the genre's main features. I will also note, schematically, the characteristic emotions, interpersonal stance, social organization, and virtues commonly associated with the genre. From there, I will give literary examples. I have chosen some examples from Shakespeare since his work is presumably most familiar and accessible to Anglophone readers. I have also included non-Western cases, despite their likely unfamiliarity for most readers, to give some degree of cross-cultural coverage. Depending on what seemed most helpful, I have sometimes treated one work in greater depth and at other times treated several cases more briefly.

### Heroic Narrative (*Mahābhārata*)

Again, the heroic prototype has two parts: the usurpation–restoration sequence and the threat–defense sequence. In its full, comic version, the former treats the overthrow of the legitimate leadership of the in-group (frequently intensified by making the usurper an attachment object, such as a sibling), the exile of the legitimate leader (sometimes his or her death or association with death), and the restoration of the legitimate leader (or some heir or follower). The threat–defense sequence involves the defeat of the in-group by an enemy out-group (sometimes with the collaboration of the usurper), the subsequent revival of the in-group (commonly by the usurped leader), and the defeat of the enemy out-group (often resulting in an idealized society). The main heroic story is sometimes followed by an "epilogue of suffering." War leads to much undeserved misery. After the heroes' victory, there is often a recognition of all that has been lost. A concluding section may simply express grief over the dead or may involve an acknowledgement that even the heroes have sinned and need to engage in some sort of penance before normal social life may begin again.

The primary motivating emotions in the main heroic story are pride and what might be called "public shame," which is to say, shame before some body of observers, either the in-group (conquered) society, the out-group (conquering) society, or both. The humiliation of the main characters is likely to inspire anger, which drives the revival of the usurped leadership and the conquered in-group, thereby leading to the restoration of both. The epilogue concerns grief and a sense of guilt or sinfulness, though it does not necessarily include remorse, as the work may suggest that there were no other viable options for the hero or heroes.

As to readers' interpersonal stance, the genre tends to foster a sort of energetic enthusiasm for the in-group, often a muscular mirroring of the sort one sees at sporting events when spectators can barely refrain from running down the aisles in parallel with the athletes they are observing. (This attitude is well captured by the Sanskrit idea of *vīrarasa*, roughly an empathic feeling of heroic engagement and energy; on *vīrarasa*, see, e.g., Ingalls 1990.) As the sporting analogy suggests, the heroic prototype tends to very strongly endorse identity categories, specifically through the threat–defense sequence. It equally values social hierarchy, principally through the usurpation–restoration sequence. The former emphasizes such virtues as bravery; the latter cherishes loyalty.

The one work we have considered in detail thus far, *Julius Caesar*, is a heroic story, but it is a highly *critical* one in the sense that it appears to partially challenge the usual heroic ideals, rather than simply celebrating them. The challenge arises principally because it is never clear just which group defines the norm for usurpation or invasion. One feature of heroic plots is that they commonly define two things: an initial social norm and an uncaused beginning to the conflict. Put crudely, the leadership cannot be challenged legitimately by any other claimant, and the enemy attack is unprovoked. These two features are crucial to the patriotic ethics of heroic emplotment. If the enemy's attack on the in-group were actually a retaliation for our prior attack on that enemy, then the (in-group) reader's ethical evaluation of and response to the situation would be different. The ethical operation of heroic emplotment often relies crucially on the assumed absoluteness of the beginning of the conflict. *We* did nothing wrong; the entire blame falls on *them*.

The usurpation sequence of *Julius Caesar* most obviously treats Caesar as the legitimate leader since he is murdered by conspirators. The assassination even includes an attachment betrayal by Brutus. But, of course, the conspirators see themselves as forestalling an imminent usurpation by Caesar, his overthrow of the Republic. This is prepared for by Murellus's early reminders of Caesar's (usurpatory) conflict with Pompey. Moreover, the "restoration" of rule, through Augustus Caesar, does in fact end the Republic. Thus, it is not really a restoration but a usurpation of what went before – albeit a usurpation in part precipitated by the conspirators' (putatively usurpation-preventing) act.

The threat–defense sequence is similarly murky. In the backstory to the events of the play, Caesar had famously crossed the Rubicon as in effect an invading force (see the account of subsequent events in Plutarch 1959, 210–212). In keeping with this, the conspirators are initially in the city, whereas Augustus is outside. This geographical organization suggests that the conspirators – and, before them, Pompey – are the representatives of the in-group society ("us"). However, the conspirators are soon driven out of the city, and the subsequent war puts them in the place of the enemy invaders. On the other hand, this series of events could equally be construed as the standard exile of the legitimate in-group leadership.

Moreover, neither side is established as morally exemplary in relation to heroic norms. Cassius condones bribery and may engage in it himself (IV.iii.1–12), and the Roman triumvirs dictate extrajudicial executions with little or no concern for what, if anything, might justify such killing, in cold blood and unforced by the dangers of battle (IV.i). In short, both sides violate basic moral precepts of the heroic plot and lack important heroic virtues.

We find a more standard use of heroic emplotment in the central battle of the Indian epic *Mahābhārata* (attributed to Vyāsa 1993). Of particular relevance here is the subsection known as the *Bhagavad Gītā* or Song of God, which directly addresses ethical issues, such as the evaluation of conflicting ethical construals in a particular situation. The main story of the *Mahābhārata* in effect treats the usurpation sequence of the heroic structure. Two sets of cousins, the Pāṇḍavas and the Kāuravas, are in conflict over rule of the society. In fact, the lineages are complicated and a case can be made for either side. However, the perspective of the poem largely treats the Pāṇḍavas as the legitimate ruling family and the Kāuravas as usurpers. Even more clearly, the reception history of the epic supports the Pāṇḍavas. This leads commentators such as Barbara Stoler Miller to characterize "the triumph of the Pāṇḍavas over their cousins" as "the triumph of order over chaos" (1986, 5), due to "the legitimate right" of a Pāṇḍava "to be king" (4). Winthrop Sargeant more simply identifies the Pāṇḍavas as "the Good Guys" (1994, 24) and the Kāuravas as "the Bad Guys" (25).

The narrative perspective that identifies the Pāṇḍavas as the in-group and the Kāuravas as an out-group is manifest in many ways. For example, it appears in the names of the characters. The Pāṇḍavas have names that suggest being "steady in battle" (Sargeant 1994, 24) and "[a]ccompanied by the gods" (25). The Kāuravas, in contrast, have names indicating "Dirty Fighter" and "Bad Commands" (26). The Pāṇḍavas also have the supreme deity, Kṛṣṇa, on their side. (Divine preference for the in-group is typical of heroic narratives; see Hogan 2009, 118–123.) For our purposes, a key feature of the heroic emplotment of the epic is that the unethical behaviors of the Pāṇḍavas are rationalized in part by the Pāṇḍavas's divine calling, which is stressed particularly in the *Bhagavad Gītā*. In other words, the poem illustrates a central feature of the ethics of heroic emplotment. Specifically, what we would ordinarily consider ethical concerns are largely subsumed under the overarching, divinely sanctioned need to defeat the enemy. The defeat of the enemy may even be represented as the necessary condition for there being any possibility of a genuinely moral decision or action in the future. In keeping with this, heroic stories tend to displace ordinary empathic responses in favor of heroic enthusiasm.

Again, the *Mahābhārata* is an unusual heroic text in that it includes an explicit discussion of ethics and ethical conflict in the section called the *Bhagavad Gītā*. As I noted briefly earlier, the account of *dharma* (ethical duty) in Sanskrit treatises on the topic distinguishes various sorts of ethical duty (see O'Flaherty 1978; Parekh 1989). These may be broadly divided into *sādhāraṇadharma* (universal dharma), alternatively, *mānavdharma* (human dharma), and *swadharma* (literally "self" dharma, but perhaps better translated as *particular* dharma). Universal dharma includes such norms as truthfulness and nonviolence (*ahiṃsā*). Particular dharma has a number of subvarieties – family dharma (including spousal and other forms of duty), caste dharma (for each of the four large caste groups or *varṇas*), and so on. There are also specific duties to ancestors, teachers, and the gods. Caste duties differ, depending on whether one is, say, a priest or a warrior/ruler (*kṣatriya*). As should be clear, different sorts of dharma often bear on different sorts of narrative. Familial narratives tend to involve family dharma. Sacrificial narratives may suggest priestly caste duty. Heroic narratives routinely connect with *kṣatriyadharma*. Finally, it can easily happen that different sorts of dharma come into conflict with one another. For example, kṣatriyadharma is regularly in conflict with universal or human dharma, most obviously in the latter's imperatives of truthfulness and nonviolence.

The kṣatriyadharma versus mānavdharma conflict is clear in the *Bhagavad Gītā*. However, the text does not address it. Instead, it focuses on the conflict between kṣatriyadharma and familial dharma. I take it that this is the result of two factors. First, the authors or compilers did not wish to give mānavdharma any support, even inadvertently, since the purpose of a heroic work is typically to support war on behalf of the in-group; even mentioning an approach to ethics that is universally human would work against this goal. Second, family bonds are perhaps the types of moral commitment that are most likely to inhibit an individual's full commitment of his or her life to the larger society, especially in the case of war. Thus, it becomes particularly socially important to encourage people to place kṣatriyadharma above familial dharma in cases where the two are incompatible.

The *Bhagavad Gītā* opens with its location – Kurukṣetra (the field of the Kurus, a geographical place), which is also "dharmakṣetre" (I.1),[1] the field of dharma. That metaphorical location virtually identifies what follows as a treatment of ethics. The Pāṇḍavas and the Kāuravas face one another across the field. In the middle, the Pāṇḍava warrior Arjuna stands in a chariot that is guided by the god Kṛṣṇa. Before him is the "evil-minded" enemy (I.23). But when Arjuna looks, he sees "kinsmen" (I.27). He feels he cannot fight, and he pleads with Kṛṣṇa that nothing good can come from killing one's kin. Specifically, Indian tradition distinguishes four goals that animate human action – pleasure (*kāma*), power or wealth (*artha*), ethical duty (*dharma*), and spiritual realization (*mokṣa*). Arjuna begins his complaint by saying that he desires neither "kingship" nor "pleasures" (I.32) – thus, neither artha nor kāma – particularly if it involves killing his relations.

Worse still, killing these kin would be a sin, a commission of evil (*pāpam*), and thus hardly a fulfillment of dharma. Indeed, it would be "adharmo" or a-dharmic (immoral), specifically a violation of "kuladharmāḥ" (I: 40), familial dharma. Indeed, the "great evil" (I.45, "mahat pāpaṁ") is even more dire than this seems. The fulfillment of duties to ancestors – such as performing rituals bearing on ancestors – is contingent on the preservation of familial dharma, (I.42) and even the preservation of caste dharma (as well as the subcaste or occupation dharma [*jātidharma*]) is contingent on familial dharma (I.41, I.43), as caste is passed on through offspring, thus families. In short, Arjuna contends that familial dharma is fundamental. It must supersede other forms of dharma because those other forms of dharma cannot exist without familial dharma.

Kṛṣṇa has the task of arguing that the kṣatriyadharma that Arjuna putatively owes to society should supersede other obligations, including moral obligations to one's family. Kṛṣṇa begins by taking aim at Arjuna's character, suggesting that he is fainthearted (II.2) and cowardly (II.3),

---

[1] This and subsequent citations of the *Bhagavad Gītā* refer to the text and translation in Sargeant (1994).

thus lacking in the key heroic virtue of courage. Kṛṣṇa also seeks to appeal to status concerns, claiming that Arjuna's doubts are "not befitting an Aryan" or noble and would lead to "disgrace" or "infamy" (II.2). He goes on to say that Arjuna's attitude is "base" (II.3).

Arjuna responds quite reasonably that the principles of dharma are all confused in this situation. This apparently leads Kṛṣṇa to try appealing to the fourth goal of life, spiritual realization. In connection with this, he maintains that the self is eternal. In consequence, killing someone apparently is not really a matter of killing him or her at all (II.19, 21). Understanding this involves achieving an uncommon level of spiritual understanding, hence the possible implication of the fourth goal of life.

Kṛṣṇa soon retreats from this approach, returning to dharma as such. He refers to Arjuna's "swadharma," or one's particular dharma. He appears to imply that swadharma is confined to caste dharma, for he immediately identifies Arjuna's swadharma with his duty as a "kṣatriya." In connection with this, he once again suggests a criticism of Arjuna as unheroic by saying that he "tremble[s]" before his swadharma when he is faced with a dharmic "battle" (II.31). He repeats the status appeals by saying that the battle enables a kṣatriya to achieve "glory" (II.33). Moreover, if Arjuna does not fight, he will suffer "disgrace" or "infamy" (II.34), for other warriors will believe he succumbed to "fear" (II.35). From here, Kṛṣṇa returns to the goal of spiritual realization. He maintains that Arjuna's fighting is inseparable from achieving the wisdom of detachment that will free him "from the bondage of rebirth" (II.52). This is precisely what happens with spiritual enlightenment.

There is little point in continuing with Kṛṣṇa's full argument. It should be clear that there is a close interconnection between the martial, ingroup-oriented ethical principles espoused by Kṛṣṇa and the heroic narrative structure in which those principles are embedded. Also, it should come as no surprise that, despite the weaknesses in Kṛṣṇa's argument, the socially exemplary figure of Arjuna is presented as being convinced. In the end, he goes on to fight the war.

Of course, wars have dire consequences, not only for the losers, but for the winners as well. Once the war is over, these are likely to become salient, and their associated emotions – of grief, disgust, remorse, even fear – are likely to return, perhaps very strongly. This is what gives rise to the epilogue of suffering. Depending on the author, such an epilogue can function to undermine the heroic ethics that dominated the prior story. This is particularly likely in independent works, which is to say stories by one author that are responses to stories by other authors. For example, I take it that Euripides' *Trojan Women* has this sort of anti-heroic function. However, in works where the epilogue is part of the same text as the heroic story – as we find in the *Mahābhārata* – the function is usually quite different. Specifically, in most such cases, the epilogue appears to operate principally to mitigate distress over the harms done by war, in order to allow a more untroubled moral commendation of the victorious in-group.

The *Mahābhārata* is a massive poem, and a great deal occurs after the Pāṇḍava victory. Perhaps the first thing to note is that the victory comes at a truly unimaginable cost, as almost all the fighters in both massive armies have been slaughtered. The Pāṇḍava heir, Yudhiṣṭhira – the literal child of the god Dharma and thus the metaphorical offspring of dharma or moral duty – immediately laments that his "victory" is simultaneously a "defeat." He has "incurred the sin of … slaying our kinsmen and friends" only to be faced with such "misery" (Sauptika Parva 28). Soon, the reader encounters "thousands of wailing" women who have lost husbands, fathers, and sons and are "deprived of their senses by grief" (Stree Parva 15). They accost Yudhiṣṭhira, criticizing the killing of "sires and brothers and preceptors and sons and friends" (Stree Parva 17). Gandhari, the mother of the Kāuravas, is particularly vehement. Yudhiṣṭhira approaches, saying, "I deserve thy curses, for I am the cause of this universal destruction." In response, Gandhari "cast[s] off her wrath" (Stree Parva 22). This is exemplary of the general operation of the epilogue. After the dangers of war have passed, it is difficult not to recognize that "the Good Guys," the in-group heroes, have committed sometimes gravely immoral acts. A ritual of self-abasement, such as that performed by Yudhiṣṭhira here, in effect shows that an in-group hero's character is morally exemplary, suggesting that his or her crimes really were necessary and are certainly forgivable.

But, again, the *Mahābhārata* is a long and complex work. Gandhari goes on to eulogize the fallen Kāuravas. She concludes by chastising Kṛṣṇa, explaining that despite his great power and authority – which made him "competent to prevent the slaughter" – he allowed the Pāṇḍavas and the Kāuravas both to be "exterminated" (Stree Parva 39). She curses him with what is by and large a version of karma – suffering the same pain he inflicted on others. Specifically, she says that he will see "the slaughter of [his own] kinsmen and friends and sons" (Stree Parva 39). Gandhari's critical judgment is given some weight by the fact that Kṛṣṇa does experience the fate she spells out; that may be taken to suggest the karmic validity of her assessment. On the other hand, Kṛṣṇa responds to Gandhari, explaining why he accepts – indeed, himself chooses – this sequence of events. He goes on to argue that she and her children were the source of the nearly two billion deaths of the war (Stree Parva 40). Gandhari is reduced to silence. This is in keeping with the rehabilitative function of the epilogue.

In fact, the epilogue is not confined to the Stree Parva. For example, it subsequently extends to the afterlife of the characters. Initially, we meet the Pāṇḍavas being punished in hell. This clearly suggests their criminality, especially as the Kāuravas are in heaven. However, the situation quickly changes, with the Pāṇḍavas entering heaven and the Kāuravas being thrown into hell. (As this indicates, within Hindu theology, residence in hell or heaven is not eternal.) Here, once again, we see the acknowledgement of sin leading to rehabilitation – all in keeping with the ingroup-based ethics of the heroic structure. The point is particularly clear when the reason for all this is explained. Specifically, "He whose sinful acts are many, enjoys Heaven first," whereas the reverse is the case for those whose good acts are many (Swargarohanika Parva 5). Thus, the ethical superiority of the Pāṇḍavas is actually demonstrated by the fact that they are initially in hell.

## Revenge (*Hamlet* and *The Zhao Orphan*)

Again, the revenge prototype begins with the hero suffering some grievous wrong. This is most often an attachment loss, such as the death of a loved one (e.g., the murder of a parent or child) or betrayal by a loved one (commonly, the sexual infidelity of a spouse). The revenger sets out to punish the perpetrator, usually aiming to kill him or her, possibly after causing him or her severe pain (e.g., through making him or her suffer a parallel attachment loss). Since the revenger is acting extrajudicially and without the consent and cooperation of the larger society, he or she must undertake the revenge covertly. This often leads to missteps in which the revenger harms innocent people on the way to punishing the person who committed the initial crime. In the end, the revenger often dies after killing the target of his or her wrath. Even if he or she does not die, the ending is often ambivalent as it is difficult to see how anything is better due to the "hero" having accomplished his or her goal. Put differently, revenge is a genre that is very difficult to turn into a comedy (in the sense of a work with a genuinely happy ending). More generally, however, much as we may sympathize with the revenger, we often recoil from his or her violence, especially as that violence frequently involves harm to innocents and may initiate cycles of cruelty. (For further discussion of the revenge genre, including its ambivalence, see Hogan 2011, chap. 4.)

In some ways, the revenge plot is a version of the heroic plot. Here, wrong done against an individual (rather than a nation) prompts that individual (rather than that nation) to respond to the offense, typically with violence against the offender (e.g., by setting out to kill him or her). However, there are two crucial differences. First, as indicated in the summary, the offense and response are individual; they do not bear on the well-being of society as a whole. Or, rather, they often bear on social well-being principally insofar as the revenger's actions disturb social order. Thus, the revenger may be more of a threat to society than the initial criminal. The second crucial difference is that the aim of the hero is not to restore the initial status quo. Indeed, that is often impossible since the initial crime is typically irreversible. Rather, the aim of the revenger is to inflict comparable or greater pain on the initial criminal.

The character emotion that dominates the genre is enduring hatred provoked by attachment violation, with more punctual spikes of anger or rage sometimes driving particular (often rash) acts. The interpersonal stance of readers is sympathetic with the hero, insofar as he or she suffers attachment loss. But this sympathy is often tempered by a critical attitude toward his or her vigilantism, with its tendency to harm innocents and to disturb the larger social order. This is not the enthusiastic commitment of the heroic genre. In keeping with the heroic genre, the revenge narrative tends to elevate the virtues of loyalty and bravery – or, more properly, to particularly denigrate the vices of disloyalty (issuing in betrayal) and cowardice (typically manifest in the way that the initial criminal harms the hero, not through open confrontation, but through concealment and deceit). Finally, the social organization favored by the revenge narrative is somewhat complicated. Specifically, the hero's actions typically involve individual willfulness in opposition to larger social norms, sometimes in direct violation of legal restrictions. Moreover, works in the genre usually foster some degree of sympathy for such willfulness. Indeed, some works favor the individual revenger over the encompassing system of social justice. But, more often, the revenge merely adds new harm to old harm. Thus, in many cases, revenge stories implicitly value rules and hierarchies of social authority by showing the consequences of their suspension in crime and revenge.

The most famous revenge drama of English literature is undoubtedly *Hamlet* ([1600] 1997). That play is, I believe, rather less ambivalent than is common in revenge stories. I do not mean that it is without ambivalence. As Robert Watson points out, in the course of the play, "[w]arfare itself—killing provoked by a sense of duty to ghosts of our fathers in armour—is brought into moral question, along with all the smaller-scale forms of revenge" (2002, 171–172). We certainly are not supposed to accept Hamlet's murder of Polonius. However much he may have been confused, this is at best the sort of "collateral damage" that is common in revenge stories and that violates moral norms. But Hamlet appears to remain very sympathetic for most audience members, who seem to want him to get on with killing his adoptive father and king, Claudius. (The latter point may be inferred from the critical obsession with why Hamlet delays in committing this murder; that obsession appears to suggest that audience members are in effect rooting for the revenge.) This would appear, then, to be a case where the revenge story is developed in such a way as to reduce, rather than increase, its usual ethical orientation against revenge and toward criminal investigation.

Before going further with *Hamlet*, I would like to bring in a famous Chinese drama, perhaps the best-known revenge drama from China, *The Great Revenge of the Zhao Orphan* (趙氏孤兒大報仇, *Zhàoshì Gū'ér Dà Bào Chóu*; hereafter, *The Zhao Orphan* [13th century CE]). In this play, Tu-an Ku, as part of his pursuit of political power, murders an entire clan except for a single child, who is raised to take revenge on his parents' murderer. The complication is that the foster father of the child, concealing the boy's identity, brings him to Tu-an Ku, who becomes a second adoptive father for the boy. This play is no more ambivalent than *Hamlet* and possibly less ambivalent; it at least apparently endorses revenge, though – like *Hamlet* – it involves the hero murdering a father figure.

The case of *The Zhao Orphan* might appear to be explained by the high place given to filial piety in Confucian thought and practice. Indeed, *The Classic of Rites* (禮記, *Lǐjì*; 1885) includes the following admonition: "With the enemy who has slain his father, one should not live under the same heaven" ("Qū Lǐ" I: 70). However, there were always contradictory tendencies in Chinese thought, as there were in Europe, and opposition to vengeance is found in China (as support for revenge is found in the West). Thus, Anne Cheng explains that "murder carried out by vengeance is problematic and has, in fact, never ceased to give food for thought to experts both on classical sources and on legal texts" (2004, 29). As we would expect, "imperial law ... prohibit[ed] murder for the sake of social order" (38).

I would suggest that the partial mitigation of the problems with revenge has the same source in both plays; moreover, that source may partially explain the success of both plays. Specifically, both works involve not only a personal harm, but also a crime against the socially definitive in-group. In *Hamlet*, the murder of King Hamlet is not only a personal loss to Prince Hamlet, but simultaneously a regicide that is part of Claudius's usurpation of the throne. Thus, the play includes one of the two primary story sequences that form the heroic narrative prototype. These are, again, the usurpation and invasion sequences, in which the legitimate authority structure of the in-group is violated (usurpation) and the autonomy of the group is lost (invasion).

Perhaps the two most important emotions for in-group definition and cohesion are pride (regarding the in-group) and loyalty or devotion (regarding the social hierarchy). (In Confucian thought, the latter is captured by the concept of *zhōng* [忠].) These involve ideals for both the individual feeling the emotions and for the in-group as a whole. The individual ideals, derived principally from loyalty or devotion, would include conformity to in-group norms as well as respect for the group's authority structure. The ideals for the in-group as a whole, derived principally from pride, would include the justice of the in-group hierarchy and autonomy of the in-group relative to out-groups (or even dominance over out-groups). In keeping with these points, as already noted, the heroic plot depicts threats to in-group hierarchy (usurpation) and autonomy (invasion). The threats are of course perpetrated by villains, including disloyal and rebellious in-group members. In the comic form of the heroic story, the usurpation is followed by a restoration. One common variant occurs when the legitimate leader is killed and the restoration is left to his or her heir. This is, of course, what occurs in *Hamlet*.

Heroic stories are often to some extent ambivalent. However, even with the epilogue of suffering, they tend to be far less ambivalent than revenge narratives. This is due in part to the collective nature of the harm. The threat is faced by the entire group. In consequence, the response is not egocentric or selfish; it concerns the well-being of the whole society. Moreover, when the entire social structure is violated, the legal system is typically not a viable alternative for pursuing the ideals of the associated emotion systems. For example, there is no such system available to Hamlet regarding Claudius; thus, a criminal investigation story is not possible. Finally, cultivating loyalty to the in-group and fostering deference to social authority – as well as bravery in opposition to the out-group – are important social functions of heroic stories, which serve to develop these virtues as part of the narrative's ethical ideal. In contrast, discouraging individual violence outside the legal system – thus, egocentric revenge – is an important social function of revenge stories. As such, we would expect the heroic structure to support *social* "revenge," which is to say social restoration and retribution for the in-group as a whole, whereas the revenge structure discourages *individual* revenge.

*Hamlet* takes up both the individual revenge story and the heroic usurpation story. It thereby renders the former less ambivalent and the latter more personal, and perhaps more appealing. At the same time, it complicates the heroic story by highlighting its connection with revenge, making that heroic structure more emotionally and thematically complex and ambivalent (as Robert Watson's [2002] comment on war and revenge suggests).

The situation is at first slightly less clear with *The Zhao Orphan*. There is certainly something akin to usurpation by Tu-an Ku when he murders the Zhao clan. However, the murders are done with the consent of the emperor (Chi 1972, 46; Ji 2014, 21), even if the latter has been deceived into thinking that the Zhaos were involved in a plot to usurp the throne.[2]

---

[2] As to the nature of Tu-an Ku's act, it is important to point out that early Chinese imperial law included "[c]ollective punishment of kin ... known by the technical term 'destruction of the lineage.'" Lewis explains that this was bound up with the practice of revenge, which could lead to "the destruction of entire families" through "reciprocal vengeance" (2007, 233).

On the other hand, the key issue is not the initial harm to the orphan's family, but the act of revenge itself. As the play develops, the orphan's revenge coincides with the full-fledged usurpation plot of Tu-an Ku, who conspires to "put the Emperor to death and seize his throne" (Chi 1972, 69; cf. Ji 2014, 43). Thus, the individual revenge of the orphan is justified by the threat to the social hierarchy of the in-group. Moreover, the play eliminates any selfish motivations on the part of the orphan by having Tu-an Ku decide to turn over his own current position to the orphan upon usurping the throne (Ji 2014, 43).

Perhaps even more significantly, like many Yuan dramas, *The Zhao Orphan* strongly hints at an allegorical reading. As Liu remarks, during the period of Mongol domination over the Chinese (i.e., during the Yuan Dynasty, when this play was written), "[t]he drama was ... the weapon of the conquered" (1972, 10). As to this particular play, Liu explains that "[i]t has been suggested that the Chao family symbolized the House of Sung ... conquered [thus, usurped] by the Mongols, and that the vengeance was the vengeance of the Chinese people upon the Yüan tyrants" (24). A key part of the connection derives from the fact that the surname of the Sung Dynasty rulers was Zhao (or Chao, depending on the transliteration system one is using). In keeping with this, the Yuan Dynasty printing of the play ends with the orphan "filled with a desire to take revenge" (Idema 2001, 804). But, in the (later) Ming Dynasty version, thus at a time when the then-current emperor was more generally considered legitimate, the orphan "reports T'u-an Ku's planned rebellion to the throne and requests permission to take revenge . . .. When this permission is granted, he proceeds ... to capture and execute Tu-an Ku." Indeed, changes throughout indicate that the Ming version does not condone vigilante-style revenge, but it affirms "the exclusive power of the state to settle such conflicts" (Idema 2001, 804), making it into a sort of criminal investigation narrative as well. (For further analysis of *The Zhao Orphan*, see Hogan 2022a.)

Thus, in both *Hamlet* and *The Zhao Orphan*, the partial mitigation of revenge appears to derive from genre mixing, particularly the integration of the revenge story into a heroic story. That integration extends the range of emotions in the play, altering the story's ideals and associated ethical norms. This is a particularly striking case because it involves ethical attitudes that, in the case of the Chinese play, would initially appear to result from culturally defined and thus socially distinctive principles, such as the elevation of filial piety in Confucianism. However, on further consideration, it seems that both the Chinese and English cases are more effectively analyzed in terms of largely cross-cultural patterns in emotions, ethical ideals implied by those emotions, and story prototypes that are bound up with the emotions and ethical ideals.

## Criminal Investigation (*Selling Rice in Chenzhou*)

It should be obvious that the revenge genre and the criminal investigation genre are closely related to one another, though also in some ways sharply opposed. Specifically, attachment loss caused by others (such as that featured in prototypical revenge narratives) has three associated ideals. First, there is restoration of the loss, preferably by the perpetrator, insofar as that is possible. Second, there is prevention of future attachment losses. Third, there is some sort of compensatory punishment for the perpetrator and only the perpetrator. But revenge, being socially unregulated and driven by hatred and rage, is unlikely to satisfy these desiderata. Indeed, as already noted, it is likely to repeat the original problem through the harming of innocents (in "collateral damage," as it is called in warfare). The common social solution to these problems is to turn over the authority for punishment to some civil body (a legal system) that may respond to wrongdoing in a way that, in principle, should minimize the harm to innocents, maximize the deterrence, and define appropriate sorts of compensation and punishment when possible. Thus, the legal system should be able to treat the situation in such a way as to maximize the realization of the ideals connected with feelings of grief and anger resulting from attachment deprivation. Though the revenge and criminal investigation genres are most often separate, they are joined and contrasted in just this way, as already noted, in one of the most important and one of the earliest works of European drama, Aeschylus's *Oresteia*.

The criminal investigation genre, then, involves an attempt to achieve these desiderata in as high a degree as possible. Its full, comic version begins with some serious harm done within the society, continues to a socially legitimated investigation of the harm and its perpetrators, and concludes with a socially legitimated response to the harm – most often (deterrence-enhancing) punishment, but sometimes restoration of the victim's losses as well. (I am referring to the actual events of the story, not the way they are recounted. Obviously, one can recount the events out of chronological order.) The emotions driving characters – and engaging readers – in criminal investigation stories may involve empathic versions of the emotions that drive revenge narratives. However, the most important emotions for this genre define a complex affective response for which there seems to be no good name in any language I am familiar with. It is the motivation that leads us to experience pleasure in observing conformity to rules and displeasure in observing deviation from rules. This motivation is surprisingly general, ranging from the aesthetic experience of music to very practical matters of human cooperation. In the latter case, it is bound up with our ability to predict routine behavior by others and our ability to trust them. Note that "trust" here includes not only such intimate matters as the sexual fidelity of romantic partners, but also such routine matters as anticipating that other, unknown drivers will drive on the proper side of the road, stop at red lights, and so on. The usual interpersonal stance fostered by the genre involves defining identity categories by reference to rule conformity and rule violation for in-groups and out-groups, respectively. In keeping with this, the social organization valued by the genre is one of systematic regulation governing the relations among group members generally and defining the social positions (e.g., police detective) tasked with assessing those relations in terms of social norms. (There may, of course, be complications when norms conflict and require hierarchizing, as with police shows where the "good" officer "bends" the rules in order to put an end to the far worse offenses of the criminal.) Finally, the moral virtues include selflessness and incorruptibility; the former distinguishes the criminal investigator from the revenger, whereas the latter distinguishes the ideal investigator from investigators in critical versions of the story structure. (The criminal investigator should also be unusually astute; however, that does not seem to be a specifically moral virtue.)

Criminal investigation stories developed extensively in China, through such figures as Judge Bao. Like an American detective, Judge Bao tries to ascertain who committed a crime by seeking various forms of evidence, which sometimes involves going undercover. When I mention this to American colleagues, they almost invariably suggest that, despite the apparent similarity to Western detective stories, the Judge Bao mysteries must be quite different because the culture is so different. In support of this view, the name "Confucius" is sometimes mentioned. It is certainly true that the ethics of, say, *Selling Rice in Chenzhou* – the anonymously authored Yuan drama to which we will turn in a moment – are not identical with the ethics of, say, Edgar Allan Poe's "Purloined Letter." But that point is almost trivial as the ethics of this story are not identical with those of *The Hound of the Baskervilles* or an episode of *Miami Vice* – or Poe's own "Murders in the Rue Morgue," for that matter. It is also true that one is likely to gain a greater understanding of *Selling Rice* by examining its cultural and historical background. Indeed, in the preceding section, we saw an instance of just this sort, provided by the political context of Yuan drama.

However, one great problem with the focus on "cultural context" is that people routinely see out-groups as far more uniform than in-groups (see Duckitt 1992, 81; Richeson et al. 2007, 16). We recognize the diversity of "us," but we tend to think of "them" as all pretty similar. Even if we like and admire "them," we have a strong inclination to take a reductive view of their culture. While Rú Xué (called "Confucianism" in the West) has been the most salient philosophical system in much of Chinese history, there are numerous competing schools of thought and indeed numerous versions of Rú Xué. Moreover, even when Rú Xué is invoked by Chinese writers or politicians, they may be drawing on other philosophical traditions, including traditions that are very critical of Kǒngzǐ's views.

Consider, for example, views of governance in Chinese tradition. In the *Analects*, Kǒngzǐ is famously recorded as having said, "By nature, men are nearly alike [or close together[3]]; by practice, they get to be wide apart" (17.2). I have already noted his criticism of a punitive approach to governance, along with his advocacy of kindness (2.3). Such comments may be taken to suggest that Kǒngzǐ had a fundamentally positive view of human nature. Such a view is explicit in the writings of Kǒngzǐ's early and influential intellectual heir, Mèngzǐ ("Mencius"), who explicitly insisted that people are fundamentally good and that one needs to act in such a way as to avoid causing them to lose that goodness. In Mèngzǐ's case, that goodness was to a significant degree based on natural empathy. Thus, Mèngzǐ maintains that "[a]ll men have a mind [or heart {xīn, 心}]] which cannot bear to see the sufferings of others" ("Gong Sun Chou" I: 6 [2A: 6]). He goes on to illustrate his assertion by noting how anyone would feel on seeing a child about to fall into a well.

In contrast, Xúnzǐ, Kǒngzǐ's other early and influential philosophical heir, believed that human beings are fundamentally evil. For example, he wrote that "[p]eople's nature is bad" (2014, 248). Thus, people's natural inclinations had to be reformed (though Xúnzǐ did indicate that nature provided people with some natural inclinations that could form the basis of later ethical thought and behavior as well).[4] Two of Xúnzǐ's most famous and influential students – Hán Fēizǐ and Lǐ Sī – abandoned Rú Xué in favor of what came to be called "Legalism." These writers repudiated Kǒngzǐ's view that social authorities should govern primarily by virtuous example. They advocated, instead, a strict regimen of punishments and rewards set out in an inflexible legal system that the people could comprehend and would be strongly motivated to follow. (There were also Daoist thinkers, who, for example, sometimes advocated nonaction [wúwéi, 无为] on the part of rulers, which was interpreted in turn as either minimal interference in the people's lives or as actual abandonment of society [see Irene Bloom 1999, 78–79]. There were also followers of Mòzǐ, with his doctrine of universal love [see Burton Watson 1999]. Later, there were the many schools of Buddhists – and so on.)

Legalism was the official legal philosophy in China for only a very brief period (during the Qín Dynasty [221–206 BCE]). But the influence of

---

[3] See de Bary and Bloom (1999, 61).
[4] For a helpful discussion of the ethics of Mèngzǐ and Xúnzǐ in relation to emotion, see David Wong (2017).

Legalism was quite extensive. Indeed, Legalism represents a way of thinking about society that tends to arise periodically in China and elsewhere, as would seem to be suggested by its consistency with some versions of the criminal investigation genre. In keeping with this consistency, while there is some influence of Rú Xué in *Selling Rice*, this legal mystery tale seems to be more in line with Legalism. Specifically, the play clearly favors harsh punishment and unmitigated enforcement of the law, along with reverence for social hierarchy. (Such reverence is largely in keeping with Kǒngzǐ's teachings; however, it seems to go against Mèngzǐ's stress on the replaceability of the emperor when he or she behaves unethically [see Chan 1963, 62 on *Mengzi* 1B: 8 ["Liang Hui Wang" II: 15].) This does not mean that individual readers or audience members will agree that the capital punishment of criminals in the play (or in the real world) is justified; it means only that the play encourages us to adopt that view. In connection with this, the play advertises a central principle of equity in Legalism – that the law applies with no less stringency to government officials, including judges, than to ordinary people. As one Legalist text (*The Book of Lord Shang*) puts it, "Punishments should know no degree or grade, but from ministers of state and generals down to great officers and ordinary folk, whoever does not obey the king's commands, violates the interdicts of the state, or rebels against the statutes fixed by the ruler ... should not be pardoned. Merit acquired in the past should not cause a decrease in the punishment for demerit later" (in de Bary and Bloom 1999, 197).

Again, there is arguably a hint of Rú Xué in the play. Judge Bao is an exemplary figure – selflessly impervious to any form of corruption and therefore a model for all other judges. This modeling function is in keeping with the principles advocated by Kǒngzǐ. However, the precise nature of Judge Bao's exemplary character is not especially Confucian. For example, it has nothing to do with ritual propriety or such cardinal virtues as *xiào* ("filial piety"). Nor does it show any hints of the empathy and compassion stressed by Mèngzǐ. Indeed, Judge Bao often seems particularly lacking in empathy and compassion. This point applies not only to his treatment of criminals, but also to his behavior toward subordinates, and even toward the victims of crimes. (He treats the last with due consideration of their injury and the appropriate legal remedies, but without sentiment.) Rather, Judge Bao's imperturbable rectitude is more a matter of striking fear in potential criminals, who see no possibility of avoiding his harsh retributions even if they are wealthy and can offer extravagant bribes to mitigate his rigor.

Thus, even this apparently Confucian aspect of the play is more consistent with Legalism than with Rú Xué. Of course, this is exactly what we would expect given the preceding analysis. That analysis indicates that philosophical doctrines such as Legalism derive in part from the prior tendency of their exponents to understand ethical and social issues in relation to a criminal investigation story model. Conversely, storytellers who favor that model are likely to be thinking of moral dilemmas in terms of the law already. (Again, there is typically no simple and absolute origin; the emplotment directs the abstract reasoning, but the emplotment is also oriented by such reasoning. To ask which is prior is to ask a "chicken and egg" question.)

The play begins with Minister Fan explaining that he has "mastered" the classic texts of Rú Xué (Anonymous 2014, 110). Of course, he could be mistaken or deceitful in stating this. But he goes on to say that he has achieved the "highest" honors (110) in the examination system, which supports the claim that he has mastered the classics. Indeed, he repeats the information. Assuming the statement is true, by Confucian principles, this mastery should suffice to make him an excellent administrator. In contrast, Legalists would say that such mastery is irrelevant and may even be a handicap to effective governance. Indeed, Hán Fēizǐ states bluntly that "men of literary accomplishment should not be employed in the government" (de Bary and Bloom 1999, 201). The course of the play will suggest how we might adjudicate this difference of opinion.

As it happens, there is a severe drought in Chenzhou. It has been ongoing for three years. In consequence, the emperor has tasked Fan with remedying the situation. This is in keeping with general principles of Rú Xué, including those of Kǒngzǐ, but perhaps especially those of Mèngzǐ. Were this a story of Mèngzǐ-like ethics, it would presumably focus on the famine itself, reaching resolution when the people had enough to eat. It may at first appear that the story is moving in that direction as Fan explains that he must send "two honest officials" to Chenzhou "to open the granary" and sell the grain at an affordable price (Anonymous 2014, 110). It is already interesting that the drought has continued for three years while the government has kept a locked granary. The play might have focused on prior government policy or on such issues as land distribution (emphasized by Mèngzǐ; see *The Book of Mencius* [3A: 3] in Chan 1963, 68). But none of this is the play's concern. Its ethical focus is much narrower.

The play goes on to introduce the other members of Minister Fan's council. First, there is Duke Han, another prodigy in learning the classics of Rú Xué. He is followed by Lü Yijian, also a classics scholar. By Confucian lights, this should be a most able group. The fourth member of the committee is Master Liu, who is marked immediately not as a top scholar, but as "top among dissolute rakes" (Anonymous 2014, 111). The audience has no trouble discerning Liu's nature. But such discrimination is denied to the scholars of Rú Xué, who agree to Liu's suggestion that his own son and son-in-law be deputed to the famine-ravaged region. It does not require great discernment on the part of the audience to see that the "Confucian" learning of the ministers has not trained them to be wise administrators. In fact, they have failed abysmally at the task. Liu's relatives are introduced to the council, and the son (Dezhong) shows himself to be an utter buffoon. A Chinese idiom states that a fool does not know how high the sky is (Anonymous 2014, 145n.17). To prove that he is not a fool, Dezhong explains that he will "climb the ladder to take a look" at the height of the sky (112). Of course, he is not a complete fool; he explains that he and his brother-in-law will use his father's social position to "extort what we can" (112). To be fair, I should note that Dezhong communicates all this to the audience before entering the council. Moreover, Duke Han expresses skepticism over their appointment. But Liu's relatives are appointed anyway.

Following this apparent failure of Rú Xué, Fan in effect introduces the Legalist theme when he instructs Dezhong and his brother-in-law (Yang) that they "must... respect the laws" (Anonymous 2014, 113). He appears to qualify this in a Confucian manner when he tells the two, "Do not resort to punishment" (113). However, he soon gives them the authority to use a "mallet... to quell [popular] unrest, no questions asked" (114). In an aside, subsequent to the statement that they must obey the laws, Liu instructs them that they must, instead, "use this official mission for our private gain" (113). This is an almost comically anti-Confucian moment. Kǒngzǐ famously maintained that the value of *xiào* (filial piety) is so great that a son should not report his father to the authorities when he has committed a crime (*Lún Yǔ* [*Analects*] 13.18). Hán Fēizǐ responded to this by noting that filial piety and broader social commitment are not always compatible (see *The Han Feizi* in de Bary and Bloom 1999, 201). Hán was clearly on the side of broader social commitments during such conflicts; in our terms, he set the scope variable at the national rather than familial level. This scene presents an even more extreme case. The father is not guilty of the crime himself. He is telling his son and son-in-law to break the law. Thus, he is in some degree relying on their commitment to xiào since in this case such filial piety would seem to commit them to actively breaking the law. Of course, Kǒngzǐ would not have condoned such behavior, by Liu or by his son and son-in-law. He would have insisted that the young men remonstrate with the father, albeit respectfully. If this did not succeed, he would presumably urge them to withdraw (like the advisors to a corrupt government [see *Lún Yǔ* {*Analects*} 8.13]). But, in fact, it is a bit of a dilemma for a Confucian system. After all, if the legal system does not preempt xiào when the father has committed a crime, it would seem to adjure at least passive complicity when the father is undertaking a crime. And, given this, it is not entirely clear why the legal system should preempt xiào when the father is instructing the son himself to actively commit a crime – which is, in effect, the sort of issue Hán Fēizǐ is addressing.

To make matters worse, Dezhong has the unexpected insight that the people themselves might object to this mistreatment. So Liu appeals to the council to give his sons a means of controlling the people. Here, there is possibly a slight complication in the general ethical schema of the play. As already noted, Fan gives Dezhong and Yang absolute authority "to quell unrest, no questions asked" (Anonymous 2014, 114). To this point, Fan had appeared to be a Confucian (e.g., in urging the avoidance of punishment). This sort of punitive authority, however, is clearly more characteristic of Legalism than of Confucianism. But it is misplaced in this instance – due to the poor character of the two young men (Dezhong and Yang) who are given administrative authority. This small bit of the play, then, might slightly qualify the general anti-Confucianism of the piece, suggesting the importance of exemplary virtue on the part of the administrators. On the other hand, Legalist writers recognized this themselves (see the Legalist *Book of Lord Shang* in de Bary and Bloom 1999, 197–198). Moreover, as already indicated, the vicious character of the government appointees may be construed as a sort of filial piety, thus as a fault derived from Rú Xué, rather than opposed to it.

The scene now shifts to Chenzhou. Here is the point where different modes of emplotment most obviously make a difference in our ethical evaluation of and response to a situation. A sacrificial emplotment of famine might point toward social sinfulness and in-group contamination by an out-group (as we will see in the case of *Nosferatu*). A family separation narrative might cultivate compassion for the famine victims by priming the attachment memories of audience members (as we will see in the case of Markandaya's novel). *Selling Rice* focuses instead on the rule of law and the violation of law, especially the violation of law by representatives of the state.

The play introduces some granary hands, who enable the corruption perpetrated by Dezhong and Yang, suggesting that the rule of law may be subverted by the interaction of central and local administration, both of which should be strictly subordinated to the legal system in which they are supposed to operate. The peasants soon complain about the injustice of the government food aid. Dezhong responds with violence.

The peasants find a particularly articulate champion in one of their own class (thus not a scholar of Rú Xué), Zhang Piegu. This role is performed by the "male lead," who also performs the role of Judge Bao (Anonymous 2014, 109). This suggests the close connection between the characters. Zhang denounces Dezhong, Yang, and the granary hands, explaining that "they misuse public resources for private gain" and should not be be "let .. off so easily" (Anonymous 2014, 117), a point consistent with the Legalist stress on punishment (and with the fundamental ethical division between egocentric and allocentric). In part enabling such punishment, Zhang inhibits empathy with this moral out-group by taking up dehumanizing models. Specifically, he characterizes them as "vermin depleting the grain store/And bloodsucking, pus-sucking flies" (Anonymous 2014, 117).[5] Zhang goes on to calculate the consequences of the officials' corruption, estimating that each "one-tenth of a unit of rice/Is tied up with eight or nine lives" (Anonymous 2014, 119). This unsentimental, mathematical approach to ethical issues fits well with both Legalism and the criminal investigation narrative. For example, the prominent Legalist Shang Yang stresses the importance of "numerical calculations," maintaining that "[n]umbers provide the true method for directing the people," including numbers bearing on "weights" and "scales" (in de Bary and Bloom 1999, 196) – precisely what are at issue in the sales of rice in the play (where numbers are in fact highlighted in the dialogue).

Dezhong and company beat Zhang to death. However, before dying, Zhang predicts the inevitability of his "just punishment," which will lead to the Liu family being "gone" and Dezhong's "household ruined," suggesting the sort of collective punishment advocated in such Legalist works as the *Guanzi* and the *Book of Lord Shang* (see de Bary and Bloom 1999, 192, 197). In keeping with this, Zhang poses the rhetorical question of whether the Liu "family does not follow the imperial law" (Anonymous 2014, 121).

Just before he dies, Zhang adds to his analysis of the situation a philosophical tradition that I have not discussed, though it has also been highly influential in China – Buddhism. Specifically, Zhang explains the inevitability of Dezhong's and Yang's punishment by reference to the doctrine of "karmic retribution" (Anonymous 2014, 122), which is often viewed as a sort of cosmic principle of punishment and reward, with a person's good and bad acts matched with compensatory experiences. This karmic retribution will be worked out in "the courts of the underworld" (Anonymous 2014, 122), which are associated with the mythic deity Yama (see Hsia, Li, and Kao 2014, 108, 269). In this appeal to Buddhism, Zhang and the author of the play appeal to aspects of Buddhism that overlap with Legalism. Rather than taking up, for example, nonviolence (a very non-Legalist ideal), he refers to the almost

---

[5] It is interesting to note that when Dezhong responds that Zhang is a "bandit" (Anonymous 2014, 117), he uses a Mongol word (145n.26). This serves to associate the Liu family with the Mongols, thereby potentially extending and intensifying the out-grouping for the initial audience.

numerical calculations involved in karma (in one very common view of karma). Moreover, he links this directly with criminal investigation by placing the calculations in a court of law. Indeed, there is a further connection here. As Li points out in her introduction to the play, Judge Bao is "widely worshiped as a deity in popular religion." Specifically, "In many accounts he is said to preside as Yama judging the dead in the underworld" (Anonymous 2014, 108). It is fitting, then, that Zhang's son, Young Piegu, concludes that he has no option other than appealing to Judge Bao, due to his "uncompromising justice" (122). It is worth noting that Young Piegu also announces that he must "avenge" his father's death, a Confucian point, as we saw in discussing *The Zhao Orphan*. However, the revenge in this case is entirely Legalistic since it consists only in reporting the crime to the proper legal authorities. In the end, Judge Bao allows Young Piegu to strike the blow that kills Dezhong, but here too this is revenge that is entirely subsumed under the law.

The second act returns us to Minister Fan. The emperor has gotten wind of the situation in Chenzhou and has "commanded" Fan and his council to replace Dezhong and Yang (Anonymous 2014, 123). This may be due to the intervention of Duke Han and Lü, who ended the previous council scene with some skepticism over the appointment of Liu's relatives, perhaps suggesting some softening of the play's criticism of Confucian scholar-administrators. Even so, the emperor's response is squarely Legalist, delegating to the new appointee the power to punish by execution. Here, again, it is striking that the play treats the problem entirely as a matter of violation of the law – in keeping with the criminal investigation prototype – as if the famine itself were a secondary issue.

The act continues with a bit of mistaken identity, where Young Piegu believes Liu is Judge Bao and therefore initially makes his complaint to exactly the wrong person. However, this does not undermine the workings of karmic retribution, as one might initially have feared. Ultimately, Judge Bao is chosen to go to Chenzhou and rectify the situation there.

The dialogue emphasizes Bao's loyalty to the state, but it also includes a list of advisors who were killed by cruel emperors. I am inclined to see this as a further, critical allusion to the Mongol rule of China, a hint at the officials who died at the hands of their (out-group) rulers (not, say, an acceptance of Mèngzǐ's more general questioning of monarchial authority). In keeping with this, before Judge Bao leaves for Chenzhou, he engages in the sort of dehumanizing, moral out-grouping that we already saw with Zhang. Specifically, he refers to "those benighted ones" – whom we know to be Dezhong and Yang – who are "no better than birds and beasts." Given their nonhuman moral status (as "beasts" [*qínshòu*, 禽兽]),

it comes as no surprise that he "will not hesitate to lop off their treacherous heads" (Anonymous 2014, 130; later, he refers to them as "vermin" [143; *dù*, 蠹{beetles}). Though Liu appeals to him, Bao's integrity is imperturbable, "unyielding" (130). Judge Bao then says something that might hint at an indirect, but harsh criticism of Rú Xué, and from the present perspective an equally harsh criticism of familial emplotment of ethics. Specifically, he attributes the evil of Liu's family to the fact that they "equate household [*jiā*, 家] and state [*guó*, 国]" (130). Within the play, Bao is simply criticizing the Lius for placing family above the nation, as when they enrich kin at the expense of the people. But of course elevating the family above the nation is one criticism that Legalists leveled at Confucians (as I noted, regarding Hán Fēizǐ's criticism of *Lún Yǔ* [*Analects*] 13.18).

Bao does go on to assert that he "will relieve the plight of the people of Chenzhou" (Anonymous 2014, 130). However, that relief appears to consist entirely of reestablishing conformity to law (in keeping with the genre). It does not seem to have any relation to resolving the issues of the famine itself or to involve anything along the lines of Mèngzǐ's empathy. Of course, conformity to law will guarantee that the people are able to purchase rice at the reduced rate, which will certainly improve their condition. My point is not that Legalism is without benefits, just that its ethics – in keeping with the criminal investigation prototype – are different from those of, say, Mèngzǐ's version of Rú Xué (and from associated forms of emplotment).

The third act begins with Dezhong recapitulating how he and his brother-in-law are following his "father's advice" (Anonymous 2014, 132), thus implicitly reminding the audience that they are in effect observing the requirements of xiào. The focus quickly shifts back to Bao and his assistant, Zhang Qian (to whom I will refer as "Qian" to avoid confusion with Zhang Piegu). Qian laments Bao's lack of compassion. Bao expects Qian to be as selflessly devoted to serving the law as Bao is himself. It is difficult to ascertain the precise attitude of the play toward this complaint. I find myself sympathetic, particularly to Qian's complaints about being underfed. Moreover, Bao's response to overhearing Qian seems to me little short of cruel. (He pretends that he is going to relent and indicates that he will give Qian more than he has received in the past, but it turns out that it is more punishment, not more food.) This might lead one to conclude that the play is somewhat critical of Legalist rigorism and lack of empathy at this point. But a later scene shows that Qian has a tendency to corruption, and the play may be designed to suggest that only strict enforcement of laws will prevent such tendencies from manifesting themselves in immoral and anti-social behavior. Indeed, Bao's overreaction to the trivial insubordination of Qian's complaint recalls the Legalist insistence that minor transgressions should be overpunished to prevent them from growing into major transgressions (see de Bary and Bloom 1999, 196).

The play then introduces a prostitute. It turns out that Dezhong and Yang are squandering all their ill-gotten gains at the local brothel. It seems that this is designed to add sexual disgust to the moral outgrouping of the play's villains. It is particularly vile that they pawn their official paraphernalia – the property of the state – at the brothel when they run low on funds. Thus, they are in a sense cheating not only the common people but even the emperor in order to indulge their lusts. These points should make it easier for audience members to accept their eventual fate, itself suggested by Bao's statement that he has been executing people for decades in service to the emperor (Anonymous 2014, 134).

Bao goes undercover as an employee of the brothel's madam in order to ascertain just what is going on in Chenzhou. What he learns fills him with "anger" and "rage" (Anonymous 2014, 136). Contrary to what I have been claiming, he also says that it fills him "with pity for the people" (137). However, the anger is more obvious in what follows, and in any case the pity seems confined to the effects of legal violations.

Eventually, Dezhong and Yang have Bao tied up and readied for a beating, as they do not know who he is. It is at this point that Qian returns and, unaware that Bao is nearby and can overhear his conversation, indicates to Dezhong and Yang that he might help them for a price. As already noted, this puts Bao's earlier harshness with Qian in a different light.

The act ends with Bao reiterating the criticism of Dezhong and Yang, "who rob the people" (Anonymous 2014, 139), and reemphasizing the disgust-provoking quality of their behavior, "covet[ing] money for whores" (139). Though addressing Qian onstage, he is equally appealing to the audience when he adjures his interlocutor, "Do not blame me for not showing mercy" (140). As should be clear, the point is fully consistent with Legalism. It is worth noting, however, that eschewing mercy is not in any way required by the criminal investigation genre, though it is a plausible specification of the genre. Indeed, the fact that the genre does allow for mercy is presumably one reason why this play devotes special attention to discrediting mercy (in a Legalist manner).

The final act begins with Bao arresting and beating the prostitute – to my mind, gratuitously, but at least some audience members would feel she merits the beating due to her (for them, disgust-provoking, immoral) profession. Yang quickly confesses that he pawned imperial property for pastries (Anonymous 2014, 140). In keeping with Legalist attitudes toward small crimes and Bao's promise not to show mercy, Yang is beheaded. Following this, Bao has Young Piegu bludgeon Dezhong to death with the same mallet the latter had used to murder Young Piegu's father. Bao claims that this is the only way that "peace and order" will be "restored to Chenzhou" (141). Again, it is striking how the criminal investigation genre isolates the criminal violation as the ethical and practical problem and punishment of the perpetrator as the ethical and practical response, as if the famine were morally irrelevant.

I must confess that I find the final page of the play somewhat confusing. After virtually ordering Young Piegu to perform the execution of Dezhong, he has him arrested. Fortunately, Liu appears with a general pardon from the emperor. Liu intended that the pardon would save his son and son-in-law, but they are already dead. Instead, it saves Young Piegu. Bao attributes these happy coincidences to "heaven's justice" (Anonymous 2014, 143), which is a bit more optimistic than one expects from Legalists. On the other hand, it may fit with the small Buddhist element in the play, marked by its assertion of "karmic retribution" (122).

## Romantic Stories

Romantic stories concern two people who fall in love and face social opposition (commonly intensified as parental opposition), frequently because they belong to different identity groups (e.g., races). The lovers are separated, with one often being exiled, the other being confined, and both somehow risking death. In some cases, there is a love triangle in which one of the lovers is supposed to marry some third person. The lovers work to be united, sometimes recruiting the aid of a sympathetic figure with some degree of social authority. In comic versions of the story, the lovers are reunited and the various parties are reconciled. The motivating character emotion is, of course, romantic love, which is (roughly) a combination of attachment bonding and sexual desire. The interpersonal stance of the reader, as cultivated by the genre, is typically a form of personal identification in which the reader responds to the characters' longings and frustrations as congruent with his or her own experience; in this way, the genre, when successful, tends to heighten empathic parallelism. The social organization suggested by the genre rejects identity categories and maximizes individual freedom of choice. In keeping with this, the genre stresses the ethical value of caring for other people's emotional well-being, especially their attachment needs. It particularly highlights the virtues of unselfish deference to other people's wishes for the conduct of their own lives, as well as intense and enduring personal commitment to those with whom one has attachment bonds.

In Chapter 6, we will look in detail at one romantic comedy, Shakespeare's *A Midsummer Night's Dream*. In examining that play, I will address the tacit ethical criticisms of Theseus and Hermia's father, the ways in which Shakespeare deals with the love triangle and inconstancy, and other relevant topics. Here, we might briefly consider a few other works, with particular attention to the issue of individual liberty, especially in relation to group norms.

As just noted, romantic stories involve both sexual desire and, much more importantly, attachment. In romantic love, attachment is linked with what I have called "reward dependency" (Hogan 2011b, 83), the contingency of goal seeking and enjoyment on, in this case, the presence and reciprocated affection of the beloved. Even in cultures where individual choice in marriage is not the norm, stories of romantic love almost invariably favor the lovers over blocking figures representing society and the usual social norms. Moreover, that preference is ethical. As already indicated, when people emplot human relations in terms of affiliative bonding, their strong inclination is to favor individual liberty over structures of authority.

For example, in Christianity, a founding commandment is "Honor thy father and thy mother" (Exodus 20:12, King James version). Yet, in *Romeo and Juliet* ([1597] 1980) – one of the most widely appreciated works of English literature – the lovers defy their family, winning the sympathy of the audience as well as that of the representative of religion in the play, Friar Lawrence. In India, custom strongly favored the arrangement of marriages. But in the most renowned classical drama of India, *The Recognition of Śakuntalā* (*Abhijñānaśākuntalam* [5th century CE]), the lovers meet and "marry" without arrangement or ceremony (i.e., they have sex). Their enduring union is deferred by a disagreeable holy man but receives strong religious approval through the reunion in heaven that closes the play. Filial piety (xiào, 孝) is a cardinal Confucian virtue. Despite this, *The Peony Pavilion* (牡丹亭, *Mǔdān Tíng* [1598]; Tāng 1980), "the masterpiece of Ming-era aristocratic theater" (Knight 2012, 80), treats a man and woman who marry without consulting her parents. Moreover, the father of the woman treats the husband with cruelty that audience members are likely to find horrifying. The father only retains our sympathy as he does not understand precisely what he is doing. In the end, the union of these lovers too is celebrated.

Readers familiar with these exemplary romantic stories are likely to be struck by a range of other similarities. One of the most interesting concerns the separation of the lovers. As already noted, romantic stories prototypically involve a separation of the lovers, and that separation is often assimilated to death, even when there is a comic resolution (see Hogan 2003, 101–109). All three of these dramas in some way intensify that connection with death. In *Romeo and Juliet*, I am not referring to the actual deaths of the lovers at the end of the play. That is unsurprising in tragedy; indeed, its association with tragedy is precisely why it appears in the middle of a comedy. The hint of possible tragedy should serve to make the reunion of the lovers all the more joyful. I am referring, rather, to the staged death of Juliet that should have allowed the (intensified) comic reunion of the lovers. In the case of *The Recognition of Śakuntalā*, one of the lovers is assumed into heaven in a scene that involves leaving the mortal world, which ordinarily happens only in death. As a result, the lovers are reunited in a heavenly hermitage. Finally, in *The Peony Pavilion*, one of the lovers actually does die before she is revived by her beloved. I take it that in each case, the point of the intensification is to enhance the emotional response of the audience and to increase the authority of the union. Again, in *The Recognition of Śakuntalā*, the reunion is divine. In *The Peony Pavilion*, it is explicitly allowed by an otherworldly court, which judges that the dead lover "share[s] a marriage affinity" with her beloved; she is therefore "release[d] ... from this City of the Wrongfully Dead" and may "search" for him while her "fleshly body" is "guard [ed] ... from corruption" (Tāng 1980, 133, 134). In *Romeo and Juliet*, the staging of Juliet's death also allows Shakespeare to establish parallels between her and Jesus, enhancing the moral approbation of the lovers' choice (see Hogan 2011b, 91, 96, 106–107).

In short, romantic story structure is principally connected with intense attachment feelings and associated reward dependency. The attachment feelings establish norms for the lovers. These include reciprocation and exclusiveness. These are tested in the love triangle narrative, a frequent addition to the main romantic narrative, often deriving from the parents' preference – as in the choice of Paris for Juliet in Shakespeare's play. (Sometimes a lover's real or apparent death serves as a way of escaping from forced infidelity to his or, more often, her beloved, as with Juliet's faked death to avoid marriage to Paris or Zhù Yīngtái's descent into Liáng Shānbó's grave on her way to be married into the Ma family [e.g., see Tsai 2004].) In these cases, the attachment feelings also establish norms for the larger society, principally a sort of libertarianism and a rejection of identity group divisions, such as the Montagues and the Capulets (or at least mitigation of antagonism across such groups).

The ethics of such narratives can easily extend to a criticism of other group norms by reference to individual needs. For example, in political contexts, the romantic distrust of identity categories tends toward internationalism and thus opposition to war (see Hogan 2009, chap. 7). Or consider the status of women, and particularly the issue of women's education, as developed in the story of Liáng Shānbó and Zhù Yīngtái. Particular instances of this story often present a strong case for the value of female higher education, both for the women themselves and for the larger society (for discussion, see Hogan 2018). They also may take up sexual preference, transgendering, and other topics, challenging standard assumptions about sex and gender identity categories (see Hogan 2018, 59–68).

As noted earlier, prototypical genres often have critical versions. For example, there are anti-heroic stories as well as heroic ones, though the latter appear to be much more common. Similarly, there are anti-romantic stories. However, anti-romantic stories appear to be particularly infrequent relative to other genres. An exception to the last point is the familial genre, for which critical versions also seem uncommon. Indeed, the relation between the two genres suggests the reason for this relative rarity. Both genres concern reciprocal attachment bonds, and we (humans) seem to cherish such bonds virtually without qualification. Indeed, when we seem to have come across a critical version of a romantic story, we almost invariably discover that it is not a genuine romantic story at all. There is, rather, some problem with the attachment feelings in the work.

Consider, for example, another Yuan period play, this by one of the most renowned Chinese dramatists, Guan Hanqing (ca. 1214–ca. 1300), *Zhao Pan'er Uses Seductive Wiles to Rescue a Sister Courtesan* (hereafter, *Rescuing a Sister*). (For information on Guan and on this particular work, see Lee's introduction to this play; on Guan's status in particular, see Li 2014, 270.) The play is a progressive work, criticizing the disabilities placed on women in the author's society, not entirely unlike some versions of the Liáng Shānbó and Zhù Yīngtái story. In this thematic respect, the work is consistent with some aspects of romantic emplotment. Moreover, the first half of the plot superficially follows the romantic script. Song Yinzhang is a young courtesan who wishes to marry Zhou She. She is opposed in this by her mother, and by her friend Zhao Pan'er, who prefers the scholar An Xiushi. An pursues Song, giving us the predictable love triangle. However, Song secures her mother's permission and weds Zhou. Unlike the usual romance, things do not end there. Zhou brutally mistreats Song, leading Zhao to devise an elaborate plan to seduce Zhou so that he divorces Song (who is not free to divorce on her own). This may seem to be a straightforward anti-romantic work. However, I have left out the characters' emotions. Zhou does not "love" Song in the sense that, though he desires her, he does not have a genuine attachment bond with her, the sort of bond that would secure and intensify a parallel, empathic interpersonal stance and associated caring behavior. Similarly, we have little reason to believe that Song has strong attachment feelings for Zhou, though she does appreciate his attentions and appearance (see Guan 2014, 276). In contrast, An appears genuinely attached to Song, and there are some suggestions that Song at least formerly reciprocated those feelings. If this were a genuine romantic story, then, the protagonists would be An and Song, not Zhou and Song. Rather, Zhou would be the rival in the love triangle.

What, then, has resulted in Song marrying Zhou? In keeping with Guan's political concerns, it is in effect a matter of economic coercion. Song chooses Zhou simply because he has money. As she herself explains, if she were to marry An, they would end up as beggars (Guan 2014, 275). One version of the play's title refers to Song as "a Seduced Courtesan" (Guan 2014, 292), suggesting that the play is better categorized in the seduction genre. The main difference from prototypical instances of this last is that the seduction in this case is not a matter of deception about romantic love, but of straightforward economic self-interest. In any event, the key point is that apparently "critical" treatments of the romantic genre are often not romantic at all, but instances of the seduction prototype. This is important because the play actually suggests the usual ethical valorization of the young lovers' free choice in marriage, but Guan goes further than many writers by highlighting the economic constraints on that free choice, constraints that may be far more effective – and far more destructive – than the more standard parental coercion.

## Seduction and Sexual Assault (*All's Well That Ends Well* and *Hamlet*)

The seduction genre involves the seduction or sexual assault of one character by another, typically the seduction or rape of a woman by a man. In the seduction version, the woman forms an attachment bond with the man and usually believes that he reciprocates her feelings. In the sexual assault version, she may have no attachment to the man but may understand that her continued existence in society requires that she marry her violator (if she is not to be ostracized by society or reduced to prostitution and beggary). In either case, she is abandoned by the man, whom she typically pursues. The resolution of these events is never entirely happy. Either at least one of the "lovers" dies or they are united in a marriage that audience members can hardly view positively. The man usually does not wish to marry. This and his prior behavior do not lead us to expect the marriage to be a happy one for either partner.

The main emotion on the part of the man is typically sexual desire, though the seduction or assault does sometimes involve other emotion motivations, such as anger (perhaps a desire for revenge). The emotions of the woman typically include desire, as well as attachment and shame. Works in the seduction genre commonly cultivate audience responses of disgust for the seducer and the "fallen woman." However, they most often develop the audience's pity for the woman as well. (I say "pity" rather than "compassion," as the feeling often involves a sense of moral superiority over the woman.) This is due in part to our general empathy for anyone suffering attachment loss and in part due to the man behaving deceitfully, as well as the unfairness of the situation due to sexual double standards. The virtues associated with the genre are largely indicated by their violation. They include honesty or sincerity and disciplined self-denial, particularly in chastity, or what Haidt (2012) refers to as *purity*. The social organization favored by the genre is not entirely clear. However, it often suggests that individual liberty should be restricted. In this way, it works in the opposite direction from the romantic genre.

Shakespeare provides some excellent instances of a complex seduction story. Consider, for example, *All's Well That Ends Well* (Greenblatt 1997) – a highly ironic title, given the extreme ambivalence many audience members are likely to feel about the ending. Helena loves Bertram, but Bertram does not reciprocate her affection. He explains, "I cannot love her" (II.iii.141; he also considers her an inopportune match [II.iii.111]). When Helena devises a way to wed him anyway, Bertram leaves after the ceremony, refusing to consummate the marriage. Helena follows in the hope of genuinely securing Bertram as her husband. This is a striking variation on the seduction plot. Rather than sex without marriage, due to the plotting of the man, this story – in Shakespeare's version and in its source from the *Decameron* – presents us with marriage lacking sex, due to the plotting of the woman. In both the standard case and this variation, the man flees, pursued by the woman. In exile, Bertram falls in lust with Diana and sets out to seduce her. Helena learns of the plot and arranges for Diana to agree to a silent assignation (silent as neither will speak during the meeting) that will occur under cover of total darkness. Helena takes the place of Diana at the meeting, thereby leading Bertram to consummate their marriage. Bertram leaves, apparently abandoning Diana after deflowering her. Later, faced with Diana's accusations, Bertram denies her. In short, Bertram enacts a standard seduction story with Diana, or rather what he intends to do constitutes a standard seduction story. What he in fact does is confirm his marriage to Helena.

So the play begins with a woman plotting marriage the way the man plots seduction in one common story. It continues with the man plotting to seduce and abandon another woman, only to find himself deceived into the very marriage he was trying to avoid. At the end of the play, it is difficult to say just how one should feel. Helena does love Bertram. But she has deceived him into a lifelong commitment that he does not desire. I, at least, can hardly approve of this part of Helena's behavior. On the other hand, one can hardly feel sorry for Bertram, given his plot to ruin Diana's life by seducing her.

The seduction prototype begins with such a degree of negativity that it is difficult to imagine how it might be developed critically. But *All's Well*

*That Ends Well* presents us with just such a critical version. Specifically, the standard version is likely to provoke disgust in readers. That disgust may take different forms. In a misogynistic context, it seems likely that it would provoke disgust at the woman's sexual indulgence. In connection with this, audience members might tacitly condone the man's deceit, justifying his abandonment of the woman due to her unchastity (even though he is less chaste and is the cause of her sexual indulgence). In this play, however, none of the women is unchaste (Helena only has sexual relations with her husband and only after marriage). Thus, there should be no issue of misogynistic disgust at women's sexuality. In this way, the play sets aside the double standard in sexual morality. It focuses instead on the aspect of plotting and deceit.

Obviously, different audience members will have different responses to the events of the story, depending on their different moral (and other) inclinations. But the story is structured in such a way as to directly parallel Bertram's deceitful plot and Helena's. This should in principle challenge audience members to reconsider their own spontaneous ethical judgments about these plots. One imagines that men in the audience would be more sympathetic with Bertram's attempts at convincing an attractive young woman to sleep with him. Similarly, one imagines that women in the audience would be more sympathetic with Helena's attempts at leading a man she loves to marry her. The paralleling of the two makes it difficult for audience members to ignore the similarities. On the other hand, the play does not make the two equal. Bertram's ploys, if successful, would have proven (literally) sinful for both Bertram and Diana and ruinous for the latter. In contrast, Helena's (successful) ploys serve to prevent sin (other than the deception itself) and to save Diana from social degradation. (They also involve curing another character of a dangerous disease.) Thus, the play is much more critical of the misogynistic tendency, which is certainly appropriate, given general social and ethical inclinations at the time.

Thinking about moral issues in terms of the standard seduction story, then, often involves misogynistic disgust at unchaste intentions or behavior by women. The focus on female sexuality in particular may be associated with a morally indulgent attitude toward male "conquest" (of the "boys will be boys" variety). Alternatively, the centrality of the seduction prototype in one's ethical thought and action may be connected to disgust with sexuality more generally. The latter is consistent with some views of morality that stress sexual "purity" (thus, disgust avoidance) and that tend to inspire much less actual moral concern with nonsexual, or at least non-disgust-related, issues. More generally, a broad, moral condemnation of sexuality is often connected with an ethics of opposing unmerited pleasure (rather than opposing unmerited pain).

The seduction story can also be developed in such a way as to criticize male deceit and to promote sympathy with the woman who is deceived. Both patriarchal and, so to speak, "feminist" specifications of the prototype are available to authors and to readers, sometimes even in a single story. Again, individual preferences in this regard probably vary in part with the sex of the reader, with women more likely to adopt the "feminist" view and men more likely to adopt the patriarchal view. But the alignment is certainly not complete (e.g., I personally am always inclined to identify with the character who falls in love and is discarded, whether that character is male or female). In any case, both versions tend to stress specifically sexual morality and disgust.

Shakespeare's presentation of this structure in *All's Well That Ends Well* is critical for two reasons: First, it sets aside the sexual issue, therefore avoiding the problem of double standards. Shakespeare does this without being anti-sex since there is sex in the play (confirmed by pregnancy), but the sex is legitimated by prior marriage. Moreover, he includes an early speech on virginity that effectively criticizes an anti-sex attitude. Specifically, Paroles engages in sexual banter with Helena about virginity. The scene is very funny as Shakespeare clearly mocks Paroles's disingenuous attempt to convince Helena that she should not remain a virgin. But, at the same time, Shakespeare puts many valid points into Paroles's speech. For example, Paroles rightly asserts that the only way to have virgins is for some women to have children. Conversely, he explains that a wholesale condemnation of sexuality would thereby be a wholesale condemnation of all our mothers. As he puts it, "To speak on the part of virginity is to accuse your mothers, which is most infallible disobedience" (I.i.128–129). In this way, for this particular work the moral issue is not really sex at all.

The second way in which Shakespeare's version is critical is that he establishes parallel schemes for the male and female characters. This seems likely to encourage a greater degree of critical self-reflection on the part of audience members, whether they would be disposed to indulge the irresponsibility of the man or the so-called "wiles" of the woman. At the same time, he does not treat the two tendencies – patriarchal and feminist – as equal. He clearly sympathizes more fully with the woman than with the man and thereby implicitly appeals to us to do the same.

Before going on, it is worth making a few brief comments on another, more standard version of the seduction story, though admittedly not a wholly standard version. One subplot of *Hamlet* is the relationship between the prince and Ophelia. Hamlet clearly presents his interest as romantic, and Ophelia appears to accept it as such. However, Laertes and Polonius both caution Ophelia against taking Hamlet at his word.

Polonius is particularly clear in saying that Hamlet cannot wed Ophelia due to their difference in status. Of course, this is itself ambiguous between the seduction story and the romantic story, for we could interpret Polonius here as playing the role of the parent who prevents the lovers from uniting. At the very least, he justifies his separation of Hamlet and Ophelia by reference to the seduction story, worrying that Ophelia will end up pregnant and abandoned. Subsequently, Hamlet himself taunts Polonius with the idea that his daughter might become pregnant. This could be taken to suggest that he has learned about Polonius's worries and resents them, though it could also be taken to suggest that Hamlet has indeed had sexual relations with Ophelia. There is a similar ambiguity in Hamlet's dialogue with Ophelia. When he adjures her to go to a "nunnery" (III.i.122), which is invariably annotated as a euphemism for a brothel, he could be taken to imply that she is sexually tainted. But his subsequent claim,"be thou as chaste as ice, as pure as snow, thou shalt not escape calumny" (III.i.136–137), would seem to indicate, rather, that she is unseduced but will always be suspected due to social prejudices.

To this point, it is unclear whether the Hamlet–Ophelia subplot is a (very troubled) romantic story or an (elliptical) seduction story. Eventually, Hamlet is exiled by Claudius after (mistakenly) killing Ophelia's father. Ophelia goes mad; this is commonly taken to be the result of her father's death. However, in her madness, she sings about a maid who trusted a young suitor and succumbed to his seduction, only to be abandoned by him (IV.v.45–64). This seems to rather strongly suggest that Ophelia is in that situation herself. Moreover, she subsequently commits suicide, which is the sort of response one might reasonably expect to find in a seduction story, where a young, unprotected woman has been impregnated and abandoned.

However, Shakespeare actually continues the ambiguity, suggesting a romantic narrative, when he has Hamlet profess his love at her burial. Thus, even in this case, Shakespeare presents us with a complex and challenging version of the story type. This is closely related to the main storyline, concerning Hamlet, his parents, and his uncle. There, too, we encounter an ambiguity over whether a particular relationship is a matter of romantic love or seduction. Claudius indicates at various points that he is in fact deeply attached to Gertrude. But Hamlet construes the relationship as a sexual seduction, albeit one in which the woman is not abandoned. Specifically, Hamlet clearly thinks of the marriage of Claudius and Gertrude in solely sexual terms. Moreover, his response to that sexuality is profound disgust, as indicated, for example, in his imagination of them "[i]n the rank sweat of an enseamèd bed" (III.iv.82). Part of Hamlet's attitudes and actions might have been significantly different if he – and those around him – had imagined the world more fully and more consistently in terms of a romantic narrative.

## Family Separation and Reunion (*Follow the Rabbit-Proof Fence* and *Nectar in a Sieve*)

The family separation and reunion prototype concerns the splitting up of parents and children (or, less often, siblings). This separation may last for many years, during which one or the other (i.e., parents or children) may seek reunion. Even comic versions of the story often have a melancholy undertone because when the family is reunited, there is no real possibility for a "happily ever after" ending, due to the parents' age and inevitable death. Moreover, the nature of the separation affects the quality of the reunion. Specifically, there are three common reasons for separation. First, there are cases of selfish abandonment, when the parents abandon the children or the children abandon the parents in order to pursue their own self-interest (as when the prodigal son of the parable [Luke 15:11–32] takes his inheritance and leaves home to live pleasurably). Second, there are cases of self-sacrifice, most often cases where a parent gives up the child in order to give that child a better future (as in King Vidor's paradigmatic 1937 melodrama, *Stella Dallas*). Finally, there are cases where external circumstances – beyond the control of either party – lead to the separation. In the most ethically significant cases, those conditions are typically social (as in Margaret Atwood's *The Handmaid's Tale*), but they may be of any sort (e.g., a storm and shipwreck, as in *A Comedy of Errors*).

The primary motivating emotion in the family separation genre is attachment. Attachment is what drives the family members to seek one another. But it is also what drives the parent to give up the child for that child's well-being in the altruistic or self-sacrificing version of the structure. Specifically, attachment encompasses two related but sometimes contradictory components. One is the need for the attachment object's accessibility and engagement with one's own well-being; the other is the desire for the attachment object's well-being. Put differently, one is a matter of receiving care from a particular person (the care cannot be supplied by just anybody); the other is a matter of giving care to a particular person (the care cannot be supplied to just anybody). The self-sacrificing version tends to occur when the long-term well-being of the child at least appears to require his or her separation from parents, though the pain of that separation is often so great – not only for the parents, but even more importantly for the children – that readers may find the self-sacrifice naïve and the consequences more negative than positive.

As to interpersonal stance, the family separation genre involves perhaps the strongest elicitors of pity that are available to us. The attachment vulnerability of children and the pain of their separation anxiety are possibly the fundamental triggers for our protective and nurturant responses – our caregiving – maternal or paternal. Note that this interpersonal stance of protection and nuturance has immediate ethical implications. First, it draws our attention to attachment relations and tends to support very strongly an ethical attitude of preventing unmerited pain, through its enhancement of empathic response. Second, it provides us with a general orientation for ethical response in empathic simulation, pity, and caregiving. I say "pity" here, rather than "compassion," because the solicitude involved does commonly presuppose some sort of superiority of the caregiver (parent) over the target (child). This is one reason why members of dominant groups seem more likely to rely on the genre for political purposes than do members of dominated groups (e.g., think of Harriet Beecher Stowe's treatment of slavery in contrast with Frederick Douglass's; for discussion of these cases, see Hogan 2020, chaps. 5, 7).

In keeping with the enhanced empathic response, this genre tends to foster an attitude of forgiveness (e.g., as with the prodigal son), as well as admiration for successful caregiving, whether that of parents or children (the latter commonly in the form of filial piety). It often values the virtues of selflessness, protectiveness, and personal loyalty. As to social organization, it tends to favor the autonomy of the family unit over the larger society in much the same way that the romantic plot favors the romantic couple.

A narratively straightforward – but emotionally somewhat unusual – example of the family separation and reunion story may be found in Shakespeare's *Comedy of Errors*. A husband, wife, and twin sons (along with twin servants) are all separated in a shipwreck. After many years, the family is reunited when the husband and one of the sons separately seek the others. The bulk of the story focuses on the sons and, in consequence, does not dwell on attachment issues since the sons were separated at such a young age that they have no recollection of their parents or of one another. On the other hand, one does not have to be too psychoanalytically inclined to see the marital problems of one son as, in part, attachment issues that might be viewed as originating in his early attachment deprivation. The play does, I believe, effectively develop audience feelings of empathy and forgiveness.

I have discussed the ethical implications of this genre elsewhere, particularly in connection with Rabindranath Tagore's work and its foregrounding of attachment in ethical response (see Hogan 2011b, chap. 7; Tagore's view appears to have been similar to Batson's very plausible suggestion that "altruistic motivation is based on cognitive generalization of human parental nurturance" [Batson 2012, 49], though I would have said "emotional – and sometimes cognitive – generalization"). Here, I would like to briefly consider two somewhat unusual, but I think revealing versions of the genre – Nugi Garimara's (2002) *Follow the Rabbit-Proof Fence* and Kamala Markandaya's (2002) *Nectar in a Sieve*. Both address ethical and political issues related to colonialism.

Nugi Garimara is an Australian Aboriginal woman. Her *Follow the Rabbit-Proof Fence* recounts a story from the life of her mother (Molly) and two other relatives (Daisy and Gracie). As girls, the three of them were taken away from their families and sent to the Moore River Native Settlement to be educated in the skills necessary for becoming part of Euro-Australian society, though the part to which they would be allowed access was quite restricted (e.g., much of it was service work, such as housecleaning). The girls escaped from the settlement and over the course of the following months made their way by foot toward home, covering roughly 1,000 miles. Molly and Daisy succeed in being reunited with their families, though Gracie does not.

Thus, Garimara had a familial separation and reunion story ready to hand in her own family. However, she faced several possible problems, in part because she was addressing both Aboriginal and white Australian readers. With regard to the former, she presumably wished to recount a story that would not be overly pessimistic. Put simply, she did not want to foster any greater feeling of despair – which is to say, she did not wish to prolong or intensify a disabling sense of helplessness – in her Aboriginal readers. (On the sources and consequences of such a sense of helplessness, see Nussbaum [2003, 100–103].) She presumably wished to give such readers a sense of empowerment. As just recounted, the main story should for the most part do that, and indeed Garimara strongly emphasizes the success of Molly and Daisy. Even the story of Gracie, who is returned to the settlement, attends principally to her skill and endurance. Also, without blaming the young girl, Garimara does suggest that Gracie too would have gotten to her home if she had persevered in following Molly's leadership. Thus, even her case contributes to the overall empowering quality of the book.[6]

---

[6] Unsurprisingly, other critics have identified some of the same basic thematic points. For example, Klein's approach, with its influences drawn from poststructuralist affect theory and mainstream postcolonial theory, is quite different from mine. Still, in exploring Garimara's critique of white racist ideology, she concludes, among other things, that "the text transforms [indigenous Australians] from victims into agents" (2016, 602). Similarly, Fu argues that the memoir "discloses a history of disruption imposed by European settlement, but, perhaps more importantly, registers Aboriginal peoples' strength to resist, adopt, and reconnect" (2019, 167).

On the other hand, Garimara presumably does not wish to support some sort of voluntarism, an overly optimistic view that people can accomplish almost anything with a bit of pluck. Thus, we learn in a very brief final chapter that the girls were, ultimately, not as successful as the rest of the text implies. The family reunion was not enduring. Gracie never managed to return home. Molly was eventually abducted again and sent back to the settlement. At this time, she was the mother of two girls (one being the author of the book); those girls were also abducted. Several of Molly's relatives died at this time, including at least one as a kind of suicide provoked by the abduction (Garimara 2002, 131). Molly escaped with the younger daughter, who was herself stolen once more. After that second kidnapping, Molly never saw her younger daughter again. Garimara provides us with this information but does not elaborate on it in the manner of the main story.

In this regard, then, the orientation of this familial separation story is somewhat different from the usual one, in part because it is prudential rather than ethical. It involves the assertion of the possibility of agency, of acting even against what appear to be overwhelming forces. At the same time, this sense of empowerment is (prudently) qualified by a clear indication that not everything is possible.

That sense of restricted possibility is even more important for Garimara's other implied audience – people of European (rather than Aboriginal) descent. Insofar as this family memoir appeals to the moral decisions and actions of white people, it seems important to indicate that the moral ideal – here represented by the attachment-based unity of the family – cannot be established by Aboriginal people acting on their own. After all, if it were entirely in the hands of Aboriginal people, there would be no need for white people to be involved at all in rectifying relevant injustices. But here another problem arises.

Like colonialism anywhere, colonialism in Australia was often simply dehumanizing of indigenous people and rapacious with regard to the natural and human resources of the place. Also like colonialism elsewhere, there was resistance to this dehumanization and systematic robbery. That resistance came not only from colonized people, but from some members of the colonizing society as well. Unfortunately, the liberal anti-colonialism of Europeans often substituted paternalism for dehumanizing exploitation. Though certainly preferable to brutalization, paternalism still involved depriving colonized people of fundamental rights, and it typically continued colonial expropriation, if perhaps in a reduced degree. As Stuart Macintyre explains, from the early nineteenth century, "some whites" saw their compatriots as engaging in "inhuman conduct." In consequence, they called for Aborigines to be "protected" (2004, 64). I certainly do not wish to suggest that anyone who used the term "protection" was thereby being paternalistic. However, I do wish to suggest that the idea of protection can easily be developed in paternalistic ways – and, indeed, it was developed paternalistically by the Australian colonial administration.

Specifically, the government established positions for "protector of Aborigines" (see Garimara 2002, 66). The aims of the position were laudable (if limited). But the design of the protection clearly presumed that, like parents treating children, the Europeans knew what was best for the native Australians. However well-intentioned, the "protection boards" that developed from these initiatives were rather sinister. They made Aborigines "wards of the state" and "were empowered to prescribe their residence, determine conditions of employment, control marriage and cohabitation, and" – what is most crucial for Garimara's memoir – "assume custody of children" (Stuart Macintyre 2004, 145).

Unsurprisingly, the model of Aboriginal people as minors was sometimes explicit. Stuart Macintyre quotes "The Victorian Board of Protection" as saying that Aborigines are "but helpless children whose state was deplorable enough when this country was their own but is now worse" (2004, 104). He goes on to quote a "sympathetic" scholar of Aboriginal culture as commenting that "[t]he blacks should, when necessary, be coerced, just as we coerce children" (105).

Clearly, Garimara did not wish to reinforce European practices of modeling Aborigines as children or the paternalism associated with such modeling. Rather, she needed to expose the traumatic nature of her mother's and other relatives' experiences without encouraging the sort of demeaning pity that was part of the problem to begin with. Liberal paternalism is based on a degree of empathy with out-group members. However, that empathy is distorted by the paternalists' interpersonal stance of assumed superiority over the out-group. With regard to her white readers, then, Garimara's task was to extend their empathy – particularly by reference to attachment loss – while simultaneously cultivating respect for Aborigines. She pursued the latter goal by two means. First, in the opening chapters of the book, she presents a very positive – indeed, virtually Edenic – account of pre-European Aboriginal life; she contrasts this with the degrading results of European colonization. In other words, she develops a historical narrative of social decline in which the cause of the decline has nothing to do with internal features of Aboriginal traditions. It is, rather, solely a matter of European violence, which extends to the (putatively benevolent) violence of separating mixed-race children from their Aboriginal mothers.

The second technique is more interesting, as it is intrinsic to the story itself. Garimara represents Molly, an Aboriginal child, as decidedly more rational, disciplined, and competent than the Europeans who have authority over her. In other words, in the liberal colonialist imagination, even literal Aboriginal adults are children when compared to Europeans. Garimara in effect turns this on its head. She tacitly suggests that even literal Aboriginal children may be more adult than the Europeans who patronize them.[7]

Garimara also uses other techniques more locally. For example, she systematically models the European school on prison, perhaps thereby recalling the criminal convictions of many Europeans who first arrived in Australia – a striking contrast with the abducted Aboriginal girls. She also develops the affinity between the Aboriginal girls and Australian nature, suggesting that they have a relation to the place that is not shared by Europeans. This also strongly reinforces the idea that the Aboriginal children should not be removed from their native environment and transported (like convicts) to the, in effect alien, European environment of the (prison-like) school.

These points all serve to specify and complicate Garimara's emplotment of colonial and racial relations in Australia. As such, they indicate the flexibility of genres. But their ethical point remains much the same. Most obviously, the story values the family, stressing the cultivation of empathy, especially empathy for attachment vulnerability (recall that the European-Australian, paternalistic liberals ignored such bonds, appropriating the position of parent to themselves through their bureaucratic "protectors of Aborigines"). At the same time, in her appeal to an Aboriginal readership, Garimara fosters a sense of empowerment through the character of Molly by depicting the parental skills that are part of Aboriginal knowledge and the parental effectiveness of Aboriginal traditions in their cultural and geographical context. The ethical preferences that follow from such emplotment are clear as soon as one thinks of how differently colonial and racial relations would appear in a heroic or sacrificial narrative.

At the level of story events, Kamala Markandaya's *Nectar in a Sieve* is a less prototypical family separation story than Garimara's memoir. At the level of its emotional development, however, it is more prototypical. Markandaya clearly sets out to foster the reader's empathy through parallel interpersonal response – indeed, identification with the characters in their attachment vulnerabilities. Markandaya's approach is aptly characterized in terms of Sanskrit aesthetic theory, the long-standing

---

[7] Though developed differently, in a different theoretical context and idiom, the basic idea has been recognized in criticism. Thus, Lovrod – referring to several works, including Garimara's – writes that "the wit and courage the young people show in their arduous journeys toward some kind of autonomy, subvert projected and internalized forms of colonialist infantilization" (2015, 68).

account of aesthetic emotion that extends from classical Indian drama through contemporary *rāga* performance (see Deva 1980, chap. 8). Specifically, she has written a work dominated by *karuṇarasa*, the empathic emotion of compassion for another's sorrow.

Not unlike Garimara, Markandaya begins by painting a somewhat Edenic portrait of precolonial rural India, stressing the connections of the people with nature. Influenced by the Marxist ideas of the All-India Progressive Writers' Association (AIPWA), Markandaya takes the reader through the developments of political economy that destroy this Edenic life (on the AIPWA, see Coppola 1974). The indigenous (roughly) feudal tenant farmer system is highly problematic, but even worse harm comes with colonialism and (European) industrial capitalism. The book is designed to systematically expose the suffering caused by these developments, particularly the last. That suffering, endured by the main characters, includes many sorts of harm, from debilitating hunger to malarial fever. But the most wrenching pain they suffer is from attachment loss.

In Garimara, the family separation is straightforward, and the cause of the separation is straightforward. The three children are forcibly removed from their families by government officials in accordance with Australian law. In Markandaya's novel, the separations are not as simple, and their causes are largely invisible matters of political economy. The narrator and her husband, Rukmani and Nathan, are landless tenant farmers. The fact that they own no land is stressed throughout the novel. This lack of ownership makes Nathan far more economically vulnerable than he might have been, due to the insecurity of his land tenure and due to the amount of rent he owes (even during a bad harvest year). This discourages their sons from working on the land. Their only choice, then, is wage labor. Two sons end up working far away in Ceylon (now Sri Lanka). They claim that the separation is temporary, but in fact Rukmani and Nathan never see them again. Another son takes a job at the local tannery, though handling dead animal skins violates religious restrictions for him. He is eventually killed, evidently trying to take one of the skins during a famine. This is obviously not a prototypical separation, but its effect is much the same. A fourth son finds employment in an Indian city (a significant distance from Rukmani and Nathan's village, but far closer than Ceylon and in principle accessible to them). When Rukmani and Nathan eventually lose their tenancy – as the land has been purchased by a European-owned factory – they go to join this son. However, they discover that he has abandoned his wife and is untraceable.

In each case, and in other parts of the novel as well, Markandaya develops the attachment relations and the pain of separation in such a way as to greatly intensify the reader's empathy. She does this with the aim of encouraging not only social transformation (presumably in a socialist direction), but also charitable giving. The latter is highlighted by the value the novel places on the building of a hospital in the village. The hospital – funded by charitable donations – is, in effect, the diametrical opposite of the factory and, more generally, industrial capitalism. The hospital is a social institution that can contribute effectively to the reduction of unmerited pain (in terms of the valence parameter).

The novel ends with a reunion – not with the sons who left for Ceylon or the city (and, of course, not the one who is dead). It is a reunion of Rukmani with the remaining son, who has taken a job at the hospital, and her daughter Ira, along with her daughter's illegitimate son. I wrote earlier that Markandaya paints an idyllic portrait of the precolonial, precapitalist village. This is only partially true. Markandaya certainly acknowledges problems with precolonial traditions (in keeping with the manifesto of the All-India Progressive Writers' Association; see Coppola 1974). Her criticisms of tradition include Ira's abandonment by her husband due to supposed infertility, a clear violation of an attachment bond, and the social prejudice against the illegitimate child (named Sacrabani) ultimately born to Ira, social prejudice due to his illegitimacy and his albinism. Both Ira and Sacrabani are crucially part of the final family reunion, which thereby rejects the sexual disgust that might have affected the reader's response to Ira and the color prejudice that might have stigmatized Sacrabani.

Even more important, Markandaya includes a street orphan, Puli – a tough child, despite the fact that his fingers have been partially eaten away by leprosy. When Rukmani and Nathan are in the city and cannot find their biological son, they are helped by Puli. They eventually form an attachment bond with him and in effect adopt him. Rukmani brings him home to the village, and to the hospital where their remaining son works. This familial, but not biological, connection points toward the ethical importance of generalizing the caregiving that is central to attachment – here, in a rejection of disability-based out-grouping. It suggests that the scope variable is set at human, even though the ethical model of attachment in this genre is the family.

## Sacrificial Narrative (*Nosferatu, a Symphony of Horror*)

The sacrificial prototype concerns a transcendent principle, such as a divine precept, that is typically in some way fundamental to an in-group society's relation to the world. That precept is violated, either by a representative figure in the society (e.g., the leader of the society) or by the citizenry in general. The violation is often provoked by temptation from some out-group. This violation leads to the devastation of the society, commonly the devastation of its relation to nature (e.g., through famine). The devastation can be ended only by a sacrifice. That sacrifice may be "purgative," ridding the society of some or all of the transgressors (especially the out-group tempters). Alternatively, it may be "penitential," in which case, the scapegoat is an innocent member of the group.

The obvious example here is the Judeo-Christian story of the fall and redemption of humankind. Adam and Eve are forbidden by God from eating the fruit of the Tree of the Knowledge of Good and Evil. Tempted by Satan (clearly an out-group member), they violate the law and suffer the loss of Edenic plenty. As they represent all humankind, their punishment is extended to the entire group. All of them must labor to produce food and to produce offspring. They are restored only by the sacrifice of the innocent victim, Jesus, and (in his second coming) the purging of sinful humans as well as the out-group of fallen angels, Satan and his cohorts.

The emotions driving the characters include feelings of remorseful guilt over the transgression (and, of course, whatever emotion drove that transgression), perhaps shame over one's sinfulness (i.e., self-disgust), as well as disgust at the out-group tempter. The emotion of an innocent but willing victim is a little more difficult to define. Often it is something like a generalized attachment feeling for the entire society (or the entire in-group), motivating equally generalized caregiving; alternatively, it may be something like all-encompassing awe before God or the divine. In both cases, the scapegoat loses all egocentric feeling. (On the other hand, this holds only for voluntary scapegoats. Forced victims may experience first terror, then eventual resignation.) Stories in this genre tend to foster parallel emotions regarding the in-group, thus empathy with the in-group sinners and admiration for the innocent but willing scapegoat. At the same time, at least in its purgative mode, the genre tends to intensify out-grouping and disgust at the out-group. That disgust is connected with the tendency of the genre to foster moral out-grouping (the delimitation of in-groups and out-groups on the basis of supposed moral probity), though the groups at issue may initially be identified by national, ethnic, or other (nonmoral) categories. The social organization favored by sacrificial narratives may form around a transcendental authority that renders identity groups meaningless, except those based on moral divisions. However, especially in its purgative version, it more often intensifies the sense that the national or other in-group is crucial, in part because it is naturally morally good, failing only through lack of vigilance about seduction by the out-group. The genre tends to present obedience (properly keyed to the highest authority), steadfastness (in the face of temptation), and selfless devotion to the in-group (alternatively, to God) as the paradigmatically praiseworthy virtues.

## Sacrificial Narrative (Nosferatu, a Symphony of Horror) 133

I will consider one case of this genre and do so in somewhat greater detail than the examples I have considered elsewhere in this chapter. The purpose of this extended elaboration is to spell out some of the more subtle cognitive and affective processes that are nonobvious parts of emplotment and to indicate what sorts of ethical consequences they may have. This is particularly important because my treatment of the other genres has focused solely on the broad ethical structures of those genres, with little attention to how these structures might affect more concrete cases of ethical response. Specifically, I will examine F. W. Murnau's (1922) *Nosferatu* and its relation to the larger discourse that helped to foster the development of Nazism in Germany, no doubt unintentionally on Murnau's part.

As noted earlier, our response to moral problems in life would appear to involve a process whereby we tacitly link some features of current conditions with some narrative prototype selecting and construing other features in terms of that prototype, which is then specified and to some degree altered by those features, and so on. Thus, we might begin to think of and respond to one ethical dilemma in terms of a heroic narrative and another in terms of a romantic plot. The prominence of a particular story prototype in this process is not solely a matter of individual disposition and the obvious, directly relevant features of a given situation (e.g., there being a war). Story prototypes are activated across a range of conditions and elicit responses that are socially patterned. For example, anything along the lines of an attack on an in-group tends to trigger the heroic prototype. In contrast, the sacrificial structure tends to be activated by conditions of social devastation. This is particularly likely when that devastation is readily associated with paradigmatic cases of physical devastation in famine or drought. Thus, it is unsurprising that the sacrificial narrative has had such importance in Ireland and in India. For example, in Ireland, the Great Hunger or potato famine of the 1840s has remained the most salient exemplum of the devastation caused by British colonialism.

Triggering of a story prototype also results from a history of particular stories. Different narrative traditions may instantiate prototypes in different proportions (e.g., having more heroic stories than other traditions). The cumulative effect of a particular history is to make some ways of emplotting events or construing characters more likely than others. In a neural or "connectionist" model of mental architecture, such a history alters relevant "connection strengths" linking various cognitive structures and emotional responses, thereby altering the likelihood that any given prototype will be activated. In this model, a particular mental process (e.g., retrieving memories of some friend) is activated when another, strongly connected process occurs (e.g., seeing the friend). In keeping with this, a particular society may stress sacrificial stories in national history, making that prototype unusually salient through multiple strong connections. In addition, a history of particular stories may instantiate the prototypes in patterned ways, cumulatively stressing a particular outgroup, isolating it as uniquely significant, associating it with a recurring threat, and so forth. For example, during the Cold War, this was arguably the case for the United States with regard to the national enemy of the U.S.S.R. or the out-group of Communists. This occurs not only in historical writing, but in fiction also, and not only in print, but in other media. Over the last century, visual media, beginning with film, have been particularly prominent in defining and developing such narratives, narratives that, as a group may be highly consequential for our ethical imagination and our actions based on that imagination.

In the remainder of this section, I will argue that F. W. Murnau's 1922 film classic, *Nosferatu, a Symphony of Horror*, was a narrative that contributed to the prominence of a particular emplotment of consequential ethical topics. Specifically, in conjunction with other films, stories from novels and political speeches, anecdotes from ordinary speech, and other features of German social discourse (in a roughly Foucaultian sense of "discourse"; see Foucault 1972), it helped to prepare the way for the purgative sacrificial emplotment of social conditions that took on such virulent form in the Nazi period. In making this argument, I am not claiming that either Murnau or Henrik Galeen, the scriptwriter, in any way intended the film as supporting Nazism or, more generally, a sacrificial emplotment of German society. The film, as I shall argue, manifests a sacrificial way of thinking about communal suffering, and it implicitly links that suffering to Eastern European Jewry. In more narrowly cognitive terms, it presents the viewer with complexes of properties that would be likely to prime (i.e., partially activate) links between the sacrificial structure and stereotypes about Jews, as well as thoughts about infection and memories of national devastation. The priming of these links is allowed by the prior presence of the stereotypes, even in the minds of people who would reject the stereotypes self-consciously. (A stereotype we disavow nonetheless remains a structure in our cognition and can influence that cognition, particularly at times when we are not self-consciously inhibiting such influence; for an overview of some relevant research, see Hinton [2017].) Moreover, as the plot works itself out, the priming of those links serves to increase their connection strength for many viewers (e.g., making it more likely that they will implicitly connect Jews with epidemic disease). This, in turn, makes the interrelations more subjectively plausible, more acceptable and more accepted, and more likely to guide thought and behavior in the future. The period before the rise of Nazism was marked by many developments of just this sort.

For example, Baxmann, drawing on a different theoretical terminology, notes that films in the 1920s included "an elaborate discourse on the body," with a "character typology" that made use of a racist "arsenal" of "signs" (1995, 361, my translation). Collectively, these processes helped to prepare ordinary Germans for the Holocaust.

It is important to emphasize that this process unfolds without any self-conscious plan. As already suggested, we can model the process in terms of connectionist circuits or associative networks in which a range of features and emotional responses are more or less strongly linked, thus more or less likely to be activated simultaneously. The general form of story prototypes, as well as the specification of such prototypes in literary traditions, may be conceived of in these terms as well. The development of such networks, and the associated specification of prototypes, occurs spontaneously, and it tends to be self-perpetuating. Ethnic or racial prototypes (in this case, stereotypes) are defined by high connection strengths among various properties or "nodes" (e.g., among the nodes for Jewish, Eastern European, and a range of particular physical features). These links lead writers and directors to choose the properties of characters (e.g., properties of their physical appearance) in certain ways. For example, in casting someone for a particular role, the director might choose someone who "looks the part," relying on these associations (e.g., regarding the shape and size of the actor's or character's nose) without realizing that he or she is doing any such thing. Indeed, not only is intent not required, but in many cases the effect is facilitated by the absence of self-consciousness about the implicit links. Reflective awareness may lead to the rejection of spontaneous, stereotyped associations.[8] In short, Murnau's and Galeen's self-conscious attitudes toward Jews or toward fascism are largely irrelevant to the following analysis. The important point here is that when they thought about communal suffering, what they came up with was a sacrificial structure that ultimately fit Nazi ideas quite well.

In general, it is unsurprising that the story of a vampire could be recruited to sacrificial use. Masters has noted a general link between vampire legends and sacrifice, especially human sacrifice, and also with the sort of collective suffering that gives rise to sacrifice (1972, 11–12, 14). Florescu and McNally explain that "[w]hen unparalleled and persistent tragedies occur in a specific village, or if there is a period of unprecedented drought ... then inevitably the people suspect the presence of a vampire haunting the vicinity" (1973, 171). Moreover, the vampire fits well with the demonization of the out-group. For example, Florescu and

---

[8] On bias correction, see Berkowitz et al. (2000).

McNally explain that "Dracula" is Romanian for "son of the devil" (9) and "the Dracula image has, from the outset, been connected with Satan" (175). Of course, *Nosferatu, a Symphony of Horror* makes its own particular use of vampire stories and the sacrificial plot, and that is our concern here. In principle, the movie could have overturned these tendencies. In fact, it intensifies them.

The action of the film takes place in the "Swedish port of Visborg" (Bouvier and Leutrat 1981, 299). I take it that Murnau and Galeen are referring to the Fortress of Visborg, one of the largest castles in Scandinavia. Technically, the town itself is not Visborg, but Visby.

Visby may seem to be an odd choice, at least if the film is related to German nationalism. But, in fact, given the particular problems facing German nationalism after the First World War, the choice is ideal. Many Germans at the time felt that Germany was, in effect, dismembered. Simply put, too many Germans were living in non-German states. The initial rallying cry of *Mein Kampf*, published only a few years after this film appeared, was "[c]ommon blood belongs in a common Reich" (Hitler 1940, 3). Visby, though in Sweden, had a significant German population (represented in the film) and a strong historical connection with Germany, having been founded by German merchants. In this respect, Visby is more relevant to the German nationalism of the period than some straightforwardly German towns in Germany proper.[9]

The film begins with a reference to a terrible plague that struck Visborg in 1838. This is, of course, just the sort of devastation that tends to trigger a sacrificial narrative. This too bears on German nationalism of the early 1920s, due to the devastation of the First World War and its immediate aftermath. Beyond the horrors of the combat outside the country, Manvell explains that, for a time, Germany "faced the serious possibility of civil war," thus horrors of combat *within* the country. "Violence," he explains, "was an everyday occurrence in the streets" (1973, 8) Then there was the decline in the economy. Consider one symptom of this decline – the value of the mark, which fell from "4 to the dollar to 130,000,000,000" (1973, 8). Perhaps most important, as Schivelbusch explains, during the war, the "Allied food blockade" had resulted in a "starving home front," with deaths comparable to those of combatants (2003, 235). Beyond these material afflictions, Germans suffered an acute sense of military despair. After the devastating end of the First World War, they had no reasonable hope of imagining their nationhood – and, with it, the end of their miseries – in heroic terms. Though hardly identical with the plague

---

[9] See the UNESCO web page "Hanseatic Town of Visby" (https://whc.unesco.org/en/list/731/, accessed September 15, 2020) and the 2015 *Encyclopedia Britannica* article "Visby" (www.britannica.com/place/Visby, accessed September 15, 2020).

victims of Visborg, many Germans watching Murnau's film might easily have felt that their situation was not entirely unlike that of their fellow Germans three-quarters of a century earlier.

Following the opening reference to the plague, and to Nosferatu, the film presents us with some happy shots of the loving Hutters, with Thomas picking flowers for Ellen. The point of the sequence is, in part, to humanize these characters and to develop identification. It also establishes a norm of life in Visborg, to contrast with the time of the plague.

Subsequently, Hutter walks to his office, exchanging a few words with Professor Bulwer. Meanwhile, at work, Knock, a real estate agent, is scrutinizing a letter from Orlok. The letter is not written in any identifiable script and is clearly alien. It is a series of symbols, including alchemical images, emblems from the tarot, and, according to Bouvier and Leutrat, "signs from the Hebrew tradition," including the Hebrew letters lamed and samek (1981, 306).[10] There is also a clear Star of David. Though not narrowly identifiable, the script in part suggests Jewish antecedents and therefore may prime the idea of the so-called "secret" or "hidden language of the Jews,"[11] at least for some viewers. (It is perhaps worth noting that Galeen directly linked secret language with Jewish necromancy in *The Golem*, though Paul Wegener and Carl Boese did not choose to represent this in a peculiar script.) In any case, it serves to link Orlok with "the Hebrew tradition."

When Hutter enters, Knock explains that Orlok wishes to buy a home in Visborg. He will be Hutter's neighbor. Ultimately, it is Orlok's arrival in Visborg that brings the plague to that town. Thus, it is the entry of the Eastern European alien – specifically, the alien who is associated with Jewish tradition – into the heart of one's "home," the entry of this foreigner as one's "neighbor," that leads to the destruction of the home society. The idea was commonplace. In the first volume of *Mein Kampf*, Hitler refers to what he considers only a first step in expelling "the Jew," which is to say, "the eternal blood-sucker" (i.e., vampire): "In order at least to prevent the worst, one begins to take the soil out of his usurious hands by making the acquisition of soil legally impossible for him" (1940, 427). Thus, Hitler urges a ban on precisely the sale of real estate undertaken by Knock and Hutter. In these passages, Hitler obviously draws on the standard anti-Semitic association of Jews with usury and thus with metaphorical "blood sucking." But the commonplaces of anti-Semitism have further connections with the film as well. Specifically, as Gilman points out, there was a

---

[10] In the upper left of the front page of the letter, somewhat above the Star of David, there is a circle that contains a clear beth and perhaps other Hebrew letters (e.g., the letter above the beth may be an aleph).
[11] See Gilman (1991, chap. 1).

"traditional association ... of the Jews as the 'cause' of the Black Plague" (1991, 221). This association seems to have inspired Hitler also. He repeatedly employed the metaphor of the plague to characterize the devastation of Germany after the end of the First World War, a devastation which, of course, he blamed on Jews (1940, 76, 314, 327, 342). Indeed, at one point, he directly connects the "plague" of social devastation with the "bloodsucking tyranny" of Jews (1940, 426).

But how are Germans guilty in this view? Why are they punished with the plague, and why is a sacrifice required of them? The explanation is explicit. Hutter agrees to a long journey in a land of "ghosts" and "phantoms" because he will make a great deal of money. It is, then, desire for wealth that seduces the otherwise decent German to bring the foreigner into the homeland. This idea too was not uncommon. In *Mein Kampf*, Hitler traces the decline of Germany back to a point where "money became the god whom now everybody had to serve and to worship" (1940, 316). This *hamartia* or tragic error is highlighted subsequently when the coachman refuses to bring Hutter into the "land of the phantoms." He explains that he would not do such a foolish thing "even for a fortune."

Departing for Transylvania to complete the fateful transaction, Hutter leaves Ellen in the care of their friends, the Hardings. At an inn on the way, he finds a copy of *The Book of Vampires*. Here, Nosferatu is represented as the offspring of the demon Belial. It is worth noting that the demonization of an enemy, though widespread, is more common with respect to some groups than others. In the West, Jews have been particularly likely to be imagined in satanic ways. More exactly, as I argue in *The Culture of Conformism*, a limited number of cognitive models have been prominent in defining out-groups and organizing or rationalizing behavior toward out-groups (Hogan 2001, 134–155). The use of these models tends to follow fairly consistent patterns. For example, Africans have largely been assimilated to animals.[12] In anti-Semitic writings, Jews have been routinely assimilated to devils (e.g., see Hitler 1940, 82, 447).

Beyond setting out Nosferatu's ancestry, *The Book of Vampires* explains that humans often fail to recognize a danger sensed by animals. This is illustrated when a group of horses flees from a threatening evil to which Hutter responded with a carefree laugh. Even when Hutter looks out the window and sees the horses scattering, he fails to understand the implications. Indeed, Hutter repeatedly responds with a smile or laughter to warnings of grave danger – for example, when the coachman refuses to

---

[12] This leads, for example, to Black/animal hybridizations in horror films, as discussed by Noël Carroll (see 2003, 88–107).

take him further, or when he first discovers the marks of the vampire on his throat. This suggests a more general point – that basically good-hearted Germans have failed to comprehend the danger of welcoming the foreigner into their homeland. It is worth noting that this is not some peculiarity of Murnau's film. As Eric Hobsbawm has pointed out, the idea of "innocence and simple-mindedness ... readily exploited by cunning foreigners" was incorporated into the German view of the German "national character" and was even represented in the national figure of the "Deutsche Michel" (1983, 276). The idea turns up in Hitler's writings, as we shall see.

The next day, Hutter travels to Orlok's castle. Here, for the first time, we see Orlok. He is in every way foreign. His coat and especially his hat are strange. His physique is even odder than his clothing. His fingernails are absurdly long. Bouvier and Leutrat (1981) refer to them as "Asiatic" – clearly, they are intended to be Eastern in some way. (The "Easternness" of Jews was an anti-Semitic commonplace; for example, Herder stated that "in Europe," Jews are "an Asiatic folk foreign to our continent" [cited in Greenfeld 1992, 383].) Orlok stands and walks in a peculiar manner; indeed, he contrasts strikingly with Hutter in both ways. In keeping with this, anti-Semitic commonplaces regarding the supposed misshapenness of Jews' feet and legs led to a stereotype of Jews as having a "faulty gait" and "pace," as Gilman explains (1991, 39). Orlok's eyes fit the stereotype of the "bulging ... Jewish eye" (Gilman 1991, 69) as well. Most strikingly, he has a huge hooked nose, emphasized at several points in the film through profile shots – here, in contrast with a profile of Hutter. Whatever one makes of the other characteristics, the nose indicates that he is not simply foreign. He is the physical stereotype of a Jew. The feature is in part taken from the original novel, where it has been recognized as a sign of "xenophobia over the influx of Eastern European Jews," as Barbara Belford puts it (1996, 228). Gilman explains that "the nose came to be the sign of the pathological Jewish character," something that "everyone at the close of the nineteenth century associated with the Jew's visibility" (1991, 181); especially "in Germany it was the Jewish nose ... that was the salient sign of difference" (219). Orlok must suggest the stereotyped Jew to any viewer familiar with that stereotype, including viewers who would never think of Orlok as literally Jewish. In other words, the portrayal of Orlok must prime this associative network – indeed, it will probably activate much of the network (even if only briefly) – reenforcing the links that define it.

Some readers have been confused by the point. Specifically, they have asked whether I am interpreting the film or discussing how German audiences interpreted the film. I am talking about German viewers. However, I am not saying anything about how they *interpreted* the film.

For example, I am not claiming that any viewer thought Orlok was, literally, a Jew in the fictional world of the film. Rather, my claims concern lexical and mnemonic connections. My argument forms a sort of cognitivist parallel to Foucaultian discourse analysis. Such analysis places a particular work in a context of overlapping ideas and practices. The claim of such an analysis is that the entire discourse produces effects, not that individual viewers perform a discourse analysis, self-consciously linking the work at hand to the patterns of the encompassing discourse. *Nosferatu* contributes to the cognitive interconnection of Eastern European immigration, plague, particular physical features, blood sucking, and so forth. Given the usual operation of human cognition, the film could fail to interconnect these ideas only if viewers failed to understand the basic plot, not realizing that Orlok brought the plague, not recognizing Orlok as the one with the hooked nose, and so on. In addition, given the close relation between Orlok and physical stereotypes for Jews, along with the associations between Jews and Eastern Europe, it seems almost impossible – again, given ordinary principles of cognitive operation – that these properties would not have at least primed ideas about Jews. An idea is primed when it is partially activated but not brought into direct, self-conscious awareness. Its partial activation, however, makes it consequential for one's thought and action. Finally, in this case, that thought and action are guided by the ethics of the sacrificial story prototype as instantiated in the film.

In the following scenes, Orlok not only behaves in a bizarre fashion, but also it becomes clear that he is sucking Hutter's blood while the latter sleeps. Yet Hutter continues ignorantly laughing at the danger – unable to recognize the threat even when it slaps him in the face, or rather bites him in the throat. He goes on to complete the sale. Hutter's collaboration with evil is due to ignorance, but it is a culpable ignorance. Soon all of Visborg will suffer for his error in introducing this alien into their community. It is only after the sin has been committed (in the signing of the contract) that Hutter comes to understand the true nature of Orlok.

Orlok packs up a half-dozen coffins, placing himself in one, and ships the lot to Visborg. The coffins are filled with earth. He will not set down his "roots" in the new land, but will still remain rooted in the old soil – a common criticism of Jews.

Hutter escapes from Orlok's castle, only to find himself in a hospital, attended by a nun. Hutter's miraculous and hardly explained arrival in the hospital and the presence of the sister, wearing a large and visible crucifix, are clearly designed to stress that divine providence – specifically Christian providence – serves Hutter even when he has erred.

The next scene returns us to the coffins. We now discover that Orlok's soil is filled with rats. Here, we have our first sign of the coming plague. Orlok's transportation of the plague is directly related to his status as an alien, for he brings the plague by carrying his "alien land" along with him.

Professor Bulwer's lectures follow. He is treating different sorts of "vampirism" in nature, such as that of carnivorous plants. The parallels do not appear to make a great deal of sense. However, their significance becomes clear in the following scene, when we find that Knock has lost his mind. Knock's madness is a form of regression to a primitive biological state. He spends his time catching flies in his fingers and eating them, repeating the actions of the carnivorous plant. The entire sequence calls to mind Nazi attempts to bolster the dehumanization of various undesirable groups by reference to often ludicrous biological and psychiatric pseudoscience. Indeed, Hitler was insistent on the necessity of treating such groups "scientifically" (see Weinreich 1999, 82). Jews figured prominently in the resulting "research," but so did the "hereditarily-ill" (36), including the mentally ill. The point here is that if Orlok is demonic, Knock is equally nonhuman. Murnau does not have Knock killed. Nonetheless, this characterization feeds directly into the subsequent Nazi view that the mentally ill have regressed to a potentially dangerous subhuman condition and that, as such, they may and indeed must be exterminated. In the case of Knock, the derangement also suggests that the real collaborators with the foreign bloodsuckers are degenerated madmen.

We now find Ellen seated on a park bench in what is evidently a seaside cemetery. The dunes around her are dotted with crosses, aptly suggesting her own connection with the cross of Jesus and with sacrificial death. (I believe I do not need to remind the reader of what group was blamed for the death of Jesus in anti-Semitic propaganda.) Ellen receives a letter from Hutter. After Ellen reads and embraces the letter, we shift back to the hospital, where Hutter is now well – presumably due to providence, the good offices of the nun, and the prayers of Ellen. Much of what follows simply indicates the parallel journeys of Hutter (traveling by land) and Orlok's ship, the *Empusa*. At one point, Knock picks a newspaper from the pocket of a guard and reads about the progress of the plague, which has begun in "Eastern Europe." The victims all have the mark of a vampire bite on their throats. From this general report, we turn to the origins and development of the plague onboard the *Empusa*.

Eventually, the idealized sacrificial figure, Ellen, realizes by spiritual intuition that Hutter is approaching. In the immediately following scene, her opposite, the mad collaborationist, Knock, realizes by a sort of demonic connection that Orlok has landed. When Hutter arrives, he rushes to join his wife. As Hutter holds Ellen, Orlok grasps his coffin.

The opposition of life (the embrace of the married couple) and death (the embrace of the coffin) is clear. Profile shots emphasize Orlok's nose yet again. Watching the film after the Nazi period, it is difficult not to see the degenerate Eastern European Jew bringing death to the couple who (as Nazi propaganda tirelessly emphasized) should be creating new life for the fatherland. Subsequent scenes involve the discovery that the *Empusa* has brought plague, and the spread of plague to the town.

Just after we see some doors in the town marked with a cross, and the beginning of a funeral procession, the scene shifts to Ellen. The conjunction is apt, repeating that of the seaside cemetery, for Ellen is, again, the Christ-like victim. The present scene begins the sequence of events that will lead to Ellen's self-sacrifice. Though she promised her husband that she would not read *The Book of Vampires*, she has been unable to "resist temptation." The phrasing is peculiar, as it puts Ellen in the position of a disobedient Eve. But, far from leading to the Fall, this is precisely what undoes the Fall. It is Hutter's caution that is blameworthy, not her boldness. She reads that only "a woman with a pure heart" can end the terror by willingly "offer[ing] her blood to Nosferatu and keeping him by her side until the cock crows" (Bouvier and Leutrat 1981, 416). The image seems odd at first, for it suggests a sort of sexual self-abandonment to the enemy. But it is in fact the opposite of the sexual abandonment that is so often linked with the original sin of sacrificial tragi-comedy. It is self-abandonment to a sort of sacrificial anti-sexuality, a self-abandonment to horror and disgust, not desire.

We are next faced with a peculiar interlude in which Knock escapes from the asylum and runs through the streets, further exhibiting his madness and degeneracy (though in a rather more athletic way than one might have expected). Back home, Ellen is embroidering a cloth with the words "Ich liebe Dich" (Bouvier and Leutrat 1981, 422). Several things are interesting about this. First, it is in German, reminding us that the Hutters are part of the German minority community in Visborg (or Visby) – thus part of greater Germany. (The text of the embroidery is visible in the scene itself, not merely in an intertitle.) Second, insofar as the message is addressed to her husband, it suggests that Ellen already knows that she is about to sacrifice herself. It is a sort of farewell. At the same time, it expresses the motivation for her sacrifice – love. That love links her once again with the Christian paradigm of self-sacrifice, Jesus, for she is manifesting the greatest love spoken of by Jesus, laying down one's life for one's friends (John 15:13). Here, the "friends" are, first of all, Ellen's family. But they are also her community. As Gregory Waller points out, she "acts because she sees, as we see, the effect of Nosferatu's presence" on her city (1986, 190). It is, of course, relevant that this scene of domestic (and, by implication, communal) devotion is intercut with Knock's antics. Knock and Ellen are, again, paired opposites – the insane collaborationist who destroys society and the inspired victim (or scapegoat) who redeems it.

This leads to the final sequence in which Ellen sees Orlok looking out from his new home. Opening her window, she in effect invites him to come, as an unfaithful wife might invite her lover. In keeping with this motif, she sends her husband away. Again, however, this is not a matter of lust. It is, indeed, the opposite of lust, as we see from Ellen's look of horror. By pairing it with adultery – perhaps the ultimate betrayal of one's home – Murnau highlights Ellen's action as the ultimate sacrifice for her home and, beyond that, for her homeland. As Ellen lies on her bed, Orlok embraces her, sinking his teeth into her neck. The cock crows. Orlok turns. In his cell, Knock calls out, but it is already too late. The sun has risen. Orlok tries to leave, but he burns away into a few wisps of smoke, for vampires are killed by exposure to the sun. One is reminded of Hitler's characterization of Jews as "that race which shuns the sunlight" (1940, 116). Ellen sits up briefly, just long enough to realize that Orlok is dead and that her husband has returned. She collapses, dying in Hutter's arms. The film ends with the sacrificial delivery of the home society: "And the miracle shall be told in truth. At that very hour the Great Death ceased and the shadow of the vampire vanished as if overcome by the victorious rays of the living sun." The health, not only of the home, but of the entire homeland, all of Visborg, has been restored due to the self-sacrifice of one bold, loyal, and pure member of the home society and through the extermination of the demonic foreigner, the disease-bearing bloodsucker, who had managed to infiltrate that society. This was the very message of individual and collective, personal and national hope that so many suffering German people desired at the time. Unfortunately, it was a message of national hope emplotted in a tacitly xenophobic sacrificial narrative of just the sort that would help to produce such unmitigated terror in two decades.

It is worth recalling here that self-sacrifice was, in principle, no less central to Nazism than genocide. Leiser (1968) explains that "dying for Germany" was "a main theme of Nazi propaganda," including feature films. In *Mein Kampf*, Hitler insists that all culture is dependent on the sacrifice of the individual for the sake of the community, that, indeed, this is "the first prerequisite for any truly human culture" (1940, 409). He particularly celebrates the "will to sacrifice" that culminates in "giving up one's own life for the existence of the community" (410). Indeed, he goes so far as to see this as the definitive Aryan trait. The Aryan, he maintains, "is greatest, not in his mental capacities," but in "service of the community" (408). Specifically, the "will to sacrifice ... his own life for others, is most powerfully developed in the Aryan" (408–409). Most significantly, in the culminating chapter of the first volume of *Mein Kampf*, Hitler describes just the sort of sacrifice that would restore greatness to the fallen Germany and the "peoples oppressed by the Jew." This statement applies equally to the end of *Nosferatu*. Specifically, Hitler claims that "[w]ith the death of the victim the vampire [*der Vampir*] will also die" (451, altered; see the German text, 1943, 358).

It is also worth noting that the notorious Nazi propaganda feature film *Jud Süß* is a sacrificial narrative with a plot in many ways very close to that of *Nosferatu*. Indeed, one could almost see *Jud Süß* as systematically transforming *Nosferatu* such that what is magical or metaphorical in the earlier film is given some literal correlate in the later film. Of course, *Jud Süß* is not literally a transformation of *Nosferatu*. However, it is a variation on the same structure that *Nosferatu* helped to particularize. At the beginning of *Jud Süß*, Duke Karl Alexander, greedy for cash, agrees to allow one wealthy Jew, Süß, into his city. Thus, we have our collaborationist, our tempter, and the initial crime for which the entire society will suffer. We also have our healthy German couple, Dorothea and Faber. Süß immediately establishes a connection with Dorothea, explaining to her that he has no homeland. Though he is not from Eastern Europe, the crucial point is that he is not truly German. Having established himself with the duke, Süß proceeds to fill the city with his fellow Jews, who pour through the town gates, not entirely unlike the vermin in *Nosferatu*. He also bleeds the people – in this case metaphorically, through taxation, rather than literally, through vampirism. Faber fears the worst, worrying that Germans are not smart enough to deal with Jews. Eventually, Süß coerces Dorothea to have sex with him. She surrenders herself in order to save the life of her husband. Afterward, she kills herself. Since this is not a mystical story, Dorothea's self-sacrifice does not directly save German society. However, it does inspire the people to rebellion. Roused by her death, they finally challenge the duke, who suddenly dies, evidently from a heart attack. Süß is put on trial and executed. The Jews are evicted from the city. Though scarred by the initial sin and by the necessary sacrifice of the innocent Dorothea, the people can now regain their ordinary life.

Needless to say, there is a vast difference between Murnau's film and Nazi policies, or even such overtly hateful films as *Jud Süß*. Again, I am not blaming Murnau for the Third Reich. However, the discourse that included the sacrificial narrative of *Nosferatu* – and other, similar sacrificial narratives – helped to orient and specify the way German people defined the scope of ethical thought and action (national, not broadly human); the way they imagined paradigmatic evil (seductive out-group members); the consequences they envisioned as the result of succumbing to evil (national devastation, modeled on epidemic disease); and the

*Sacrificial Narrative (Nosferatu, a Symphony of Horror)* 145

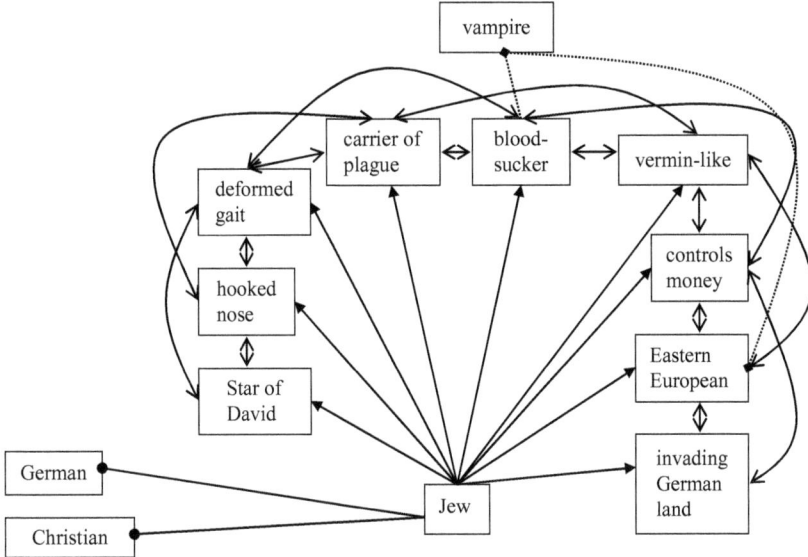

Figure 4.2 A modified and simplified connectionist model of an anti-Semitic associative network. Inhibited connections are represented by lines ending in solid circles. Facilitated connections are marked by single- or double-headed arrows. Priming is marked by lines ending in a solid diamond.

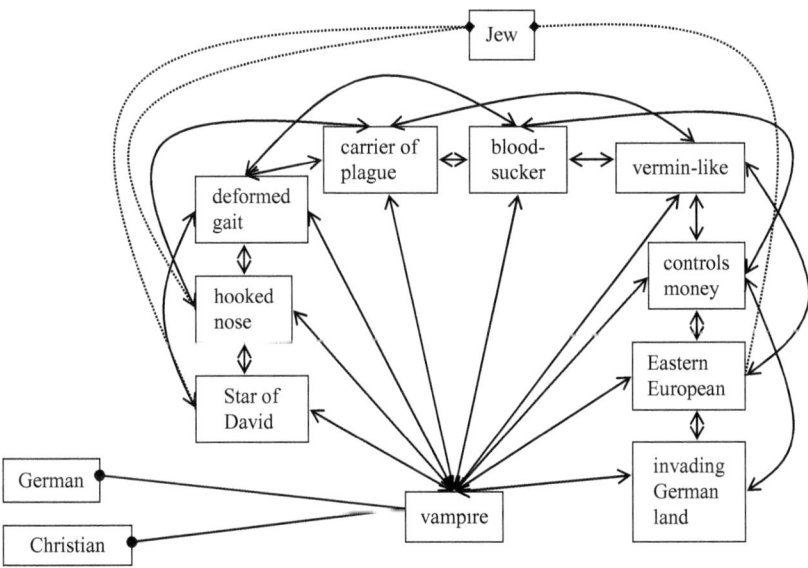

Figure 4.3 A modified and simplified connectionist model of the associations fostered by *Nosferatu*.

virtues they prized as exemplary (self-sacrifice for the national in-group), as well as the punishments they counted as needful (the purgation of the seductive out-group and in-group self-sacrifice). Moreover, they tacitly drew these connections in the context of persistent anxieties regarding the devastation of their society, anxieties that were already likely to prime a sacrificial prototype. (For a schematization of key points from the main argument, see Figures 4.2 and 4.3.)

**Spiritual Realization (*Atsumori*)**

Before going on to normative ethics, I should make a few brief remarks on another possible cross-cultural genre suggested by one pattern of the preceding genres (see Figure 4.1). I will refer to this as the *spiritual realization* genre. It appears to begin, prototypically, when ordinary material life is disrupted by some tragic experience. This leads to the hero's alienation from society (parallel to the geographical exile found in other genres, and often manifest in something very much like exile). This alienation is ended by some supramundane experience that alters the protagonist's attitude toward the world, resituating him or her in relation to spiritual goals, which he or she at least partially achieves. The most obvious example here would be the life of the Buddha. However, we also find something along these lines in the life of Jesus, with his baptism by John, his retreat into the wilderness, his resistance to temptations, and the subsequent beginning of his ministry (see the Gospel of Matthew, chaps. 3, 4).

The spiritual realization story seems to be driven by a sense that ordinary enjoyments, including those that guide the other genres, do not produce enduring happiness. The goal of the protagonist's actions in this genre is the realization of such enduring happiness, sometimes conceived of ecstatically, but sometimes viewed as a matter of peace or contentment. The realization of this state typically involves a sort of epilogue in which the spiritually realized protagonist shares his or her knowledge and practice with others. The audience's interpersonal stance cultivated by such works tends to be something like emulative admiration in which the reader experiences wonder over the protagonist's accomplishments, but does so in such a way as to allow the possibility of pursuing the same course of action himself or herself. The virtues celebrated by such a genre would include something like stoicism (here, an intensified ability to modulate one's emotional response to both positive and negative events), perseverance, and selfless devotion to the well-being of others, with well-being understood as spiritual. The social organization associated with this prototype would most obviously involve the existence of social networks that support the withdrawal of individuals from society in pursuit of spiritual realization.

A lovely example of this genre may be found in Zeami Motokiyo's (1998) Noh drama, *Atsumori*. In fact, this play combines the epilogue of suffering with the spiritual realization genre (and, in a more limited way, the revenge genre). In battle, Kumagae killed the young, flute-playing, enemy soldier, Atsumori. Filled with remorse, he renounced the world, becoming a Buddhist priest. To compensate partially for his actions in the war, he returns to the battleground to offer prayers for Atsumori's soul. The ghost of Atsumori enters as a laborer with other laborers, accompanied by flute music and a chant about the "misery" (131) of mundane life. When most of the laborers are gone, Kumagae asks the one remaining laborer who he is. The latter, who is in fact the ghost, responds that he is "related to" Atsumori (133). Kumagae calls on Amida Buddha. Following this, both Kumagae and the ghost, quoting a text of Pure Land Buddhism (see 133n.12), recall Amida Buddha's vow that no one who calls him by name will be abandoned; through its quotation, they perhaps suggest that if they achieve enlightenment, no one who calls them by name will be abandoned. (In Pure Land Buddhism, "salvation" is not a matter of self-discipline alone, but also involves "faith in the saving power of the buddhas," which may be activated by "the simple invocation" of a buddha's name, as indicated by a famous vow by Amida, echoed by Kumagae and Atsumori here [de Bary and Bloom 1999, 482].) This prayer is moving in part because we may sense (in cognitive and affective empathy) that both characters feel as if they were abandoned at a crucial moment – Atsumori because he was killed, and Kumagae because he did the killing. Atsumori indirectly informs Kumagae of who he is, then departs.

There is an interlude between the two acts of the play, at the place where the battle had occurred. Kumagae meets a local resident and asks about Atsumori's death. The resident recounts what he has heard. He ends his story by explaining that Kumagae is said to have renounced the world and devoted himself to praying for Atsumori's soul. But, the fellow continues, this seems to be a lie; if Kumagae had such concern for Atsumori, he never would have killed the boy to begin with. He concludes by suggesting that Kumagae should himself be killed, if he ever returns to the site of the battle. Kumagae identifies himself to the man, explaining that he has indeed come to pray for Atsumori's soul.

The second act of the play begins with Kumagae praying that Atsumori's soul will achieve "enlightenment" (135). Atsumori now appears in his own form. The two speak together of overcoming the karmic effects of past sins and achieving salvation. Then Atsumori recalls the battle as if he is reliving it. At the crucial moment, he is about to revenge himself by striking the now defenseless Kumagae. But he stops, seeing that Kumagae is "returning good for evil" by praying for his soul. He announces that the two former enemies will be "reborn together/on a single lotus petal" (142), presumably in Amida Buddha's Pure Land, free from the distractions that impede self-realization (on the Pure Land; see de Bary and Bloom 1999, 481–482).

Thus, we find Kumagae living his ordinary (here, heroic) life. This is disrupted by the trauma of realizing that he has killed young Atsumori. This leads to his alienation from society and self-exile, culminating in the vision of spiritual self-realization made possible by his selfless devotion to the well-being of others, specifically Atsumori. At first, the play may seem to be an instance of the heroic epilogue, and in fact that is how I have analyzed it in the past. However, its spiritual conclusion indicates that it is not dealing with the social domination goals that animate the heroic genre; its purpose is not to repair past harms in order to live in a revived nation. Rather, it suggests that the heroic goals are in fact a violation of Buddhist dharma or ethics and are, in keeping with that, imprudent as well, for they tie one to the fleeting world and the suffering that is inevitable in that world. In contrast, the play orients ethical evaluation and response toward bodhisattvic peace, the peace that comes from a selfless devotion to other people's spiritual realization, crucially including one's enemies. Moreover, this is enabled by the key principles of Buddhist dharma, which – very much unlike heroic emplotment – centrally includes nonviolence (see Keown 2005, 14–15).[13] In any case, it should be clear that the prominence of a spiritual realization narrative structure – temporarily (in a given context) or enduringly (as part of one's more general inclinations) – entails different ethical ideas and attitudes than other narrative structures. As such, and as a possible narrative universal, it would appear to be a likely candidate for one of the key ethical prototypes. Moreover, it extends the parallel with Haidt's (2012) moral foundations, in this case parallel to Haidt's sanctity, but taking up sanctity in a manner different from that found in the related, sacrificial prototype.

## Conclusion

The universal story prototypes include heroic, revenge, criminal investigation, romantic, seduction/sexual assault, family separation, penitential sacrificial, and purgative sacrificial genres. They may also include a

---

[13] On the other hand, one might argue that the epilogue of suffering takes up the spiritual realization genre, revising it often – though not always – in the service of heroic ethics and politics.

spiritual realization genre. Each of these structures establishes norms for ethical thought and action and fosters particular emotions bearing on those norms. Obviously, most ethical decisions one faces do not occur in situations with the same literal properties as any given prototype (i.e., they usually do not concern, say, foreign invasion or family separation). However, these structures are not confined to literal application. If one broadly favors the heroic prototype, one will tend to understand and respond to a wide range of situations on the model of warfare. In keeping with this, one's ethical aspirations and evaluations will tend to stress the moral values of in-group loyalty and courage in the face of group enemies. Similarly, a preference for familial emplotment is likely to make one particularly sensitive to the impact of a given situation or activity on attachment relations (e.g., the impact of slavery on parent–child bonds for Harriet Beecher Stowe).

As the preceding points indicate, individuals appear to have broad, ethical preferences for some story structures over others. The same point holds for some groups. For example, the counterculture of the 1960s, with its slogan "Make love, not war," favored the romantic above the heroic, both literally and as a model for a range of ethically demanding situations. On the other hand, all these prototypes appear to be available to everyone, with general preferences being open to change in specific situations. Moreover, it is always possible for individuals to adopt a critical approach to a given prototype, altering its values (e.g., representing war in a way that undermines heroism).

Finally, though it seems that we have a strong general inclination to think about or respond to ethical issues by relying on salient narrative structures, we are not confined to the cross-culturally prominent prototypes. Sometimes, we draw on culturally specific prototypes or on exemplars (e.g., critical particularizations of prototypes, or stories that are not prototypical at all); at other times, we may reason through an issue, based on our fundamental orientation, along with principles of logic and empirical study. In cases of the last sort, we draw on narrative only in the basic sense that we seek to isolate particular causal sequences. Story prototypes define broad tendencies, not absolute constraints. But they are, it seems, very strong and consequential tendencies.

CHAPTER 5

# Emotion and Empathy

With this chapter, I turn from descriptive to normative ethics. As already indicated, my focus in this part is on empathy. However, before we can treat ethics and empathy in any detail, we first need to gain a greater sense of the nature and operation of emotion, since empathy – or, more precisely, affective empathy – is largely a matter of emotion. This is particularly important because emotion is widely assumed to be a much simpler psychological process than is in fact the case. We also need to clarify the nature and varieties of empathy, which are no less likely to be oversimplified. Explicating emotion and empathy is the task of this chapter.

### Emotion

We can define "emotion" in different ways. I use the term to refer to a motivation system that prototypically has a set of specifiable, recurring features. I say, "prototypically" because not all emotions share all the relevant features. In consequence, there are some motivation systems that we would characterize as better cases of emotion than others (contrast, for example, anger and thirst).

In referring to motivation systems, I am adopting the systems approach to emotion rather than the dimensions approach. According to dimension theorists, what we call "emotions" are culturally variable clusters of properties defined along a number of dimensions, often two or three (for a concise account, see Fontaine 2009). The dimensions commonly include "valence" and "arousal." Valence is the degree to which an emotion is positive or negative, thus (usually) leading to approach or avoidance. Arousal is the degree of intensity. "Bliss" and "happiness" are positively valenced emotions that differ in intensity. I am skeptical about the possibility of explaining emotions based on a small number of dimensions. However, it is clear that emotions involve such dimensions. After all, if they did not share properties, they would not all count as emotions.

The systems approach views different emotions as different systems. These systems have neurological specificity (e.g., disgust is associated with the anterior insular cortex [Kelly 2011, 17]; note that neurological specificity does not mean localization, as emotion systems involve patterns of distribution across the brain, though one or a small number of regions may be particularly significant for a given emotion). They also have functional consequences (e.g., reduction of the likelihood of poisoning or infection, in the case of disgust). Thus, in their basis, they are genetic and universal. I have not referred to this as a discrete emotions account, as is sometimes done, because it seems clear that systems can be partially activated, activated in combination with other systems, partially activated in connection with specific (cognitive) information, and so on. Thus, romantic love involves at least the attachment, sexual desire, and reward systems. (The reward system includes both "seeking" behavior and pleasure, with the former connected with dopamine and the latter with endogenous opioids.) Jealousy involves the (emotional) attachment system along with the (informational) idea that one's attachment object has attachment feelings for someone else. Thus, by my account, emotion systems are distinct in neurological operation and in evolutionary function; moreover, they are, as such, universal. However, what we refer to as particular emotions can combine different systems, and their conceptual identification can vary from language to language.

Emotion systems may be activated or inhibited (or neither). The activation of some systems leads to the inhibition of others. For example, disgust activation typically inhibits hunger. Activation may occur at different time scales. If, relative to other people, one ordinarily has an elevated or reduced level of sensitivity to activation for a particular system, that defines a personality trait or disposition. For example, someone who is prone to activation of the anger system may be viewed as irascible. A propensity to arousal (or to resistance to arousal) that is of more limited duration and is unusual for the person in question may define a mood. For example, if I do not find something amusing that I would ordinarily enjoy, my depressive mood may have led to an inhibition of the system (or systems) that bear on mirth. The most intense emotion activation defines an emotion *episode*, when we experience an emotion – for example, when we are angry or mirthful.

Within affective science, "affect" is commonly used to refer to all forms of emotion. In other words, it has a broader scope than the term "emotion," when that term is confined to episodes (and thus not used for dispositions or moods). Sometimes, however, it is used in almost the precise opposite way, as a form of emotion-like experience that is temporally more limited than an emotion episode. As Haidt puts it, affect in this sense comprises "small flashes of positive or negative feeling that prepare us to approach or avoid something" (2012, 63). This is more or less the sense in which the term is used in poststructuralist affect theory.

Here, however, I will use "affect" in the broad sense that is common in affective science.

An emotion episode commonly involves a sequence of arousals and inhibitions interspersed with "modulation," or attempts to alter the trajectory of one's emotional experience. The initial arousal may have various sources, prominently perceptions and memories. Such an episode is often materially realized in subcortical areas of the brain (i.e., areas below the neocortex, which are older in evolutionary terms and have less involvement with cognition than neocortical areas). In contrast, modulation is primarily a matter of effects on subcortical areas resulting from activation of neocortical areas – as when we try to reason ourselves out of an irrational fear. Churchland presents an apt example affecting the behaviors that result from an emotion. As she explains, "a basic lesson for survival in the bush is never to run from a bear.... Standing still despite a powerful impulse to run requires an unholy effort in self-control, but humans can do this. During the encounter, your frontal cortex will be highly engaged with your [subcortical] basal ganglia, as it draws on its acquired skills to suppress instinctive behavior that would be deadly" (Churchland 2019, 36).

Perhaps more important, emotion episodes involve a number of functional components. These begin with the following:

(1) *Eliciting conditions* are experiences that arouse emotion systems or combinations of emotion systems. For example, seeing a dangerous predator moving toward you is an eliciting condition for fear.

Emotion elicitation is commonly taken to be a function of *appraisal*, which is the assessment of a condition or an experience as having a particular sort of impact on one's well-being or one's goals (see Nussbaum 2003, chap. 1). For example, fear would result from an assessment of some event or condition, such as the sudden appearance of a predator, as posing an immanent threat to one's goal of staying alive. Appraisal theorists stress that appraisals need not be self-conscious and indeed are probably automatic in most cases. One problem with this account is that since appraisal can be unselfconscious, it is difficult to say what it is. Moreover, there seem to be many cases where our emotions are clearly incompatible with our self-conscious assessments (e.g., when we know that a plane is safer than a car, but we fear flying more than driving).

The account of emotion elicitation I adopt is different. By this account, elicitors – like most components of emotion episodes – have three sources. First, they may be innate or innately prepared. For example, there is reason to believe that we are innately sensitive to other people's emotion expressions. This sensitivity allows children to learn adaptive emotional responses without having to experience the suffering (and likely death) that would result by judging everything through direct experience. Thus, by observing a parent's expression of disgust at a particular object – for example, something in the garbage – a small child may experience disgust and associate it with features of the object, leading to avoidance of similar objects in the future, all without having to experience food poisoning.

Early acquisition of emotional responses provides the second source for eliciting conditions – critical period experiences. A critical period is a developmental stage when key features of a system are defined in an enduring way through interaction with the environment. For example, one's bonding relations with one's early caregivers may be "secure" or "insecure," depending on whether one feels that the target of the bond is trustworthy in intent and reliable in capacity (e.g., will be willing and able to come to the rescue when one is in danger). This sense of security or insecurity tends to orient one's later attachment bonds as well (see Waters, Weinfield, and Hamilton 2000; see also Holland and Roisman 2010).

Finally, particular experiences after the critical period leave emotional memories, which is to say memories that, when activated, revive the feelings of the initial experience (see LeDoux 1996, 180–181) or perhaps feelings with the same valence; for example, an emotional memory of boredom may be aversive, though it does not precisely make us bored. Emotional memories are commonly connected with episodic memories (i.e., recollections of particular experiences). But that is not always the case. Thus, we may sometimes experience emotions because a current situation activates an emotional memory, but we may not know what the source of the emotion is, as we do not recall the associated episode. (Indeed, we may not even have a memory of the associated episode; see LeDoux 1996, 180–181.)

As we consider postcritical period emotions, we may distinguish traumatic from nontraumatic experiences. Among other things, traumatic experiences are more likely to prove indelible in the way critical period experiences tend to be; indeed, they may reverse propensities developed through critical period experiences. More exactly, in *Imagining Kashmir* (Hogan 2016, 203–207), I have argued that the activation of emotional memories (e.g., fearful memories) is functional to the degree that such activation conforms to three restrictions. First, it must have a narrow scope. Fear memories should probably slightly overpredict threat (on the "It's better to be safe than sorry" principle), but only slightly (in order not to miss opportunities). Second, such activation should be accompanied by a reasonable sense of the likely causal trajectories of the situation and appropriate actional outcomes (e.g., fleeing in a certain manner and in a certain direction). Finally, the intensity of the activation should be in the range where it can motivate action but is still subject to appropriate modulation. Thus, it should not generally be so strong that it overwhelms one's ability to act (as when one is paralyzed with fear when escape is needed) or blocks one's ability to modulate one's response when that is appropriate. Traumatic experiences lead to violations of all three restrictions. The traumatic memories tend to arise in a very wide range of circumstances. They do not involve a sense of the causal trajectory of relevant events (thus, we experience the events as inexplicable) and in consequence we have no sense of possible actional outcomes. Finally, they are largely impervious to modulation.

In all these cases, there is some perceptual, bodily experience that is at the source of the emotion elicitation – the perception of someone else's emotion expression, the experience of pain or pleasure in connection with a target (e.g., being mauled by a dog) that forms an emotional memory (leading us to feel fear when that memory is activated in the presence of a dog), and so on. (For this reason, Caracciolo [2022] reasonably classes my account as an embodied theory of emotion.) By this account, we do not experience an emotion due to abstract calculation of the likelihood of an outcome (e.g., I may fear a dog that I know is harmless). This is not to say that appraisal can have no emotional consequences. It can and does – but only insofar as the appraisal process activates emotional memories, leads to perceptual simulations that bear on innate sensitivities, or otherwise produces sensory or "embodied" consequences of the relevant type. (As Gallese and Guerra point out, "Imagining or representing something really does activate the areas of our brain linked to the related experience" [2019, 41]; they therefore refer to "embodied simulation" [48] as central to cognitive and affective processing.)

Moreover, the logic of appraisal plays a role in my account as well. Specifically, I see myself as spelling out some of the evolved *mechanisms* that operate in emotion. These mechanisms approximate an adaptive *function*. That function is (more or less) what is given in an appraisal. More exactly, functions explain how a process increases the likelihood that an organism will pass on its genes. For example, a particular mutation may affect one's leg muscles, thereby increasing one's speed in running. The function would be something like *escaping danger*. But the mechanism is not "escaping danger"; it is an alteration in leg muscles that improves running. Evolution never produces functions as such. Rather, evolution proceeds as mutations produce mechanisms that, relative to alternatives in the gene pool, more closely approximate adaptive functions than do currently existing alternatives. Appraisals in effect articulate the functions of emotions (e.g., responding to an imminent threat to one's well-being). That is important. But it is also important that appraisals are

*Emotion* 155

not the mechanisms themselves. (There is less that needs to be said about the other components of an emotion episode, which follow.)

(2) *Attention orientation* is the narrowing of our interests to targets relevant for the aroused emotion system. This narrowing of interests may bear on, among other things, perceptions (e.g., in scanning the environment for threats when afraid) and memories (e.g., in "mood-congruent processing," where memories of danger become prominent when one is afraid; e.g., see Oatley 1992, 201; Kringelbach and Philips 2014, 177).
(3) *Action readiness* is preparation to behave in such a way as to change an aversive situation (e.g., fleeing in connection with fear) or sustain a hedonic one. When the action is undertaken, it is termed an *actional outcome*.
(4) *Physiological outcomes* are physiological changes (e.g., in pulse or respiration rate) produced as part of the emotion system activation. These contribute to action readiness and/or expressive-communicative outcomes.
(5) *Expressive-communicative outcomes* are facial, postural, or other external manifestations of the emotion (e.g., weeping in sorrow) that do not involve acting directly on the situation but convey one's emotional state to others. For example, the facial expression of fear does not alter the aversive situation in the manner of an actional outcome such as fleeing, though it may indirectly aid one in communicating the need for help. (Some behaviors, such as shrieks of fear, may have both direct and indirect functions. They count as both actional and expressive-communicative outcomes.)
(6) *Processing strategies* are ways in which we organize and integrate information. For example, in positive emotional states, we tend to employ "top-down" processing, beginning with and favoring prior generalizations, whereas in negative emotional states, we tend to favor "bottom-up" processing, beginning with particulars rather than assuming general principles (see Forgas 2000, 15–17).
(7) *Phenomenological tone or feeling* is our experience of what it is like to have an emotion (e.g., to be angry or to be afraid).

*Reason versus Emotion?*

Before going on, it is important to say a few words about the supposed opposition between reason and emotion. In my view, the idea of opposing reason and emotion is entirely misguided. This claim is consistent with the views of many current theorists. However, I do not reject the thinking–feeling dichotomy primarily for the reasons most commonly cited in affective science today. Specifically, Antonio Damasio (1994) has famously argued that emotion is in fact necessary to functional cognition, citing cases where the disruption of emotional response leads to irrational, ultimately self-destructive actions. To some extent, Damasio is merely stating a version of the "affect as information" thesis – the idea that we sometimes use our emotions as the basis for more abstract judgments, as when we won't enter into a contract with someone that we have a "bad feeling" about. Given that the affect heuristic (i.e., the use emotion as information) evolved, it is probably the case that it provides us with quick intuitions that are on the whole more beneficial than if we had to rely solely on (nonintuitive) calculations. On the other hand, it is ironic that Damasio's work would point in any way toward the affect heuristic, as it is one area in which the "reason versus emotion" idea would seem to have some validity. Specifically, when we have time to investigate and calculate, it is clear that, in comparison with the affect heuristic, investigation and calculation are much more likely to lead us to valid conclusions. Of course, even here, the division is not an absolute opposition, but a division of labor. We should rely on the affect heuristic (or other, evolved shortcuts) when time is limited and the stakes are high. Even so, we should adopt self-conscious research and calculation when possible.

Nonetheless, for the most part, Damasio's (1994) claims are not related to the affect heuristic. For example, in a study commonly cited as providing strong support for Damasio's view, Bechara and colleagues (1997) tested people's responses to a gambling game. In the game, there were four decks of cards – A, B, C, and D. The decks were arranged so that the "winning" results from A and B gave larger rewards than those from C and D. However, the overall result of choosing A and B was worse than that of choosing from C and D. Eventually, emotionally neurotypical subjects came to avoid A and B. However, the patients who had brain damage affecting their emotional response persisted with A and B. The former group avoided A and B even before they had any "hunch" that the decks were rigged (Levy 2007, 31). In contrast, the ventromedial (brain-damaged) subjects remained "more likely" to choose decks A and B even after they "did ... work out how the decks were arranged" (32). Following Damasio, Levy summarizes the experiment as showing that the emotional response proved "beneficial to cognition" (32). But this is a strange conclusion. Neurotypical test subjects started avoiding decks A and B prior to drawing inferences about them. This suggests the usual operation of motivation, specifically a feeling of apprehension regarding decks A and B that motivated avoidance, in keeping with our usual enhanced sensitivity to threats. Conversely, ventromedial patients were able to come to the proper inferential or "reasoning" conclusions about the decks, though they would often persist in choosing decks A and B. Thus, it does not appear that the reasoning of either group was affected by their emotional response. Rather, their *action* was affected by their emotional response. But that is just what we should have expected all along. Specifically, changes in motivation alter action. The study does not show that emotion benefits cognition. It shows that (evolved) motivation systems drive action and do so, for the most part, adaptively. The ventromedial subjects suffered from a motivational problem, not a cognitive – or information-processing – problem.

So why then do I say that the reason–emotion opposition is entirely misguided? The answer is implicit in what I have just written. Reason is information processing. As such, it concerns facts – particular facts, general laws, statistical tendencies. Emotion, in contrast, concerns the motivations we have for altering or sustaining a current (factual) state of affairs. The two are, of course, different, but they are not contradictory. Only particular complexes of the two are contradictory.[1]

Consider the standard case of future discounting, where I opt for some pleasure in the present even though it is likely or even certain to go against my long-term interests (see Ahmed 2020; Dunning 2012, 260). For example, suppose I decide to eat yogurt even though it will probably produce digestive distress later on. My behavior in this case – like my behavior in any other decision – involves reflection on and simulation of the alternatives. Specifically, I draw inferences about and imagine eating the yogurt, enjoying its taste, and so on. I also draw inferences about and imagine the digestive sequelae, including sometimes not insignificant pain. In each of these cases, I feel some associated emotion – respectively, hunger (in the sense of a desire to experience a particular taste; on the different sorts of hunger, see Roderick Wong 2000, chaps. 4, 5) and apprehension. The emotion with the greater motivational force wins. If my hunger for the yogurt is stronger than my fear of digestive pain, then I eat the yogurt. If, on the other hand, my apprehension is stronger, I opt to abstain.

Note that my consideration of these choices involves both information processing and emotion. It is not the case that one alternative is all

---

[1] One possible objection to my argument here would be that we have "cognitive motivations" (see Beswick 2017 for a valuable discussion of this topic). But cognitive motivations are simply motivations that yield some sort of reward (or that we imagine will yield some sort of reward) when we achieve some cognitive goal (e.g., isolate a pattern in a musical composition). They do not indicate that reasoning is in part a matter of emotion. Similarly, we have "fiscal motivations," but these are simply motivations that yield some sort of reward (or that we imagine will yield some sort of reward) when we achieve some financial goal (e.g., acquiring a lot of money). They do not indicate that money is in part a matter of emotion.

emotion while the other is all reason. There is, therefore, nothing that can be called a conflict between emotion and reason. There is, rather, a conflict between one cluster of inferential and emotional processes ("I will have the yogurt [because it will taste good]") and another cluster of inferential and emotional processes ("I will abstain from the yogurt [because it will upset my digestion]").

The same point holds even for a case where I blatantly choose preference over evidence. Suppose I want to believe that, say, cholesterol is not relevant to health, and I end up deciding that it is not relevant to health. Since I ignore many sources of evidence to reach this conclusion, it may seem that this is a case of emotion versus reason. But here too both alternatives involve information processing and motivation. I have motivation to continue eating many saturated fats, and I selectively read articles noting that such-and-such a population has high cholesterol but low heart disease rates. On the other side, I have motivation to understand what is true about my health, and I have my doctor's testimony, along with a series of articles I have chosen not to read. When I decide on the issue of cholesterol, I have chosen between one emotion–information complex and another emotion–information complex.

Another way of putting the point is that information processing is not opposed to emotion, but the two are often invoked in discussing the difference between deliberation and spontaneity. We tend to think of spontaneous judgments as governed by emotion, probably because spontaneous decisions are more likely to occur in time-constrained circumstances where one is experiencing significant motivational arousal. That is, after all, what spontaneous responses are for. Thus, the emotion is salient in this case. But they involve both emotion (i.e., the motivational arousal) and information processing (i.e., our understanding of the circumstances, and of ourselves in relation to those circumstances). Similarly, we tend to identify decisions following deliberation as the product of reason. Here, the reasoning process is more salient. But, in fact, however much we reason, we will only act on a decision if we experience some motivation, thus some emotion. Again, one element is more salient in each case, but both are present in both cases.

Of course, one may make "irrational" decisions in the sense that one may fail to follow scientific procedures (as in the cholesterol example). Moreover, this irrationality involves emotion (e.g., my motivation to rationalize an unhealthy diet). But, again, both alternatives include emotion and reason. To say that I am motivated by a desire to continue eating high-fat foods is equivalent to saying that my emotions of, say, fear of heart disease are weak. By that construal, we could say that the problem is not lack of reason, but lack of (a particular sort of) emotion.

## Empathy

In Chapter 6, we will look in some detail at the processes involved in empathy. However, it is important to clarify some basic terms and distinctions before turning to that discussion.[2] Fundamentally, empathy is a process that – when successful – allows a person to achieve some explicit or implicit knowledge of the mental states of other people. The most basic distinction in types of empathy is between cognitive and affective empathy (on the former, see Spaulding 2017; on the latter, see Maibom 2017). Cognitive empathy is equivalent to what many writers refer to as "theory of mind" (ToM). (Sometimes, it is used more narrowly to refer to ToM applied to emotion [e.g., see de Waal 2006, 39].) Specifically, ToM is our attribution of mental states to others. For example, if I see someone's hand moving toward a glass as the person's head is oriented in the direction of the glass and the person has his cupped hand open just a bit wider than the glass, I do not directly perceive his intention to pick up the glass. However, I ascribe that intention to him. I am able to do this because I have ToM or cognitive empathy capacities.

I have chosen a simple example of ToM to remind us that, in the vast majority of cases, ToM works very well. We generally do understand one another. This is what we would expect as our ToM capacity has evolved and is adaptive. However, we tend to be unaware of the successful operation of ToM. On the other hand, errors do occur and we often notice them, though not always. Errors are increasingly likely as we move from simple intentions to experiences and thoughts of greater complexity, such as those that are the ordinary concerns of literature. Thus, it is important to be sensitive to the limitations of our ToM capacities as well.

Unfortunately, writers are not uniform in defining the difference between cognitive and affective empathy. But the most common usage identifies the latter as shared experience, rather than a belief about the target's state. In this usage, if I think that you are sad, I am exercising cognitive empathy. If, however, I feel sad because I take it that you are sad, then I am exercising affective (or emotional) empathy. I have phrased this as "exercising" cognitive or affective empathy because, in ordinary speech, "having" empathy seems to imply that the cognitive attribution

---

[2] I should note that I do not believe that I am drawing the only valid or useful distinctions in types of empathy, just the types that bear most on the current analysis. Other distinctions (e.g., see Matravers 2017, 19–24) may be very valuable in other contexts. For instance, Matravers importantly differentiates using empathy to ascertain what someone is feeling versus using empathy to get a sense of someone's experience after we know from other sources what he or she is feeling (19). Readers interested in a lucid, scholarly, and rigorous introduction to work on empathy may wish to take up Matravers's valuable book.

or emotional experience is accurate to the target's thought or feeling. But it is important to recognize that one may engage in the same cognitive and affective processes in cases where one is right and cases where one is wrong (e.g., I am exercising affective empathy in the case just mentioned, even if I am mistaken and you are not sad at all).

One standard way of defining emotional empathy involves having "the same" emotion as the target (e.g., see Bloom 1999, 40). As a loose approximation, this generally works well enough if we mean to refer to the broad emotion category, such as *fear* or *anger*. It clearly does not work for the particularity of an emotion episode. For example, suppose I am angry to see someone praised as an anti-racist when I know that she had repeatedly treated my wife and other non-Europeans in racist ways. If someone empathizes with me simply at the level of feeling anger, that does not involve anything like the precise emotional nuance and the associated sequence of memories that shape my anger.[3]

It is worth pausing for a moment over the possible identity of people's emotional experiences in empathy. In recent years, it has become common to claim that mirror neurons allow us to share other people's emotions. Thus, Armstrong writes, "I literally can feel your pain" (2013, 60, though see 61 for a partial qualification). Goldman writes that due to "the discovery of mirror neurons ... there is much less room for skepticism" that "the feeling states of receivers [are] exactly the same as those of their targets" (2011, 33; note the adverb "exactly"). Even Gallese and Guerra claim that mirror neurons provide "a neurobiological foundation for a direct modality of access to the meaning of the behavior and experiences of others" (2019, 3).

But this is clearly wrong. Mirror neurons may allow Smith, for instance, to experience some very limited activation of her anger system when witnessing my expression of anger. But they do not give her anything like a precise simulation of the relevant sequence of events, the same emotional memories and formative, critical period experiences, or even the genetic particularities that contribute to my individual emotional dispositions. At best, mirror neurons allow only a general parallelism in the primary emotion systems involved in the two cases. Unsurprisingly, the claims for mirror neurons have been disputed by psychologists and philosophers. Matravers presents a clear and balanced criticism of the extrapolations from empirical research (2017, 50–54, 137–139). Debes (2017) offers a compelling critique of the idea that mirror neurons allow great depth of "understanding" with regard to other people's emotional states.

---

[3] For an insightful discussion of the various ways and degrees in which empathy may (or may not) approximate the experience of a target, see Roughley and Schramme (2018, 20–26).

On the other hand, I think Debes (2017) might give mirror neuron theories too little credit. Fundamentally, saying that mirror neurons allow me to "understand" Jones's grief (for example) does not necessarily mean that I have deep insight into the particularity of his emotional experience. It means that mirror neurons allow me to know what sort of thing grief is. The understanding at issue is, first of all, just having a sense of what it is like to experience grief. Contrast, say, an emotion term one encounters in another culture – for example, "qurtob." We learn that there is a characteristic facial expression – perhaps slightly opening one's mouth and placing the tip of one's tongue on one's upper front teeth. With practice, we come to be able to recognize when people are feeling qurtob. But until we connect the concept with some first-person experience, we cannot say that we understand qurtob because we have no sense of what it feels like. Whether or not mirror neurons explain that understanding in the case of grief and other emotions, that is the fundamental kind of understanding at issue here.

In any case, affective empathy is not a matter of sharing the same emotion anyway. Thus, Kelly, for example, states that the emotions of the empathizer and target need only be "type-similar" (2011, 91). As Marsh explains, "Empathic emotional responses include both matching emotional responses—you feel sad, so I feel sad—and compatible responses—you feel pain, so I feel anxiety" (2012, 192). Again, it is important to stress that even "matching" does not mean "identical," since the emotional memories and other factors that contribute to my empathic pain will differ from yours, only sharing the broad category of "pain." More significantly, the relation of empathy to mere compatibility may be illustrated by a simple example. If I empathize with a four-year-old who is bored at a concert of avant-garde music, I do not have to feel boredom myself. Rather, I empathize with him insofar as I have a feeling of the same valence (positive or negative) and that feeling is derived from experience of the same emotion category. It is true that I may empathize with the boredom of the four-year-old because I am currently bored. However, I may empathize with him simply because I have felt bored in the past and the emotional memories – activated by a perception of the child's boredom – make me reexperience, in an attenuated form, some of the aversive qualities (e.g., some fidgetiness) of boredom. This is why, in my overview of emotion, I characterized activated emotional memories as rearousing the relevant emotion system or perhaps only its valence. What I would say at this point is that, when activated, emotional memories give rise to the earlier experience of valence, with some properties of the initial emotion – sometimes many of those properties. Instead of saying that these are the same emotion, we may signal the differences and similarities by referring to the empathic emotion as *congruent* with the target emotion (or as aiming at such congruence, for, again, one's empathic response may be mistaken).

All this points to a definition of *affective empathy* as, minimally, the sharing of valence derived from a source with some degree of similarity to the source of the target's feeling. For example, when empathizing with a person in mourning, we may achieve some degree of empathic congruence from any experience of sadness; we are likely to achieve a greater degree of congruence insofar as that sadness derives from the death of an attachment object.[4] Needless to say, "some degree" is vague. The point is that the degree of similarity will vary, and this will have consequences for the quality of our empathic response. Indeed, this account of affective empathy has the benefit of allowing us to explain different degrees of affective empathic precision and accuracy. Empathic precision is the fine-grained quality of our emotional response to the target. Suppose I am sixteen and seeking to empathize with a classmate in her grief over the premature death of a parent. If I draw on various experiences of sadness, the emotional source of my negatively valenced feeling is likely to be rather vague. If I relate it to the death of my grandmother, then it is likely to increase in precision, being linked with a more distinctive set of attachment feelings and a loss related to them.

In the case just mentioned, the increase in precision is likely related to an increase in accuracy as well. Accuracy is the degree to which the features of my empathic experience are distinctively parallel with those of the target. Precision does not always increase accuracy; for example, my relationship with my grandmother may have been limited and nonconflictual. In contrast, my classmate's relationship with her deceased parent may have been profound and combative, leaving her with a sense of loss compounded with feelings of resentment and regret or even guilt. On the other hand, it probably is the case that, on the whole, increasing precision of empathic sources increases empathic accuracy, insofar as the increase in precision bears on features relevant to the target's experience. Thus, someone who has had a parent die prematurely is generally able to empathize more accurately, as well as more precisely, with someone whose parent has died prematurely.

A further variable in one's empathic response is *intensity*. My experience of a congruent emotion is almost always lesser in degree than that of

---

[4] I take this to be consistent with the neurological research on, for example, empathy for pain. As Guo explains, "brain regions activated by empathy for pain are the same ones implicated in processing the affective and motivational aspects of pain" (2017, 46). These regions are common across experiences of pain; the overlap between empathizer and target does not extend to, say, particular memories, simulated anticipations, and so on.

my target. (I say "almost always" because it sometimes happens that one feels the sorrow or fear of an attachment object – such as one's child or spouse – more intensely than the other person does himself or herself.) This intensity is in part open to our modulation. We may dwell on relevant memories, recollecting details, or distract ourselves quickly. Moreover, empathy does not derive solely from memories in themselves. It also involves, for example, the perception of relevant conditions (e.g., the experience of having dinner without the parent who had always been there previously). Of course, we never experience exactly what the target experiences. However, we can to some degree approximate his or her experiences through effortful simulation. Indeed, this is an area in which literature is directly relevant. One way in which literature excels ordinary thought and speech is that it often involves the elaborate development of simulation (or imagination) in such a way as to produce particularly precise, vivid, and intense empathy. This may be one of the reasons why literature is often successful in fostering empathic feelings across identity group divisions (e.g., see Hakemulder 2000; Paluck 2009).

The idea of empathic accuracy is, of course, complicated in the case of literature. It is important to remark briefly on this complication before going on. Since fictional characters do not really exist, it is most often wrong to say that one's empathy is mistaken (or incongruent), at least in the usual sense. However, it does make sense to say that one's empathy is or is not "well-grounded" (to borrow a term from Nussbaum 2016, 35), which is to say well supported by the evidence available in the work. That evidence includes uncontroversial mental state attributions provided in the text (e.g., "Jones recognized the man who just entered the bar"). But it is frequently a matter of drawing on common connections from real life in order to understand characters in the fictional work. To take a very simple example, if someone cries in real life, that is commonly correlated with his or her feeling sad. In keeping with this, we assume a weeping character in a story is sad, unless we are given reason to suspect that the weeping may be duplicitous (e.g., due to an earlier statement that the character could cry on cue) or may have another source. Indeed, the idea of well-groundedness applies to real-world situations as well. Real people have real emotions, which is not the case for literary characters. Nonetheless, a real person's thoughts and feelings may be profoundly inaccessible. For this reason, we most often need to evaluate our ToM attributions (e.g., that Harry has a crush on Sally) by whether they are well-grounded, not whether they are precisely true, though the latter is, of course, our ultimate goal.

This leads us from the broad definition of empathy to the issue of how empathy operates in practice. In the cases just mentioned (e.g., in literary interpretation), we may engage in rational discussion about the best way to understand a target. Whether we are speaking of a real person or a literary character, we cite the same sorts of behavioral or other evidence. On the other hand, it is important to recognize that empathy does not usually arise in reflective processes of self-conscious evaluation and dialogue. Although our empathic responses certainly may include self-conscious choices and articulation, they operate most often as part of an ongoing process of response to real-life interactions or to our engagement with a literary work. As such, they are generally not self-reflective and explicitly articulated. To understand empathy in practice, we need to examine that response or engagement. This is what situated cognition and enactivist theorists refer to as "embedded" cognition, or cognition as it unfolds in our ongoing interaction with the world. That embedded engagement involves three key psychological elements: information integration or inference (often referred to as "theory"), simulation, and interpersonal stance.

By "inference," I mean the various processes by which different particular or general forms of knowledge or belief are integrated to yield new information. Principles of both deduction and induction guide inferential processes in this sense. We clearly use inferential processes in empathy, as when we reason that someone was out of the room when a particular announcement was made and therefore is likely to be unaware of that announcement. Simulation is the process whereby we imagine a particular causal sequence with some degree of perceptual representation, as when we envision how we might lift a heavy piece of furniture, sometimes even moving our hands and feet as we picture different possibilities for where to stand and how to grip the object.

It is a commonplace in discussions of ToM that there are two competing accounts of cognitive empathy. These are "theory theory," which asserts that ToM is a matter of inference, and "simulation theory," which asserts that it is a matter of simulation. Current treatments of this topic are likely to conclude that now we recognize that ToM involves both (e.g., see Matravers 2017, 48, discussing Alvin Goldman's views; see also Doherty 2009, 48). It certainly does involve both. But the entire discussion may make it seem that the two could in principle constitute mutually exclusive alternatives. However, I believe that opposing the processes in this way is misleading. These two processes are so integrated with one another and with a range of other cognitive and affective processes that it is almost impossible to separate them in practice.[5] (We will return to these two processes, especially simulation, in Chapter 6.)

---

[5] Research discussed by Zaki and Ochsner (2012) suggests this point. Zaki and Ochsner distinguish a "shared representations system" and a "mental state attribution system," which are at least parallel with simulation and inference. They explain that the two

In and of itself, *interpersonal stance* is the simplest of the three key elements in empathic activity. It is also by far the least widely discussed or even recognized. However, it is pivotal for the entire operation of affective empathy and such related feelings as compassion and care. Interpersonal stance is the attitude that we take up toward a target that determines the relation we have to his or her emotions. It is a sort of parameter setting. We may in some manner share a person's feelings, be indifferent to them, or feel something else in their regard. In the most obviously consequential cases, our relation to someone and his or her circumstances may be such that we experience the same general type of emotion or some contradictory emotion. I will refer to the former as "parallel" and the latter as "complementary." For example, if Jones is angry, I may feel the parallel emotion of anger directed at the same target (e.g., Smith). Alternatively, I may feel a complementary emotion of anger at or fear of Jones.[6]

One of the crucial variables – perhaps the only crucial variable – governing interpersonal stance is *identity category*. If I categorize myself and Jones as part of the same identity group (thus, an in-group), I will be very likely to adopt a parallel emotional stance toward him or her. If, however, I class him or her as a member of an out-group, then it is much more likely that I will adopt a complementary stance toward him or her. Suppose Smith and Doe are in a mixed group of soccer fans watching a match. Suppose further that Smith exhibits mirth. Doe is more likely to have a parallel response to Doe's mirth (e.g., a degree of happiness) if she identifies herself and Smith as partisans of the same team. In contrast, if she categorizes herself and Smith with different teams, the likelihood increases that she will have a complementary response (e.g., irritation). In keeping with this, empirical research shows that test subjects are more likely to respond with schadenfreude to the pain of people they categorize as fans of a rival team (see Hein et al. 2010; see also Gazzaniga 2011, 164; Hess 2009, 253–254). Along the same lines, Robert Sapolsky (2017) stresses the relation between "in-group loyalty and favoritism," on the one hand, and "an enhanced capacity for empathy" on the other. Of

---

systems are neurally distinct, and separable in very simple tasks, but they are not dissociated in complex, social interactions.

[6] Parkinson distinguishes reciprocal, complementary, and antagonistic emotions (2019, 135). This is a perfectly reasonable way of dividing emotions. However, his use of these terms is different from my own. For example, imagine Jones is angry with Doe and Doe feels guilty. For Parkinson, Doe's guilt is complementary to Jones's anger. For me, however, Doe feels guilt over what he has done; empathy is not directly relevant here. In contrast, the empathically relevant cases would involve Doe's response to Jones's anger – parallel if Doe shares Jones's anger at himself (i.e., at Doe) or complementary if Doe is angry with Jones.

course, the point applies not only to sports fans, but also to a wide range of identity group divisions, such as race. Thus, Sapolsky explains that, in an experiment involving two racial groups, "among subjects of both races, there's more activation of the (emotional) medial prefrontal cortex when considering misfortune befalling a member of their own race than of another race" (86). As an example, he cites the fact that "the amygdala activates when viewing fearful faces, but only of [in-]group members; when it's an out-group member, Them showing fear might even be good news" (395).

I should point out immediately that this does not mean that we are condemned to respond to others in a racist way. We can modulate our spontaneous tendencies when we make an effort to empathize with out-group targets. For example, Sapolsky explains that "perspective taking ... enhances identification with Them" (2017, 419).

As the case of schadenfreude indicates, interpersonal stance need not result in some specific emotional pairing (e.g., of fear relative to a target's anger). It is often more likely to involve only valence. In that case, we may refer to the alternatives as empathic or antipathetic interpersonal stance and congruent or incongruent emotional experience. Thus, we may have an orientation toward another person's emotions (an interpersonal stance) that leads us to share the aversive or hedonic quality of that emotion, commonly as indexed to roughly parallel experiences. For example, with a parallel interpersonal stance, we may briefly share the dissatisfaction of the bored child at the symphony, tacitly recalling similar experiences from our early years (though not feeling bored ourselves now). Alternatively, with a complementary stance, we may feel indifferent, or perhaps happy, as the child's reaction confirms our argument to her bullheaded parents, whom we judge to have made an absurd choice in thinking that a four-year-old would enjoy an evening of Schoenberg's serial compositions ("One could imagine taking her to a program of Webern, but – really! – late Schoenberg? What on earth are you thinking?")

This is not to say that the particular emotions of the target are irrelevant. Sometimes, they are crucial. For example, Richeson et al. note that we distinguish some emotions as uniquely human and others as shared with animals. We are "reluctant to attribute uniquely human emotions to outgroup members" (2007, 18). Thus, in some cases, our interpersonal stance in effect involves the exclusion of out-group members from an entire set of humanizing emotions, such as love or hope, and a corresponding over-attribution of, so to speak, "animal" emotions, such as fear, anger, and sexual desire.

I mentioned that identity categorization is one of the key variables in defining interpersonal stance, perhaps the only key variable. At the very least, most conditions or events that affect proneness to empathy will do so by affecting identity categorization. Of course, there are factors such as fatigue that make it less likely that we will engage the effort to simulate a target's emotional state. These limit our empathy without affecting interpersonal stance. But at least some factors that initially appear different from identity categorization may ultimately operate through such categorization.

For example, research indicates that we are less likely to empathize with someone's suffering if we believe him or her to be responsible for that suffering or "blameworthy" (Maibom, 2017, 29). This initially seems to be separate from identity categorization. However, I suspect that it is not. First of all, sometimes learning of someone's apparent responsibility does not really affect our empathic response at all. Indeed, it may even enhance that response, as we imagine the person suffering from both the condition (e.g., addiction) and remorse for having brought it on himself or herself. I suspect that in many cases, such responses are a function of whether we take ourselves to have the same sorts of fallibility as the target.

Related to this, one of the most consequential identity categorizations is ethical. Moral out-grouping involves dividing the world into the good *us* (or perhaps the flawed-but-basically-good *us*) and the bad *them*. It is one of the most effective means of blocking empathy (cf. Morton 2011, 318). It is also distressingly easy to foster. As Boyer explains, "a moralized description of a situation is likely to result in coordinated opinion, more so than other possible understandings of what is going on" (2018, 84); for example, "stating that someone's behavior is morally repugnant creates consensus more easily than claiming that the behavior results from incompetence" (85).

In treating congruent/incongruent emotional experience and empathic/antipathetic interpersonal attitudes, I have acted as if the only important factor is the general form of identity group categorization. In fact, the stereotypes and models through which we respond to identity groups also have consequences. (This division – between out-grouping and stereotyping or modeling – is roughly parallel to that between abstract ethical orientation and the activation of the more specified, ethical–narrative prototypes. Such parallels are what one would expect, given human cognitive architecture, including types of categorization process.) These stereotypes and models not only have representational content (regarding, say, the putative intelligence of out-group members); they also have emotional coloring. Specifically, we tend to begin with an increased inclination to have a particular emotional response to members of a given out-group. This *default* attitude affects how we understand and respond to their emotions; thus, it affects both our cognitive and emotional empathy. As Maitner, Smith, and Mackie explain, "three emotions—fear, anger, and contempt/disgust—have been studied extensively as important contributors to intergroup conflict" (2017, 115). There has been particular attention to fear-based and disgust-based attitudes toward out-groups (see Bergh and Akrami 2017, 440, 445). For example, disgust tends to be particularly important with regard to sexual, aesthetic, or health-related out-groups. In keeping with this, research finds a correlation between anti-gay (sexual) and anti-disabled (health and aesthetics) prejudices (Maitner, Smith, and Mackie 2017, 115–116).

In contrast, white out-grouping of blacks – at least black men – is often fear-based. This is presumably one reason why white test subjects are more likely to see a playful nudge from a black to a white person as aggressive, in comparison with a playful nudge from a white to a black person (Kunda 1999, 347). This attitude of fear is in part a matter of "hostility attribution bias," our tendency to assume that members of certain out-groups will be hostile (Lukianoff and Haidt 2018, 158). The point is bound up with the empirically established psychological association of blacks, especially black men, with weapons and violence (see Banaji and Greenwald 2016, 105–107).[7] This too is a matter of empathy, as it concerns test subjects' inferences about and/or simulations of the mental states of other people. More precisely, it is a specific case of *interpersonal stance attribution* – our (usually tacit) understanding of someone else's interpersonal stance toward ourselves. In many cases, the crucial factor in adopting an antipathetic stance toward another person is our prior assumption that he or she has an antipathetic stance toward us. It is important to note that this response is not confined to an initial feeling. As Banaji and Greenwald explain, we recover more quickly from an initial fear of other in-group members than from an initial fear of out-group members (2016, 135). Thus, whites are more likely to fear blacks than to fear whites, and they are likely to sustain fear longer when the target is black than when the target is white.

Presumably, anger will, on the whole, arise more readily through a nonparallel interpersonal stance. In keeping with this, one common trigger for anger is a sense of shame or humiliation. When a person feels that he or she personally or his or her in-group has been shamed by an out-group, that person has an increased likelihood of reacting with rage against the out-group (e.g., see Ray, Smith, and Wastell 2004 on shame,

---

[7] The fear associated with hostility attribution bias need not concern physical violence. For example, Ickes (2009) points out that men who abuse their female partners are "more likely than nonabusive men to presume that women are harboring critical and rejecting thoughts and feelings about their male partners." Such men presumably fear emotional hurt rather than physical pain.

rage, and racist violence). This appears to be one recurring factor in certain types of terrorism.

*Some Related Concepts*

In Chapter 6, I will focus on the processes of "embedded" empathy – empathy as it develops in actual changing conditions, as stressed by situated cognition and enactivist theorists. However, before going on to that, it is important to distinguish empathy from some related phenomena. I should stress at the outset that my aim here is not to say what terms such as "care" might "really mean." I do not believe that terms "really mean" anything in particular.[8] Given this, I take it that debates over what "care" – or "compassion" or "sympathy" – "really is" are pointless. Rather, there are certain concepts that it is important to isolate and define. We then give names to those concepts. The names are likely to fit the ordinary sense of the terms only partially. But that is unimportant since we are using the words in the stipulated, technical senses. This is generally recognized in the sciences. No one objects to the use of the word "atom" in physics on the grounds that it does not capture the "real meaning" of "atom" as we use it in ordinary language. In fact, such objections make no more sense in psychology, narratology, or literary theory.

The first concept that we need to contrast with that of empathy – or, more exactly, emotional empathy – is that of *emotion contagion*. As Eisenberg, Huerta, and Edwards point out, "empathy ... is not mere contagion of affect without understanding the source of the vicariously induced emotion; to experience empathy the individual must realize that the emotion he or she is responding to affectively is another's emotion" (2012, 147). To clarify the difference between emotion contagion and empathy, we need to return to the difference between *egocentric* and *allocentric* emotions. An egocentric emotion addresses my condition directly, functionally bearing on my own well-being. An allocentric emotion addresses my condition only indirectly, as a function of someone else's emotion, functionally bearing on that person's well-being. Empathy is allocentric. For example, in empathic fear, I worry over the well-being of another person whom I view as in danger. I resolve my empathic fear by

---

[8] The same point holds for "empathy." Thus, if I use "empathy" as someone else uses, say, "sympathy," that is theoretically inconsequential. The only theoretically consequential issues concern the delimitation of concepts, not the pairing of concepts with a particular sequence of letters. For example, Echols and Correll distinguish empathic understanding from empathic concern (2012, 56); these are largely independent of one another, but they may readily confound discussion if both are referred to simply as "empathy."

addressing this person's conditions and apprehensions. Emotion contagion, in contrast, is egocentric. If I experience fear contagion, for example, I do not fear empathically for the other person. Instead, I am afraid for myself. Suppose Jones is being considered for tenure, whereas I already have tenure. I learn that there are some weaknesses in his file and that he is afraid he might be turned down. If I begin to feel fear also, it is not fear that I will not get tenure, but fear for Jones. In contrast, suppose Jones and I are on a wilderness trail. He suddenly screams and flees, apparently having spied something threatening ahead on the trail. I feel afraid and flee also. I am not worried about Jones. Even if I do not think about what Jones saw or reflect on the situation in any way, my behavior shows that I am afraid for me. For example, I do not stop to defend Jones against the danger. Feeling egocentric fear and fleeing to protect myself result from emotion contagion.[9,10]

Emotion contagion and empathy are both related to and distinct from *personal distress*. Personal distress is our feeling of aversion when faced with someone else's emotion. That distress may be due to egocentric concerns that have resulted from emotion contagion. However, it may also derive from allocentric concerns of empathy. The important point about personal distress is that it can exceed the optimal level for effective response to a situation and, as a result, impede or even prevent pro-social action. As I noted with respect to trauma, our emotional response to a situation should be strong enough to motivate an appropriate action, but not so strong as to produce an overreaction (e.g., leading to flight when mere caution is needed) or prevent appropriate sorts of emotion

---

[9] I should point out that this distinction is consequential in a number of areas. For example, Schulz's (2017) valuable analysis of the evolution of empathy isolates two distinct sources for empathy. However, one source seems to apply to emotion contagion only, whereas the other applies only to empathy (as distinguished from emotion contagion). This would appear to suggest that the sources he isolates are actually sources for distinct phenomena (though they presumably do share some component psychological processes, which benefited from both sets of selective advantages – and perhaps others – in the course of evolution).

[10] One of the referees for this volume observed that some writers would see this as "social appraisal," not emotion contagion. I find the idea of social appraisal even more obscure than appraisal as ordinarily understood (as individual), except in cases where it is explicit and deliberative. My view about social appraisal is the same as my view of appraisal more generally (as already discussed). Various mechanical processes produce emotions. Those processes have arisen because they are adaptive. They are adaptive because they approximate the functions (e.g., survival) that would be satisfied by appraisal under ideal conditions. Social appraisal is therefore a valuable idea. But it is valuable not, in most cases, as an account of an actual process. It is valuable as a way of thinking about the functions that are partially approximated by emotion contagion and other mechanical processes.

modulation. When it becomes intense, personal distress can do both, even when it is allocentric. One result of this is that in some circumstances, a person with particularly strong empathic feelings may be less capable of acting pro-socially than someone with more moderate feelings. In keeping with this, relative to some unrelated physician, a parent may find it much more difficult to, say, reset a child's dislocated shoulder due to the parent's having increased personal distress over the child's pain.

On the other hand, personal distress is not the only factor that prevents people from acting on sincere empathic concern. At any given time and in any particular circumstance, we have egocentric concerns. This is true even in cases where we have empathic concerns as well. As the egocentric motives become more intense or numerous, we become increasingly likely to act on them rather than on allocentric motives. This is one reason why research shows that simply being in a hurry to get somewhere significantly reduces helping behavior (see Darley and Batson 1973).

Personal distress is often contrasted with another important concept, *altruism*. Altruism is commonly defined as acting with no self-interest whatsoever. Various authors claim that much research shows that people behave altruistically. As I explained in Chapter 1, this seems to me untrue. What the research shows is that people are often motivated by allocentric self-interest. For example, Hoffman explains that "observers' empathic distress decreases more quickly and they feel better when they help than when they don't" (2011, 231). This clearly suggests self-interest, albeit self-interest that is not egocentric.

Specifically, the research treating putative altruism commonly involves putting people in a situation where they see that someone is in pain; the test subject may aid the person, but he or she may more easily leave the situation altogether. It turns out that even though they could leave easily, people are more inclined to aid the suffering person. This is taken to show that the test subjects are not guided by self-interested motives. If all they wanted was not to feel badly due to the suffering of the target, then they would simply leave the situation. Thus, for example, Batson states that it is possible to test whether a person has any goals relevant to his or her own aversive feelings by arranging the test situation so that the "potential helper can—without helping—easily escape continued exposure to the other's suffering" (2009, 44). But this is a strange interpretation of the research. It would be a plausible interpretation if the test subjects had no memory and would not recall the other person's suffering after they left the situation. But, given that people remember things, it seems clear that, after leaving, test subjects would be likely to remember the other person's expressions of pain and would feel some continuing empathy with him or her, now potentially combined with guilt and remorse. Moreover, test subjects know that this will happen (evidently unlike the researchers running the tests). Put differently, if there were absolute altruism, then the test subjects would help people for whom they felt absolutely nothing; they would be entirely indifferent to a person's suffering but would still seek to alleviate it.

Another valuable distinction is that between our inclination to empathize with other people's negatively valenced emotions and our inclination to empathize with other people's positively valenced emotions. Empirical research, in keeping with our everyday experience, suggests that it is much easier for us to empathize with other people's pain than with other people's joy (see Royzman and Rozin 2006). There are some apparent exceptions to this. For example, we respond differently to our favorite sports team winning and to that team losing. A striking case of this may be found when "after a victory of their college football team, students were more likely to wear school colors, and were more likely to use the first person pronoun, 'we,' than the third person pronoun, 'they,' in referring to the football team" (Ortony, Clore, and Collins 1988, 136, citing the research of Cialdini et al. 1976). This may be in part a matter of our relative inclination to empathize or not to empathize with the team or with members of the team.

Some writers mark this division between sharing negative emotional valence and sharing positive emotional valence with the terms "sympathy" and "symhedonia." I will on occasion use these terms when it would clarify the analysis. I should note that authors differ greatly in the ways they define "sympathy." I am using it in this narrow, technical sense – empathy with negatively valenced emotions – principally as it readily allows us to distinguish sharing of suffering (the "pathy" of "sympathy") from sharing of joy or pleasure (the "hedonia" of "symhedonia"). Fundamentally, sympathy and symhedonia involve a congruent emotional stance toward the target. This terminological distinction may also help to sensitize us to the possibility that there are differences in what is required to establish a parallel interpersonal stance in these two cases. Indeed, as already suggested, one's interpersonal stance in negatively valenced emotions may actually contradict one's interpersonal stance for that same target's positively valenced emotions (e.g., I may be inclined toward some degree of congruence with the sufferings of a rival but jealous incongruence with his or her joys).

Another concept that is applied in a great variety of ways is *compassion*. I will use the word "compassion" to refer to one specific consequence of putting oneself in the target's place. It is important to distinguish between putting oneself in another person's shoes (as Goldie 2011 phrases it) and trying to imagine the other person's experience. Obviously, we erroneously attribute our attitudes or ideas to other people all the time. The distinction I am marking here, however, does not result from an error, but a decision. That decision can have a range of purposes. One of these is particularly relevant to ethical judgment. That purpose is to evaluate the target's emotion, including any associated behavior. This evaluation involves comparing the target with the way that I see myself in his or her circumstances. If I judge him or her to be inferior to me in feeling and response (e.g., less stoical), then I may "lose sympathy" entirely (i.e., not feel empathy at all) or I may feel a sort of patronizing empathy, which we commonly refer to as "pity." When I see the target as roughly equal to me in his or her response, we may refer to my emotion as "compassion." Finally, I may judge the other person's response as significantly superior to my own, in which case I am likely to feel something like a sense of sublime wonder or inspiration, viewing him or her as a model for my own aspirations. (These points are complicated by the fact that in such circumstances, I may also evaluate myself against social norms or prototypes. Suppose Jones is more courageous than I am. I will evaluate and respond to him differently if I see myself as substantially less courageous than is typical, or as courageous as is typical, or as more courageous than others.)

It is important to note that these comparative assessments are often problematic. I take it that the drawbacks of pity are clear. But even an admiring attitude can limit our empathic response by, in effect, dehumanizing the target – as when some men may elevate a subgroup of women to the status of self-sacrificing angels. Though he discusses the topic in a different theoretical context, Morton clearly articulates some of the problems with such evaluative comparisons – which can easily lead to moral out-grouping – when he comments on the way in which perhaps the great majority of us are likely to respond morally to a pedophile. We imagine that "were we to have his desires we would force chastity on ourselves with a rigor fuelled by horror of the alternative." Morton adds that this is how we would proceed, "even while being distantly aware that there is something unrealistic and self-deceptive in what we are telling ourselves" (2011, 321). Later, Morton cites Hannah Arendt on the participation of ordinary people in Nazi genocide and Stanley Milgram's experiments on obedience to show that in the right circumstances, "just about anyone will acquiesce in acts that in other contexts they would find morally repugnant" (325).

Finally, I would like to distinguish what I will refer to as *care*. By "care," I mean empathy that motivates action that is shaped by one's concern for the well-being of the target. That well-being may address either the reduction of suffering or the promotion of happiness. Thus, it may be a function of either sympathy or symhedonia. The paradigmatic case of care is that of a person's relation to an attachment object, such as a parent's relation to a child.

### A Note on Peter Goldie's Objections to Some Forms of Empathy

As is probably clear to readers familiar with Goldie's views on the topic, the preceding points suggest a rather different evaluation of empathy than that of Goldie. Since Goldie's work is influential, it is valuable to consider this difference in some detail. I have generally located my response to critiques of empathy in Chapter 6. However, Goldie's critique is in part a matter of analyzing types of empathy and empathy-related concepts, which is one task of this chapter.

Specifically, Goldie distinguishes "empathetic perspective-shifting" from "in-his-shoes perspective-shifting" (2011, 302). The former involves trying "to imagine *being* the other person," whereas the latter involves imagining how you yourself would feel "if you were in the other's circumstances" (302). In my account, neither is necessarily problematic, morally or otherwise. Either may involve mistakes, and false empathy or false pity, compassion, or inspiration can be problematic because false anything can be problematic. (We will return to the problem of false empathy in Chapter 6.) However, it seems clear that, on the whole, "in-his-shoes perspective-shifting" poses potentially greater problems due to its connection with pity and wonder. Goldie's view is the precise opposite. He objects, not to "in-his-shoes perspective-shifting," but to the empathetic variety.

More exactly, Goldie has both cognitive or informational objections to empathetic perspective shifting and more specifically ethical objections. Though he presents a range of cognitive arguments, they all appear to reduce to a single objection – that we can never fully understand another person or adopt his or her perspective. That is undoubtedly true, and it does have the consequence that we should not be overly confident about our conclusions regarding other people. (In fact, much the same point applies to our self-understanding, as a great deal of research has shown [e.g., see Bargh 2007, 560; LeDoux 2015, 81; Toates 2014, 168–169].) But this has no bearing on whether or not we should pursue empathetic perspective taking. As Clifford Geertz (1973) pointed out in another context, arguments of this sort are fallacious. The fact that we cannot achieve an ideal in no way implies that we cannot improve or achieve greater approximation to that ideal. (As Geertz puts it, we would not opt to have surgery done in the "sewer" on the grounds that "a perfectly aseptic environment is impossible" [30].) It seems clear that we can take traits of a target into account and that relying on our own feelings in another person's situation will often be quite distortive.

Imagine, for example, that I am asked to empathize with a gay man living in a place that does not allow same-sex marriage. By Goldie's argument, I can imagine myself in the person's circumstances, but

I should not – and, in effect, cannot accurately – try to imagine what he feels. So I imagine anti-sodomy laws in my state. It turns out that they would have no consequences for my well-being. Based on this, my feeling toward the gay man in question is one of simple indifference. But I can also seek to imagine his or her experience of being gay in such a state. The resulting imagination of his feelings is likely to be wrong in many ways. However, it is likely to be more accurate than confining myself to my own feelings in the imagined, sexually intolerant society. Moreover, wherever it is distorted, my imagination of his emotions can be improved, as long as I am interested in understanding his attitudes and have not dismissed the entire project as impossible. As Matravers rightly points out, this is in part a matter of simulating the situation and then self-consciously "correct[ing] for the differences we know there are between" ourselves and the target (2017, 40).

As to the ethical issue, Goldie objects to the use of the empathetic variety of perspective shifting "for prediction, for explanation, or for understanding" because this "usurps the agent's own first-personal stance" (2011, 303). Indeed, at the end, he goes further and asserts that empathetic perspective taking "usurps" the target's "agency" (316). I don't know what to make of Goldie's claim here. I can see such usurpation if someone says, "You don't have to ask Jones what candidate she'll vote for; through my infallible empathetic powers, I can vote in her place." But the problem there is denying the person the right to speak for herself. It wouldn't be any better if the usurper had said, "You don't have to ask Jones what candidate she'll vote for; if I were in her place, I'd vote for Smith – so we can just put that down as her vote."

What about the more specific cognitive issues of predicting, explaining, and understanding? Goldie develops his point by treating very broad character traits, such as "being a kind person" (2011, 311). He also maintains that one is typically not self-conscious about these traits oneself. For example, if Doe is kind, he simply acts kindly; he does not decide on his action based on a judgment that he is kind (see 310). In fact, "kind" seems to me too vague to guide simulation. But we can easily treat Goldie's points by taking up traits that are more simulation-friendly.

Consider prediction first. My argument in this book in no way indicates that empathy is a good way of predicting future behaviors, outside of simple cases (e.g., if someone's child dies, he or she is likely to feel grief). But I fail to see why our fallible simulations are necessarily more objectionable if we try to imagine other people's feelings and behaviors, rather than confining ourselves to our own feelings and behaviors in their circumstances. Suppose, for example, that I believe I am the sort of person who is likely to get irritated if someone is condescending and that I am likely to be undiplomatic when irritated. Suppose Jones is notoriously condescending and I am on a committee that needs to communicate with Jones. Now, suppose that Doe is generally polite and reserved in conversation, no matter what her interlocutor is like (even when she is angered by that interlocutor). I cannot see what is wrong with members of the committee simulating Doe's and my likely interactions with Jones and concluding that it would in all likelihood be safer to ask Doe to talk with Jones. Moreover, I cannot see how this judgment would be rendered less legitimate by the fact that Doe does not think, "I am reserved" or "I have equanimity" when she does not make ascerbic replies to Jones.

The difference between Goldie's two sorts of perspective shifting (i.e., imagining oneself in the target's place versus imagining being the target) may be a matter of inference or simulation. Goldie's discussion appears to stress the latter, so I will focus on that. The difference between these two sorts of simulation – "in-his-shoes" and "empathetic" – may be understood in terms of setting parameters in general principles. Suppose little Billy is sobbing. When little Sally thinks that in Billy's place, she would want her teddy bear, she is not shifting parameters for disposition, only for circumstances. When she thinks that Billy would probably want his own teddy bear, she is shifting dispositional parameters as well. Through that added shift in parameters, she is changing from in-his-shoes to empathetic perspective shifting. I'm afraid that I'm simply bewildered as to why this might be objectionable. Such an objection would seem to commit Goldie to the strange view that Sally is behaving better when she brings Billy her teddy bear, rather than Billy's own teddy bear, even though the latter would be far more comforting for Billy. Stranger still, as already indicated, it seems to suggest that a straight person is behaving more morally if he or she imagines what life is like for a straight person in a homophobic society and dismisses the possibility of imagining what it is like for a gay person.

Goldie's (2011) view may appear to receive some support from Vorauer's valuable research and analysis. Vorauer (2019) presents considerable evidence that the injunction to empathize can enhance the mutual alienation of identity groups. She favors "perspective taking" instead. But her objection to empathy is a result of the way she is using the word "empathy." Specifically, Vorauer stresses the divisive effects of an empathizer focusing on the target's hostility to people who share an identity category with that empathizer. For example, a white person seeking to "empathize" (in Vorauer's sense) with a black person may be overwhelmed by a sense of black anger toward white people. This would clearly generate or intensify hostility attribution bias.

But the problem here does not result from empathy in the sense in which I am using the term; indeed, in Vorauer's usage, "empathy" crucially involves "the empathizer's egocentrism" (2019, 23). More exactly, empathy, in Vorauer's usage, involves "imagining how [a target] feels" and "try[ing] to feel the full impact" oneself. In contrast, perspective taking involves "trying to get inside the [target's] head and ... imagin[ing] as clearly and vividly as possible what your reactions would be if you were [that person], taking into account everything that you know about him/her and trying to adopt his/her own way of looking at things" (30). The second approach, Vorauer tells us, avoids many of the problems with "empathy," as she defines it.

In Vorauer's account, then, there is a problem when one first begins with an imagination of the target's attitude and then tries to experience the "impact" of that. By this definition, a feeling of empathy would preserve the initial sense of difference between the empathizer and the target, which is precisely what Goldie advocates. The result is that the empathizer readily comes to feel that he or she is one of the objects of the target's anger. Since Vorauer's perspective taking involves imagining "what your reactions would be," it may seem at first that it is parallel to Goldie's "in-his-shoes" approach. But Vorauer goes on to stress that it is your reactions "if you were" the other person. Vorauer's perspective taking clearly involves what I have referred to as setting the various parameters to avoid self–other differences. Indeed, Vorauer stresses that this requires us to draw on all our knowledge of the target, and that its goal is "to adopt" that target's "own way of looking at things" (2019, 30). In short, Vorauer's research and analysis support empathy in my sense and in Goldie's sense, while opposing forms of response to others that maintain the difference between self and target, such as Goldie's "in-his-shoes" perspective shifting. This is initially obscured because she uses the relevant terms very differently than Goldie and I.

But, again, Goldie is right that our simulations of other people's experiences are highly fallible and, indeed, always inaccurate in some degree. Caution is warranted in assuming even general accuracy in one's understanding. Thus, it is widely recognized that there is often something problematic and sometimes even morally offensive about telling someone that you "know what it is like" to undergo the experiences he or she has undergone. Claiming that one "knows what it is like" – say, for a man to assert (or to simply believe) that he knows what it is like to be sexually harassed – often suggests not only error, but underestimation of the severity of the target's pain. Thus, such a claim of understanding may lead to a patronizing attitude and a judgment that the target is inferior. "I can only imagine what that might be like" or "I can't even imagine what that is like" connotes a degree of salutary humility and a presumption of respect for the target. On the other hand, such assertions also suggest that one needs to make some sort of effort at such empathy. In connection with this, the claim that "I can't even imagine what that feels like," while seeming to be an expression of humility, may be a way of excusing oneself from trying to empathize with the other person.

## A Literary Example

Before going on to the dynamics of empathic response in Chapter 6, we might consider a briefer literary example of the sorts of problem raised by Goldie. In my course on the literature and culture of China, I sometimes teach the poem "Táo Yāo" (桃夭) from the *Classic of Poetry* (*Shījīng*, 詩經).[11] The poem treats a young woman's departure from her natal home to the home of the man with whom her marriage was arranged. One way of thinking about the poem would involve my male students saying that they cannot possibly imagine what it would be like to be a woman in China during the Zhōu Dynasty and my female students saying that they cannot possibly imagine what it would be like to live in that time and to be in such a marriage system.

Alternatively, we could acknowledge that we will never know exactly what it was like, but that we can make an effort to get some sense of the young woman's situation. In class, we have already spent several weeks on cultural and historical materials. In connection with this particular poem, I then explain, for example, that arranged marriages often involved a bride and groom who did not know one another and might not be particularly compatible – though they also might be very compatible. The bride was often very young (say, fourteen or fifteen). As it was patrilocal, the system almost always involved the young woman moving into the house of another family, whom she may not know at all. Moreover, that new house was often far from her parents' home. I remind them that at the time there were no telephones, no automobiles, and no email, and that this separation often meant that the young woman would have no communication with her family for months. She would enter into a hierarchical system where she would be subordinate to the men and older women in the household. She may be resented by her mother-in-law (for the same reasons new brides are sometimes resented by their mothers-in-law today).

The poem comprises three stanzas of two repeated and two variable lines. (Every line has four characters.) The first variable line in each stanza suggests the stage of life of the young woman. In the first stanza, this is the time of her wedding. The governing metaphor of the poem overall assimilates the woman to a peach tree; thus, this initial youthful stage is suggested by flowers blooming on the peach tree. The middle stage of the

---

[11] Available at https://ctext.org/book-of-poetry/tao-yao (accessed September 27, 2019).

marriage, given in the second stanza, is represented by fruit. This points to her fertility – giving birth, becoming a mother. The third stage, in the third stanza, is depicted as an abundance of leaves, representing her full maturity.

The second variable line in each stanza concerns the young woman's status in the home at each of these stages of life. Each of these lines begins by saying that the bride is "suitable" ("yí," 宜) for something. What the bride is suitable for, in the first stage, is "shì jiā" (室家). In the second stage, it is "jiāshì" (家室). In the third, it is "jiārén" (家人). "Shì" means "room" and "jiā" means either "house" or "family." Placing "shì" before "jiā" would seem to stress the physical meaning of "jiā," thus "room in the house." "Jiāshì," in contrast, means either "family" or "home," thus suggesting greater integration. Finally, "jiārén" means "family member" (more literally, "family person"), suggesting that she is fully part of the home.

Thus, the poem represents three stages of this young bride's life. First, there is her marriage, when she has a place in the house but does not really fit in. Students can both infer and simulate the apprehensions and loneliness of the young woman in these conditions. They can develop this further upon reading later poems where, for example, the new bride is able to undertake a visit to her natal family and enthusiastically prepares for a trip she has not been able to make since marrying.

On the other hand, my students are also able to have some sense of the excitement a young woman might feel when faced with the new possibilities of married life, including sexuality and motherhood. (The relevant forms of empathy here are both sympathetic and symhedonic.) This is brought out in the second stanza, where the suggestion of her giving birth is connected with greater integration into the household. Then there is the longer-term prospect of her children growing up and establishing her in a position more definitive of the family, the position currently held by her mother-in-law.

This last stage represents a natural change from a subordinate to a more dominant position, ideally accompanied by the respect due to the elder generation from the younger generation in Confucian tradition. The poem is very brief and obviously does not allow for detailed development of character and associated fostering of identification. Nonetheless, when accompanied by historically and culturally guided simulation, it can help students to empathize with women in this character's position. Moreover, it does so in such a way as to help them recognize and have some emotional sense of both the problems with such a system and the rewards it promises. (This is particularly true if we contrast the trajectory of the young bride's imagined life with nuclear family life in the United States.)

I offer my students the following translation, which draws on William Nienhauser (2008) and James Legge especially,[12] but alters earlier translations considerably:

> *Tender, tender peach tree,*
> *Bright, bright its flowers.*
> *The child goes to marry,*
> *Good enough for the family's house.*
>
> *Tender, tender peach tree,*
> *Its fruit grown full.*
> *The child goes to marry,*
> *Fit for the family home.*
>
> *Tender, tender peach tree,*
> *Its leaves luxurious.*
> *The child goes to marry,*
> *One of the family, right at home.*

I explain that I keep "tender," the usual translation, to suggest the tender age of the young woman. That emphasis is also why I opt for "child" in the third line. The youth of the bride is, I believe, particularly important to emphasize for modern Western readers, who may otherwise imagine her to be a decade older. I treat the changes in the fourth line by stressing the physical space and the minimal tolerance that might greet the new bride – a stranger to the women of the house. For this, I adopt the phrase "Good enough for the family's house." The change in her status with the birth of a child (especially a son) is indicated by her now having a place in the clan or lineage. Finally, when she eventually assumes her position of full respect, her place will not merely be tolerated in the house, but will (ideally) be central to the family home. Throughout, I try to phrase the translation in such a way as to foster an empathic simulation of what the "child" would be imagining, fearing, and hoping for, as she goes to her wedding.

## Conclusion

Affect encompasses a range of phenomena, including dispositions, moods, and emotion episodes. The last may be analyzed into eliciting conditions, attention orientation, action readiness and actional outcomes, physiological outcomes, expressive-communicative outcomes, processing strategies, and phenomenological tone or feeling. The eliciting conditions are in part a matter of innate perceptual sensitivities (e.g., to emotion

---

[12] Legge's translation may be found at the Chinese Text Project, https://ctext.org/book-of-poetry/tao-yao (accessed September 18, 2020).

expressions), but they also derive from critical period experiences and emotional memories (of which, traumatic memories are particularly consequential). In each case, eliciting conditions are embodied in the sense that they are based on bodily experiences, rather than appraisals of one's prospects for well-being. (Such appraisals do, however, indicate the functions of emotions, functions that are approximated by the mechanisms through which emotions operate.) Perceptual sensitivities, propensities derived from critical period experiences, and networks activating emotional memories bear not only on direct perception but also on simulation, the quasi-perceptual (and thus embodied) imagination of particular causal sequences. Emotions operate to motivate action and thus cannot be opposed to reason, understood as a form of information processing (though, of course, complexes of motivation and information can lead to actions that are imprudent).

Empathy, though defined in different ways by different writers, may be broadly characterized as (part of) our response to other people's mental processes, based on inference and simulation. Cognitive empathy or theory of mind is our understanding of other people's thoughts and feelings. Affective empathy is our partial sharing of other people's feelings. Specifically, affective empathy involves at least a shared valence (positive or negative), derived from some emotional source (e.g., a set of emotional memories). The emotional valence may be connected with a more or less precisely delimited emotion and with circumstances that are shared in greater or less detail (e.g., sadness versus grief at the premature death of a parent). Affective empathy results from interacting processes of simulation and inference within the ambit of a particular interpersonal stance. Interpersonal stance is one's attitude toward the target, insofar as this attitude defines one's response to that person's emotions. Perhaps the key variable in determining interpersonal stance is identity category. One responds to in-group members with parallel (empathic) emotion while responding to out-group members with complementary (in some way antipathetic) emotion.

Empathy must be distinguished from emotion contagion; the former is allocentric, whereas the latter is egocentric. It should also be distinguished from personal distress, which may have egocentric or allocentric sources. It is often valuable to recognize the different operation of sympathetic empathy and symhedonic empathy. Finally, there is often an evaluative component to empathy, which may lead to (demeaning) pity, (egalitarian) compassion, or (admiring, but sometimes dehumanizing) wonder. This evaluative component and its consequences seem to suggest that it is misguided to value "in-his-shoes" perspective shifting over empathetic perspective shifting, as does Goldie (2011).

CHAPTER 6

# The Dynamics of Empathic Response: Simulation and Inference in *A Midsummer Night's Dream*

In Chapter 5, I mentioned the idea that our cognitive and affective processes need to be understood in the context of actual engagement in the world. This position is, in one form, referred to as "situated cognition" and, in another form, as "enactivism" (on the former, see Robbins and Aydede 2009; on the latter, see Noë 2012). In both cases, it is widely taken to stand opposed to "classical" cognitive science in, for example, rejecting the latter's work to isolate enduring rules that are internal to the mind. In my view, there is no necessary opposition between the two, just as there is no necessary opposition between the isolation of grammatical principles in theoretical linguistics and the study of moment-to-moment language use in pragmatics. Both are valuable, indeed necessary, for understanding language. The same point holds for the isolation of enduring structures and processes of empathy in the human mind – the cognitive and affective architecture of empathy – and the careful description and explanation of ongoing, particular experiences of empathy.

Up to this point, we have focused on the enduring structures and processes. I would like to turn now to the "enactment," the situated or embedded operation of these processes in an unfolding experience of empathy. Such an act involves continual changes in the configuration of inferences, simulations, and other operations. These changes proceed through the usual sequence of initial processing followed by modulation. In connection with this sequence, it is important to recognize that empathic engagement can be spontaneous or elected. In other words, it can be initiated by circumstances or by one's choice. As indicated in Chapter 5, we are more likely to find ourselves empathizing spontaneously with in-group members than with out-group members. But we can (partially) compensate for this bias by deciding to empathize with out-group targets. Moreover, empathic processes can unfold automatically or through effort. Thus, we self-consciously simulate someone else's experience at a certain level of detail as a matter of course. But we may decide to press our simulation further, seeking to take up more of the target's experiences, with greater intensity and precision. This difference too is often particularly great with respect to in-groups and out-groups.

Literary experience manifests these differences as well, and not only with respect to in-group and out-group characters. For example, our first reading of a work or our viewing of a play is likely to involve primarily spontaneous and automatic processes. However, our critical engagement with a work in subsequent readings is likely to involve elective and effortful processes. Part of our response to other people – in real life or in fiction – involves the isolation of patterns in their thought, feeling, and behavior that have predictive and explanatory functions. The isolation of such patterns is part of our empathic understanding of and response to other people. For example, recognizing that a given individual is particularly sensitive about some physical trait (e.g., weight) may lead us to feel a sort of empathic embarrassment with him or her when some situation draws attention to that trait, even when the person gives no sign of feeling embarrassed at the time. In literature, our processes of cognitive and affective empathy apply most directly to characters, but they are often extended to the author, especially in critical rereading. A simple – though in some ways puzzling – case of this occurs when we view a character as treated unfairly by an author, as when we think the author suffers from in-group prejudice against a character. (We see cases of the latter in rewritings of canonical works that treat, say, women or African characters more sympathetically than the original author, as in Jean Rhys's *Wide Sargasso Sea*, which takes up the character of Bertha from Charlotte Brontë's *Jane Eyre*.) Finally, in scholarly reading, we are often concerned as well with extending our theory of mind (ToM) attributions to different audiences, especially those that would have been contemporary with the author. Thus, we are often concerned to modulate our own attributions of mental states to characters or to the author by reference to what we infer or simulate about the mental states of the various readerships addressed by the author – for example, the different constituencies of audience members attending one of Shakespeare's plays. Thus, we may respond to a character differently depending on our sense of what the original audience would have felt about him or her. Here, too, the point holds for real-life cases and, for instance, culture. To take a very simple example, we will judge and empathically respond differently to a naked Jain monk in India if we learn that it is acceptable for a Jain monk to appear naked in public.

In the following pages, I examine these and related empathic processes that I go through in a reflective rereading of *A Midsummer Night's Dream*. My intention is to give an example of the sort of operations that are involved in empathy as an enactive engagement with the world. Such an engagement is embedded in a complex of cognitive and affective processes. Two of the central processes involved here are inference (in a rather broad sense) and simulation, briefly introduced in Chapter 5. Before turning to *A Midsummer Night's Dream*, we need to consider the latter process in a little greater detail.

**A Note on Simulation**

Again, I take simulation to be, first of all, the cognition of particular causal sequences (as opposed to a generalization about causal patterns). The sequence in question may concern physical objects, nonhuman organisms, or people, and one may or may not be involved in the sequence oneself. That cognition of particular causal sequences has a quasi-perceptual quality in that it involves neural activations that overlap with the activations caused by sensory observation or one's own motor activity. Such simulation is guided by partially innate systems of causal construal for inanimate objects (called "folk physics"), organisms ("folk biology"), and humans along with some animals ("folk psychology"). For example, folk psychology leads us to understand and explain human action in terms of dispositions, emotion-related goals, beliefs about the world and about oneself, and so on. This guidance by folk physics, folk biology, and folk psychology necessarily involves inference to some extent. For example, to engage in simulation, we necessarily take up some prior ideas about the world and apply or modify them in particular ways.

Our simulations are of three main types. First, they may complete actual causal sequences, filling in unobserved details concurrently or piecing together fragments from memory. Second, they may generate hypothetical causal sequences. Or, third, they may vary actual causal sequences in counterfactuals.

The guiding structures for simulation may be particulars, prototypes, or more strictly defined rules. In other words, the guiding structures, like concepts, are of these three types (on these as the three types of concept, see Murphy and Hoffman 2012, 166). The structures recur at different levels of complexity. At the most basic level, they include simple rules defining minimal causal connections (e.g., the physics of one billiard ball hitting another). But at more advanced levels, they involve such cognitive structures as story prototypes. For example, Shakespeare undertook many types of simulation over many days when creating *A Midsummer Night's Dream*. The structures for these simulations included countless causal rules, prototypes, and instances at many levels. The particulars undoubtedly included, among other things, individual people whom he knew, specific literary sources, and memories of particular places. The larger structures included a romantic prototype in which lovers are separated by a domineering father who has chosen another groom for his daughter. But such particulars, prototypes, and rules do not simply appear simultaneously before simulation begins. They are necessarily to some extent the result of selection or induction from simulations. For example, a guiding, biographical source for Helena might have occurred to Shakespeare because he had previously begun to simulate the story in a certain way.

A key element of simulation is the setting of parameters and the changing of variable properties to produce, for example, counterfactuals. This setting of parameters is a central feature of empathy, as it is a necessary part of any attempt at imagining another person's point of view. Take the simple case of optical point of view. In order to imagine what you can see, I take the general principles that govern sight for both of us (e.g., that we cannot see around corners), but I change the parameter of observer location. This is the sort of thing that occurs when I ask you to look at something and then after a moment add, "You'll need to come over nearer to me; you won't be able to see it from there." (Of course, the resetting of parameters is not confined to simulation. If I engage in some sort of calculative inference about your position, that too involves changing the values of variables.)

Shifting parameters in empathy is not limited to spatial location. A wide range of elements – indeed, probably all isolable elements – in any given structure are in principle open to variation. To take an extremely simple example, I feel sad when I have to leave my wife every fall because we teach 1,200 miles apart. When I empathize with someone else in a similar situation, I do not feel badly that he or she has to live 1,200 miles from my wife. I feel badly on his or her behalf because he or she has to live at a noncommutable distance from his or her spouse. I reset the parameter from my wife to his or her partner.

One important aspect of such parameter resetting is that just what we "parameterize" – that is, just what elements we engage in resetting – can change and develop. Consider the prototypical sequence of development in a young child, Sally. Billy cries when he cannot find his teddy bear. Initially, Sally experiences emotion contagion upon hearing him cry. Thus, she responds egocentrically, as if there is some threat to her well-being (even though there is not). In keeping with this, she responds by hugging her teddy bear. Subsequently, she comes to parameterize just who is threatened. When she hears Billy cry, she realizes that there is something distressing from his point of view, not from her own point of view. She knows that when she is distressed, she finds comfort in her teddy bear. In consequence, she brings her teddy bear to Billy. He pauses, stares dourly at the doll, drops it to the ground, and, to Sally's bafflement, begins to wail even more piteously. Sally remains confused on subsequent occasions until she parameterizes the object of comfort and, seeing

Billy's teddy bear behind the sofa, retrieves the prized item and offers it to the brokenhearted lad, immediately making him her love slave for life (cut to Billy in first grade carrying Sally's books; dissolve to Billy in college carrying Sally's books and then proceed to complications until Sally realizes that she has been in love with Billy all along and they get married and live happily ever after, making sure all their children have teddy bears, as shown in the concluding shot of the film [roll credits, play happy theme song]). (Note how I cleverly drew on structures of cinematic storytelling and film technique to guide a brief, illustrative *simulation*, specified by the *setting of parameters* in keeping with the example.)

As is well known, several lines of research suggest that the study of literature may enhance our empathic capacities (see Kidd and Costano 2013; Kidd, Ongis, and Costano 2016; Mar, Oatley, and Peterson 2009). Literature commonly demands that we take up various points of view – not only perceptual, but also emotional, philosophical, psychological, and others. It seems possible that part of the empathic benefit of literature may be a matter of extending our parameterization in two ways. First, it may lead us to parameterize more parts of a guiding structure. Second, it may lead us to envision more variability in the parameters and thus a greater range of values for a given variable. For example, from early on, romantic love stories have parameterized the people who fall in love, allowing them to be particularized differently and to differ from parental preferences. However, it is only much more recently (at least in mainstream works) that the possible alternatives for the values of the variables came to include same-sex couples. This parametrization is not confined to literature; however, literary instances seem likely to play a particularly important role in expanding people's sense of what parts of a structure can be varied and in what ways.

A Midsummer Night's Dream

Shakespeare begins his play with the entrance of Duke Theseus and his captured fiancée, Hippolyta, Queen of the (defeated) Amazons. There are clearly many ways in which this scene could be staged and acted. Each would contribute in different ways to the audience's simulations, inferences, and cognitive and affective empathies. For example, an audience member's response would result in some degree from the emotionally expressive qualities of the actors' facial expressions, postures, pitch contours in speech, and many other factors. I will focus only on the text, leaving aside the performance features. Though certainly important, these will vary from production to production.

It is a commonplace of cognitive analysis that our selection of information from the world – including that of literary works – is not only in part a function of intrinsic qualities of objects and events in the world, but also in part a function of our interests. Since this is a romantic comedy, I will be paying attention to the gender relations in the play. I will be particularly attentive to the romantic preferences of the characters. This is an empathic concern that is central to the romance genre. Moreover, it is part of the romantic prototype that has particular consequences for the ethical implications of the romantic story. As we saw in Chapters 3 and 4, romantic stories tend to elevate freedom of individual choice as an important social good. The genre commonly suggests that in matters of emotionally significant personal life – especially matters of attachment bonding – individuals are ethically bound to refrain from coercing others and societies are ethically bound to foster individual freedom at least in this area.[1]

Theseus enters and immediately laments that he craves marriage to Hippolyta, but he must still hold off another painful four days. The relatively narrow sexual interest of Theseus does not take terribly complex ToM processing to infer. The task is rendered simpler by Theseus's own reference to "my desires" (I.i.4). He then criticizes the "old moon" for this slow passage of time (I.i.4), identifying the moon as female and comparing her to a stepmother or "a dowager" who spends part of the money that a young man might have inherited (I.i.6). This is a rather disagreeable statement. He basically complains that some old women live too long when they should get around to dying so that young men can inherit more money. When we recall that Theseus has just engaged in a literal war against women, one begins to sense some degree of antipathy toward women on his part. For readers sensitive to these points, even unselfconsciously, this seems likely to affect their interpersonal stance toward the duke. Of course, many readers may not engage in a particularly effortful attempt to discern his intentions and attitudes and might therefore take the speech as nothing more than a formulaic assertion of his enthusiasm for marrying his beloved Hippolyta – despite the fact that he does not show much evidence of genuine affection at this point.

We then turn to Hippolyta, who does not feel that time moves too slowly but proclaims that it "will quickly" pass (I.i.8), which begins to suggest that her attitude toward the marriage is different from that of Theseus. She compares the moon on the night of their wedding to a "bow/New bent in heaven" (I.i.9–10). The image is ambiguous. Theseus is free to interpret Hippolyta as referring to the bow of Cupid. But we might also see it as the bow of war, perhaps suggesting that she has been

---

[1] In connection with this, it is worth noting that *A Midsummer Night's Dream* has received some attention to ethics, but with a rather different focus. For example, Hawley (2010) explores the play in relation to Hegel and Jean-Luc Nancy.

forced into this marriage at the tip of an arrow. She ends by referring to their wedding, what Theseus called the "nuptial hour" (I.i.1), naming it their "solemnities" (I.i.11). While "solemnities" is a perfectly acceptable word for ceremonies, including celebratory ceremonies, it does not convey something we would be likely to characterize as enthusiasm on Hippolyta's part. Thus, we may begin to have a sense that Hippolyta is dissatisfied with this marriage but – for the same reason that she is dissatisfied – must engage in adequate impression management not to confront Theseus with her feelings.

Theseus goes on to make a comment about Athenians – that they should be mirthful, reserving melancholy for funerals. This may suggest that Theseus has some sense that Hippolyta is herself melancholic about their solemnities. Or it may indicate that he has simply gotten some inkling of melancholy without engaging in adequate empathic effort to realize that the source of the melancholy he senses is his own fiancée. The statement about funerals seems to be either pathologically insensitive or simply mean, given that the defeated Amazons must have recently seen many of their number through the burial ceremonies caused by Theseus. He then goes on to say that he "wooed" her using a "sword" (I.i.16). Perhaps because swords are outmoded weapons associated with noble knights engaged in chivalry, some readers appear to view this as innocuous.[2] But here we might think about the situation from Hippolyta's point of view, comparing how we would respond to a man claiming today that "I wooed her with a gun." When he says that he "won thy love doing thee injuries" (I.i.17), we may wonder whether he is threatening her with renewed injuries if she indicates that he cannot have her "love."

Here, again, for readers who engage in effortful inference and simulation, especially simulation of Hippolyta, this is likely to further intensify an interpersonal stance that is antipathetic to Theseus. I cannot claim that there is enough vivacity in Hippolyta to foster much genuine empathic concern about her. But what little there is seems likely to be positive. This construal of Theseus as coercing Hippolyta, and Hippolyta somewhat quietly acquiescing, seems to receive further support from what happens next. Egeus enters and introduces a love story in which he is clearly the villain. His daughter, Hermia, is in love with Lysander, an admirable youth. The feeling is reciprocated and the two wish to marry. However, Egeus prefers Demetrius, a well-off but fickle young man who previously vowed his affection for Helena (who retains her love for Demetrius).

---

[2] I was first sensitized to the implications of this speech early in graduate school, on reading Gohlke's reference to "the rape metaphor that informs Theseus' words to his captured queen" (1980, 179).

Egeus not only wishes to force his will upon his daughter – he actually appeals to Theseus to execute the girl if she does not comply. This may point toward part of a backstory between Theseus and Hippolyta, suggesting that Hippolyta may have been offered a similar alternative following her defeat. After all, killing an enemy leader in a war seems far more ordinary than killing one's own daughter.

Egeus makes a predictable claim about the boyfriend he disprefers – that they did not really fall in love, but Lysander "bewitched" her (I.i.27). Specifically, he gave her "rhymes" (I.i.28), which is to say poetry. Since the playwright was, of course, a poet – indeed, a poet who wrote "rhymes" for much of this play – we seem justified in imagining that he felt a sense of identification with Lysander and has conveyed that identification, with all that it says about authorial favor, in part through this statement. Egeus goes on to make the standard criticisms of poetry, that it is mere "feigning" (I.i.31), not the expression of feeling but the pretense of feeling – a pretense associated not only with "verses" (I.i.31) but with drama and acting as well. Having insisted that Lysander's love is false, Egeus goes on to manifest his own, presumably more genuine paternal feelings by claiming that Hermia "is mine" in such a way that he "may dispose of her" (I.i.42), including by demanding her death – as if she is "his" in the way a chicken or goat is his.[3]

Thus, here too, we begin to infer and simulate the ideas and attitudes of the characters, forming our interpersonal stances toward them. We also begin to think about the author's mental states, and this reacts back to some extent on our thoughts about and attitudes toward the characters. It is, of course, expected in romantic comedies that most of the audience would develop a parallel stance toward the lovers and an antipathetic

---

[3] I am very grateful to Paul Fried for pointing out to me that there are traditions familiar to Shakespeare that awarded fathers this sort of authority. For example, he cites Deuteronomy 21:18–21, according to which a son may be stoned to death for disobedience, at least if he is "a rioter, and a drunkard" (21:20 in the 1599 Geneva Bible [available at www.biblegateway.com/versions/1599-Geneva-Bible-GNV/ {accessed June 12, 2020}]). (For discussion of this passage in Jewish tradition, see Avioz 2020.) This does to some extent mitigate Egeus's blameworthiness by giving divinely sanctioned precedent for his cruelty, thereby suggesting that at least some people at Shakespeare's time may have found his behavior acceptable. (This is mitigating only in the sense that it indicates Egeus may not have been so extreme for his society as we are likely to imagine today.) However, Hermia's case does not appear so serious as that suggested in Deuteronomy (e.g., we hardly have reason to conclude that she is a drunkard, or a "rioter"). More importantly, such precedents are not exculpatory in the context of the play. Rather, they may be taken to suggest that Shakespeare's clear development of sympathy for Hermia (and not for Egeus) has broader social implications, going beyond the usual distaste we feel for the unlikable *senex iratus*, or irate oldster, who blocks the lovers' union in Roman New Comedy.

stance toward the interfering father figure and the rival. Shakespeare complicates this by making the rival part of another romantic story, so that an unequivocally antipathetic attitude toward him could make that second story appear less than comic when those two "lovers" are united.

At this point, Theseus speaks again. He begins by making a claim about the relation between parents and children that, though common enough among conservatives, should strike many readers as almost blasphemous for a Christian audience. Specifically, he says, "To you your father should be as a god" (I.i.47). In addition to the blasphemy, readers familiar with Jesus's comments on parent–child relations are likely to recall Jesus's statement that "If any *man* come to me, and hate not his father ... he cannot be my disciple" (Luke 14:26).[4] In short, we have at least some reason to infer that Shakespeare may have been hinting at a problem with Theseus's ideas here. Theseus goes on to draw on the Aristotelian view of conception, according to which the mother supplies the matter for the child while the father supplies the form (see Henry 2006, 426). He concludes that since Egeus provided her "figure," he is entitled to "disfigure" her (I.i.51). The claim is a non sequitur, and also extremely brutal. For at least some readers (like me), this will contribute to an ongoing interpretation of Theseus and Egeus as misogynistic and enhance an inclination to adopt an antipathetic interpersonal stance toward both of them.

Theseus may slightly modulate our assessment of him when he points to a possibility for Hermia, other than obedience or death – entering the nunnery. The fact that this associates Theseus with Catholicism complicates things, given the anti-Catholicism of most of Shakespeare's audience and his own complex, though in part sympathetic, relation to Catholicism (e.g., discussed by Greenblatt 2004). (In the play, the cloister is not literally Catholic; however, it would almost certainly have been associated with Catholicism by Shakespeare and his audiences. Thus, Catholicism is germane to our attribution of mental states to the author and to members of the original audience.) But, at a more basic level, I imagine that most people at most times would rather live a celibate life than be executed. Thus, Theseus does appear more humane than Egeus. In addition, his cruelty is not aimed at his own daughter and thus does not involve attachment betrayal.

At this point, Hermia speaks. She employs none of the equivocal indirectness of Hippolyta. Rather, she asserts her commitment to Lysander and her unequivocal rejection of Demetrius, whom she does not love and who (we learn soon thereafter) should properly wed Helena

---

[4] King James Version, available at www.kingjamesbibleonline.org/Luke-Chapter-14/ (accessed June 8, 2020).

anyway. There is no art involved in either inferring Hermia's thoughts or simulating her feelings, for she is explicit about both. Moreover, the play is clearly designed to foster a parallel or empathic interpersonal stance in her regard. To some extent, this means that we will feel compassionate. But to some extent, our judgment elevates her above ourselves, leading perhaps more to admiration than to compassion (which would perhaps have inhibited the comic spirit of the play). In the context of the references to Catholicism and to obeying Egeus as "a god" (I.i.47), it seems likely that I am not the only reader to associate Hermia's integrity and defiance with the integrity and defiance of martyrs who, whatever their denomination, refused to acquiesce in what they did not believe, even in the face of death. Moreover, the terms in which Hermia takes her stand recall and rebut some of the patriarchal implications that preceded. Specifically, recalling how her father treated her as "his" in the way chattel would be his, she rejects taking on the "yoke" of Demetrius (I.i.81). This stresses the degree to which, in accepting this marriage, she would accept subhuman status, akin to an animal in harness. In addition, she rejects Demetrius's "sovereignty" (I.i.82), much as we suspect Hippolyta might wish to reject Theseus's marital sovereignty, and did try to reject his political sovereignty.

So, thus far, we have three men – Theseus, Egeus, and Demetrius. All three seem to have no empathy for women. Indeed, Shakespeare makes this clear when he has Hermia in effect appeal to the empathic capacities of her father, saying, "I would my father looked but with my eyes" (I.i.36). But Theseus answers, "Rather your eyes must with his judgment look" (I.i.37). Interactions such as this suggest that the men's interpersonal stance toward the women is at best one of indifference. (Note that we conclude this by using our ToM capacities to attribute mental states to them, in the first place implicitly but then explicitly in criticism.) Their stance – of indifference or antipathy – allows them to seek to control women like chattel. In contrast, we have two women who have their own interests and recognize that these are completely different from those of the men just mentioned. In one case (Hippolyta), the woman largely suppresses her discontent. In the other (Hermia), she expresses it and refuses to cooperate with patriarchal imperatives.

The first scene goes on to treat another man and woman – Lysander and Helena. Lysander shows us that men do not necessarily have the attitudes of Theseus, Egeus, and Demetrius. His argument that Demetrius and Egeus should marry is, in effect, the complement of Hermia's lament that they have no empathy for her, even though she would be one of the marriage partners. While Hermia stresses the exclusion of her point of view, Lysander stresses the exclusive focus on the points of view of Egeus and Demetrius. Perhaps more significantly, Shakespeare first hints at

Theseus's misogyny with the reference to a dowager who wasn't dying fast enough to give a young man maximal inheritance. Now Lysander refers to a real "dowager," his childless aunt who treats him as her son (I.i.157–158). Far from resenting her longevity, Lysander looks to her as a great help and her home as a refuge. The difference in attitude from Theseus is striking and further affects our interpersonal stances. Indeed, the inverse parallel goes further. Hippolyta responds to Theseus's comments on the dowager by referring to a bow, suggesting the violence of war. In her reply to Lysander, Hermia also refers to a bow. But, in this case, it is explicitly "Cupid's" (I.i.169) and thus a symbol of love, not violence. Finally, in a peculiar development, as soon as Lysander and Hermia have a plan to escape and be united, the verses begin to rhyme. This may suggest the association of hope with the rhyming Egeus earlier criticizes in Lysander. Though the pattern does not appear to be sustained, at least here it seems possible that this formal feature contributes to our emotional response to the goals and attitudes of the characters (e.g., our compassion or admiration) and our interpersonal stances toward them.

Thus, Lysander presents us with an alternative to Theseus, Egeus, and Demetrius. To some extent, Helena – who enters at this point – does the same for women. On the one hand, her skepticism about the value of romantic love is salutary. When she states, "Love looks not with the eyes, but with the mind" (I.i.234), she affirms a central point of the play and a principle that facilitates certain sorts of ToM inference. That principle is that intense romantic love leads us to idealize the beloved, either ignoring or fetishizing his or her flaws and exaggerating his or her virtues. For example, as my students regularly note, the idea is later illustrated by Titania's infatuation with Bottom (though I will somewhat disagree with the most obvious way of understanding this). However, her insight here does not affect her behavior. More significantly, she turns out to be spiteful and disloyal. Specifically, she resolves to reveal to Demetrius the plans of Lysander and Helena. Thus, she will prevent her friends from being united. To make matters worse, in doing so, she presumably realizes that she is condemning her childhood confidant and "sweet playfellow" (I.i.220) to the legal wrath of her father. Here, once again, we both infer and simulate Helena's thoughts and attitudes, forming an idea of her broader dispositions as well as her particular intentions and feelings in specific contexts. We also develop our interpersonal stance toward her and our associated emotional response.

This case is complex, however. I do not feel indifferent or wholly antipathetic to Helena. I am sympathetic with her sorrow over Demetrius, but not with her spite against Hermia. On the other hand,

I recognize that jealousy can lead us to unfair evaluations and behaviors. Thus, I would say that my attitude toward Helena is broadly parallel. However, that parallelism is strongly qualified by a critical evaluation of her jealousy (based in some degree on the sort of comparative assessment that is part of compassion). The mixed quality of my response to Helena helps to make her final union with Demetrius more unequivocally comic. If Helena had been a wholly benevolent, thus sympathetic character, I may have been disturbed by her marriage to the inconstant Demetrius (in the way I am disturbed by the marriage of Mariana and Angelo in *Measure for Measure*). (On the other hand, the play suggests that Oberon's magic has changed Demetrius forever, guaranteeing his continued love for and loyalty to Helena, making this less of an issue.)

There is no reason for me to go through the entire play in this detail. The complex interaction of multiple cognitive and affective processes in cognitive and affective empathizing should already be clear from the analysis of the first scene. I will therefore confine my discussion of the rest of the play to some key points that may further nuance our understanding of empathic processes.

The second scene turns from aristocrats to commoners. It also turns from stories of romantic (or unromantic) love (or lust) to a story about people representing a story of romantic love. Put differently, we begin with real actors representing fictional lovers. This is replaced in the second scene with real actors representing fictional actors representing fictional lovers. It is all very "meta," as we might say today. Thematically, the representational embedding in the second scene may serve to make us more aware of two things: First, lovers, even when sincere, are, like actors, engaging in impression management, trying to guide other people's ToM attributions; the point applies to authors as well. Second, much of the self-expression of lovers – and indeed much of their self-understanding and understanding of others – is guided by stories that we tell about romantic love.

The first scene of the second act takes us from aristocrats and commoners to superhuman beings. While the previous scenes concerned romantic love and patriarchal control of lovers, this scene turns to a different aspect of male–female relations, though one that still involves men violating women's attachment bonds. Titania has taken an Indian boy as a changeling and is raising him as her son. She "makes him all her joy" (II.i.27), evidencing the usual sort of maternal attachment bonding, though he is not her biological offspring. Oberon is "jealous" (II.i.63), but it is not the jealousy of romantic love. Audience members can readily simulate the situation, drawing on their own experiences or situations they have observed. It is not difficult to understand that this is the jealousy of a husband faced with a rival in the form of a child.

Oberon concocts the wacky plan of bewitching Titania – recalling how Lysander was supposed to have bewitched Hermia – so that she falls in love with whatever she first sees. This story has remarkable resonance with maternal bonding. Though Shakespeare could not have known this, the attachment of mothers to newborns is enabled by the neurochemical changes produced by pregnancy and parturition; in other words, maternal neurochemistry operates in a way not that dissimilar to Oberon's love potion. Regardless, the result is much the same in the two cases, as they "madly dote" (II.i.171) upon the object of their affection. Titania falls in love with Bottom, who has the head of an ass and thus (as they say) a face that only a mother could love. It is interesting that here – as with Theseus and Egeus – the socially dominant male seeks to control the woman's attachment relations. Only in the case of Oberon and Titania does the patriarchy completely win, in the sense of (apparently) altering the woman's feelings (here, returning Titania to Oberon). Perhaps this is because the ideal of a mother–son relation (unlike that of spouses) is not one of a lifelong, exclusive union. Rather, the son at some point must leave the mother and become independent of her. Titania would at some point have to part with the Indian boy, presumably returning to Oberon. The same point does not hold for Hermia with regard to Demetrius and Lysander.

Much of the subsequent humor of the play depends on our ongoing empathic understanding of and response to the characters' very different knowledge. Hermia's ToM processing falters when she wakes to find Lysander in love with Helena. Helena, knowing nothing of Oberon's magic, tries to puzzle out just what is happening, only to infer that the other three have joined together to mock her through their playacting. In keeping with this, we must understand that she simulates unobserved aspects of the current scene, consistent with her knowledge, as when she suspects that they "Make mouths upon me when I turn my back" (III.ii.239).

By the end of the third scene, the basic ToM principles we develop for this particular play are fairly well set, as are our basic interpersonal stances. We have established what we take to be the character traits and sustained emotions of the characters. What follows involves us only in more local inferences and simulations. For example, when Demetrius and Helena enter, the former avers his intent to "slay" his rival (II.i.190), reiterating the violence involved in patriarchal "romance," introduced at the start of the play by Theseus. Subsequently, addressing Helena, he expresses the opposite emotion from attraction – disgust ("I am sick when I do look on thee" [II.i.212]). In contrast, Helena expresses reward dependency, the contingency of reward system activation on the beloved, which is effectively a form of addiction. None of this alters the general principles of our inference and simulation as developed earlier in the play.

One question that we might wonder about, however, is just what we are to make of the transformation of Lysander. He appears to be entirely devoted to Hermia. But the love potion turns him away from her and leads him to behave cruelly toward her in his pursuit of Helena. Indeed, he parallels Demetrius in this respect, simply inverting the latter's shift from Helena to Hermia. Does this mean that we are being guided to simulate and experience these characters as, ultimately, the same? Is falling in love a random process, such that one has virtually no control over one's subsequent behavior? Or is this another case where the men in the play prove brutish in their domineering and insensitive treatment of women? After all, Helena and Hermia are not fickle. Titania is affected by the love potion, but in her case (as we have seen) the infidelity is really maternal rather than romantic.

A final, small point is worth noting. In the last act, the aristocrats serve as audience to the commoners' play. The former mock the latter mercilessly, clearly out-grouping them on the basis of economic class, and thus adopting an interpersonal stance toward them that is far from fully parallel. It is not antipathetic but condescending, the sort of stance an adult might have toward a child. Only Hippolyta is different. She feels "pity" (V.i.279, arguably sympathy, as defined in Chapter 5.) for Pyramus as Bottom clumsily enacts his pain at the (apparent) bloody death of his beloved. In connection with this sympathy, we in the audience may recall her recent losses in battle and her unwelcome solemnities.

## Conclusion

The processes of empathic understanding and response are highly complex when we are engaged in any real-world activity. That complexity involves repeated cycles of perception, recollection, inference, and simulation that are inseparable from one another as, through those cycles, they actually provide the conditions for one another's operation. Simulation is a quasi-perceptual imagination of particular causal sequences that may be hypothetical and/or counterfactual, or may simply serve to fill in unobserved aspects of an ongoing situation. These variations in simulation may be understood as the setting of parameters (e.g., for point of view) within otherwise constant principles. In at least some ways, improvements in empathic precision and accuracy can be understood as matters of parameterization, changing constants to variables and changing what values are available to set those variables.

All these inferential and simulative processes are on display in our spontaneous and elective, automatic and effortful empathic processing of literature. That processing is usually aimed at characters, but our response to characters is often inflected by our empathic responses to the author or a particular audience for the work (commonly, the audience for the work's initial composition). Through the analysis of *A Midsummer Night's Dream*, I hope to have illustrated some aspects of this complexity, thereby making the situated and enactive character of actual empathic engagement more comprehensible (without downplaying the importance of more enduring cognitive and affective structures and processes, which in fact enable that situated, enactive, empathic engagement).

CHAPTER 7

# Evaluating Empathy

A fundamental, often unmentioned premise of work on empathy – including work on literature and empathy – is that empathy is ethically and politically good. This is often just assumed because the case for empathy seems pretty straightforward. If I mistreat someone, I am typically not taking his or her feelings into account; I am certainly not sharing those feelings. There is an intuitive appeal to the idea, manifest in parenting, when the mother or father urges the selfish child to "just think how Sally must feel when you won't share your toys with her."

There are academic arguments in favor of the value of empathy as well. Some of these arguments are indirect. They concern the apparently deleterious consequences of a lack of empathy. For example, disgust and empathy tend to be mutually inhibitory. As Paul Bloom states, "Disgust is the opposite of empathy" (2014, 140). Moreover, he explains that "disgust is a powerful force for evil. If you want to exterminate or marginalize a group, this is the emotion to elicit" (131). If one opposes disgust, then, one favors empathy. For example, Martha Nussbaum analyzes dehumanizing disgust aimed at gays and lesbians. She explains, "Disgust relies on moral obtuseness. It is possible to view another human being as a slimy slug or a piece of revolting trash only if one has never made a serious good-faith attempt to see the world through that person's eyes or to experience that person's feelings" (2010, xvii).[1] More strikingly, Ickes (2009, 62) notes that "violent husbands have an empathic deficit."

There are more direct arguments also, arguments that empathy does good on its own. Vorauer explains that research "found that perspective taking enhanced individuals' recall of an outgroup member's stereotype-inconsistent behaviors and led them to make more internal attributions for

---

[1] Nussbaum is doubly relevant here because she is perhaps the most eloquent supporter of literature as a means of training moral sensibility. In keeping with this, she asks, "How ... do we ever become able to see one another as human?" She replies, "Only through the exercise of imagination" (2010, xvii), later adding that "the capacity for imaginative and emotional participation in the lives of others is an essential ingredient of any respect worthy the name" (xix). For Nussbaum, literature helps make such participation possible.

such behaviors; perspective taking also enhanced their pursuit of stereotype-inconsistent information. Other research has demonstrated that empathy can enhance the perceived injustice of discrimination toward minority group members" (2019, 4). As C. Daniel Batson explains, "The proposal that other-oriented emotion felt for someone in need produces altruistic motivation to relieve that need has been called the empathy–altruism hypothesis." This hypothesis has been extensively researched. Batson summarizes the results: "In the past several decades, more than 30 experiments have tested this hypothesis against various egoistic alternatives. Although still controversial, results have been remarkably supportive of the empathy–altruism hypothesis" (2009, 27). Martin Hoffman cites research indicating that "empathy and empathy-derived emotions ... have been found to motivate some of the Germans who saved Jews from Nazis ..., American Civil Rights activists in the 1960's," and others (2011, 231). Haji puts the point more simply and generally, writing that "empathy is essential to being good persons; its lack is correlated with future bad behavior (whether criminal or immoral), aggressive behavior, and causing pain to others" (2017, 253).[2]

### Humanists against Empathy? Some Recurring Claims

On the other hand, there are criticisms of empathy, both within and outside literary study. One objection that I hear with surprising frequency involves references to "compassion porn" and "voyeurism." Sometimes these references are academic, as when Zembylas refers to "the numerous dangers that have been pointed out about empathy leading to ... Voyeurism" (2012, 120,citing Boler 1999 and Zembylas 2008). Others appear in popular, political, or journalistic outlets, as in the title of a *Village Voice* article on "Oscar-Feted Compassion Porn" (Taylor 2011). Authors using these phrases would perhaps explicitly defend only the banal point that sometimes empathic appeals make us feel happy with ourselves but lead to no real, beneficial change. The rhetoric of the statements, however, suggests something far from banal – that appeal to empathy is really a covert appeal to a sort of voyeuristic desire on the part of recipients, who turn records of trauma into a sort of pornography, while claiming to understand the suffering of the traumatized people they are leering at. Personally, I find this view not only implausible, but distressing. It manifests and rationalizes a form of self-righteousness that can readily demean people who feel genuine compassion and pursue humane goals,

---

[2] Empathy can also have unexpected benefits in other areas. For example, Feshbach and Feshbach (2009, 88) point out that "positive relationships between teacher empathy and indices of academic achievement" have been found in both early education and college.

driven by that compassion. Such rhetoric tends to discredit the entire project of trying to define and in some degree approximate a parallel emotional response to other people's suffering. It thereby risks disabling an important source of motivation for pro-social behavior.

Some problems with these characterizations are immediately obvious. The metaphor of voyeurism, though certainly rhetorically effective, draws implicitly on psychoanalytic ideas about unconscious fantasies and on the expansive psychoanalytic concept of unconscious desire, which (like much else in psychoanalysis) seem either implausible or overgeneralized. Moreover, there does not appear to be any evidence of anything sexual in the vast majority of cases of empathy with trauma victims or others who have experienced severe suffering or oppression. (The authors who make use of these characterizations may not wish to defend the sexual implications of the terms; however, the rhetorical force of the claims relies in some degree on those implications with their associated suggestions of disgust.)

Nonetheless, the argument – or claim – has two significant implications. The first has to do with audience. I do not at all believe that empathic appeals to dominant groups are pornographic or voyeuristic. However, it does seem clear that there will be sometimes profound differences in readers' responses to works, depending on whether they belong to the same group as the victimizers or the same group as the victimized. For example, I was teaching Lillian Hellman's *The Children's Hour* in my undergraduate American literature class. The play concerns two women who are wrongly accused of having a lesbian relationship. The accusation and consequent public hysteria lead to their social isolation and the ruin of the school they run. In the course of these events, one of the women, Martha, realizes that she is indeed in love with the other, who does not reciprocate her feelings. Socially isolated, deprived of her livelihood, and rejected by the woman she loves, Martha kills herself.

I respond to the play as a compassionate representation of the cruelty of homophobia, and a sharp criticism of the hypocrisy of sexual bigots. I probably do get some small boost in self-esteem from my affectionate response to the lesbian character depicted in the play and my identification with her despair over unrequited love, but that seems to me either innocuous or beneficial, not voyeuristic. It is probably the case that this particular work on its own did not have any significant, specific consequences for my practical actions; nonetheless, it forms part of a larger complex of empathic works that have contributed to shaping my outlook and behavior. The entire configuration of works seems likely to have had beneficial effects, even if the consequences of any single work are very slight. However, I had a student who was genuinely disturbed by the play and objected to reading a work that (in her view) said that the only thing a lesbian could do is kill herself. It struck me then that, though the tragedy of the work was not pornographic for me, it was more deeply painful for readers who may have experienced homophobic cruelty and suicidal despair themselves. *The Children's Hour* was an effective political work for one audience, but not for another.

Generalizing the point, we might say that if the implied audience of a novel or play is different from the group whose suffering is being depicted (e.g., if an American slave narrative is written primarily for white people), then it might be designed most appropriately to develop the audience's empathic response. If, however, the two groups are the same (e.g., in a novel about discrimination against women aimed principally at women readers), then one wants to foster a sense of hope (or to combat a sense of despair) and/or to foster solidarity among members of the group. These tasks – cultivating empathy versus cultivating hope and solidarity – are not only not the same; they may even be contradictory in particular cases. They certainly call for different rhetorical strategies.

The second point to be gleaned from the "voyeurism" argument has to do with the emotional complexity of works that seek to cultivate empathy with suffering (rather than – or in addition to – cultivating hope or solidarity). Specifically, the "voyeurism" argument suggests something about the nature of empathy with other people's suffering that allows us to understand empathic processes more fully. The valid point in the argument is that we are indeed attracted to some texts that present us with suffering. We do not simply turn away when we encounter a terrible story of pain. We continue reading, often with increasing absorption.

But this is not a problem with empathy. It is, rather, a version of the so-called "paradox of tragedy" (Ridley 2005, 413). A tragedy represents events that we do not wish to happen and that we find sad. Nonetheless, we enjoy tragedies. How can we possibly enjoy something that we find sad? The paradox of tragedy is related to the so-called "paradox of fiction" (see Feagin 2011, 149). We know a story is fictional. Even so, we experience emotions with regard to its (nonexistent) events – rejoicing in the hero's escape from death, grieving over his or her ultimate demise. I have argued that the solutions to these supposed paradoxes are straightforward (see Hogan 2013, 6–10; 2017; 2022a). Fiction is a form of simulation, the process of imagining unperceived, hypothetical, and counterfactual particulars and particular causal sequences. One of the primary evolutionary functions of simulation is to help us to avoid threats without actually exposing ourselves to the threats. Simulation does this by allowing us to envision the likely consequences of various courses of action. For example, Jones simulates robbing the liquor store but envisions being caught, convicted, and imprisoned, and thus forced into degrading and humiliating conditions. In consequence, he does not rob the liquor store.

But what exactly is it that leads to this avoidance? The effects of simulation are not merely the effects of abstract knowledge, which would make simulation redundant (e.g., since Jones knew about the threat of prison all along). They are, rather, the result of our experience of emotion in response to the simulation. Thus, it is necessary to the evolutionary functionality of simulation that we experience the same sort of emotion in simulation as we would in real life; indeed, a good deal of our putative experience of real life is actually experience of simulation, as we fill in aspects of the world we do not perceive (as when a police officer shoots someone because – tacitly relying on a racist prototype – he thought he saw the victim pulling out a gun). This is consistent with the embodied quality of much of our cognition. When we hear the word "hammer," for example, areas of the premotor cortex connected with the act of hammering are activated (Pulvermüller 2002, 58, 62); when we imagine an object, our patterns of neural activation significantly overlap with those that occur when we perceive the object (see Kosslyn 1994, 295, 301, 325). Our simulations are, so to speak, phantom perceptual experiences. It is hardly surprising that they would foster the same sorts of emotions, presumably through the same means (e.g., the activation of perceptually related emotional memories).

But what about tragedy? Imagine the following situation. We feel emotions of the same sort in simulation as in reality. In order to have their evolutionary function, some simulations must give rise to aversive emotions. We, of course, experience the aversive emotions directly in connection with the simulation. In consequence, we stop the simulation as soon as we begin to experience aversive emotions. But, if we do this, won't it incline us to engage in the risky (unsimulated) actions, thereby undermining the evolutionary function of simulation? For example, suppose Jones simulates the robbery. However, he avoids simulating the possible arrest and imprisonment as soon as that particular causal sequence begins to distress him. Though that initial distress is mild, it is strong enough to lead him to end the simulation, and therefore he does not reach the stage where the aversive force of the simulation is great enough to dissuade him from robbing the liquor store – especially because he continues to simulate what he will do with the money from the liquor store, making the robbery increasingly attractive.

Clearly, then, there must be some impetus to drive the aversive part of the simulation. In other words, I need a motive – thus, an emotion – that will lead me to continue a simulation that has become painful. As it happens, there is evidence that the simulation of other people's suffering involves just such a motive. Specifically, the reward system is activated in compassionate responses to other people's distress (see Kim et al. 2009). The distress we are responding to in those cases is, of course, always in part simulated distress since we never experience the other person's pain directly. The same sort of reward system activation is presumably what provides the motive force for simulating emotionally aversive events or conditions bearing on our own actions and conditions as well. After all, imagining myself in the future involves a form of empathy, just as imagining someone else does. Thus, such reward system activation would seem to be what enables our simulation of aversive, egocentric scenarios (e.g., Jones's simulation of imprisonment) as well as our reading or viewing of tragedies about other people, both real and imagined.

Does this mean that empathy is some sort of paraphilia, rightly denounced by moral invigilators? No, not at all. The pleasure that we experience in such cases – whether concerning ourselves or others – is simply what enables us to consider likely or possible suffering with detailed and sustained attention adequate to produce emotional aversion and thereby to motivate action. It is the evolutionary condition for functional simulation. Is it possible that some people read real stories of trauma and are largely unaffected by their reality, focusing only on the reward system activation and the story's (tragic) pleasures? Of course, it is. But, in that case, the recipients' empathic response is restricted. It bears on the victims only to the extent that their suffering is represented in the story. It does not extend that simulation to their ongoing conditions or to the current misery of others like them, conditions and misery that could in principle be changed. In this way, the evolutionary function of the simulation has been inhibited. This, in turn, suggests the need for enhancing – not repudiating – empathy, continuing it beyond the confines of the story.

It is, of course, also possible that some readers of, say, Holocaust narratives (e.g., Nazis) or other traumatic experiences will not experience aversive emotions at all with respect to the victims. But this, too, is a case of too little empathy, not too much. Specifically, it is a case where the recipient's interpersonal stance is not parallel (thus empathic), but antipathetic or neutral. Here, too, the argument does not oppose but supports the cultivation of empathy.

In sum, these common, psychoanalytically modeled objections to empathy do suggest some features of empathy that we might otherwise have missed. However, they do not provide us with any good reason to reject empathy. Rather, they only further the case for its cultivation.

Another objection to empathy, common in literary study, is based on Bertolt Brecht's idea of epic theater and the *Verfremdungseffekt* ("alienation effect" or "estrangement effect"). According to Brecht, theater has traditionally drawn its audience into an unthinking, emotional identification with a character or set of characters. Brecht's contention is, roughly, that this identification leads to unreflective immersion in the fictional world rather than cultivating our thoughtful response to the real world and its real politics (see Brecht 1992, 986–996). Therefore, the author needs to estrange the viewer from the events, provoking reflection during the work and debate about its issues after the final curtain.

Reformulating Brecht's (1992) ideas in terms of the theoretical principles we have been using, we might say that Brecht is undoubtedly correct that spontaneous identification and empathy often function to support oppressive ideologies and unethical attitudes and actions (e.g., when we automatically empathize with members of a racial or other in-group, at the expense of out-group members). However, there are two problems with his conclusions. First, a play may be developed in such a way as to foster a parallel interpersonal stance and empathy with characters that we might otherwise dehumanize or simply ignore. Thus, the cultivation of unreflective empathy may work against politically and morally objectionable prejudices and toward our sense that oppressive conditions consistent with those prejudices should be changed. Second, if we are fully estranged from the characters, we will probably not care to think or debate about them. We reflect on and discuss the politics and ethics of a work *because* we are emotionally engaged by the work, not despite that engagement. Consequently, we do not need estrangement or "distance" from emotional response, as critics sometimes say. Rather, we need to systematize that emotional response, modulating it in cases of such spontaneous tendencies as emotional bias against out-groups. That is more likely to occur by fostering more complex and varied empathic responses (e.g., fostering empathy with members of out-groups) and by encouraging empathic effort beyond spontaneous and automatic response, rather than by estranging the audience from empathic responses. Here too, then, we find that the anti-empathy argument not only fails to undermine the case for empathy; it rather supports the case for extending empathy.

One of the most cogent defenses of a Brechtian view was articulated in a talk by Joshua Landy at a session on empathy at the 2018 annual meeting of the Modern Language Association (a session in which Paul Bloom and I were the other participants). Landy argues that there are politically committed works that actually block empathy and that may be more effective because of that blocking. Unfortunately, as I write this, Landy's lucid and insightful essay has not been published. Therefore, it is not possible to respond in a definitive way to his arguments. However, I would still venture to make two points in response. First, Landy is concerned with what is likely to produce the best results for society. I, of course, am also concerned with that. However, in this book, I am focusing solely on ethical decisions, not social prudence. (Ethics might have only a very limited role in producing a better society.) In that respect, we are addressing different issues.

The second point I would make in response to Landy concerns *empathy blocking*. Specifically, we may distinguish two general types of case that he categorizes as such. One of these is exemplified by Radio Raheem in Spike Lee's *Do the Right Thing*. I agree with Landy that Lee inhibits empathy for Raheem. However, I believe this is not because empathy is ethically harmful or irrelevant. It is, rather, because Lee is sensitive to the response of his African American viewers. Specifically, many African American audience members are likely to respond with intense feelings of identification when faced with the image of a black man strangled by a police officer. This identification is not only painful, but also likely to provoke debilitating personal distress and to encourage a feeling of despair. Put differently, a large part of his audience already has empathy for black victims of police violence; there is no need to cultivate empathy in this case. On the other hand, this does suggest that dwelling on the target's suffering is likely to become counterproductive after some amount of time. This is an important point; we will return to it in connection with Bloom's (2016) criticisms of empathy.

The other type of empathy blocking identified by Landy is, in my view, not empathy blocking at all. It is, rather, an attempt to avoid a particular sort of empathy blocking. Specifically, it is an attempt to foster empathy for morally imperfect characters, characters whom we would be likely to out-group on moral grounds. For example, Landy refers to Bigger Thomas in Richard Wright's *Native Son*. Wright makes Thomas a rapist and murderer. Landy argues that Wright thereby inhibits our empathy for Thomas. However, in my view, the novel as a whole does develop our empathy for Thomas. The point of making Thomas behave reprehensibly is not to block our empathy for him or African American men in real life (though it is important to remark that the latter is a potential danger of Wright's decision here; as Landy recounts, Baldwin [1955] noted just this). The point, rather, is almost the exact opposite. The point is to expand nonblack readers' empathy beyond angelic out-group members. The risk of a character such as Stowe's Uncle Tom is not that such a character will foster racial subservience (Stowe's character is not "an Uncle Tom," as the phrase is commonly used). It is, rather, that it will extend white readers' empathy only to saintly black men, leaving real human beings without their compassion. (In fairness to Stowe, I should note that she was trying to oppose slavery; in that context, it may have been most effective to cultivate an image of saintly, martyred slaves.)

## False Empathy: Richard Delgado

As Suzanne Keen (2022) has pointed out, one of the most common objections to empathy is that it is often mistaken. This is the "false empathy" problem, perhaps most famously discussed by the legal theorist Richard Delgado. In an engaging fictional dialogue with the legal firebrand "Roderigo," Delgado articulates the problem with interracial empathy, as he sees it. The problem is that, in empathy across races, "a white believes he or she is identifying with a person of color, but in fact is doing so only in a slight, superficial way" (1996, 18). Prima facie, this seems to be a simple issue. White people are not making adequate empathic efforts. They are projecting their own preferences onto blacks. Subsequently, Delgado writes, "False empathy is worse than indifference, Professor. It encourages the possessor to believe he is beyond reproach" (21). But this seems to get the causality wrong. It seems unlikely that having some sort of spontaneous empathic response would lead an otherwise humble, self-critical white person to assume he or she is infallible. It seems much more likely that a white person would begin with an interpersonal stance toward blacks in which he or she views blacks as simple, childlike creatures who can be understood easily. In other words, the paternalism that Delgado rightly criticizes (28) presumably precedes the superficial empathy, fostering that superficiality, rather than deriving from some effort at empathy.

Though Delgado does not address this issue directly, his general argument suggests one possible response. If interracial understanding is genuinely impossible for whites, then in a sense it does not matter whether or not they are self-critical. They are always going to get things wrong. Thus, Delgado writes that "when a white empathizes with a black, it's always a white-black that he or she has in mind—someone he would be like if he were black, but with his same wants, needs, perspectives and history, all white, of course" (1996, 18). The implication seems to be that there is a white perspective and a black perspective, and whites can never adopt the latter. A first, obvious response to this is that no one could possibly know this if it were true because everyone would be trapped in their own race-bound consciousness. But Delgado has a response to this. Specifically, "Most whites lack double consciousness. They have little practice in seeing things two ways at once," whereas blacks do this all the time (19). I should note that this modifies the prior claim since it is not about what whites "always" do, but about "most whites."

At this point, we might isolate two separate issues. First, suppose that white people always – or perhaps mostly – project their own preferences onto blacks. Is this actually worse than a complete absence of empathy, as

Delgado (1996) maintains? Clearly, false empathy is worse than true empathy. If I think you are hungry for steak when you actually want tofu, that is worse than if I think you want tofu. But is it really better if I simply do not bother about whether you are hungry at all? Isn't some effort at empathy better than none? Here, the answer would seem to be that it depends on just how incapable whites are of adopting a black person's perspective. But even that is not clear. If a white supremacist "empathizes" with a black person and bizarrely decides that the black person wants white domination, will that in fact make the white supremacist's behavior any worse than if he or she does not consider what the black person thinks? Won't he or she pretty much just pursue white domination as he or she would have done otherwise – perhaps doing so less efficiently, due to underestimating the opposition? Of course, in some individual cases, the outcomes will be worse. But it seems very unlikely that they will be worse on the whole. Moreover, with even the slightest inclination toward a sincere effort at getting things right – and with even the most otherwise routine, minimal self-criticism – whites should be able to improve their accuracy well above the level of chance. In short, it seems extremely unlikely that white people would act more beneficially if they just set empathy aside entirely – though, of course, they would act more beneficially if they overcame a tendency toward self-certainty. All too often, criticisms of empathy involve arguing in effect that actually existing empathy is harmful, when tacitly contrasted with the alternative of ideal intergroup relations. But in fact, the relevant contrast would lead us to ask, "Would actually existing conditions be improved if we removed empathy?" It seems clear that they would not be improved, but worsened.

The second issue is – just what sort of idea or attitude are we talking about here, and is it really true that nothing can be done to improve empathic accuracy across racial lines? What sorts of interests do blacks have that are inscrutable to whites? Delgado gives the following example: "lawyers working on behalf of black groups would often pursue a strategy favored by the litigation team – say, desegregated schools – when what the client really wanted was better schools, ones with more resources" (1996, 18). But this is strange. Surely, white people are able to understand what a better school would be and what would constitute having more resources. Moreover, it is pretty easy to find out whether this is what any given client wants – you just ask the client what he or she wants. (Of course, the legal system may in effect require the lawyer to pursue desegregation rather than superior funding, in keeping with what Delgado rightly argues later in the chapter. But that has no evident bearing on empathy.)

I entirely agree with Delgado (1996) that whites very often fail at empathizing with blacks. Indeed, I would say that we (humans) like to think well of ourselves. If we are liberal, we like to think that we are empathic. We also like to feel superior to others. Thus, we will often misunderstand others in a self-congratulatory way. Moreover, I agree that this danger is enhanced when the empathic target is an out-group member. However, the problems arise uniformly at those points where empathy is in fact constrained, where a sincere, effortful attempt at empathizing is blocked, typically by unself-critical egoism or out-grouping. Thus, Delgado's arguments too do not serve to dispute empathy; rather, they highlight the problems with common psychological (and social) processes that work against empathy. I should also note that Delgado ends his article by discussing strategies for anti-racist work. Thus, he too raises the issue of what the best strategy would be for changing society. That is obviously a deeply important issue, arguably far more important than the issue of what constitutes a valid moral choice for an individual. However, once again, the present focus on empathy is on ethical value, not on strategic value.

## Cognitive Science against Empathy (I): Jesse Prinz

Despite his criticisms of false empathy and interracial empathy, Delgado (1996) sees empathy as potentially beneficial. Some critics, however, have a more encompassing critique of empathy. Probably the most plausible and well-considered arguments against empathy more broadly have been offered by cognitively oriented philosophers and by cognitive scientists. One influential case against empathy is made by Jesse Prinz. First of all, Prinz distinguishes between taking empathy as foundational for moral judgment and taking empathy as crucial for moral motivation (2010, 213). As to the former, Prinz articulates a series of important general principles that undoubtedly do count against establishing unmodulated, spontaneous empathy as definitive for ethical assessment. For example, "empathy is prone to in-group biases" and "subject to salience effects" (2010, 226, 227). Martin Hoffman explains these biases well, writing that people "empathize more with kin, friends, and their own ethnic group." As to saliency, "people empathize more with victims who are physically present than with absent victims or potential victims" (2011, 251). Again, empathic response is mediated by interpersonal stance, which is to say the attitude we have toward the other person's emotions. As already discussed, that attitude may be parallel (e.g., when he or she is sad, I am sad) or complementary (e.g., when he or she is sad, I feel schadenfreude). Clearly, the former is conducive toward empathy while the latter is not. We tend to begin with a parallel interpersonal stance toward in-group members and a complementary (specifically, antagonistic) interpersonal stance toward out-group members (for research indicating this, see Hein et al. 2010; see also Gazzaniga 2011, 164; Hess 2009, 253–254).

Prinz is right that it is extremely important to acknowledge empathic biases. Among other things, these points respond in a compelling way to some unreflective celebrations of all things empathic. For example, suppose we are faced with a choice between an action that will mildly harm a friend and one that will not harm the friend but will greatly harm some unknown person. Our spontaneous and automatic empathic response might very well lead us to judge the second act more moral, though on reflection most of us would consider the moral value to be precisely the opposite of this. Alternatively, take a real, political – rather than narrowly personal – case. After the 9/11 attacks, Americans had enormous empathy for the victims (e.g., for their terror before dying) and their families (for their grief), as of course they should have. But Americans by and large seem to have had very little empathy for innocent victims of the US "War on Terror." This was in part because the out-grouping of those victims tended to promote a complementary rather than parallel emotional attitude and in part because the experiences of the foreign victims (in Iraq or Afghanistan) were not salient (e.g., we did not generally read their individualized stories). But this means that the responses of most Americans were ethically problematic.

So does this show that empathy is not needed for ethical judgment – indeed, that it may even be harmful? I do not think so. In fact, the examples show the opposite. Empathic responses in these cases were ethically biased. However, in both the personal and political examples, the problem is not that people had empathy for some; it was that they did not have empathy for others. The problem was that they relied on spontaneous and automatic empathy rather than choosing to undertake the effortful process of empathizing with those they would not ordinarily consider, such as strangers and out-group members. It is certainly important that we not assume spontaneous and automatic empathy is unbiased and comprehensive. But that means we need to modulate our spontaneous and automatic empathy through deliberate perspective taking and simulation of other people's experience.

Indeed, effortful empathy is crucial to the process of ethical evaluation. Extended, effortful empathy is the fundamental means by which we determine what constitutes harm and how different sorts of harm compare to one another. Returning to the friend/stranger case above, suppose one action will cause a friend to have a temporary headache, whereas the alternative will cause a stranger to lose a leg. We evaluate the former as less of a harm than the latter, and thus we judge the former action (causing the friend to have a headache) to be less unethical because we have an empathic sense of the suffering caused by each form of harm. I should perhaps note that we do not necessarily need to engage in actual processes of empathic experience in every instance. Sometimes, we have made the relevant judgments in the past and simply return to those judgments, with their sense of relative harm, in the present case. But the past judgment was contingent on empathy at the time. Moreover, its application to the present case requires enough simulation of the stranger's experience to call to mind the relevant past judgments. On the other hand, it is important that it does not require that we dwell on the person's possible pain (a topic to which we will return).

In any case, the point is that Prinz's (2010) argument does not debunk empathy (or nonegocentric, emotional parallelism) as crucial for ethical judgment. Rather, it brings out the importance of modulating spontaneous response precisely by engaging in effortful empathy in ethically relevant cases. As Shoemaker writes in his compelling response to Prinz, "All of the faults cited – in-group bias, preferential treatment, proximity effects, manipulability – are bad things that could be eliminated or mitigated simply by more empathy, by increasing the range of those with whom we empathize.... It's not that empathy itself is bad or causes bad things; rather, it's the incomplete or improper deployment of empathy that does so" (2017, 247).

A similar point holds for the second focus of Prinz's criticism, the importance of empathy for motivation. Here, I need to draw a distinction between what I will call "normative outcomes" and "moral choices." A normative outcome is an event that conforms to some ethical principle, independent of how it came about. In contrast, a moral choice is a decision that conforms to an ethical principle, no matter what its actual result may be. Suppose there is a famine and Jones happens to have stored a great deal of food. Distributing the food to the hungry is a normative outcome; it is a good thing, whether Jones decides to do so freely, hoping to alleviate the people's suffering, or is convinced to do so by an offer of ten times the food's ordinary market price. In contrast, if Jones feels compassion for the people's suffering and determines to distribute the food to alleviate their hunger, he has made a moral choice. It remains a moral choice even if the food ends up not being distributed (e.g., due to a fire in the granary or a robbery).

I agree with Prinz that if our goal is establishing a society with maximum normative outcomes, the cultivation of empathy is probably not the most efficient way of achieving this goal. We are better off passing legislation, including legislation that embodies what Thaler and Sunstein

(2009) call "libertarian paternalism" (which takes advantage of people's tendency not to change a default option, and pretty clearly has little to do with people's moral attitudes and decisions, though it does bear on moral outcomes). Thus, empathy is generally not necessary for motivating moral action in the sense of producing normative outcomes. However, it is, I believe, crucial for moral choice. Again, empathy is precisely what makes a decision not egocentric, which is, I have argued, the definitive feature of moral decision. Of course, empathy is consequential for some forms of normative outcome. For example, in a democracy, it is likely to be important that the populace support legislation aimed at producing normative outcomes. In many cases, it will be important to cultivate empathy in those who do not themselves benefit (egocentrically) from the legislation. This would include much affirmative action policy, disability rights law, and the like. Thus, it is not irrelevant to producing normative outcomes, even if its primary role is in motivating moral choices.

After criticizing empathy, Prinz proposes anger in its place – specifically, the form of anger called "indignation" (2010, 225; for a literary version of Prinz's advocacy of anger, see Sue Kim 2013). He supposes that this would help the "victims" of "economic injustice" (Prinz 2010, 225). But he writes this shortly after citing research indicating that anger promotes an advocacy of "harsher punishments" (221). This suggests an ethics aimed at ending the unmerited pleasures of the rich, rather than ending the undeserved sufferings of the poor. Maybe being angry with the wealthy would eventually help the poor. But for one even to wish to help the poor (as opposed to harming the wealthy or merely helping oneself), one needs to feel compassion for their poverty, not merely anger at, say, the sexual decadence of the feudal aristocracy. In any case, it seems clear that anger is subject to the very same cognitive problems with which Prinz tasks empathy – including in-group and saliency biases. We are much more likely to be angered by salient doing of harm, such as flying airplanes into buildings, than at diffuse and obscured harmfulness, such as causing deaths through embargos (despite the fact that the number of the dead may be vastly greater in the latter case; e.g., see Crosette on Iraq). Moreover, it is clear that the complementary emotional stance toward out-groups fosters anger against them, just as in-group identification fosters empathy. In some cases, anger may intensify anti-racist attitudes among liberals (Banks 2014, 11), though I suspect that this anti-racism is often subject to a rebound effect, with racism increasing for a time after the anti-racism (see Kunda 1999, 344–345). More significantly, Banks argues that "anger is the dominant emotional underpinning of contemporary racism"; indeed, "anger and racial prejudice form such a strong bond that evoking anger should activate this racial belief system from memory" (2014, 3). In other words, at least among conservatives, any form of anger is likely to activate and intensify racism.[3]

In short, Prinz makes a good case that spontaneous and automatic parallelism in emotion is inadequate for ethical action. Indeed, in some cases it may be deleterious. However, his arguments do not appear to hold against effortful empathic processes that modulate spontaneous and automatic tendencies. Indeed, his arguments would appear to suggest the ethical importance of effortful empathy. Moreover, his alternative of anger appears more problematic than spontaneous empathy.[4]

## Cognitive Science against Empathy (II): Paul Bloom

An argument similar to that opposing Prinz can be made regarding Paul Bloom's (2016) *Against Empathy*. This is a rigorous, erudite, and thought-provoking work. I of course disagree with Bloom's assessment of empathy and its role in ethics. However, like Prinz, Bloom shows us a range of problems with the ways in which we often think about these topics. His book is therefore valuable in helping us to formulate a more adequate integration of empathy and ethics.

Part of my disagreement with Bloom is the result of terminological differences, which I should note briefly at the outset. In this case, the differences are not trivial, for they help define what we consider to be alternatives. As discussed earlier, empathy is not simply feeling what the target is feeling. That is how we often talk about it in theorizing about empathy. But it is not how we use the term. Bloom writes, "If you feel bad for someone who is bored, that's sympathy, but if you feel bored, that's empathy" (2016, 40). But this is clearly not how we use the word "empathy" and the associated concept. To return to my previous example, suppose a young child is brought to a concert of Schoenberg's serial compositions. He begins to fidget restlessly shortly after the concert begins. I might infer that he is bored, through theory of mind reasoning. Alternatively, I may simulate his perspective, thereby activating emotional memories of boredom from my own past. In this simulation, I may briefly reexperience a form of the aversive feeling I had when my

---

[3] For a differently focused, but also powerful indictment of the moral consequences of anger, see Nussbaum's (2016) *Anger*.

[4] Jackson offers a more mixed assessment of anger than does, say, Nussbaum (see Jackson 2021, chap. 9). In keeping with Jackson's arguments, it would be unreasonable and ultimately disabling to try to train everyone never to feel or even simply to express anger. However, this does not mean that anger is morally admirable, even in cases where it is expedient for fostering normative outcomes. The preceding, moral problems with anger remain.

class in grammar school went to a concert of the Saint Louis Symphony Orchestra. Even if this occurs, it does not mean that my predominant emotional condition during the current concert is boredom, even at the moment of the simulation. It merely means that my emotional response to the simulation of the child's condition involves my own limited activation of an emotional memory from childhood and, as a result of that, my sense of sharing with the child, in that respect, a negatively valenced feeling derived from the same category of emotion. Again, empathy does involve emotion sharing, but in a way that is usually limited to the valence of a relevantly associated source (e.g., an emotional memory of the same general type); it does not extend to other aspects of the target's emotion, nor is it necessarily predominant or enduring. Indeed, these differences are part of what distinguishes empathy from emotion contagion; I don't "catch" the child's boredom.

As with Prinz, the centerpiece of Bloom's (2016) argument against the ethical value of empathy is that empathy is severely biased. Put in terms of psychological processes, this comes down to an argument against relying on the affect heuristic in moral evaluation (on the affect heuristic, see Slovic et al. 2002). The affect heuristic is, roughly, relying on your gut. Bloom is undoubtedly right that we need to be more empirical, logical, systematic, and self-critical when making decisions about what is an ethical issue and what is right or wrong. Indeed, it is hard to overstate the deleterious consequences of relying on spontaneous emotional response in making ethical evaluations. Consider again an experiment carried out by Thalia Wheatley and Jonathan Haidt (2005). Test subjects were hypnotized to experience a feeling of disgust upon seeing a particular word (e.g., "often"). They were then given stories to evaluate ethically. The test subjects, on average, made harsher ethical judgments of the people and actions when their cue word appeared than when it did not. Worse still, they did not restrict their condemnations to actual cases of ethical misbehavior. In one story, a student council president was reported to have chosen topics for events so that they would be of interest to students and faculty. Of the test subjects who read the version with their cue word (e.g., "often"), one-third condemned the student council president for this behavior (Haidt 2012, 61–63, referring to Wheatley and Haidt 2005), even though there was nothing morally objectionable about it. As this indicates, the affect heuristic is often highly misleading.

As in this case, the majority of biases identified by Bloom (2016) affect spontaneous and automatic empathy. As such, they support arguments against, precisely, spontaneous and automatic empathy, not against most views of the value of empathy in ethics. Advocacy of empathy in ethics is generally an advocacy of *cultivating* empathy for moral purposes, not of relying on whatever empathy we would have felt anyway. Put differently, the entire purpose of advocating empathy is to enhance effortful empathic response, not to remain content with spontaneous, automatic, highly biased empathy, which there is no need to advocate since it occurs spontaneously and develops automatically. Moreover, related to this, as far as I am aware, no significant contemporary theoretician self-consciously advocates spontaneous and automatic empathy as a moral criterion. Indeed, the foundational writers on this topic – David Hume and Adam Smith – recognized the need for what we now call "effortful empathy." As Kauppinen puts it, "Hume and Smith agree that making moral judgments on the basis of empathy involves counteracting some of our natural tendencies. In contemporary terms, it demands a form of emotion regulation: we need to both up-regulate our empathic reaction on behalf of strangers and down-regulate our empathic reaction on behalf of those close to us" (2017, 217). (Actually, I don't believe we need to down-regulate empathy for anyone. We need to compensate for our spontaneous, empathic biases. In addition, we need to recognize that part of our concern for those close to us is egocentric, not empathic.)

Of course, people – philosophers, cognitive scientists, politicians, and others – do often unreflectively use spontaneous empathy as a moral criterion. Bloom helps make us aware of that, and of the very serious problems that go along with it.[5] In an empathically oriented ethical theory, defensible moral criteria should govern where we exercise effortful empathy, rather than being defined by spontaneous and automatic empathy.

This does lead us to a question. How do we decide what is an ethical issue and what is right or wrong for that issue in relation to the goal of fostering empathy? By the criteria of Chapter 1, "A value judgment and associated action are more prototypically ethical to the extent that they oppose egocentric self-interest." This principle does not set the parameters discussed in Chapter 1. Thus, it does not in itself determine the level at which one should forego egocentric self-interest in cases of conflict. Again, an advocate of patriotism would put the relevant level at the nation, whereas an internationalist would set the parameter at humanity as a whole, viewing national commitment as a sort of extended egocentrism. As already noted, I favor the more encompassing alternatives. The range of possibilities is important to maintain in descriptive ethics. However, in normative ethics, I believe a reasonable case can be made

---

[5] Similarly, Daniel Kelly (2011) argues compellingly against the use of disgust – in effect, the contrary of empathy – as a moral criterion (thus, evaluating the immorality of an action by reference to the intensity of disgust it provokes in us). This is probably an even more common and almost certainly more destructive practice.

for breadth of inclusion in setting the scope parameter. As noted in Chapter 1, the anti-egocentric nature of ethical prototypicality would seem to suggest that we should generally include more targets in the scope of our ethical response. In other words, it would seem to suggest that the burden of proof lies with those who would restrict the universality of ethical concerns – in our case, the universality of our empathic efforts. Indeed, it seems to me to suggest that anyone who stops short of the Mahāyāna Buddhist view – exemplified in the bodhisattva's commitment to "all beings" (Keown 2005, 19) – needs to defend that restriction. Just to keep the discussion simple, I will not be treating issues of animal rights, which I certainly support. I will, however, presume that the default scope for moral evaluation – including the moral scope for empathic effort – is (at least) humanity.

To clarify these and other points about the relation between empathy and ethics, we need first to recall some basic elements of ethical deliberation and action. Specifically, there is an information-processing component to ethical decision and action and a motivational component. Motivation or emotion involves a range of elements, including cycles of spontaneous response and modulation. In the case we are considering, the information-processing component directs the modulation of empathy. Specifically, it guides us in the extension of our empathy, the systematic engagement with other people's concerns. That information-processing component may itself be developed in different ways, stressing, for example, intrinsic moral value (as with Kant) or practical effects (as with Utilitarians), as specified in the method parameter. But one thing that makes all the options ethical is the opposition to egocentric self-interest.

Empathy – more precisely, emotional empathy – involves at least two things. First, in order to elicit emotions (by the account of emotion given in Chapter 5), it requires simulation of another person's condition and interests – not merely an abstract inference to what he or she is experiencing, but an imaginative recreation of that experience. Second, this simulation must take place in the context of a parallel interpersonal stance, rather than a complementary interpersonal stance. (Empathic accuracy also requires some degree of emotional congruence or compatibility between empathizer and target, but I will leave that aside.) Again, an ethical appeal to empathy does not leave empathic response to our spontaneous inclinations and their automatic processes. It encourages us to elect to take up other people's points of view, effortfully simulate their experiences, and respond to them from a parallel interpersonal stance. Generalizing such an approach, as just suggested, would appear to respond to many of the biases discussed by Bloom and Prinz. The point is in keeping with Hoffman's views. As Hoffman argues,

> Empathy's limitations are minimized when it is embedded in relevant moral principles. Briefly, the way it works is that the cognitive dimension of a moral principle ... helps give structure and stability to empathic affects, which should make empathic affects less vulnerable to bias. The cognitive dimension should also make moral affects less dependent on variations in intensity and salience of distress cues from victims, and thus it should reduce tendencies toward empathic over-arousal (and under-arousal).
>
> (2000, 216)

Consider, for example, saliency and group identity biases. We spontaneously empathize with people we see, not with people we don't see, and we spontaneously empathize with in-groups over out-groups. These biases are the most obvious targets of the imperative to universalize simulation (extending it to nonsalient cases) and to universalize parallel stance (extending it to out-groups).

But what about, say, time-scale biases? Bloom notes that (spontaneous) empathy is "insensitive to the long-term consequences of our acts" (2016, 9). Indeed, he points out that "achieving long-term goals often requires inflicting short-term pain" (35), which appears to be anti-empathic. But this is all merely part of the generalization process for effortful empathy. Consider prudence. I may act on an immediate impulse or I may defer the impulse, acting prudently. The prudent decision is at least in some cases the result of empathy – empathy with my future self. I simulate what I will feel like in the embarrassing situation where I show up for a panel with Paul Bloom and do not have a paper written.[6] I therefore prudently decide to write the paper beforehand. Ethical considerations are of the same sort. There is no reason why my empathy with another person must be confined to the present. If I empathize with a drug addict, I not only may but should envision the consequences of his or her present acts for his or her future experience, just as I do with myself. Thus, my empathy should bear not only on his or her present suffering, which may be alleviated by going to a dealer and purchasing the drug, but also on the consequences of his or her continuing addiction.

An apparently more complex case comes with nonspecific or currently nonexistent persons. Bloom (2016) indicates that the devastation of climate change may have greater effects on unborn generations than on anyone we know. This would seem to put it beyond the scope of empathy.

But actually, this is less of a problem than it may seem. We simulate the situation of generic passersby or unborn generations all the time. Once we

---

[6] An earlier version of part of this chapter was written for a panel with Paul Bloom.

simulate, we respond emotionally, even though the simulation is fictional or explicitly counterfactual. For example, simulating and empathizing with generic people are far from uncommon. To take a banal example, one day last summer, I stood in a long line in the hot sun waiting to enter the Vatican Museums. The next day, it was about ten degrees hotter. I said to my wife that I would hate to be someone standing in that line today. In imagining their condition, I empathized with unknown, nonspecific people, drawing on my own episodic and emotional memories, just as I do with known, specific people. This sort of process is part of the generalization of effortful empathy that is central to empathic ethics (given my preferred setting of the scope parameter). In keeping with this, Kauppinen emphasizes the importance of "regulating our [empathic] emotional responses to particular cases so that we won't miss the big picture" (2017, 224–225). That "big picture" may be aptly characterized as a concern for "justice," but "our regard for justice itself stems from empathy" (225); in terms of the present analysis, this sense of justice results from effortful empathy that has been generalized.

Of course, it remains true that we are likely to feel a real, known person's suffering more acutely than that of some unknown, generic person. But here too this does not indicate that an advocacy of empathy is wrong. It indicates, rather, that we need to cultivate empathy more assiduously in relation to generic, unknown persons – one task of, for example, dystopian eco-fiction.

The foregoing observations indicate why literature may be of particular ethical value. Literature can provide us with vivid simulations of conditions that would otherwise be difficult for us to imagine. It thus may help us to respond empathically to geographically or temporally distant events (or, in the case of the future, possible events). But here Bloom cites Joshua Landy on the ways in which literature may be unethical, noting that "for every *Uncle Tom's Cabin* there is a *Birth of a Nation*" (2016, 48). Bloom is undoubtedly correct that – to put the point somewhat differently than Bloom – literature does often operate as an "ideological apparatus," disseminating sexist, racist, colonialist, or other unethical ways of thinking. That is why ideological critique is and should be an important part of literary study. Even so, I believe that the plenary simulation that is part of literary creation tends on the whole toward expanding empathy rather than contracting it (a point I have discussed in Hogan 2003, chap. 4). This fits with research suggesting the general empathic benefits of literary study (see Kidd and Costano 2013; Kidd, Ongis, and Costano 2016; Mar, Oatley, and Peterson 2009). As, for example, Paluck's (2009) work in Rwanda has shown, certain sorts of narrative may reduce prejudice against out-groups. Moreover,

Hakemulder's (2000) research indicates that the way we approach that literature (e.g., the degree to which we try to simulate a character's situation) may make an ethical difference as well.

These points are related to Bloom's observation that the story of a specific victim is likely to motivate action, whereas statistics are not ((2016, 89). Bloom sees this as an objection to a stress on empathy in ethics. But I take it to be a statement of the psychological constraints that we are dealing with when we engage in ethical thinking. Thus, I take it as a point in favor of an empathically oriented ethics. The empathic part of such an ethics is motivational – and the research appears to show that such empathic particularity is in fact important for motivation (however much we might wish it were otherwise). Part of what gives literature its ethical value is precisely its painstaking attention to emotionally rich individual cases.

On the other hand, we should not brush aside Bloom's objection that empathy is "innumerate" (2016, 9), simply noting that this gives literature a special ethical role. Innumeracy in ethical response is a complex issue, with a broad range of consequences that are usually deleterious (for insightful discussions of innumeracy, see Slovic and Västfjäll 2015; Västfjäll, Slovic, and Mayorga 2015). But it is not a problem with ethical theory. It is a problem with the actual operation of human ethical motivation, a problem for which I do not have a solution (though others have developed promising strategies; see www.arithmeticofcompassion.org). (Note that the problem of innumeracy remains whether we are "against empathy" or for it.)

However, I might remark on one aspect of the problem here. Unlike Bloom (2016), I do not find it entirely clear that innumeracy is wholly bad. Take the common example, cited by Bloom, of the group hiding from Nazis (I touched on this example briefly in Chapter 1). There is a baby who starts to cry. Should we suffocate the baby to save the others? Maybe. But at the very least we should feel that it is wrong to do so, even if we also feel that it is wrong not to do so. Our empathy for the adults should not simply extinguish our empathy for the child, nor should our moral obligations to the former annihilate our moral obligations to the latter. Among other things, we do not want to foster a society in which the killing of innocents for a greater good is emotionally easy.

Indeed, if I concretely imagine myself in the situation, I both believe and hope that I would try to prevent the child from being suffocated, especially if suffocating the child would benefit me personally. One crucial problem here recurs in a wide range of such tests of ethical intuition. The question specifies something with absolute certainty that we in fact never know with certainty – and usually not even with reasonable confidence. In a real situation, we do not know that the crying child will draw the Nazis or that killing the child would keep the Nazis from finding the people. The question simply stipulates those conditions. Whether or not this tells us anything about how we should behave in such idealized conditions, it doesn't tell us much of anything about real conditions. (It probably doesn't even tell us about the idealized conditions since, if we have prophetic capacities, we should have used them earlier to learn when the Nazis would arrive and where they would be looking for us.)

Another case raised by Bloom (2016) concerns physicians and empathy. Suppose I am seeing my neurologist. He remembers his father's decline with Parkinson's disease and feels overwhelming grief at my diagnosis with that illness. I want advice and treatment, but he sits there weeping. This shows that empathy is just what we do *not* want from physicians.

Or does it? Consider another scenario, a real one. I am speaking with my neurologist and the issue of dementia arises, for reasons unrelated to my illness. I remark that, fortunately, dementia is not inevitable in my case since my illness is tremor-predominant. He responds that I am mistaken and that it is indeed inevitable. In fact, from what I can tell, the research on Parkinson's disease and cognition does not warrant certainty of doom (if nothing else, I could be run over by a bus beforehand). More importantly, there is considerable research showing that even unsupported optimism about health outcomes improves those outcomes (see Ryff and Singer 2009, 1092). Does he have no sense of the likely impact of his pessimistic claim? Even if the claim had been indisputably accurate, the most minimal empathic effort should have produced a response along the following lines: "Well, it is not inevitable, and we will of course do all that we can to try to prevent it. But it does become very likely in late stages of Parkinson's disease, so you should keep that worst-case scenario in mind when planning for your future medical coverage." Here, empathy would have been not only humane, but it also would be likely to be therapeutically beneficial. In keeping with this, Halpern argues that empathy "makes for more effective medical care" (2012, 231). In a related vein, Doyle, Hungerford, and Cruickshank explain that "there is a strong correlation between high scores in empathy and clinical competence in nursing students" (2014, 1069) and that "poor patient outcomes are achieved when the behaviour of nurses lacks empathy" (1070). Contrary to what Bloom indicates, Nortvedt contends that "the empathic physician may ... profit from increased diagnostic accuracy" (2016, 276). Drawing on his own "background in intensive care medicine and anaesthesiology," Nortvedt goes on to explain: "Empathy with the patient in a particular situation has two important bearings upon medical therapy. It alerts and fine tunes clinical observation by raising awareness of alterations in the clinical condition. Secondly, a clinician who is empathically concerned is also motivated to conduct further clinical examinations" (2017, 278).

What is the difference between these hypothetical and real neurologists, then? The difference, I believe, is that the case of the weeping neurologist is not empathy at all, but either emotion contagion or a product of personal distress related to the doctor's loss of his father. It is an *egocentric* response. Though emotion contagion, personal distress, and empathy are closely related, it is crucial to keep them distinct conceptually. Emotion contagion and personal distress are not anything that an empathic ethics sets out to enhance and systematize.

In short, Bloom (2016) raises many important issues bearing on emotion, empathy, and ethical evaluation and action. However, his arguments "against empathy" appear to bear only on spontaneous empathic response and automatic empathic processes. Indeed, as such, they are not really against empathy at all, but rather *for (more) empathy*. Specifically, his arguments appear most obviously to provide a case for an elective expansion of empathy through effortful processes.

*Empathy and Ethical Motivation*

To recapitulate some of the points thus far, I might first recall that empathy is a process that begins with simulation of a target's emotional experience, which leads to localized, allocentric emotion sharing with that target. The emotion sharing is usually confined to valence, itself commonly derived from relevant emotional memories (i.e., emotional memories of the same type as the experiences of the target, such as the death of a loved one), and enabled by a parallel interpersonal stance. The localized emotional sharing is subject to modulation. That modulation may proceed by reference to such factors as reasonableness of the target's feeling (e.g., consider, the internet meme of the child in Norway weeping wretchedly because his parents refuse to grow pineapple trees in their yard). This process leads to some degree of care, depending in part on one's relation to the target. This in turn inclines one to take some ameliorative action.

An empathic ethics advocates (or should advocate) the effortful expansion of empathic simulation across space and time, beyond spontaneous and automatic processes. It stresses the importance of overcoming biases – such as those derived from saliency or identity categorization – and extends to generic and nonexistent persons. Finally, the nature of empathic biases suggests that the concrete simulations fostered by literature may be particularly valuable means of developing empathy ethically; the last point extends to such motivationally difficult areas as ecology.[7]

My contention about empathy's role in ethical behavior, then, is as follows. Again, we do not do anything without the activation of an emotion-motivation system. That activation may be egocentric or allocentric. Egocentric motivations, rationally considered, may turn out to be all that we need for a humane society. However, egocentric motivations do not yield moral choices (though they may lead to normative outcomes). Insofar as we are concerned with moral choice, we are concerned with allocentric motivations. It follows that ethical actions must involve some sort of allocentric motivation. The obvious case of allocentric motivation is empathy. There are other possibilities, such as obedience to the will of God or a ruler. But it seems likely that these are usually, perhaps always, based in part on egocentric fears of punishment. Empathy is perhaps the only case of a necessarily allocentric motivation; if a response is not allocentric, it is not a case of empathy, however much it might initially seem to be such.

It is not clear to me what Bloom's (2016) view of ethical motivation might be. At some points, he appears to place a lot of faith in reason alone without the involvement of any emotion-motivation system. At other points, he supplements reason with compassion. But I am not sure I understand what he means by compassion. Suppose for the moment that I have no experiential sense whatsoever about what Jones is feeling; though I have the abstract knowledge that it is aversive, I have no aversive emotional experience that I connect with Jones's experience. For example, suppose Jones is disabled and has dropped something that he cannot pick up. (This is the sort of situation experimenters sometimes contrive.) By the terms of the thought experiment, I do not in any way connect with this since I have never been disabled and no relevant memories have been activated (e.g., memories of dropping something that I could not reach). I feel nothing at all like what Jones is feeling; I do not, even briefly, share his feeling of frustration. In keeping with this, I have no aversive emotional experience that would be altered by a change in Jones's emotion (as I infer it). I may pick up the item anyway, simply as a matter of training or habit. I am walking by; Jones drops something; I automatically pick it up.

---

[7] The ethics of ecology are particularly relevant to the scope parameter. Empirical research indicates that "the extent to which individuals identify with 'the world as a whole'" is "associated with increased contributions to global (as opposed to local) shared resources" (Brewer 2017, 104). In the case of climate change, such global awareness and commitment are imperative.

But suppose I do not do it automatically. What would lead me to help Jones, even in a trivial case such as this? Prinz mentions a range of emotions that may promote ethical action. In some cases, this is merely action that conforms to moral criteria, whatever one's motive might be (e.g., if one performs the act as part of a strategy to achieve eternal life in Heaven). However, as already noted, my focus here is not on normative outcomes, but on moral choices – thus, actions that are not motivated by egocentric concerns. Of the emotions mentioned by Prinz, "concern" (2010, 211) and "guilt" (221) would be obvious candidates for allocentric motivators. But what fosters concern and guilt? Suppose I am concerned about Doe. Perhaps Doe is ill. Does my concern arise independent of empathy? For that to happen, I would have to have genuine, emotional concern about Doe (i.e., my "concern" could not simply be a matter of politely following the convention of "expressing" concern, even though I am indifferent). However, this feeling of concern would have to be independent of me experiencing a negatively valenced emotion with regard to Doe's illness, a negatively valenced emotion derived from emotional memories of the experience of being sick and a sense that this is the sort of painful experience Doe is undergoing right now. In effect, I would have to have no emotional relation to Doe's sickness. Perhaps I am simply lacking in imagination. However, I find it impossible to imagine what such concern would be like. I do not believe I have ever felt this type of concern for another person, a type of concern that is insulated from empathy. (Of course, I have felt egocentric concerns related to other people, but again those are not our topic here.)

Guilt is somewhat more complicated. However, I believe that complication is largely a matter of the ambiguity of the term. Ultimately, I agree with Hoffman that guilt is one of the "empathy-derived emotions" (2011, 231). Specifically, I feel guilty because I hurt someone – or at least that is the prototypical case. As Tangney and Tracy explain, "there appears to be a special link between guilt and empathy" (2012, 449). Indeed, "research also indicates that at both the state and trait level, guilt and empathy go hand in hand" (449). In addition, "Proneness to guilt consistently correlates with perspective-taking and empathic concern" (449). Similarly, Pinker cites research showing that guilt "goes hand in hand with empathy." In addition, "More empathic people are also more guilt-prone ... and it is the targets of our empathy who engage our guilt" (2011, 581).

The relation between guilt and empathy is bound up with the distinction between morality and social convention. Blair and Blair explain, "Healthy individuals distinguish moral and conventional transgressions" – for example, murder in the former case and cross-dressing in the latter case – "from the age of 39 months ... and across cultures" (2009, 142). They go on to cite research indicating that "it is the presence or absence of victims that distinguishes moral from conventional transgressions." In keeping with this, "moral transgressions can be associated with the distress (fear, sadness) of the victim and are more likely to elicit empathy induction by caregivers." Finally, moral transgressions are distinctively associated with "guilt."

Prinz responds to this connection between guilt and empathy when he asserts (rightly) that I might feel guilty even if my "victim" is not hurt (2010, 235). But that response is inadequate. Even brief reflection would lead us to realize that guilt bears on both perceived and simulated harm. When the harm has not occurred and we recognize this, we may modulate our feeling of guilt downward. However, our modulatory processes may also involve recognizing that our behavior very well might have caused harm, and could do so in the future, if we do not alter that behavior. This is simply part of the way that all forms of regret – including guilt – function (in evolutionary terms). For example, suppose I do something rash that might have gotten me killed. I learn from my mistake, in prudential regret, precisely because I have an emotional aversion to the harm that I might have suffered, even though such harm did not in fact occur. If this were not the case, my ability to learn from mistakes would be severely restricted. The same point applies to (empathic) guilt.

*Empathy versus Compassion and Care?*

As already mentioned, Bloom's argument in some degree rests on the difference between empathy and compassion. Specifically, Bloom (2016) maintains that compassion is differentiated from empathy as *feeling for* is differentiated from *feeling with*. Those phrases can certainly be used to mark a difference, and a significant one. But it is difficult to say just what that entails. For example, suppose Doe has left his drug rehabilitation program and scored some heroin. He shoots up and is euphoric. I witness Doe's action and feel utterly abysmal. Clearly, I am not "feeling with" in the sense of sharing his feeling at that moment. Thus, as Bloom is using the terms, I feel compassion, not empathy.

So, case closed. Empathy is bad. It would lead me to procure heroin for Doe.

No, not quite. I feel abysmal for Doe precisely because I am able to simulate the outcome of his most recent act. I do not envision Doe as remaining blissful for very long. Quite the contrary. And just what is it that I am feeling when I simulate the misery of Doe in the future? The obvious answer is empathy. Indeed, it is difficult to view my response to the simulated future Doe as anything other than empathy. Thus, compassion does not appear to be separable from empathy in practice. Here, as elsewhere, Bloom's points are instructive. They indicate that it is important not to confine empathy to present experience. We need to recognize the central importance of matching our emotional response with the target as he or she is likely to be in the future, just as we do with ourselves in prudential deliberation. But such matching shows again that empathy is crucial, despite Bloom's claims.

In connection with this, Bloom recounts studies that he says resulted in "the surprise of the investigators" (2016, 138). It turns out that if you ask test subjects to concentrate on being empathic, neuroimaging scans show activation in areas associated with the experience of pain, such as the anterior cingulate cortex (64, 139). So if you try to share someone's pain, activation increases in areas of your brain that are associated with pain. People who have this experience also tend to dislike it (just as they generally dislike pain). In contrast, when instructed to "feel positive and warm thoughts toward a series of imagined persons" (139), parts of the reward system, such as the ventral striatum, are activated (139). Moreover, people rather like this experience (just as they generally like reward). I must say that I am baffled by the idea that these results surprised the investigators. They seem to be precisely the results one would expect. Moreover, these results do not seem to lead us to cheer for compassion and recognize that empathy is some sort of villain that, for the first part of the story, we were deceived into believing was a hero (somewhat like Elizabeth's attitude toward Wickham in *Pride and Prejudice*). Indeed, they appear quite consistent with the view I have been advocating. Specifically, the warm thoughts suggest the adoption of a parallel interpersonal stance, whereas the aversion to pain suggests why we would want the target of our warm thoughts/parallel interpersonal stance not to feel pain.

Indeed, the "compassion training" Bloom (2016) describes would seem to play a role in extending our inclination to adopt a parallel interpersonal stance (though Bloom does not treat it in these terms). The research itself does not directly address this. But the goal of the training seems to be something roughly along these lines. It is worth noting that this clarifies what is at issue between Bloom, on the one hand, and Christov-Moore and Iacoboni, on the other. Christov-Moore and Iacoboni claim that empathy is a source of compassion. Bloom indicates that the experiments show the contrary. In fact, they are using "compassion" in different, though related, senses. For Bloom, compassion is "feel[ing] positive and warm thoughts" (139), which may (in my account) help to foster a parallel interpersonal stance. For Christov-Moore and Iacoboni, compassion is a (parallel, in my account) response to someone else's suffering. Developing an interpersonal stance precedes empathy for a target's pain – which in turn precedes engaging in ameliorative action to curtail that pain.

A second point that is suggested by the positive quality of Bloomian compassion is something that should have been obvious to everyone, but perhaps was not. Specifically, empathy is not an intense and detailed meditation on the target's misery, something like the spiritual exercise of imagining the suffering of Jesus on the cross as undertaken by some Christians. In other words, one might imagine a conception of empathy along the following lines. The difference between spontaneous and effortful empathy (in this conception) would be that the latter consists in dwelling morosely on the sufferings of the target of one's feelings. Such a conception might be reinforced by reading literary works that try to foster our empathy by dwelling on the torment of slaves, concentration camp inmates, or other brutalized people. In contrast, one might conceive of compassion as involving a focus on improving the target's condition. If one has something like this in mind, then of course "compassion" is superior to "empathy." But that only means that dwelling on someone's suffering, with no attention on how to mitigate it, is less productive than considering positive responses to the person's suffering. Moreover, as this phrasing suggests, one still needs to account for the "compassionate" person's motivation – which, it seems, would necessarily involve empathy (in the sense of shared valence from a related source, not in the sense of committing oneself to a course of depressive brooding).

To clarify the point, we might think of egocentric emotion. Suppose I am suffering myself, rather than considering someone else's pain. Brooding on my misery and sighing "woe is me" will not constitute a productive response to my problems. I am much more likely to do something beneficial for myself if I do not allow myself to be overwhelmed but instead "take care of myself." However, this does not mean that I am not motivated by my current (or simulated, prospective) discontent. Put differently, experiencing either egocentric or empathic emotion involves an emotion episode. Emotion episodes proceed from elicitors to actional outcomes. If I brood on elicitors, rather than focusing on outcomes, the results are likely to be bad in both allocentric and egocentric cases. The main difference between self-focused and empathic emotions is that, for the latter, I need to sustain sensitivity to the other person's pain even when that pain is not clearly present to me. Typically, this is less of an issue for oneself (most of us are excruciatingly aware of and motivated by our own pain), though it does enter importantly in future discounting, where I ignore long-term consequences for myself, as future pain is not salient for me now. (On future discounting, see Dunning [2012, 260] and Ahmed [2020].)

The issues here arise with particular force in areas such as medicine, on which we touched earlier. As Parkinson points out, "issues of empathy regulation come to the fore in the caring professions" (2019, 309), as constant experience of others' pain may lead to a loss of empathy through "burnout" (311). But this is not a special problem about empathy. Rather, empathy is like any other sort of moral concern in being open to prudential restriction. We would not say that it was immoral of Smith to violate his promise of bringing his daughter ice cream if it would have resulted in him risking his life. The point is particularly obvious in cases where the prudential restriction itself has moral consequences. This is why it is both prudent and moral for some people – for example, physicians and nurses – to seek to modulate their empathic responses when it appears that they might otherwise suffer compassion fatigue. On the other hand, this modulation is to some extent produced automatically by the shift from brooding to consideration of ameliorative responses. Indeed, Parkinson suggests the connection with (excessively, and thus imprudently) brooding over one's own problems. Specifically, he characterizes (excessive) dwelling on pathos by doctor and patient as "co-rumination" (2019, 319).

Robert Sapolsky draws on some of the same research cited by Bloom to make a case similar to Bloom's. Sapolsky acknowledges that "most of us typically require moments of piercing, frothing shared pain to even notice those around us in need" (2017, 551). This is an important admission in part because it points to a key difference between real-life situations and experimental conditions. In the latter, ordinary preoccupations are set aside as one cannot pursue ordinary goals, so the issue of motivation becomes potentially far less consequential. As a result, one might do a broad range of benevolent things in an experiment that one would not do in ordinary life, absent significant incentives.

Even having granted this, Sapolsky still concludes that "a fair degree of detachment is just what is needed to actually act" (2017, 551). But, as with Bloom's claims, this does not appear to be quite the right conclusion, unless "detachment" simply means that our response should be allocentric (i.e., empathic), not egocentric (i.e., a matter of emotion contagion). It seems much more plausible to interpret the research as telling us that it is best not to brood exclusively on the target's pain, forgetting about the question of how to mitigate that pain. Rather, in order to respond adequately to other people's suffering, we need to do three things. First, as I have emphasized from the outset (though without recognizing the possible benefits of compassion training), we need to cultivate the capacity and inclination to adopt a parallel interpersonal stance toward others. Second, we must develop empathic sensitivity to the target's experience. Again, this empathic response is what motivates subsequent ameliorative behavior. Finally, we need to think about actional outcomes that could sustain the other person's positive experiences and alter his or her aversive experiences, especially in the long term. Note that even a parent with a strong attachment bond with his or her child will act to aid the child only if he or she is motivated by a sense that the child is in pain and only if he or she (i.e., the parent) is not simply brooding on the pain, but determining what to do about it.

Bloom seeks to bolster his opposition to empathy by invoking Buddhism, explaining that Buddhism opposes "sentimental compassion" to "great compassion," and asserting that the former, dispreferred option "corresponds to what we would call empathy" (2016, 138). But this seems misleading. In her discussion of Buddhist views on empathy and compassion, McRae explains that "there is a deep recognition in Indo-Tibetan ethics of the moral significance of one's ability to 'resonate' or 'feel one's way into another' and no shortage of ethical practices of role taking, 'inner imitation,'" and related practices (2017, 123). She continues, "In these practices, empathetic imaginative projection is cultivated as a central moral and spiritual skill that provides a foundation for two pillars of Mahayana Buddhist ethics" (124). Specifically, effortful empathy is the condition for compassion. As McRae puts it, "In Mahayana Buddhist ethics compassion (karuna, snying rje) is a complex moral virtue that includes being sensitive to and feeling with the suffering of others combined with the desire to alleviate that suffering and acting in accordance with that desire when possible" (2017, 125). Presumably, Buddhist teachers would direct practitioners to experientially understand others' suffering with adequate accuracy about the kind and intensity of that suffering, but they would also stress the necessity of turning to ameliorative actions. In keeping with this, McRae explains that "empathy is the moral skill, roughly understood as 'feeling with another'; compassion is the emotional and conative response to the suffering" (125). (I might add that, in McRae's account, the Buddhist stress on empathy and compassion involves opposition to moral out-grouping along with other forms of out-grouping; in "Indo-Tibetan Buddhist ethics, all suffering beings are proper objects of compassion, regardless of their criminal or moral history" [2017, 130].)

A final point about Bloom's criticism of empathy concerns the actional outcomes that empathy gives rise to. He cites research showing that empathy tends to make people more punitive (2016, 195). This is probably not the outcome that most advocates of empathy would support. It is certainly not the outcome I would favor. Of course, in some cases, greater punishment may be salutary. For example, if rapists commonly go unpunished, then advocating some punitive deterrent is likely to be the most humane way to proceed – humane in that, if it operates as a deterrent, it will benefit at least some women in the future (and even arguably benefit the men who would be deterred from committing such an act). But, in general, our society is far too punitive (see Bruce Waller 2011, 244–247, 293–300; punishment is intrinsically objectionable and instrumentally often ineffective or actually deleterious). So, on the whole, it would seem that we should decrease rather than increase punitive inclinations.

What might be going on in the developments cited by Bloom (2016)? First of all, it is clear that empathic involvement in these cases does not include extending effortful empathy to all parties. If I consider how much Jones suffered when he was defrauded of his life savings by Smith, I am likely to share or even intensify his anger against Smith. Spontaneous and automatic empathy, especially when restricted by moral out-grouping, can readily tend toward what Lukianoff and Haidt refer to as "vindictive protectiveness," the tendency to "shame others for small things ... deemed to be insensitive ... to members of a group that" one sees oneself as "standing up for" (2018, 10).[8] Thus, in the hypothetical case just mentioned, I am likely to morally out-group Smith. Thus, my interpersonal stance toward Smith is likely to be antipathetic. Of course, I understand why Jones would object to engaging in effortful empathy with Smith, just as I understand – in a general, human way, though not in experiential detail – how a victim of sexual assault may object to engaging in effortful empathy with a rapist, a Holocaust survivor may object to engaging in effortful empathy with a Nazi, and so on. Moreover, I would agree that such empathizing can be a problem in cases where it displaces empathy with the actual victims of the person's crimes or the potential victims of future crimes of the same sort (i.e., the crimes we wish to deter). However, I take it to be a fundamental ethical principle that everyone merits empathy, that everyone merits a sincere attempt to understand and respond non-antipathetically to their conditions and beliefs. This does not mean supporting their beliefs or goals or abandoning efforts at deterrence. It means treating these people, in Kant's terms, as ends in themselves, and not only as means – means to my moral self-congratulation, means to the victim's revenge, or even means to the deterrence of future crime. Note that this does not imply that one cannot pursue any goals that treat someone in part as a means. While self-congratulation and revenge, though comprehensible, are likely to be tendencies that we would not wish to encourage, we clearly do wish to pursue deterrence; indeed, by any usual moral criteria, we are obligated

---

[8] It is important to emphasize here that the tendency is not at all confined to left liberals, as Lukianoff and Haidt appear to suggest. Indeed, it seems more prominent, or at least more violent, on the political right, as we have seen in recent conflicts over the Black Lives Matter movement, such as when a white vigilante shot protestors in the name of protecting property.

to do so. Nor does the Kantian principle entail that we cannot use the person in question as a means to achieving such goals. The maxim states only that I cannot ethically treat him or her *only* as such a means. In other words, I can treat a human being as a means to a given end only if I maintain respect for his or her basic dignity.

In any case, whether or not one agrees with my Kantian universalizing, the point here is simply that, once again, insofar as punitive tendencies are a problem, they do not result from too much empathy. Rather, they result from too little empathy. Or, rather, they result from a failure to pursue a program of empathic ethics fully. Once more, they are the product of spontaneous and automatic empathy and its biases, prominently biases of identity categorization and out-grouping.

### False Empathy and Failed Empathy

Perhaps the two most obvious objections to empathy are the straightforward points that sometimes it is false and sometimes it is absent entirely (on the basic ideas of false and failed empathy, see Keen 2010). We have already touched on the former in examining Delgado's (1996) arguments. But both merit fuller consideration.

It is often obvious, even painfully obvious, that our empathic responses are fallible, sometimes going far wrong. Even in the best cases, our response is never perfect down to specifics. But it also seems clear that sometimes we are about right in our inferences and simulations regarding other people's emotions (e.g., the child really is frightened by the dog), even if there are other times when we are obviously wrong (e.g., the person to whom you told the joke may have said nothing, but was, like Queen Victoria, not amused). The fact that we sometimes get things badly wrong cannot count as a general argument against empathy. If it did, then by the same token our mistakes in reasoning would count against the employment of reason; our mistakes in judgment would count against judging anything, and so on. As Matravers points out, "absence of true beliefs will hamper us in many of our projects, empathy included." But the consequences of this are quite banal. Thus, Matravers continues, "all we can do is to work to ensure that we are as well informed as we can be" (2017, 95).

Things would be different only if our empathy were generally false. Now, it may sometimes appear as if it is generally false. But that is because we take theory of mind success for granted and pay attention only when the smooth flow of interaction is interrupted, when mistakes occur. In actuality, our empathic processes have to operate pretty well for them to have provided a selective advantage in evolution. As Ta and Ickes point out, citing empirical research, "although it is true that we cannot have direct access to other people's minds and achieve a perfect knowledge of what they are thinking and feeling, we can – and do – achieve a limited knowledge that is often 'good enough' to sustain successful relationships with them" (2017, 360). As Shoemaker puts it, "one may need only rough or partial understanding." For example, "while one may not be able to understand what it's like to be a soldier, say, one may nevertheless be able to understand what it's like to be in danger" (2017, 245).

This does not mean that we should simply ignore false empathy. In fact, we need to be aware of the problem of false empathy, what gives rise to errors, and how we might respond to those errors. The most obvious source of empathic error occurs when we make mistakes in inference, due either to erroneous premises (e.g., factual errors about the target's interests or capacities) or to processing mistakes (e.g., in logical deduction or statistical estimation). The most pernicious forms of erroneous premises are most likely due to out-grouping biases, prominently stereotyping. The most common forms of processing mistakes are probably the result of heuristic biases – cognitive shortcuts that work well enough to serve an adaptive function, but that are far from infallible (on such biases and heuristics, see Gilovich, Griffin, and Kahneman 2002). For example, one such shortcut is the "availability heuristic" (see Kahneman 2011, chap. 12). When tasked with judging the frequency of a certain type of event, we are not usually able to engage in an actual statistical analysis. One way in which we judge such frequency is by reference to how readily instances of the type come to mind. If I can readily remember instances of airplane crashes but do not easily recall instances of train wrecks, I will be inclined to conclude that the former are much more frequent – thus, probably more of a real danger – than the latter.

Both false premises and processing errors are real issues in our empathic relations with other people. Neither suggests a particular problem with empathy as such, as they will continue to be problems whatever our approach to ethics may be (e.g., they distort nonempathic reasoning in connection with Prinz's favored emotion of indignation). However, they do call for our response. Strategies in both cases are fairly clear, though often difficult to implement. In both cases, they are largely a matter of modulatory processes, our self-conscious attempts to alter spontaneous operations. With regard to stereotyping, we may seek to substitute individuating information (which tends to supplant stereotypes; see Holland et al. 1986, 219, 221). We may also might try to counterbalance stereotypes by seeking to recalculate our inferences in compensatory ways (e.g., by self-reflectively evaluating what we would have inferred if the target had been, say, a man rather than a woman). Our strategies would be much the same in the case of cognitive heuristics.

Note that corrective inferences are likely to rely on a prior knowledge of our stereotypes and heuristics. That prior knowledge will be consequential only if we recognize that the inferential problems are not solely to be found in what other people think about us, but in what we think about them as well. In that way, inferential errors are frequently instances of another problem – inadequate self-criticism. Our empathic response to others, both cognitive and affective, should be qualified by a sort of humility. This is not self-deprecation or shame. It is simply an acknowledgment of our fallibility. In this way, humility becomes an important part of ethics, principally because it is necessary for any progress in responding to the problem of false empathy.

Of course, false empathy does not stop with erroneous inferences. It also encompasses misguided simulations, and these are almost certainly more important for emotional empathy in most cases. Again, simulation may be understood as comprising broad principles of human cognition (principles that define general types of causal sequences in folk physics, and so on) together with parameters (that define the particularity). In empathic simulation, the parameters may be roughly divided into two sorts. Some bear on the target himself or herself; others bear on his or her situation. Thus, when we simulate someone else's point of view, we need to shift these parameters to his or her (rather than my) interests, dispositions, knowledge, and so forth, as well as his or her (rather than my) circumstances. Suppose I want to understand Jones's feelings on unexpectedly coming face-to-face with Smith at a departmental party. I have to shift from my physical situation to Jones's, where he sees Smith and sees that Smith sees him and then realizes that he has to engage in some sort of interaction with her. I also need to shift my own inclinations and interests as a distant acquaintance to Jones's perspective as Smith's former romantic partner.

Several things can go awry in simulation. First, we can set the parameters erroneously (e.g., I might have somehow mixed up Smith with Jones's actual former partner, Doe). This is more or less the same problem that we encountered with inference and can be treated in the same way. A second problem is that sometimes our parameterization of the principles is inadequately extensive or fine-grained. Think again of Sally trying to comfort Billy by offering him her teddy bear rather than his own. One way of construing her error is that she does not see the comforting object as variable (comforting object = $x$, where $x = f(target)$), but as constant (comforting object = my teddy bear). This is a deficiency in parameterization. Sometimes deficiencies in parameterization result from a lack of reflection, sometimes inadequately diverse personal experience, and sometimes limited cultural experience.

In each of these cases, even that of limited reflection, the problem usually cannot be solved simply by thinking about the topic more. Typically, we need something to spur our thought about other people's interests, dispositions, and so forth. Philosophy, psychology, and other disciplines can and do advance our understanding in this area. However, I suspect that literature plays a particularly important role. Literature can lead us to imagine a range of characters that vary from one another and from ourselves in fine-grained, nuanced ways. It can also expose us to something approximating the lived experience of other cultures. As such, literature seems particularly likely to encourage the parameterization of previously fixed parts of our imagination, leading us from assuming that everyone is the same on some trait, and leading us to recognize that people may follow the same basic principle but instantiate that principle differently.

To take a very simple example, for which we do not need literature, as a child, I might start out believing that everyone takes Sunday to be a special, religiously oriented day. I may subsequently learn that there are actually two hierarchized parameters here. First, a person may or may not take one day of the week as spiritually distinctive. Second, if he or she does take there to be such a day, it may be any day, though Friday, Saturday, and Sunday appear particularly common.

A final problem that occurs in simulation does not concern the target so much as the empathizer himself or herself – or, more accurately, the relation between the empathizer and the target. It may simply be that my personal experiences do not adequately prepare me to respond to a target in an emotionally congruent way. This is one source of our underestimation of other people's pain – or, more generally, our misunderstanding of that pain, since we also make errors about our own suffering (e.g., test subjects often judge their own past or even current medical conditions as more distressing than they in fact were or are; see Kahneman 2011, 406). We try to imagine what slavery or the Holocaust was like, but our experiences are too limited. Drawing on work by Kendall Walton, Matravers explains that, "it is likely that the gap between ourselves and the targets with whom we are attempting to empathize will be smaller if we have been in the target's situation ourselves" (2017, 101). Here, again, humility is crucial. The most important thing is recognizing the constraints on our simulative capacities. However, we can also try to achieve a somewhat more adequate understanding of experience distant from our own, in part through the detailed, imaginative exercises we find in literature.

A problem apparently more severe than false empathy is failed empathy. There is an empathy failure when someone should feel empathy – or perhaps should engage in pro-social, caring behavior – but does not. This too has several possible sources, some of which are the same as those of false empathy. These include misinformation and inferential errors, which we would treat in the same way as inferential errors in false empathy. Sometimes, empathy fails simply because we have relied solely on our spontaneous response and have not undertaken the effort to infer the details of a target's experiences, to set parameters appropriately, and to simulate his or her condition and experiences concretely. Again, the entire point of advocating an ethical development of empathy is to foster that sort of effort.

More significantly, an absence of empathy is perhaps most often a result of a nonparallel interpersonal stance, itself commonly derived from out-grouping through identity categories, including moral identity categories (good *us* versus bad *them*). Here, we undertake the usual ways of challenging identity categories – for example, by stressing the individuality of the targets and/or shared humanity among the people involved. For example, regarding the former, Dovidio, Gaertner, and Pearson explain a key principle of "reducing implicit bias" in the following terms: "Encourage people to think of members of other groups more in terms of their individual qualities than as primarily members of their racial or ethnic groups. Examples of these techniques include training in perspective taking and empathic responding" (2017, 277). As to the relation between empathy and human commonality, McFarland cites research on test subjects who "on average placed greater value on American than Afghani lives"; he explains that "this ethnocentric valuation of human life correlated positively with ... identification with America, but negatively with dispositional empathy" (2017, 639). A common technique for opposing specifically moral out-grouping involves filling in the chain of events that led a person to violate moral principles, enabling us to see that, at least in many cases, this is a matter of unpropitious circumstances, circumstances in which we could perhaps imagine ourselves acting in the same way that we have condemned. As it turns out, literature is pretty good at these tasks – leading us to think about members of out-groups as individuals and clarifying how people just like ourselves might end up committing crimes that we would otherwise be inclined to see as inhuman (for some empirical work that suggests these points, see Hakemulder 2000; for related, interpretive study, see Bracher 2013).

There are two other sources of failed empathy that are in some ways more problematic, in part because they are likely to result from something that is generally good – devoted effort to understand and respond to other people's pain. The first is part of a problem brought up by Sapolsky (2017) and Bloom (2016). Drawing on a religious concept, we might refer to this as *despair*. In traditional Christian theology, a person would suffer from spiritual despair when he or she felt so sinful that he or she could not imagine any way of being forgiven and redeemed (see Chester 2006, 518). This may lead him or her to abandon any effort of the sort, and even to commit suicide (thereby ensuring his or her eternal damnation). Despairing suicide does not appear to be a common response to other people's suffering. However, either at a personal level or at a broader social or political level, we can come to feel that there is nothing that we can do to ameliorate the other person's condition. If we can imagine no productive actional outcome, then we have little choice (if we wish to preserve our own emotional equilibrium) but to, in effect, make ourselves ignore that suffering, effortfully blocking empathy rather than effortfully pursuing it. At a personal level, one might be faced with the suffering of a physically ill relative for whom one is incapable of doing anything to improve his or her condition; even simply conversing may be impossible if, for example, he or she is not fully conscious due to medication. At a social and political level, one may feel that there is nothing one can do to stanch the flow of blood from violence or to protect impoverished children from preventable diseases.

This returns us to the value of the research reported by Sapolsky (2017) and Bloom (2016). Again, that research does not appear to undermine the value of empathy. Rather, it suggests that once empathy is established, it is not a good thing to wallow in the suffering of others, just as it is not a good thing to wallow in self-pity. It is far better to think positively and constructively about the target and how to improve his or her condition. Indeed, this suggests that the political program of progressive literature may require some alteration. Literary works have often focused on conveying the suffering of oppressed out-groups, thereby fostering readers' cognitive and emotional empathy. However, they should perhaps be spending more time on presenting possible actions that readers could engage in after closing the book. Of course, one problem here is that, in many cases, the only responses we can take are fairly indirect and really would not be appropriate to tack onto a literary work. For example, during the Trump administration, a story about the mistreatment of Central and South American immigrants to the United States might have fostered in readers an intensified opposition to the president's policies in their regard. But for most people, this would involve one or more of the following actions: voting against that president and supporters of these policies in the next election; writing to senators and representatives, urging them to oppose the separation of families; attending or even organizing a rally against these policies; and sending money to relief organizations. But it seems likely that most of these activities would not fit effectively into the conclusion of a well-made novel.

There are exceptions. For example, the progressive Indian film *Garam Hawa* (Sathyu 1974) presents the plight of Muslims in post-Partition India. It ends with one of the main Muslim characters joining a mass-based political movement that is not simply Muslim, but socialist and opposed to a range of oppressive social practices and conditions. As discussed in Chapter 4, Markandaya's (2002) novel culminates in the building of a hospital in rural India, made possible by charitable giving of the sort that the reader himself or herself could easily undertake after closing the book. However, not every work develops in such a way as to allow this sort of pragmatic conclusion. After all, a play or movie, or even a novel, is not a how-to manual. Still, the research cited by Sapolsky (2017) and Bloom (2016) does suggest that politically engaged authors might wish to consider the development of practical responses more consistently and creatively than they have done in the past.

The final, and in some ways most intractable, problem of failed empathy has been addressed by a number of authors, but it is clearly treated by Ann Kaplan under the headings of "empty empathy" and "trauma culture." I do not follow Kaplan's argument in its entirety. However, I believe she has captured something about what we might call "the manufacture of empathy" in the world of global, high-speed media communication. Specifically, Kaplan maintains that we live in a sort of "trauma culture" where "representations of victims prevail" (2011, 256). Such representations are undoubtedly pervasive. Moreover, Kaplan is right that, at first, this may foster genuine empathy. However, when we continually encounter reports of new forms of suffering, the result is likely to be a "numbing" (256) of our empathic sensitivities. This is what she refers to as "empty empathy." It is not simply failed empathy; indeed, it began as real empathy. But that real experience of empathy was lost, emptied of its shared feeling and any associated pro-social caring.

There seem to be two reasons that a trauma culture would produce empty empathy. The first is despair, which we have just considered. As Kaplan explains, "Empty empathy is linked to ... [a] feeling of hopelessness" (2011, 269). In a culture where we are continually bombarded with images of suffering, we are likely to feel overwhelmed by the sheer extent of misery and bewildered by having no sense of what we could possibly do to mitigate that suffering. Part of our bewilderment is explanatory. Most of us do not really understand what is going on in Syria or the Sudan or anywhere else. Given, for example, some basic comprehension of US support for violence or oppression in different places, Americans would have some sense of what they might do to respond to some of these traumatic situations – even if it is only voting differently, attending a rally, or one of the other (admittedly limited) forms of political activity mentioned earlier. Part of our particular "trauma culture" involves the use of violent images to draw the attention of spectators or audiences, attention that can then be sold to advertisers (as when news programs try to gain greater market share, as they are more or less forced to do, given the economic realities of the news business). This sort of culture tends not to encourage sociopolitical analysis and explanation of suffering, since the suffering is what appears to draw audience attention, not such analysis and explanation. When explanations would implicate corporations or the home government, they are likely to appear even less frequently.

Such "empathic despair," as we might call it, is a very serious problem. But it is relatively easy to respond to. We simply try to formulate as accurate and comprehensive explanations as we are capable of formulating, and we try to disseminate these as widely as possible. Indeed, this is what many politically active writers are already engaged in doing – in fiction, history, journalism, and related fields. For example, to a great extent, Noam Chomsky's political writings are a matter of filling in descriptions and explanations of human suffering that are underreported. His straightforward accounts have inspired countless people to engage in political activism. This is largely because he has been able to make the causes of suffering comprehensible and thereby enabled people to understand how they might respond to that suffering.

The second reason trauma culture will often produce empty empathy is both more banal and more recalcitrant. It is basically a matter of habituation. It is part of our cognitive and affective processing that our attention and interest are drawn to novel phenomena. In evolutionary terms, this is because a novel development can suggest either a threat or an opportunity. However, as the phenomenon continues and leads to neither harm nor benefit, our attention and interest wane. Instead of being in the foreground of our thought and feeling, it drifts into the background, where we barely notice it. In evolutionary terms, this makes sense. The longer something has been around with neither harm nor benefit, the less likely it is that the object in question does in fact constitute a threat or an opportunity. (At the level of mechanisms, when a neuron is repeatedly stimulated by a particular source, its ease of activation decreases; e.g., see LeDoux 2002, 138).

There is one small qualification here. As Niko Frijda explains, there is "hedonic asymmetry" in habituation (1986, 323). Specifically, we habituate more readily to pleasures than to pains. This presumably applies to allocentric pleasures and pains as well as egocentric ones. Thus, we are probably less prone to habituate to the miseries that we encounter in electronic media than toward the benefits of current social structures (i.e., we easily come to take the latter for granted, but we find that more difficult to do with the former). Thus, in at least some cases, it should be possible to sustain sympathy longer than we might have sustained symhedonia. But that does not tell us much, especially since the experience of symhedonia is so limited anyway.

It is important to stress that the problem of habituation has no special consequences for empathy. Consider, for example, Prinz's preferred emotion of anger. We got angry when then-President Trump committed one moral or legal outrage, then when he comitted a second, then a third . . .. But as these outrages recurred, we became decreasingly outraged by them. As Bill Lueders has commented, "Donald Trump's . . . behavior is so consistently outrageous . . . that it becomes difficult to muster the appropriate level of revulsion for each new affront" (2019, 6). In other words, indignation is subject to precisely the same habituation effects. But, of course, that does not make the possibilities for empathy-based ethical behavior more robust. It merely indicates that habituation does not contribute to a critique of empathy or to the support of an alternative, such as anger.

This problem of habituation, despite its psychological and social simplicity, appears particularly difficult to resolve. It seems that for any given appeal for empathy to be effective, we have a window of opportunity when recipients would be sensitive, before habituation sets in. Moreover, this window is likely to be affected by the overall environment of empathic appeals, such that a "trauma culture" may make it difficult for any appeal to be effective, even for a limited time. Thus, one might initially have sought to respond to the problem by showing restraint in one's empathic appeals. However, since one does not control everyone else's empathic appeals – nor should one – this is likely to do little good. For example, we would undoubtedly be deeply moved by some isolated pictures of and reports about families being separated at the US–Mexico border. Similarly, we would be deeply moved by photographs of and reports about families fleeing drought in Africa or the victims of the Syrian government or people suffering from painful but preventable diseases. However, when we encounter wave after wave of such stories and images, we do not effortlessly develop our imagination of the scenes and the people involved. In addition, we are likely to feel decreasing emotional engagement with each new report of suffering, even when it is first introduced.

In relation to these concerns, Kaplan (2011) distinguishes "witnessing" as a proper response to other people's suffering. But it seems that this is simply definitional for her. "Witnessing," in her usage, just means experiencing empathy in such a way as to engage in consequent pro-social action. It is, of course, perfectly fine to use the word "witnessing" in this way – roughly the same way I have used "care," but with the emphasis on the behavior rather than the motivating emotion. But it does not tell us what is required to foster witnessing. She mentions "a certain distancing effect that is necessary for an ethical impact" (274). This could mean any one of at least three things. It might mean that the experience has to be allocentric rather than egocentric. But this only means that it has to be empathy, rather than emotion contagion. That is clearly insufficient since the problem arises precisely for empathy. Alternatively, in referring to "distancing," Kaplan might mean that we should not brood on the pain but direct our attention toward constructive responses – an important point, as we have already seen, but one that also does not appear to respond to the problem of trauma culture. Finally, it could mean that witnessing requires some emotional separation from the onslaught of trauma images, so that habituation is interrupted. This seems true as well, but it amounts to a restatement of the problem. (Kaplan [2011] could also be making a point similar to that of Brecht [1992] on alienation or to that of Sapolsky [2017], both of which we have already considered and neither of which solves the habituation difficulty.)

Perhaps a partial response to the problem may be found in a three-component strategy, which we may draw from the preceding analyses. First, we need demystifying social and political explanations, accounts of the sources of suffering that enable us to understand the causes of people's experiences and thus how we might mitigate their suffering. Second, we need a commitment to sustained empathic effort – not brooding on the targets' pain, but seeking to recognize it in a way that, in combination with understanding, motivates care and the associated consideration of actional outcomes. Finally, we are likely to need literary works to guide our simulation, to provide "instructions for mental composition," as Elaine Scarry puts it (1999, 244). Literary artists are generally far more skilled than the rest of us at simulating people's lives in their experiential – including emotional – detail. Literary works can provide us with simulations that are not only "relatable" but also explanatory, and they can do so with complexity and nuance. As such, they may displace the repetitive, even clichéd images of television news reports or social media, thereby perhaps partially overcoming the inertia produced by habituation to such affecting but superficial representations.

## The Uses of Simulation: A Note on Fritz Breithaupt

I will conclude this response to critiques of empathy with a few comments on Fritz Breithaupt's (2019) *Dark Sides of Empathy*. Breithaupt's book – like the work of Bloom (2016), Prinz (2010), and Delgado (1996) – is insightful and thought-provoking. Moreover, Breithaupt is not opposed to empathy. He sees empathy as crucial to human cognition and behavior. However, he sees it as, on the whole, morally neutral. Yes, sometimes it can be morally beneficial. However, sometimes it is morally deleterious. Specifically, following some general points about the definition and nature of empathy, Breithaupt devotes his book to examining what he sees as five ways in which empathy is problematic. My contention is that, in each of these cases, Breithaupt is either using the word "empathy" in a sense different from that employed here, thereby rendering his criticisms irrelevant, or he is tacitly referring to spontaneous empathy, in which case his criticisms in fact point to the value of empathic effort.

The first point to make here is that Breithaupt "define[s] empathy as the coexperience of another's situation" (2019, 12). Thus, Breithaupt is taking empathy to be what I and many other writers would refer to as the simulation of another person's perspective in particular circumstances. In my account, such simulation often leads to (affective) empathy. However, to do so, it requires a parallel interpersonal stance, as well as emotion systems (e.g., emotional memories) similar enough to those of the target to foster congruence in valence. It seems clear that these requirements will often not be met. In consequence, it will often be the case that "empathy" in Breithaupt's sense – "simulation" in my sense – will lead to amoral or immoral behaviors, even when systematic and effortful. For example, if one's interpersonal stance is antipathetic, then effortful simulation, when accurate, may facilitate harming or manipulating the other person.

Related to this, Breithaupt also maintains that "like most other human abilities, empathy probably serves the empathizer first and foremost and not the target of empathy" (2019, 11). There are at least four points to make here. First, in evolutionary terms, the benefits of (spontaneous) empathy do not need to accrue to the individual feeling empathy, but only to the population that has empathy-promoting genes, presumably including relatives of the person feeling empathy. This is precisely why spontaneous empathy has the range of biases it has, since these biases should, on the whole, favor kin over non-kin. Second, empathy – in the sense in which I am using the term – has an evolutionary history connected to but not identical with the evolutionary history of simulation. Third, even if there is a particular evolutionary advantage for the person feeling empathy, it does not follow that this advantage is egocentric. It may be the case that, for example, allocentric motivations in parenting are superior to egocentric motivations in securing the passing on of the parents' genes. Finally, the definition of empathy as allocentric segregates the cases where the primary benefit is not to the one doing the empathizing, and that is crucial for the ethical case.

These are two important general issues raised by Breithaupt's (2019) argument. We might now turn briefly to his five "dark sides" of empathy. For the most part, these too do not address empathy in the sense in which I am using the term. They are, therefore, largely irrelevant to my ethical claims about empathy. On the other hand, several of Breithaupt's categories are very illuminating about some closely related issues.

Breithaupt's first dark side is self-loss. This is basically a form of imprudence in which the empathizer totally abandons his or her self-interest on behalf of an undeserving target, as when a victim of terrorism uncritically supports a terrorist. This is actually a standard case of too little empathy, not too much. Most obviously, the victim who supports exonerating a still dangerous terrorist focuses narrowly on the latter's suffering, leaving aside the pain of any victims that terrorist may harm in the future. This is a failure of effortful empathy, due in part to saliency and other biases. What is interesting about Breithaupt's category, however, is that it highlights the ethical significance of prudence. Prudence is, again, in large part a matter of empathy with one's future self. While it is morally suspect because it is oneself, it is not oneself right now. Concern for one's future self is therefore in some degree allocentric. In consequence, it merits some ethical consideration. Thus, we would be likely to say that it is not only imprudent but immoral to sacrifice one's life so that someone else can have some trivial enjoyment or not suffer some insignificant pain. The idea of self-loss also recalls feminist criticisms of empathy, when urged on women, as being complicit with patriarchal oppression of women. Here, too, the problem is not too much empathy, but too little – failing to recognize that an empathic response to patriarchal mistreatment (e.g., sexual assault) may lead to future suffering (e.g., future sexual assaults) caused by the same man or other men.

Breithaupt's second dark side is group polarization, dividing the world into friend and foe. This is obviously important. But I believe Breithaupt gets the causal order wrong here. We do not generally begin by empathizing with people and then forming some identity category that manages to subsume the people we empathize with. Rather, we form the identity groups, and these define our interpersonal stance and thereby our inclination to empathize.

The third dark side is false empathy or, perhaps more accurately, pseudo-empathy. Breithaupt isolates a significant, recurring pattern in which a pseudo-empathizer presents himself or herself as empathizing while in fact he or she is engaging in a self-aggrandizing fantasy of saintliness. This is a common occurrence, rarely addressed theoretically. It carries a number of dangers. For example, one is likely to find oneself more excellent to the degree that the victim one aids is pathetic. In consequence, this sort of fantasy can readily lead to a patronizing or even demeaning attitude toward out-groups. On the other hand, I imagine that it often leads to genuinely moral actions, even if those actions are not motivated morally. Thus, I find it hard to believe that such a fantasy is so routinely harmful as Breithaupt suggests. In any event, this is clearly not a case of empathy; indeed, the whole point of it being a pretense of empathy is that it is not the genuine item.

Fourth in Breithaupt's list comes sadism. This category covers both the sexual version and schadenfreude. Schadenfreude and nonconsensual sexual sadism are not empathic in my sense because they do not involve a parallel interpersonal stance. (Consensual sadomasochism presumably can – and probably often does – involve such a stance, but, as such, I take it to be unobjectionable.) Thus, sadism too is irrelevant here. Nonetheless, Breithaupt's references to sexual sadism do serve to remind us that there are different ways in which the various sorts of interpersonal stance may manifest themselves, sometimes proceeding in counterintuitive ways (as in consensual sadomasochism).

Finally, Breithaupt refers to the sort of vicarious experience that we find when fans live a glamorous fantasy life through imagining the life of a celebrity. This too is an interesting case. It is a matter of simulation and thus empathy in Breithaupt's sense. Indeed, it is a case of the sort of thing we do all the time with literature, but concerning a real person. This does use our theory of mind skills (if often with wild inaccuracy). However, it is squarely egocentric and thus not a matter of empathy at all (in my sense). If Jones lives his life through Brad Pitt, he is probably never attending to what he imagines Brad Pitt feels. He is probably thinking something much more like, "I sure wouldn't split with Jennifer Aniston." On the other hand, if there is genuine empathy – as when a fan is genuinely worried about the health of a celebrity with COVID-19 – I believe that can foster ethical behavior, toward the celebrity or more generally (e.g., in donating money to COVID-19 research).

## Conclusion

In this chapter, I have sought to show that a wide range of arguments against empathy – though often insightful and thought-provoking on a range of relevant issues – simply do not debunk empathy, but something else. For example, there are two problems with arguments against empathy stressing its possible falsity. First, the problem with false empathy is the false part, not the empathy part. Of course, we need to recognize that empathy can be false. But that only means that we should redouble our efforts to get things right. The second problem comes with the claim that false empathy is worse than nothing. This would suggest that false empathy is, on the whole, positively harmful. But that all depends on the nature of the false empathy and the real alternatives. Obviously, false empathy is worse than true empathy. But it typically involves a benevolent interpersonal stance. Given the fact that our interpersonal relations are often far from benevolent, it seems likely that this will have a positive effect, though of course not an ideal one.

Much the same points hold for the more radical arguments against empathy. A key point in these arguments is that empathy is biased (e.g., in favor of the in-group). But that is spontaneous empathy, which favors in-groups, salient cases, and so on. The point of advocating empathy is to foster empathic effort against such spontaneous limitations. Moreover, these critics appear to assume that if empathy is set aside, what remains will be pro-socially motivating. But it seems likely that the absence of empathy will most often lead to indifference. True, empathy may have only the minimal effect of leading me to send Oxfam a check that, say, keeps a famine-stricken family alive for a month. But, in practice, eliminating empathy won't lead me to change the economic system, thereby eliminating poverty and ending the need for charitable giving. It will probably just mean that I won't send the check, and thus that family will not survive for that month. Of course, some critics of empathy urge other motivating emotions, such as anger. But anger seems to suffer from all the problems that afflict empathy and to have far greater potential for harm. (In addition, it is not clear that anger provides a specifically ethical motivation, which is the particular concern of this chapter.)

None of this is to say that there are no real problems with empathy. For example, the nature of empathic processes makes it easy for our empathic sensitivities to be dulled by habituation, as with the constant representation of trauma. But phenomena such as habituation are problems precisely because ethical response is bound up with empathy, not because a particular ethical theory stresses empathy. Moreover, the most ethically promising responses to these problems appear to be based on the cultivation of empathy, along with the development of causal analysis and understanding; the analysis and understanding, then, may guide our practical, ethical behavior while the empathy serves to motivate it.

CHAPTER 8

# The Critical Empathy of *Angels in America*

Tony Kushner's award-winning play about the AIDS crisis – "arguably the most important American play to be produced in the past 20 years" (Nielsen 2008, 1) – is particularly valuable for the study of empathy. This is in part because it faces and responds to a complex problem directly relevant to our concerns. On the one hand, Kushner clearly wants to cultivate an empathic response in audience members. But at the same time, he no less clearly recognizes that some obvious ways of cultivating empathy may prove emotionally, ethically, or politically problematic.

There are two obvious ways of trying to cultivate empathy that seem particularly likely to be counterproductive. They concern, respectively, the target and the (empathy-relevant) condition of the target. The first problematic technique is idealization. It is well established that we inhibit empathy for targets whom we consider blameworthy. Therefore, to cultivate empathy, an author needs to restrict the reader's inclination to view the target as meriting his or her suffering. The easiest way of doing this is by idealization. Arguably, this is, for example, what Harriet Beecher Stowe does with Uncle Tom. However, there are obvious difficulties with idealization. First, the reader may find the characterization implausible and thus fail to experience empathy with the character. For example, I feel empathy with Uncle Tom, but I find Eva (in the same novel) so saccharine that I can hardly bear to read the sections where she is represented. Second, if the reader accepts the idealization in the case of the character, he or she may be unable to extend empathy to real people, who after all are not ideal. In other words, if Kushner got straight audience members to empathize with a perfected gay character, that might not have any consequences for their likelihood of empathizing with real, necessarily flawed, gay people.

The difficulty with the target's circumstances is that we tend not to simulate other people's aversive conditions in detail, and, when we do, we tend to underestimate the pain caused by those conditions. An obvious response to this is to intensify representations of the target's suffering, prolonging the reader's focal attention and increasing the degree of pain. There are several problems with this approach. First, it may provoke personal distress, leading the reader simply to stop reading. Beyond this, it may lead the reader to feel disgust, which is then likely to be extended to the person, even though it was caused by the circumstances. When neither of these problems occurs, such representations may be problematic in limiting our empathy to cases of such severe pain. Put differently, ordinary suffering – pain that we would find terrible if it happened to us – may appear trivial in comparison. Finally, stressing the debilitation of a target may limit the reader's sense of that target's dignity, and potentially the dignity of others in the same identity category (racial, sexual, and so on).

These problems are perhaps unusually clear in the case of AIDS. Especially at the time the play was written, gay men were still often considered morally or psychologically deviant. For example, the World Health Organization still included homosexuality in its statistics on diseases (see Neel Burton 2015), and the Supreme Court had judged laws forbidding homosexual intercourse to be constitutional (see Weinmeyer 2014). This made it imperative that Kushner not represent the characters in a way that would encourage audience members to blame AIDS victims for having the virus. For example, this is presumably the reason why he has Louis say that he "fucked around a lot more" than Prior (Kushner 2013, 201), but Prior is the one who ended up with the disease. By the same token, however, it is important that he not make his gay men superhuman exemplars that no one could feel compassion for (as opposed to feeling wonder at) and who would potentially make real gay people appear more degraded by comparison. He does make Prior – one of the two AIDS victims in the play – less faulty than most other characters, but that does not contradict the general point. Prior's slightly superior goodness presumably facilitates our empathic response to his pain. However, he still has flaws. Put differently, he is not idealized, but his flaws do not contribute to a sense of blameworthiness.

As to the circumstances or experience, AIDS is not a beautiful disease. It involves a range of physical symptoms that are likely to appear repulsive to theatergoers. Thus, an audience reaction of both (empathy-inhibiting) disgust at the target and personal distress at the sight of the symptoms poses a significant threat, or challenge, to the playwright. Kushner responds to these issues by several means. First, he guides us through some of the most devastating results of AIDS, virtually forcing the audience to confront these results – as with Prior defecating blood, developing cancerous lesions, or soiling himself. However, the representation of these (disgust-provoking) symptoms is limited in time and largely verbal (even though the theater is visual). This helps Kushner to preserve Prior's human dignity. Moreover, Kushner divides the AIDS symptoms between the sympathetic Prior and the often antipathetic Roy

Cohn (based on the notorious McCarthyite lawyer of the same name). Kushner works to produce an increasingly sympathetic version of Roy. But, even so, the distress of audience members may be partially mitigated by this embodiment of some AIDS symptoms, and especially the play's one death due to AIDS, in a less sympathetic character. Put differently, Kushner fosters an interpersonal stance toward Prior that is strongly parallel. Our interpersonal stance toward Roy is more mixed, leaving us with an attenuated response to his symptoms, even as we recognize that Prior and others whom we favor are likely to suffer similarly.

Another technique used by Kushner is humor. Both Prior and Joe's distressed wife, Harper, treat their situation with wit. They are certainly aware of their plight – and deeply unhappy about it. But their compassion for themselves is only reasonable, and they lighten the burden on others, laudably, through humor. Kushner also draws on negative exemplars, in this case to discourage empathy-inhibiting responses, a point that is most evident with Louis. Though likable as a character, I suspect that few audience members would care to see themselves as similar to Louis, especially with regard to his reaction to Prior's HIV-positive status.

To a great extent, the sort of attitude Kushner develops in this play may be categorized as "critical empathy." By critical empathy, I mean an affective response to a target derived from a parallel interpersonal stance (thus, a rejection of out-grouping), which has the following characteristics: (1) It is effortful in seeking to extend empathy to all relevant targets, rather than succumbing to saliency or other biases of spontaneous empathy. (2) It is also effortful in seeking to extend empathy beyond the current time to likely and possible futures. In connection with this, (3) it does not dwell morosely on a target's current suffering, but attends to ways of ameliorating that target's condition in the future. (4) It neither ignores the faults of the target nor uses those faults as a reason to inhibit empathy (through specifically moral out-grouping). (5) It recognizes the fallibility of every empathic response and involves further efforts to identify and correct one's empathic errors. Note that critical empathy most often responds to the key points of critiques of empathy by enhancing or extending empathy, not repudiating or even limiting it. It does, however, involve an attempt to shift one's attention from brooding over current or future suffering to isolating practical actions that might alter harmful conditions.

Kushner's project seems to me largely consistent with critical empathy, though the play does at points deviate from critical empathy. (I will note one case of such deviation later.) In order to understand – and learn from – this project, we need to consider just what sorts of empathy the play develops and what variables it suggests are consequential in differentiating empathic (and nonempathic) responses, especially as these relate to various morally relevant emotions depicted in the play.

## Kushner's Characters and Their Roles in Empathy

Kushner represents a range of characters and situations in his play. In treating these characters and situations, he necessarily depicts some who empathize spontaneously with others and some who engage in empathic effort. He also presents instances of what we might refer to as "endogenous" and "exogenous" empathy. By "endogenous empathy," I mean empathy that arises from the attitudes or decisions of the empathizer. By "exogenous empathy," I mean empathy that is fostered or provoked in one person by someone else. Like many literary works, *Angels in America* provides occasions for endogenous empathy, but it is, I believe, designed to function as a provocation to (exogenous) empathy as well. The most obvious cases of the latter sort are signaled by moments of exogenous empathy within the story itself.

A striking case of exogenous empathy occurs when Belize asks Louis to recite Kaddish over the dead body of Roy. Louis is bewildered and repulsed by the request. However, Belize responds, "He was a terrible person," but "he died a hard death." He goes on to urge "forgiveness" (Kushner 2013, 265). This is a transparent appeal, not only from Belize to Louis, but from Kushner to the audience as well.[1] There is a difference between the two appeals, however. Belize's comment bears on a specific person in a unique context. I take it that Kushner's thematic point for the audience is more general. I doubt that Kushner really cared whether audience members changed their attitude about Roy Cohn per se. The suggestion is rather that one should have empathy for people who suffer, even if they have behaved immorally in the past. In other words, I take it to be a criticism of moral out-grouping and its associated inhibition of empathy. As this suggests, it is important to distinguish between the empathy of characters and the empathy of readers or audience members. Audience empathy is directed, first of all, at characters and then (on the basis of empathy for characters) to people or groups of people in the real world.

While audience empathy for characters is not dependent on characters' empathy for one another, the two are often related, especially in

---

[1] Since Roy is dead, this may not appear to be empathy. I take it to be empathy for two reasons. First, it involves sensitivity to what Roy felt over many months before he died; at the very least, this is empathy with Roy at that earlier time. Second, in the world of the play, it appears that Roy's spirit is still alive since he seems to pay a postmortem visit to Joe.

cases of exogenous empathy. In connection with this, it may be useful to have in mind the general contours of empathy within the storyworld of the play. Kushner tends to cluster characters into those who are primarily targets of empathy, those who are primarily sources of empathy, and those who are both sources and targets, but perhaps somewhat less important in either role. It seems clear that Prior and Harper are the primary targets of empathy in the play. Their pain is highlighted, and the moral status of most other characters is largely a function of how they respond to Prior and Harper. Prior and Harper are also sources of empathy, or rather lack of empathy, in their responses to the men who abandon them. Prior refuses to take Louis back, and Harper refuses to stay with Joe. We will consider the implications of their attitudes below. I take it that, in both cases, Kushner has made them somewhat uncompromising in order to make them human (rather than selflessly idealized) and to preserve their dignity and self-respect, as many people might consider it abject for them to accept back the men who have betrayed them.

The characters who are principally sources of empathy are Belize and Hannah. They are not wholly lacking in occasions for being the target of empathy. For example, we might feel badly about Hannah's being lost in an unfamiliar city when she arrives in New York. But neither Belize nor Hannah is presented as suffering much at such moments. Their role is almost entirely one of feeling for other characters and directing other characters (thus, indirectly, members of the audience) to feel empathy. I have already noted a case of both with Belize. Another case of directing empathy may be found with Hannah, in her sharp exchange with Prior. Prior basically begins to accuse Hannah of homophobia, based not on anything Hannah has said or done, but only on her "demographic profile." Hannah responds angrily, "You don't make assumptions about me, mister; I won't make them about you" (Kushner 2013, 240). Kushner is probably assuming that many people who would go to a play about gay men might themselves expect Mormons or members of other religious communities to be bigoted. Such an expectation would be a case of hostility attribution bias (our tendency to assume that out-group members have malevolent attitudes toward us and fellow in-group members; see Lukianoff and Haidt 2018, 158) and is connected with empathy inhibition through an antipathetic interpersonal stance. The point for the audience is clear. Hostility attribution bias is a bias, as is the tendency to take up a nonparallel stance to someone because he or she is a member of a particular religious community. This is not in itself a call for empathy. However, it is a call for readjusting our attitudes so that we can experience empathy in appropriate circumstances, rather than rejecting it due to in-group versus out-group divisions.

There are three characters who figure importantly as both sources and targets of empathy. In both respects, they are more limited than the characters just noted. In other words, they are less empathetic themselves, when compared with Belize or Hannah, and less likely to inspire empathy, when compared with Prior and Harper. Two of these are the play's temporary odd couple, Louis and Joe. Louis abandons Prior at a time when the latter needs him most. The play makes clear Louis's own pain – a variety of personal distress – over Prior's sickness, thereby explaining and partially mitigating that abandonment. In keeping with this, it fosters a degree of audience empathy with Louis. However, that empathy is definitely limited. In terms of idealization and disgust, Louis is significantly less ideal than Prior, and his suffering is significantly less also. In addition, he is more prone to self-pity, as signaled by his tendency to weep. His grief is real, but it does not inhibit him in pursuing other sexual relations – first, with a stranger in the park; then, with Joe.

Joe is more stoical than Louis, but his pain is therefore far less evident, probably making him less sympathetic for most audience members. He is similarly flawed, abandoning Harper in a way that directly parallels Louis's abandonment of Prior. Like Louis, he shows ethically inadequate sensitivity to his partner's suffering. But that does not mean he experiences no pain himself. Rather, his pain is more hidden. He cannot reconcile his sexual desires with deeply felt religious and ethical precepts that serve to regulate pleasure (with regard to the valence parameter), specifically forbidding same-sex sexual enjoyment. With an ethics oriented toward justifying pleasure, rather than preventing suffering, he is in a poor position to respond ethically to Harper since he is likely to be more aware of the putative (unjustified) pleasures of her pill taking than of her suffering in loneliness. Kushner does seem to me to cultivate empathy for Joe less than he might have. However, Joe's internal struggle with his sexual preference is affecting, and I personally feel that he suffers disproportionately at the end of the work, inspiring my empathic response. Specifically, he has foregone an opportunity for career advancement due to ethical commitments, and he has himself been abandoned by the two people with whom he has formed an attachment bond, however imperfect – Harper and Louis.

A third character figures as both a source and target of empathy, but in somewhat different and more complex ways – Roy. For the most part, Roy is not a source of empathy, but so to speak an anti-source, an exemplar of empathy inhibition. His response to his clients (such as the woman from whom he "borrowed" a half-million dollars [Kushner 2013, 69]), his heartless pursuit of Ethel Rosenberg, and his willingness to threaten his physician and colleague (see Kushner 2013, 45 and 156) with ruining their careers all suggest that Roy is empathy-challenged. He does, however, show brief moments of empathy with Joe, such as when he comforts Joe over the latter's feeling that he was not loved by his father. A particularly revealing instance of this empathy comes when Roy urges Joe not to follow his same-sex desires. At the time, Joe probably misunderstands the reasons for this, assuming that Roy has moral scruples, like Joe himself. However, it seems clear that Roy sees Joe as opening himself to great suffering – social, emotional, and perhaps most of all physical (due to the threat of AIDS). Kushner and most members of the audience are likely to think of this as deeply misguided. But I believe Kushner is also suggesting two things. First, this is a moment of genuinely empathic and ethical response on Roy's part. He has nothing to gain from this advice. It is aimed solely at Joe's well-being. In our terms, it is allocentric empathy with Joe's future self. It is mistaken advice (one cannot simply decide on one's sexual preference). But it is, to all appearances, sincere and, in its (allocentric) sincerity, a moral choice.

The second thing Kushner suggests here is that, despite his bluster, Roy has considerable emotional conflict over his sexual preference and behavior. Indeed, it seems likely that he has had this conflict for a long time, even to the extent of wishing that, when he was Joe's age, he had followed the advice he has just given to Joe. This in turn recontextualizes several events in the play. For instance, Roy responds belligerently to his physician when the latter suggests that Roy is gay. Roy threatens the physician, apparently for reasons having to do with possible public response. In light of his care for and advice to Joe, however, we can see his rage at the physician as suggesting a deep unhappiness with his own desires, a rage at being gay, not merely at being labeled "homosexual" (Kushner 2013, 45–46).

This leads us to Roy as a target of empathy. Kushner develops Roy's suffering no less than Prior's. Moreover, Roy's response to that suffering is stronger than Prior's. He boasts about his toughness (Kushner 2013, 151, 212) and appears justified in doing so. Apparently, his only sign of emotional vulnerability comes in his urging Joe not to act on his same-sex sexual desires, with its suggestions of both a genuine attachment bond with Joe and a deep sense of regret over his own sexuality. These vulnerabilities, as well as the grudging admiration we may feel for his strength in the face of suffering, make it more possible for us to empathize with Roy. That possibility is taken up when Belize tells Louis, "He died a hard death" and urges forgiveness (Kushner 2013, 265). Again, I take the point here to be that everyone who suffers merits empathy, even someone who was "a terrible person" (265). It may also suggest that forgiveness is better for everyone involved, though Kushner may exempt the actual victims of the terrible person's terror.

## Attachment Betrayal, Trust, and Critical Empathy

Kushner's play seems to imply that the victims of certain sorts of inhumanity cannot and perhaps should not reconcile with their victimizers. I say "cannot" because the anger that they feel will inhibit empathic response (anger being one of the primary emotion systems that function in this way, along with fear and disgust, as already noted). I say "should not" because Kushner may at least be indicating that prudential considerations require the victims to take precautions against future harm. Thus, we find Harper leaving Joe forever and Prior barring Louis from full reunion. These non-reconciliations occur in parallel, as parts of a split scene (V.vii of *Perestroika*). Harper tells Joe that they will probably never be in contact again. She explains, elliptically, "That's how bad" (Kushner 2013, 283). Her pain has been too great to risk repeating it in the future. Just after this, Prior explains to Louis, "I love you," but he adds, "you can't come back. Not ever" (284). In both cases, the angry resentment is a response to a particular act – attachment betrayal. Attachment betrayal destroys trust, and trust is necessary to place one's future well-being in the hands of someone else.

This breaking of attachment-based obligations, with its resulting breach of trust, is particularly stressed by Kushner. It is in some ways a particularly heinous moral crime. But it is in some ways a very ordinary moral failure as well. Louis and Joe are not bad people. Yet, they abandon someone to whom they are tied by bonds of affection and moral commitment, and they do so just at the moment when that person needs them most.

Of course, there are worse crimes. Roy Cohn was responsible for ruining the lives of many people through his prosecutions of leftists for their political beliefs. He violated legal procedures to have Ethel Rosenberg executed. Even Joe appears to consider this a case of murder (Kushner 2013, 114). In keeping with his representations of Prior and Harper, Kushner has the ghost of Ethel Rosenberg return and sit at Roy's deathbed. Kushner is clearly not judging Ethel or anyone in her situation when he has her say, "I came to forgive but all I can do is take pleasure in your misery" (253). Kushner does not appear to expect or even to encourage such forgiveness. However, the point does not extend beyond the actual victims of particularly devastating and trust-destroying crimes.

As we have already seen, Belize urges forgiveness of Roy. For our purposes, one crucial aspect of Belize's forgiveness concerns its relation to Louis. Belize has asked Louis to pray for Roy. Louis balks at the idea. Belize responds, "Louis, I'd even pray for you" (Kushner 2013, 265). Literally construed, the "even" indicates that Louis is morally worse than Roy. Of course, in one sense this is clearly untrue. Belize has a friendship with Louis; he trusts and respects Louis in many ways and has affection for him. But, in a sense, it is also true. First, we have not seen Roy betray an attachment bond, even temporarily. Thus, one might say that Roy has been incomparably more evil, but not so personally cruel. Second, and related to this, in comparison with Roy, Louis has failed more severely relative to Belize's moral expectations (of course, he didn't expect much from Roy). On the other hand, it is important to recognize that Kushner does still have Belize say that he would pray for Louis, and Prior only limits his future relations with Louis; he does not cut Louis off entirely.

In comparison with Prior's (and Belize's) response to Louis, Harper's complete abandonment of Joe – and indeed Kushner's own abandonment of Joe, whose ultimate fate is not treated in the play – may appear excessive. The reason for the difference probably has something to do with the reasons for the abandonment and breach of trust in the two cases. We can certainly feel compassion for Joe's painful feelings about his sexual desires. But it is important that these feelings are completely egocentric. He shows some consideration for Harper, more than Roy for example believes reasonable. But he does not appear to devote much thought or emotional energy to Harper's anxiety and loneliness. In my view, this remains forgivable in light of his own internal conflicts (to which we will turn in the following section). But those conflicts do cut him off from Harper (though it is also understandable that he would not wish to confess them to her; indeed, that may suggest some minimal sensitivity to her feelings since such a confession would undoubtedly have caused her considerable pain).

In contrast with Joe, Louis's abandonment appears to have been only partially egocentric. In some degree, he presumably felt disgust over Prior's physical symptoms. Indeed, Prior appears to see Louis as motivated principally by sexual desire or lack thereof. This is indicated when he explains that he should warn Joe that if he gets fat or bald, he should expect to be abandoned by Louis because "Louis ... can't handle bodies" (Kushner 2013, 234). Louis himself struggles with the question of why he "abandoned" his grandmother (24). He asks the rabbi, "What does the Holy Writ say about someone who abandons someone he loves at a time of great need?" (25). In asking this, Louis is suggesting the special moral status of attachment betrayal. The rabbi turns the question back on Louis, inquiring, "Why would a person do such a thing?" After some typical obfuscation, Louis suggests that "maybe vomit ... and sores and disease ... really frighten him, maybe ... he isn't so good with death" (25). (As this makes clear, he is already considering abandoning Prior; he is not talking about his grandmother.)

Thus, Prior suggests that Louis's problem is egocentric, perhaps a crude matter of physical desire. We might take it that there is evidence for this interpretation in Louis's affair with the gorgeous Joe, taken up after he flees from the diarrhea-plagued and lesion-spotted Prior. We may also take it as egocentric in another way. No one wants to die of AIDS, which is of course contagious. What "really frighten[s]" him could be the prospect of contracting the disease and dying a terrible death himself. This seems plausible as a contributing factor, based solely on general human nature. But it is not exonerating. After all, Prior explains later that "there are thousands of gay men in New York City with AIDS and nearly every one of them is being taken care of by ... a friend or by ... a lover who has stuck by them" (Kushner 2013, 220). Other caregivers observe the necessary precautions to avoid contracting the virus; Louis could certainly do the same. Of course, it is important to recognize that prudence is not in itself objectionable, nor confined to Louis. For example, Prior himself admits that he did not attend a friend's funeral for fear of contracting something from the corpse (102). The situations of Prior and Louis are clearly not identical. But I take it that Kushner includes this point in part to remind us that fear and self-protection are not motivations limited to Louis.

On the other hand, it seems clear that sexual distaste and prudential fear are not the only, nor even the primary, motivations affecting Louis. Louis does not ask the rabbi about abandoning somebody he formerly loved or who loves him or to whom he has a relationship commitment. He speaks of "abandon[ing] someone he loves" (Kushner 2013, 25). The clear implication is that he never stops loving Prior. Moreover, the fear that disease and death inspire in Louis need not refer primarily to himself. Indeed, Louis's comments about disease and death seem more obviously to refer to someone else, specifically Prior. In other words, the disease and death that frighten Louis are not principally his own, but those of Prior. In short, he is suffering extreme personal distress. The source of that distress is allocentric in that Louis's well-being is contingent on Prior's well-being. This is pretty clearly indicated by the fact that Louis begins to cry and deny Prior's sickness or inevitable death whenever it comes up. If his response were primarily prudential, one would expect disgust-based withdrawal rather than the expression of sorrow and denial that are characteristic of grief. Indeed, on first learning of Prior's lesions, far from withdrawing from Prior, Louis "*grab[s] Prior, embracing him ferociously*" (21, italics in the original). In keeping with this, Prior complains that whenever they talk about Prior's illness, Prior ends up having to comfort Louis (39). When Prior has a crisis that will lead to his hospitalization, Louis's personal distress – in this case, a form of anticipatory grief – becomes overwhelming. He can only mutter helplessly, "Oh help. Oh help. Oh God oh God oh God help me I can't I can't I can't" (50). Of course, leaving the situation does not solve his problem. It reduces the saliency of Prior's sickness and thus the frequency with which he experiences surges of such distress, but it does not eliminate the distress. Moreover, as we will discuss, it compounds the distress with other aversive feelings, prominently guilt.

Here, we might reasonably ask just what Kushner's representation of Louis suggests about empathy and ethics. If the preceding interpretation is correct, Louis cannot be faulted for a lack of empathy. Is the ethical problem empathy, then, as Bloom might suggest? No. The empathy is crucial for any ethical response to Prior's condition. But, in addition to ego-centric self-interest, Louis does not behave ethically toward Prior because he is prone to brooding. Whether he is concerned with his own pain or with someone else's, he is not particularly good at shifting from a focus on the feeling itself to a consideration of actions he might take in response to the eliciting conditions of that feeling.

## Out-Grouping

Perhaps surprisingly for a play focusing on gay men, *Angels in America* hardly touches on out-grouping based on sexuality. Kushner does devote some limited attention to race-based identity divisions and a bit more to ethical-religious divisions. As to the former, we find Louis and Belize at odds over racism and the attitudes of African Americans and Jews toward one another. Thus, Louis says to Belize, "You hate me because I'm a Jew" (Kushner 2013, 99). Belize counters, "You hate me because you hate black people" (99). Both make general claims about bigotry among Blacks and among Jews, accusing each other of racism on account of those generalizations. As these points suggest, the in-group versus out-group division here is centrally a matter of hostility attribution bias. It involves a particular form of nonparallel interpersonal stance that renders distrust more likely.

Somewhat surprisingly, there is a small hint of racial out-grouping on Prior's part, a hint that is noticeable principally due to its (temporary) impact on Belize. Specifically, Prior and Belize are engaged in what strikes me as a sort of sweet, affectionate flirtation, when suddenly Belize responds somewhat angrily (*"With an edge"*) that "all this girl-talk shit is politically incorrect" (Kushner 2013, 64). Evidently, the trigger for Belize's change in attitude is Prior's preceding reference to him as "ma belle nègre" (64; "my beautiful negress"), which certainly may be taken as racially objectifying.

But Prior is teachable. I have already made reference to a particularly striking moment of identity-based out-grouping and hostility attribution bias, this time based on religion, which occurs later in the work. Prior is with Hannah, a Mormon. Prior tells her that "it's repellent to me. So much of what you believe." Hannah reasonably asks him to elaborate. He begins, "I'm a homosexual. With AIDS. I can just imagine what you – " But, before he can finish, she interrupts, telling him that he cannot imagine, and (as noted earlier) countering the hostility attribution bias with the insistence, "You don't make assumptions about me, mister; I won't make them about you" (Kushner 2013, 240). Prior immediately agrees. Subsequently, Hannah proves herself to be one of the most humane characters in the play, helping Prior in particular. The point of the entire sequence appears to be the same as that between Belize and Louis, and that between Belize and Prior. It is merely clearer in this case. The out-grouping of others based on identity categories in fact creates the hostility that it claims to warn us against.

Something similar happens in the case of Louis with regard to Joe, whom he repeatedly reduces to a mere instance of his religious identity. For example, he apparently laments the fact that he has "spent two whole weeks in bed with a Mormon!" (Kushner 2013, 194). The crucial difference is that Louis never learns that a complex human being cannot be reduced to a simple stereotypical category. Moreover, Louis's out-grouping of Joe is not simply religious, but moral as well. Louis sees Joe as immoral for his political attitudes, which he in part explains by reference to Joe's religion (see 195). The moral out-grouping becomes particularly intense when Louis reads Joe's legal opinions and simply views them as ethically repugnant, though it is clear that he does not have any clue about the legal issues involved in the cases, such as the doctrine of suspect classification (248). This is particularly important because it bears on Louis's own attitudes and behaviors. The doctrine of suspect classification states that there are certain sorts of categorization that call for greater scrutiny in determining the constitutionality of legal procedures that invoke those categories. For example, it is generally unconstitutional to target members of a particular religion in legislation; however, it is generally not unconstitutional to target, say, people who have committed a felony. This is relevant to Louis because he clearly does not scrutinize his own judgments of people based on religious classification. Of course, Louis is not writing laws; his attitudes are not (and could not be) unconstitutional. However, they do reflect the sort of bias that the doctrine of suspect classification is designed to counter. As such, it is significant that he is not only ignorant about the doctrine, but ignorant about his ignorance, and in effect arrogant about his bias.

On the other hand, it is important not to condemn Louis too thoroughly. We would then risk engaging in the same sort of moral out-grouping as he engages in. Perhaps unsurprisingly, Louis is sensitive to moral out-grouping when he is its target. Indeed, he even articulates its consequences for interpersonal stance, complaining that Belize experiences schadenfreude in seeing "how unhappy I am" (Kushner 2013, 228). Schadenfreude may be an overstatement in this case. But it is clear that Belize has a partially nonparallel interpersonal stance toward Louis based on moral evaluation of Louis's attachment betrayal of Prior.

**Moral Emotions: Guilt and Shame**

The condemnation of Louis, though far from undeserved, may be too harsh. The abandonment of Prior is clearly a deep violation of a desirable normative outcome (in this instance, attachment-based caregiving for the sick). It is also a culpably immoral choice on Louis's part. However, the immorality of the choice is significantly mitigated by the fact that it is precipitated by Louis's largely allocentric personal distress. This motivation is further indicated by the fact that Louis's departure does not ultimately succeed in relieving him from emotional pain. It certainly reduces the immediate empathic distress that resulted from seeing Prior's decline and being continually reminded of his likely death. However, it replaces this – what we might call "panic distress" – with "guilt distress." Guilt distress results from Louis's recurring recognition that, far from helping the person he loves, he is actually exacerbating that person's suffering. This sense of guilt is based on an empathic response that he cannot suppress, in part due to attachment bonds.

Empathy-based guilt is clearly an important moral emotion in Kushner's play, and the case of Louis shows that it has a significant moral function. On the other hand, Kushner's representation of guilt is fairly limited. He devotes more attention to the far more problematic consequences of another emotion related to moral sensibility – shame. "Shame" is commonly understood to refer to a global attitude toward the self (unlike guilt, which concerns a particular act or series of acts), specifically an attitude of disgust or a sense that one is the object of other people's disgust (see Sapolsky 2017, 502; Tangney and Tracy 2012, 447–448). Kushner tacitly develops two types of shame linked with two types of disgust – physical and moral (on the two types of disgust, see Haidt 2012, 121–124; Nussbaum 2019, 114–115). Both bear on the experience of empathy – one's sense of other people's empathy, one's empathy for one's own past or future self, and one's empathy for others.

The less harmful sort of shame concerns physical disgust. Prior clearly considers himself physically disgusting to others, particularly after he is abandoned by Louis. This is, of course, to some degree true. That sort of physical shame is certainly unfortunate. But it does not appear to be, in and of itself, consequential for empathy or moral response. That is where it becomes important that shame targets the entire self. Prior's sense of his body's disgust-provoking properties leads him to blame himself – not merely his body – for Louis's behavior. We see this when he talks about how other men's lovers stayed with them and asks, "What's wrong with me?" (Kushner 2013, 220). This is why, even early on, he dreams of Harper telling him that the problem is not his self, assuring him that, "deep inside you, there's a part of you, the most inner part, entirely free of disease" (34). Kushner has Prior respond to this shame with the purifying fancy that he has been chosen as a prophet, thus one of the most holy, the most elevated and spiritual, rather than the most bodily and shameful. In this context, it is important that Prior ultimately rejects the role of prophet, evidently reconciling himself to his human, bodily condition and in large measure overcoming his bodily shame.

Joe may not be so fortunate. There are moments when Prior's feeling of shame leads him to feel disgust at his own sexuality, and at gay sexuality generally, most obviously when he says that "faggots; we're just a bad dream the real world is having" (Kushner 2013, 158). However, these seem to be isolated moments – perhaps only one isolated moment. In contrast, Joe is profoundly ashamed of his sexual preference. In connection with this, Joe's disgust at his self is not physical, but moral. We learn about Joe's sexual shame early on. Confronted by Harper, he responds that they should pray together. But Harper presses the – unarticulated, but clearly implied – issue. Joe indirectly admits his sexual preference, and his shame over it, saying, "I might be one thing deep within." The key point for Joe is that this deeply concealed self has no consequences, "no matter how wrong or ugly that thing is, so long as I have fought, with everything I have, to kill it" (40). In keeping with the sense of shame that makes one overly sensitive to observation from others (on shame and social withdrawal, see Scheff 2011, 455), Joe insists that he has not transgressed "in the eyes of God" (Kushner 2013, 41).

Subsequently, however, we find that Joe is not so confident that God sees a good man in him. His shame is clear, not only when he admits to being "ashamed" (Kushner 2013, 180–181, 183) or says that he is a "terrible person" (123), but also when he explains his prayer to God. Even before he begins his affair with Louis, Joe prays "for God to crush me, break me up into little pieces and start all over again" (51). One could hardly ask for a clearer representation of the effects of a global disgust with one's self. Moreover, like Prior, Joe tries to oppose this with an imaginary purity. As he puts it, "I wanted to be one of the elect [those chosen by God], one of the Blessed" (56). However, he is incapable of following it through; the self-disgust is too profound. It is significant that Joe wanted to be, specifically, "one of the elect," which is to say a soul chosen by God. This special love from God is particularly important for Joe because it would be an absolute and perfected attachment bond that could substitute for the failed bond with his father.

It seems clear that, despite his sexual alienation from Harper, he is genuinely fond of her. Yet, this fondness does not prevent him from treating her cruelly, however unintentional that cruelty might be. In part, this is a direct result of shame over his sexual preference since he would never have married her in the first place had he accepted that sexual preference. But, after they are married, he responds to Harper with an almost pathological absence of empathy. The suggestion seems to be, roughly, that his deep shame over his sexual urges not only depletes his psychological energy (which does appear to be limited for all of us; see Kahneman 2011, 43), but also continually directs his attention to himself. Ironically, being disgusted with one's self draws one's attention repeatedly back to one's self (when it would be better for everyone if one were able to turn one's attention to others). Indeed, there are suggestions from the beginning that Joe's general politics derive from his deep sense of shame. Most obviously, toward the start of the play, he explains his enthusiasm for Reagan, telling Harper that there has been a great "change for the good" and, as a result, "people aren't ashamed . . . like they used to be" (Kushner 2013, 26). It seems that Joe may see hope for his own release from shame in conservative politics.

Finally, though it is much less straightforward, there are hints that Roy suffers from the same sort of shame and that this shame has so distorted his feelings that he becomes the unempathic "polestar of human evil" (Kushner 2013, 229) that Louis takes him to be. This is suggested in his insistence that, whatever sexual acts he might engage in, he is not a "homosexual." Roy's physician has clearly been loyal to Roy for many years and has treated his sexually transmitted diseases discreetly and effectively. Yet, Roy threatens to ruin his career if he labels Roy a "homosexual" even in the privacy of his office. This is somewhat ambiguous, as Roy is aware that labels, such as "homosexual," have consequences in the real world (not that Roy is all that prudent in his life generally). But it is suggestive that he threatens his physician even in a context where it seems clear that the physician has no intention of outing Roy to the general public. As I have already remarked, the point where Roy's feelings about his sexual orientation become clear, however, is when his affection for Joe leads him to urge Joe to repudiate his desires and conform to the heteronormative prescriptions of society. In addition to showing genuine concern for Joe, this almost certainly suggests shame on Roy's part. Of course, that shame does not completely explain his political attitudes and actions. But, in keeping with empirical research (Tangney and Tracy 2012, 449), the play appears to indicate that shame has an inhibitory effect on empathy, with results for one's political attitudes and ethical choices. (In its critical view of shame, the play has much in common with Martha Nussbaum's analysis of that emotion; e.g., see Nussbaum 2009.)

## Conclusion

By the end of *Angels in America*, we seem to have a view of ethical choice and normative outcomes along the following lines. A parallel interpersonal stance, empathy, and forgiveness are crucial for the ethical treatment of anyone. This point is made particularly clear through the exemplary characters of Belize and Hannah. Though not without flaws, these are highly ethically admirable characters whom readers might aspire to emulate (in contrast, Roy – the "negation" of Belize [Kushner 2013, 223] – is the figure whose behavior readers would wish to avoid). They are, metaphorically, the "angels in America" referred to in the title of the work.

But to say they are exemplary is not to say that they define absolute standards. In Kushner's play, there are times when a parallel interpersonal stance, empathy, and forgiveness are not morally required. Specifically, these ethical criteria may be qualified by prudential considerations, at least in some cases. The paradigmatic case of such qualification occurs in attachment betrayal. Depending on the nature and duration of the relevant behaviors, such a betrayal is likely to produce distrust that is justified and, in some cases, apparently irreparable. Commonly, that distrust is interwoven with anger. The anger may fade eventually, but to expect the injured party to respond to the betrayer with restored trust may be asking for angelic, rather than human, behavior. Even so, others should try to approach both parties with empathic understanding.

Attachment betrayal has a special status because attachment love provides an ideal model for empathic sensitivity. Indeed, secure attachment has "the hallmarks of joint empathic attunement" (Denham 2017, 237) and thus empathy that goes in both directions. Such attachment in childhood also "predict[s] mature empathic responsiveness" and other "morally relevant capacities" later on (Denham 2017, 237). In keeping with these points, empathy may be blocked by cognitive and emotional processes that contrast particularly with attachment bonding. As to cognitive processes, empathy can be blocked most obviously by identity group divisions, even in the rather limited form of hostility attribution bias. As to emotion, it can be blocked most completely by disgust – the virtual opposite of attachment. That disgust may be physical or moral, the latter generally being far more consequential for our empathic response to another person.

A more complex relation between emotion, empathy, and ethics may be found in the related feeling of shame. Shame involves a sense of disgust at one's self, either one's own disgust or that of others. This shame may be physical or moral. In both cases, it tends to focus a person's attention egocentrically, sometimes severely inhibiting empathic response, especially in the case of moral shame. Moral shame may be contrasted particularly with guilt, a response not to one's whole self, but to specific, immoral acts, specifically acts that cause harm to someone else. As this suggests, unlike shame, guilt is often inseparable from empathy.

As noted at the outset of this chapter, critical empathy involves the systematic, effortful extension of empathy beyond our spontaneous and automatic empathic responses. Most often this will involve reference to cognitively developed ethical principles (e.g., universalization in the scope parameter). This elective and effortful empathy should correct for biases such as our tendency to empathize with people who are present while ignoring the needs and experiences of those who are not present. Critical empathy entails an awareness that our empathy remains fallible even with effortful extension. Finally, critical empathy is distinct from brooding; it moves from shared feeling to actional outcomes, behavior aimed at altering the eliciting conditions of aversive emotions.

The nature of critical empathy becomes particularly clear in a sequence of events where Belize – and perhaps Kushner – apparently departs from some of its defining principles. Specifically, Belize tells Roy about AZT, a drug that might save him. The drug is in short supply and is rationed. Belize informs Roy that he will need to use his contacts to get the drug. Roy asks Belize why he has explained all this. Belize says he does not know (Kushner 2013, 155). The point is very important because if Roy gets the drug, then someone else – someone without contacts – will not get the drug. In this exchange, Belize clearly exhibits the biases of spontaneous empathy. Roy's case is salient for Belize. The case of the unknown person who will not get the drug is not salient. Indeed, Roy acquires a stash of AZT that would seem enough to deprive many people, not just one. Kushner has Roy claim that he is just an added person taking the drug (186), implying that no one is being deprived. But that seems implausible. Assuming someone else has been deprived of the drug – someone who may have been determined to benefit more than would Roy – it is also relevant that Roy dies. Of course, in the context of the play, this all has a happy outcome, as it allows Belize to steal the drug and thereby save Prior. We all like Prior and very much want him to live. But this merely shows that we too are liable to spontaneous empathy biases. Perhaps contrary to Kushner's intentions, the scene powerfully illustrates the importance of a specifically critical empathy, and the ease with which we can slip from critical empathy to spontaneous and biased empathy, with all its ethical problems – which are, again, problems of too little empathy, not too much.

# Afterword: The Limits of Ethics: On Free Will and Blame

It might seem obvious that someone writing a book on ethics must be a devoted advocate of morality. Thus, it may seem unquestionable that I must have a strong commitment to the value of ethical evaluation. Of course, like everyone else, I have my preferences regarding how people should act. Sometimes, those preferences are very strong and lead me to feel guilt or, in other circumstances, to express righteous indignation, depending on whether I or someone else violates those preferences. But, in fact, on the whole, I distrust morals. I have mixed feelings about guilt. Sometimes it is beneficial; sometimes it isn't. But I am unambivalent about righteousness, including my own. It is a bad thing. Enhancing self-righteousness is a continual danger of reflection on ethics. Indeed, I worry that social discourse on ethics operates more commonly to enhance self-righteousness than to foster empathic sensitivity. Therefore, I am highly ambivalent about the normative part of the present book.

The basic problem here is well stated by Steven Pinker, who writes,

> The world has far too much morality. If you added up all the homicides committed in pursuit of self-help justice, the casualties of religious and revolutionary wars, the people executed for victimless crimes and misdemeanors, and the targets of ideological genocides, they would surely outnumber the fatalities from amoral predation and conquest. The human moral sense can excuse any atrocity in the minds of those who commit it, and it furnishes them with motives for acts of violence that bring them no tangible benefit. The torture of heretics and conversos, the burning of witches, the imprisonment of homosexuals, and the honor killing of unchaste sisters and daughters are just a few examples.
>
> (2011, 622)

Oscar Wilde put the idea comically when he wrote that "morality is simply the attitude we adopt towards people whom we personally dislike" (qtd. in Sapolsky 2017, 509).

A crucial part of the problem is that any emphasis on ethics can lead easily to moral out-grouping, which is arguably the most destructive form of out-grouping. That may seem self-evidently wrong. For example, isn't Nazi anti-Semitism far more destructive than moral out-grouping? The problem is that, perverse as it may seem to us, Nazi anti-Semitism is actually a form of moral out-grouping. Nazis rationalized their genocide precisely by demonizing Jews (on the assimilation of Jews to devils and thus the extremity of evil, see Hogan 2001, chap. 4). Mussolini and Gentile put the point more generally when they wrote, "Let no one think of denying the moral character of Fascism" (2012, 31). Throughout their essay, Mussolini and Gentile stress the idea that fascism is a specifically moral system.

I have distrusted moralism for decades. But I only began to think systematically about moral out-grouping much more recently, after reading an essay by Adam Morton. Morton discusses how morality inhibits empathy. In recognizing this, he is clearly onto something. However, Morton argues that "being a morally sensitive person ... limits one's capacity to empathize with those who perform atrocious acts" (2011, 309). I do not believe that this is usually a matter of imaginative incapacity based on genuine moral sensibility. Rather, it seems to be principally a matter of interpersonal stance. Moreover, the views in question seem more aptly characterized as *moralistic*. Indeed, the moralistic undermining of parallelism in interpersonal stance enabled many of the atrocious acts Morton alludes to.

More exactly, the problem of moral cruelty has been to a great extent the problem of moralizing identity divisions, as in Nazi anti-Semitism. When we act on an opposition between identity categories – for example, a racial opposition – we do avoid narrow egocentrism. That is what makes, for instance, dying for one's country – or, for some people, dying for one's race – into a paradigmatically moral act. Indeed, as noted earlier, Brewer reports research indicating that people find in-group favoritism more moral than evenhandedness across people generally (2017, 102).

This problem of moralizing identity group divisions may be partially mitigated by the formulation of one's ethical norms. Specifically, one may reject non-meritocratic identity categories, such as those of race, sex, or sexual preference. However, at that point another, more insidious identity division is likely to appear, one that leads directly to self-righteousness precisely because it is viewed as meritocratic. This is the identity division between the moral, progressive in-group and the immoral, regressive outgroup – in short, the good guys (us) and the bad guys (them). The asymmetry in our attitudes toward in-groups and out-groups virtually guarantees that our inclination and ability to empathize with the outgroup and to critically evaluate the in-group will be severely compromised. In moral out-grouping, then, our moral evaluations will be distorted and our consequent behaviors degraded.

The problem is only worsened by the nature of moral out-grouping. First, in moral out-grouping, we are unlikely to be bothered by the nagging sense that there is something immoral about degrading the out-group. They are by definition morally degraded and therefore unlikely to inspire moral self-questioning on our part. After all, such self-questioning would seem contradicted by the criteria that define the moral in- and out-groups from the start.

Moreover, there are important extraneous – egocentric, thus nonethical or pseudo-ethical – motives to which we are more likely to surrender when convinced of our own moral excellence or the virtue of our cause. Lukianoff and Haidt (2018, 73) refer, for example, to the predominance of "virtue signaling" in political and ethical discourse. The phrase is sometimes used to criticize the left in particular, though it is in fact a nonpartisan fault. Virtue signaling is a form of impression management, our self-conscious or unselfconscious endeavor to shape other people's conception and evaluation of us.[1] Virtue signaling is the variety of impression management by which we advertise our exceptional moral excellence. It commonly involves aggrandizing one's ethical achievements in part by dichotomizing alternatives and demonizing opponents. I am more saintly to the extent that my opponent and his or her ideas, affections, and behaviors are degraded. I have to admit that I see this tendency in myself. For example, I disagree with Haidt (2012) and believe that he is mistaken about a great many things he claims regarding liberals and conservatives in the United States. But I also believe that some of his criticisms of the left are valid and some others, though overstated or misleadingly phrased, should foster self-reflection by those of us on the left. Yet, in speaking to my graduate class about his book, I find myself continually struggling not to exaggerate what I take to be faults of the book. I particularly have to (try to) prevent myself from characterizing intellectual non sequiturs as political or moral flaws, thereby appealing to what I imagine are the political preferences of my students and thereby elevating myself in their moral esteem.

Additionally, destructive emotions such as anger may be given free reign when we engage in moral out-grouping. As Berkowitz (1993) explains, when angry, we tend to engage in victim seeking. Presumably, the ideal victim would be the person who caused our anger initially. But, should he or she be unavailable or dangerous, an innocent person will often do just as well. The problem with taking out our anger on an innocent person is that we might feel guilty afterward. This difficulty is overcome in moral out-grouping. The "bad guys" deserve

---

[1] On impression management, see Banaji and Greenwald (2016, 27).

whatever they get, even if we use them as punching bags for frustrations to which they made no contribution. This is at least part of what gives rise to "vindictive protectiveness," what Lukianoff and Haidt (2018) label the inclination to harm real or possible antagonists in the name of protecting some vulnerable group. This too is often seen as a fault of the left, but cases on the political right are so commonplace and extreme that it is hard to understand how anyone could view it as a particularly left-liberal propensity. For example, President Trump's immigration policies – including the separation of families – were instituted in the name of protecting Americans; his Muslim ban was rationalized in the same way. In both cases, the protectiveness is far more vindictive than almost anything done by the US left. The same point could be made about the death penalty or a wide range of other issues. Of course, I do not mean to say that the left is innocent of vindictive protectiveness. It is not. The left also seems often more interested in hurting someone who has violated a norm (or might do so in the future, or belongs to the same identity group as somebody who violated a norm), rather than helping someone who has been hurt. Indeed, there appears to be a widespread, nonpartisan preference for gouging out someone else's eye rather than aiding the person who was blinded initially.

To take a small example, many years ago, I would regularly join protests against US policies against Nicaragua. However, I was unenthusiastic about the signs made by organizers, which tended to denounce the president or the United States. I certainly didn't care for the president, and I was generally opposed to nationalism of any sort. Even so, the posters seemed to me too negative. I therefore made my own, positive poster for one of the rallies. It read, "BEFRIEND NICARAGUA." The organizers of the rally actually took my poster when I arrived and put it aside, instructing me to take a poster from another stack. (I chose, rather, to march without a placard.) Similarly, when the Modern Language Association (MLA) was considering an academic boycott on Israel, I proposed a positive alternative to my colleagues in one section of the MLA. Instead of encouraging universities not to engage in various interactions with Israeli universities or professors, why not encourage them to institute preferential policies for interactions with Palestinian institutions and professors? I fully admit that this was merely the seed of an idea. But it inspired literally zero interest. Perhaps unfairly, I felt that part of the reason was that my suggestion offered no clear way of hurting anyone.

Whether or not I am right about the last point, it seems clear that normative ethics can very easily inhibit self-criticism aimed not only at oneself individually, but at one's in-group. It can also readily encourage us to exaggerate the faults of the out-group. This is true whether the division is initially defined by standard categories of social identity, such as race, or by specifically moral categories. Moreover, moral out-grouping can readily enhance virtue signaling and vindictive protectiveness or anger-motivated aggression more generally. For these reasons, there is a very serious ethical risk in a normative discussion of ethics, which is to say any discussion that goes beyond a descriptive treatment of ethics. Specifically, such a discussion may actually foster unethical behavior, in part by convincing us of our own righteousness.

But that is not all. In fact, my objections to normative ethics go even deeper. Put very simply, I believe moral blame is unjustified. It is unjustified because it only makes sense if people have free will, and thus may reasonably be condemned for their choices. But I also believe that people do not have free will, or not exactly.

Specifically, in *Personal Identity and Literature* and elsewhere, I have argued for what might be called "incomplete material reductionism." Let me begin with the material reductionism part and then turn to the incompleteness. Suppose you are describing me. You begin with my state as an organism at a particular moment. That organism has various neural structures and processes, as well as musculoskeletal organization, respiration, and so forth. For ease of reference, you may wish to identify the neural structures and processes as memories, skills, propensities, and so on, but there is no need to do so. All these interconnected components of the organism ("me") are situated in an environment with which that organism interacts through perception and motion. Suppose you set out to explain one of these motions. To do so, you might begin with a physical event outside the organism, tracing its effects on the organism's eyes, the consequences for the visual cortex, the networks of neuronal activation that follow from this, extending to the motor cortex, and so on, until, say, the arm lifts and swings in the direction of an approaching insect. Once you have formulated this account – assuming you have God-like access to the entire causal sequence – there is nothing left over to explain. That is all there is to my trying to swat a fly. I cannot be blamed (or praised) for that or any other act, any more than a billiard ball can be praised or blamed for careering off at a certain velocity when struck by another billiard ball.

Of course, the advocates of free will immediately object that the human brain does not operate with billiard ball causality. For example, there is quantum indeterminacy (on the idea that freedom is secured by quantum indeterminacy, see Arvan 2013; Pestana 2001). But if there is quantum indeterminacy, it also applies to the billiard balls. Quantum mechanics does not tell us that brains operate differently from billiard balls. It tells us that billiard balls do not operate the way we previously thought billiard balls operated. Indeterminacy as such does not help us with free will. If it did, then it would have to give billiard balls free will as well as people. As Dehaene puts it, "even if quantum phenomena influenced some of the brain's operations, their intrinsic unpredictability would not satisfy our notion of free will" (2014, 264). Kosslyn explains that "adding random factors would not confer free will ... simply adding indeterminacy to a system does not make its actions free" (2004, xi).[2] In Buonomano's words, "quantum mechanics provides a form of probabilistic determinism: it establishes a domain of options and their respective probabilities" (2017, 224). Indeed, probabilistic determinism has other consequences here that would seem to render the entire situation absurd. Suppose we grant that free will operates in individual instances. The overall distribution of outcomes (e.g., brain processes) would have to conform to the overall probabilities. Thus, my choices on the whole would have to fall in the right distribution curve, as would yours and mine together, and so on.

As Sapolsky points out, "Nearly everyone believes ... that we are somewhere between complete and no free will, that this notion of free will is compatible with deterministic laws of the universe as embodied in biology" (2017, 586). But this idea does not seem to make any sense. It arbitrarily removes one part of thought or action from biology, treating it as an island of free will in a sea of determinism. Sapolsky goes on to explain, "Of all the stances of mitigated free will, the one that assigns aptitude to biology and effort to free will, or impulse to biology and resisting it to free will, is the most permeating and destructive" (598). Again, it is difficult to make any sense of this separation. Clearly, the "resistance" is as much a function of neural activations as the initial impulse; if the latter is not free, the former is not either. Thus, "being a child molester [thus, not "resisting" the impulse] is as much a product of biology as is being a pedophile [having the impulse]" (598).

Of course, we can still speak of free will in a looser way. We often think of autonomy as something like an organism's tendency in routine circumstances or as an "internal" rather than "external" form of determinacy. For example, I think of my autonomy as compromised if someone holds a

---

[2] Bruce Waller appears to hold the view that random factors can constitute free will. Specifically, he imagines a situation in which behaviors are rigidly singular, with particular triggers yielding particular responses in all cases. He contrasts this with the actual operation of humans and "closely related species" (2011, 54). These species exhibit "spontaneous behavior" in which the organism sometimes responds to circumstances in an unusual way. This "occasional spontaneity" allows the discovery of potentially adaptive "new paths" (57). Leaving aside the validity or invalidity of Waller's analysis, it seems clear that this sort of (biologically caused) novel behavior is not what anyone means by *free will*. Rather than explaining free will, Waller seems to have offered an alternative way of using the phrase "free will." Moreover, this usage and associated account in effect eliminate free will as ordinarily understood.

gun to my head and orders me to hand over $100, but not if a charitable organization sends me a letter requesting a $100 donation. The internal versus external division can be quite fine-grained. For instance, I consider myself to have given in to temptation if I forego a resolution to avoid coffee in the afternoon, seeing this as an abandonment of my autonomy to desires that are external to "me," though they are part of the same organism. These uses of "free will" make sense and are useful in daily life. But they do not isolate anything that is "free" in the necessary, ethical sense. My action results as much from a series of ordinary causes and effects when I give to the charity as when I hand over my wallet to the robber. The internal versus external division is useful in daily life only because it says something about how I would ordinarily act, given ordinary conditions.[3] It is the equivalent of saying, for example, that the car is fine; it didn't start simply because the weather was much colder than usual or the battery was too old. But clearly, we would not morally blame a car for not starting even in fine weather and with a new battery. It would not make any sense to do so. Ultimately, this is my view of moral blame applied to people – it just makes no sense.[4]

Or, rather, it sort of makes no sense to blame or praise someone for their actions. This brings me to the incompleteness part of incomplete material reductionism. I began by referring to the way in which you could explain some motion of my body. I did not begin by referring to the way in which you could explain some motion of your body or I could explain a motion of my body. In those cases, a discussion of purely physical events would leave something out – our sense of subjectivity, our

---

[3] Another way of discussing free will focuses on law and the deterrent effect. For instance, I believe that the deterrent effect (along with some related ideas) is often what Hirstein, Sifferd, and Fagan (2018) end up treating under the rubric of "responsibility," though they do not conceive of it in that way. In making decisions about legal responsibility, we will be interested in, for example, types of brain damage that would render ordinary deterrents (e.g., the threat of prison) inconsequential for an agent. In those cases, the deterrent effect (for the current criminal or for someone else with the relevant brain damage) will be disabled. Thus, there is no point in pursuing deterrence in cases of that sort. If someone suffers relevant brain damage, we might *say* that he or she could not choose his or her course of action freely. But that only means that the usual effects of deterrence could not enter. Such situations tell us nothing about free will. Indeed, it is precisely because ordinary deterrents operate through the usual sorts of causal sequences that brain damage can alter behavior – by altering those causal sequences.

[4] A number of authors have articulated strong arguments against moral responsibility along different but compatible lines (see the excellent discussion in Bruce Waller 2011, chap. 2). For example, Bruce Waller summarizes Galen Strawson's argument as follows: "to be ultimately responsible for what you do, you must be ultimately responsible for the way you are. But you can't be ultimately responsible for . . . your genetic inheritance and early experience [which] shaped you" (2011, 23).

first-person experience.[5] In *Personal Identity* (2019), I have offered several arguments that it is in principle impossible for any materially reductive account of the world to be complete. In other words, it is impossible for any such account to include the entire world with nothing left over that is unexplained. Specifically, such an account cannot in principle include itself. For example, one argument is drawn from the Copenhagen interpretation of quantum mechanics. In that interpretation, the facts of a given system become definite only with observation. The act of observation defines or sections off the system to be explained, and that system is sharply distinguished from the observer. (For a discussion of these issues in quantum mechanics, see Putnam [1983].) In consequence, the observer cannot be part of the system that is being explained – unless, of course, one introduces a second observer who establishes the previous system plus the previous observer as a new system for the new observer. But, in the latter case, the new observer is not part of the new system. In each case, then, there is something that escapes to materialist reduction, an observer. (See Figure 9.1.)

What consequences does this have for free will? For each subjective point of view there is on the world, there is a subject who is not subsumed under the causal sequences of a materialist reduction. From that first-person perspective, one has free will. I do not mean that one has the illusion of free will. I mean that one actually has free will in one's own construal of the world. My claim is that this holds despite the fact that one does not have free will from any other perspective. (Note that this account solves the problem of having to grant free will to billiard balls. Billiard balls have no first-person experience and thus no point of view that is unexplained by material reduction. Billiard balls are, so to speak, completely reducible to matter.) This free will is not absolute, the free will of God. It is the practical free will of inner determination or autonomy in circumstances that we have not chosen, including, for example, the free will of resisting temptation.

Or, rather, we are sort of free in these ways. Material reductionism does not apply to my subjectivity. But my subjectivity is not eternal. Once I have done a thing, I am no longer in the midst of experiencing it as a first-person phenomenon. My past self is an object for me in much the way other people are. But the present and the future are different. They

---

[5] I was initially sensitized to the special nature of first-person experience in part by some of Thomas Nagel's work (see 1979, 165–180). However, as I point out in *Personal Identity* (Hogan 2019, 167), Nagel appears to draw very different conclusions from this than I do. His account places first-person experience within the causal explanation of the observed world (see Nagel 2012), whereas I see such experience as a condition for any such causal explanation, a condition that therefore cannot be subsumed under that explanation.

268  Afterword: The Limits of Ethics

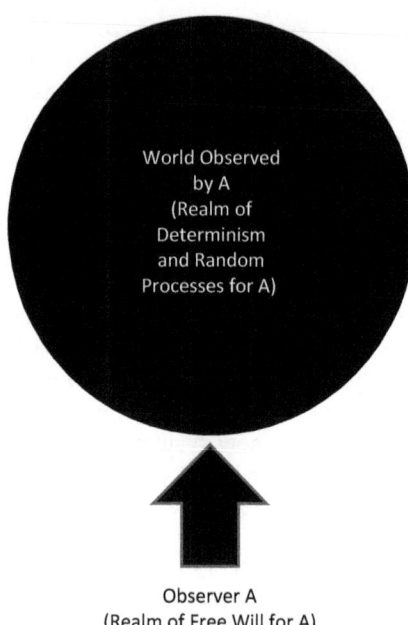

Figure 9.1 Transcendental freedom (for person A as observer).

are irreducible. The consequence is that I am morally responsible for my choices now and for my choices in the future. (The importance of the latter comes from the extension of my ethical obligations to situate my future self in such a way that I will be able to act ethically at that time [see Marcus 1980].)

So where does this leave us? First, we are all fully determined (in the relevant sense) and thus not free, except subjectively, from our first-person perspective. Even subjectively, there is a difference between the past and the future-oriented present. Thus, from a first-person perspective, our present decisions are open to moral guidance and therefore moral evaluation. Our response to harms caused by others and even to our own moral failings in the past is probably best modeled on our response to natural harms, such as diseases or earthquakes. We should not respond with anger or blame, but with effortful empathic sensitivity to current suffering (and likely future suffering), along with an attempt to mitigate that suffering in the present and to prevent future harm of the same sort. In both mitigation and prevention, we should seek to set aside such egocentric practices as virtue signaling or victim seeking. We should be concerned instead with what is effective, keeping in mind the consequences for all parties (including those who are "guilty"; again, by this account, they are guilty only in the way that the weather is guilty of preventing the car from starting).

These conclusions underlie something about my view of normative ethics that I have not stated explicitly, but that may have struck some readers. Ethical theories often operate to guide our judgments of what other people did in the past. For example, ethicists might be concerned with evaluating to what extent someone is blameworthy for some act that we consider immoral and just what our (presumably punitive) response should be to that transgression. Given the preceding argument, however, such blame is misplaced and punishment is not a matter of moral choice, but of fostering certain outcomes. Normative ethics, in my account, does not bear directly on other people at all. Indeed, it does not even bear on oneself in the past. The target of moral concern is almost entirely oneself in the present and future. I say "almost entirely" because our ethically requisite empathy with others necessarily includes a sense of their self-experience as moral agents. For example, we need to respond to their sense of guilt (which is partially retrospective, thus nonmoral, but in part bears on the present and simulation of the future, which also makes it in part moral). In this way, other people's first-person ethical decisions and actions are relevant to us. But they are relevant only to the extent that they bear on the other person's well-being – including their sense of dignity and their moral self-evaluation.

An account of this sort implies clear responses to some common objections aimed at denials of free will. As Sapolsky notes, with understandable exasperation, "If you reject free will and the discussion turns to the legal system, the crazy-making, inane challenge that always surfaces is that you'd do nothing about criminals" (2017, 608). But, of course, "People must be protected from individuals who are dangerous. The latter can no more be allowed to walk the streets than you can allow a car whose brakes are faulty to be driven" (609).

I should note that none of this entails that there are no dispositional differences bearing on normative outcomes. As Bruce Waller points out, "No one is morally responsible for being bad or behaving badly—but this does not mean that no one has a character with profound moral flaws" (2011, 5). Thus, the training of character – most obviously, in the upbringing of children – remains crucially important. Moreover, this account accepts that punishment will probably remain a part of our response to anti-social behavior, having a purely "instrumental" role, as Sapolsky puts it (2017, 610). But it is important to stress that punishment should probably be the last option (whereas, in the United States at least, it is often the first or only option considered), and it should not be accompanied by shaming. As Nussbaum points out, the United States has a virtual "obsession with incarceration" (2016, 181). For example, with "5 percent of the world's population," it has "25 percent of [the world's] prison population" (181). But there is "evidence that incarceration simply breeds hardened criminals with nothing positive to live for—thus undermining specific deterrence [i.e., deterrence of future crime by these individuals] and reform, and perhaps general deterrence [deterrence of crime by others], given the influence of such hardened offenders in their communities" (182). It seems particularly clear that there is no "special deterrent value" to "humiliating conditions, which are well known to breed hopelessness, a sense that crime is the only future" (183). Moreover, if we are actually concerned about improving the well-being of our society, there are methods, such as "early intervention in childhood education," that "diminish the likelihood" of children becoming criminals (181). Moreover, "empirical study" shows that "shame-based penalties ... actually increase violence in society" (199).

In practical terms, this treatment of free will would probably suggest an attitude toward punishment that is roughly along the lines of that proposed by Gill and Cerce. Gill and Cerce (2017) distinguish two types of free will. One indicates that a person is free to determine their own dispositions. The other indicates only that one is free to choose one's actions at a given moment. Drawing on empirical research, they argue that denying the former, while affirming the latter, helps to produce salutary effects that "reduce the urge to inflict spiteful punishments on offenders, but leave intact the urge to nonviolently guide the offender toward moral improvement" (Gill and Cerce 2017, 361). Again, I have maintained that, objectively, we are not free in either sense. Moreover, this is a problematic distinction theoretically as, presumably, the freedom of action at each point in time would accumulate to form a sort of freedom to form oneself (as the product, in part, of those prior actions). Even so, this distinction roughly captures the first-person perspective on action and in that regard does appear to orient a roughly appropriate response to other people's misbehavior. It inhibits blame and maintains respect while still seeking to improve behavior, both from the individual offender and from the society more generally.

As to concrete policies, Bruce Waller cites empirical evidence that the most socially beneficial outcomes are produced by attention to the ways in which undesirable consequences are produced by the encompassing system, without attaching blame to individuals (see Waller 2011, 287–304). This approach leads us to ask what policies are most likely to produce the results we desire in the future. In contrast, the more common moralism usually leads us to ask what suffering is appropriate for the individual who most directly caused a morally objectionable outcome in the past.

## Conclusion

In sum, it would seem to be the case that there are two ways of describing and explaining the world, neither of which can be complete. One is third-person or object-defined and deterministic (or random). The other is first-person or subject-defined and voluntaristic within limits. Since normative morality presupposes some degree of free choice, this account indicates that moral evaluation applies only to the first-person account, thus to one's own present and future. Everyone else's actions and even one's own past fall outside the realm of moral evaluation. The only qualification to this is that empathy is central to our present and future moral decisions and behaviors. In consequence, our moral obligations include sensitive attention to other people's first-person, moral well-being. If followed consistently, this view should preclude self-righteousness and moral out-grouping, while still motivating each person's commitment to his or her own ethical behavior. It should also guide each person's treatment of other people in a way that preserves sensitivity to their moral dignity, while encouraging attention to genuinely effective means of reducing social harm. Put differently, it stresses the importance of moral outcomes for everyone's behavior, but it stresses moral choice in our own future-oriented, current decisions and actions. Empathy, then, is principally an imperative for ourselves. It is an imperative we envision for others only insofar as we are (empathically) considering their dignity as a function of their first-person view on the world; as such, our concern with their moral choices is a matter of empathic prudence that is not morally evaluative and as such is inconsistent with self-righteousness.

# References

Ahmed, Arif. "Rationality and Future Discounting." *Topoi* 39 (2020): 245–256.
Ambady, Nalini, Joan Y. Chiao, Pearl Chiu, and Patricia Deldin. "Race and Emotion: Insights from a Social Neuroscience Perspective." In *Social Neuroscience: People Thinking about Thinking People*. Ed. John Cacioppo, Penny Visser, and Cynthia Pickett. Cambridge, MA: MIT Press, 2006, 209–227.
Anonymous. *Selling Rice in Chenzhou*. Trans. Richard Hessney. In *The Columbia Anthology of Yuan Drama*. Ed. C. Hsia, Wai-Yee Li, and George Kao. New York: Columbia University Press, 2014, 109–146.
Arendt, Hannah. *On Revolution*. New York: Penguin, 1977.
Armstrong, Paul. *How Literature Plays with the Brain: The Neuroscience of Reading and Art*. Baltimore, MD: Johns Hopkins University Press, 2013.
Arvan, Marcus. "A New Theory of Free Will." *The Philosophical Forum* 44.1 (2013): 1–48.
Atwood, Margaret. *The Handmaid's Tale*. New York: Anchor, 2017.
Avioz, Michael. "The Law of the Disrespectful Son and Daughter." *The Torah.com* (June 4, 2020). www.thetorah.com/article/the-law-of-the-disrespectful-son-and-daughter (accessed June 12, 2020).
Baker, Robert. *The Structure of Moral Revolutions: Studies of Changes in the Morality of Abortion, Death, and the Bioethics Revolution*. Cambridge, MA: MIT Press, 2019.
Baldwin, James. "Everybody's Protest Novel." *Notes of a Native Son*. New York: Dial Press, 1955, 13–23.
Ball, Philip. *Critical Mass: How One Thing Leads to Another*. New York: Farrar, Straus and Giroux, 2004.
Banaji, Mahzarin, and Anthony Greenwald. *Blindspot: Hidden Biases of Good People*. New York: Bantam, 2016.
Banerjee, Abhijit, and Esther Duflo. *Good Economics for Hard Times*. New York: Public Affairs, 2019.
Banks, Antoine. *Anger and Racial Politics: The Emotional Foundation of Racial Attitudes in America*. Cambridge: Cambridge University Press, 2014.
Bargh, John. "Social Psychological Approaches to Consciousness." In *The Cambridge Handbook of Consciousness*. Ed. Philip David Zelazo, Morris Moscovitch, and Evan Thompson. Cambridge: Cambridge University Press, 2007, 555–569.
Barrett, Justin. "Theological Correctness: Cognitive Constraint and the Study of Religion." *Method & Theory in the Study of Religion* 11.4 (1999): 325–339.

Batson, C. Daniel. "The Empathy-Altruism Hypothesis: Issues and Implications." In *Empathy: From Bench to Bedside*. Ed. Jean Decety. Cambridge, MA: MIT Press, 2012, 41–54.
"These Things Called Empathy: Eight Related but Distinct Phenomena." In *The Social Neuroscience of Empathy*. Ed. Jean Decety and William Ickes. Cambridge, MA: MIT Press, 2009, 3–16.
Baxmann, Inge. "Der Körper der Nation." In *Nation und Emotion*. Ed. Etienne François, Hannes Siegrist, and Jakob Vogel. Göttingen: Vandenhoeck & Ruprecht, 1995, 353–365.
Bechara, Antoine, Hanna Damasio, Daniel Tranel, and Antonio R. Damasio. "Deciding Advantageously before Knowing the Advantageous Strategy." *Science* 275 (1997): 1293–1295.
Belford, Barbara. *Bram Stoker*. New York: Knopf, 1996.
Bergh, Robin, and Nazar Akrami. "Generalized Prejudice: Old Wisdom and New Perspectives." In *The Cambridge Handbook of the Psychology of Prejudice*. Ed. Chris Sibley and Fiona Barlow. Cambridge: Cambridge University Press, 2017, 438–460.
Berkowitz, Leonard. "Towards a General Theory of Anger and Emotional Aggression: Implications of the Cognitive-Neoassociationistic Perspective for the Analysis of Anger and Other Emotions." In *Perspectives on Anger and Emotion*. Ed. Robert S. Wyer and Thomas K. Srull. Mahwah, NJ: Erlbaum, 1993, 1–46.
Berkowitz, Leonard, Sara Jaffee, Eunkyung Jo, and Martholomeu Troccoli. "On the Correction of Feeling-Induced Judgmental Biases." In *Feeling and Thinking: The Role of Affect in Social Cognition*. Ed. Joseph Forgas. Cambridge: Cambridge University Press, 2000, 131–152.
Beswick, David G. *Cognitive Motivation: From Curiosity to Identity, Purpose, and Meaning*. Cambridge: Cambridge University Press, 2017.
Blair, Robert, and Karina Blair. "Empathy, Morality, and Social Convention: Evidence from the Study of Psychopathy and Other Psychiatric Disorders." In *The Social Neuroscience of Empathy*. Ed. Jean Decety and William Ickes. Cambridge, MA: MIT Press, 2009, 139–152.
Bloom, Irene. "Metaphysics and Government in the Laozi." In *Sources of Chinese Tradition: From Earliest Times to 1600*. 2nd ed. Ed. Theodore de Bary and Irene Bloom. New York: Columbia University Press, 1999, 77–79.
Bloom, Paul. *Against Empathy*. New York: HarperCollins, 2016.
*Just Babies: The Origins of Good and Evil*. New York: Broadway Books, 2014.
Boler, Megan. *Feeling Power: Emotions and Education*. New York: Routledge, 1999.
Book of Poetry (*Shījīng*, 詩經). Trans. James Legge. *Chinese Text Project*. Ed. Donald Sturgeon. https://ctext.org (accessed January 12, 2022).
Bouvier, Michel, and Jean-Louis Leutrat. *Nosferatu*. Paris: Gallimard, 1981.
Boyer, Pascal. *Minds Make Societies: How Cognition Explains the World Humans Create*. New Haven, CT: Yale University Press, 2018.
Bracher, Mark. *Literature and Social Justice: Protest Novels, Cognitive Politics and Schema Criticism*. Austin: University of Texas Press, 2013.

Brecht, Bertolt. *Die Stücke von Bertolt Brecht in Einem Band*. Frankfurt am Main, Germany: Suhrkamp Verlag, 1992.

Breithaupt, Fritz. *The Dark Sides of Empathy*. Trans. Andrew Hamilton. Ithaca, NY: Cornell University Press, 2019.

Brewer, Marilynn. "Intergroup Discrimination: Ingroup Love or Outgroup Hate?" In *The Cambridge Handbook of the Psychology of Prejudice*. Ed. Chris Sibley and Fiona Barlow. Cambridge: Cambridge University Press, 2017, 90–110.

Brinton, Howard. *The Religious Philosophy of Quakerism: The Beliefs of Fox, Barcla, and Penn as Based on the Gospel of John*. Wallingford, PA: Pendle Hill, 1973.

Bucchioni, Giulia, Thierry Lelard, Said Ahmaidi, Olivier Godefroy, Pierre Prystkowiak, and Harold Mouras. "Do We Feel the Same Empathy for Loved and Hated Peers?" *PLoS ONE* (May 29, 2015). https://journals.plos.org/plosone/article/file?id=10.1371/journal.pone.0125871&type=printable (accessed September 10, 2020).

Buchanan, Allen. *Our Moral Fate: Evolution and the Escape from Tribalism*. Cambridge, MA: MIT Press, 2020.

Buonomano, Dean. *Your Brain Is a Time Machine: The Neuroscience and Physics of Time*. New York: Norton, 2017.

Burton, Henry. "The Worship of the Roman Emperors." *The Biblical World* 40.2 (1912): 80–91.

Burton, Neel. "When Homosexuality Stopped Being a Mental Disorder." *Psychology Today* (September 18, 2015). www.psychologytoday.com/us/blog/hide-and-seek/201509/when-homosexuality-stopped-being-mental-disorder (accessed October 10, 2020).

Cantarino, Vicente. *Arabic Poetics in the Golden Age: Selection of Texts Accompanied by a Preliminary Study*. Leiden, the Netherlands: Brill, 1975.

Caracciolo, Marco. "Cognitive Science: Literary Emotions from Appraisal to Embodiment." In *The Routledge Companion to Literature and Emotion*. Ed. Patrick Colm Hogan, Bradley Irish, and Lalita Pandit Hogan. New York: Routledge, 2022, 50–60.

Carroll, Noël. *Engaging the Moving Image*. New Haven, CT: Yale University Press, 2003, 88–107.

Chan, Wing-Tsit, ed. and trans. *A Source Book in Chinese Philosophy*. Princeton, NJ: Princeton University Press, 1963.

Cheng, Anne. "Filial Piety with a Vengeance: The Tension between Rites and Law in the Han." In *Filial Piety in Chinese Thought and History*. Ed. Alan Chan and Sor-hoon Tan. London: RoutledgeCurzon, 2004, 29–43.

Chester, Stephen. "Paul and the Introspective Conscience of Martin Luther: The Impact of Luther's *Anfechtungen* on His Interpretation of Paul." *Biblical Interpretation* 14.5 (2006): 508–536.

Chi Chün-hsiang. "The Orphan of Chao." In *Six Yuän Plays*. Ed. and trans. Liu Jung-en. New York: Penguin, 1972, 41–81.

Chomsky, Noam. *The New Military Humanism: Lessons from Kosovo*. Monroe, ME: Common Courage Press, 2002.

Chomsky, Noam, and Michel Foucault. *The Chomsky-Foucault Debate on Human Nature*. New York: The New Press, 2006.

Christov-Moore, Leonardo, and Marco Iacoboni. "Equivocating Empathy." *Boston Review* (August 20, 2014). https://bostonreview.net/forum_response/leonardo-christov-moore-marco-iacoboni-response-against-empathy-iacoboni/ (accessed January 19, 2022).

Churchland, Patricia. *Conscience: The Origins of Moral Intuition*. New York: Norton, 2019.

Cialdini, Robert, Richard Borden, Avril Thorne, Marcus Walker, Stephen Freeman, and L. R. Sloan. "Basking in Reflected Glory: Three (Football) Field Studies." *Journal of Personality and Social Psychology* 34.3 (1976): 366–375.

*The Classic of Rites*. Trans. James Legge. In *Sacred Books of the East*. Ed. Max Müller. Vol. 28, pt. 4. Oxford: Oxford University Press, 1885. https://ctext.org/liji (accessed March 20, 2018).

Coplan, Amy, and Peter Goldie, eds. *Empathy*. Oxford: Oxford University Press, 2011.

Coppola, Carlo. "The All-India Progressive Writers' Association: The Early Phases." In *Marxist Influences and South Asian Literature*. Vol. 1. Ed. Carlo Coppola. East Lansing: Asian Studies Center of Michigan State University, 1974, 1–41.

Crossette, Barbara. "Iraq Sanctions Kill Children, U.N. Reports." *New York Times* (December 1, 1995), A9.

Damasio, Antonio. *Descartes' Error: Emotion, Reason, and the Human Brain*. New York: Avon, 1994.

Darbha, Poosha. *The Illustrated Dictionary of Sexology*. Samalkot, India: Ramsha Institute of Sexuality, 2002.

Darley, John M., and C. Daniel Batson. "From Jerusalem to Jericho: A Study of Situational and Dispositional Variables in Helping Behavior." *Journal of Personality and Social Psychology* 27.1 (1973): 100–119.

de Bary, Theodore, and Irene Bloom, eds. *Sources of Chinese Tradition: From Earliest Times to 1600*. 2nd ed. New York: Columbia University Press, 1999.

Delgado, Richard. *The Coming Race War? And Other Apocalyptic Tales of America after Affirmative Action and Welfare*. New York: New York University Press, 1996.

de Waal, Frans. *Primates and Philosophers: How Morality Evolved*. Ed. Stephen Macedo and Josiah Ober. Princeton, NJ: Princeton University Press, 2006.

Debes, Remy. "Empathy and Mirror Neurons." In *The Routledge Handbook of Philosophy of Empathy*. Ed. Heidi Maibom. New York: Routledge, 2017, 54–63.

Debes, Remy, and Karsten R. Stueber, eds. *Ethical Sentimentalism: New Perspectives*. Cambridge: Cambridge University Press, 2017.

Decety, Jean, ed. *Empathy: From Bench to Bedside*. Cambridge, MA: MIT Press, 2012.

Decety, Jean, and William Ickes, eds. *The Social Neuroscience of Empathy*. Cambridge, MA: MIT Press, 2009. (Unpaginated Kindle edition.)

Dehaene, Stanislas. *Consciousness and the Brain: Deciphering How the Brain Codes Our Thoughts*. New York: Viking, 2014.

Denham, Alison. "Empathy and Moral Motivation." In *The Routledge Handbook of Philosophy of Empathy*. Ed. Heidi Maibom. New York: Routledge, 2017, 227–241.

Deva, B. C. *Indian Music*. 2nd ed. New Delhi: Indian Council for Cultural Relations, 1980.

Doherty, Martin. *Theory of Mind: How Children Understand Others' Thoughts and Feelings*. New York: Psychology Press, 2009.

Dovidio, John, Samuel Gaertner, and Adam Pearson. "Aversive Racism and Contemporary Bias." In *The Cambridge Handbook of the Psychology of Prejudice*. Ed. Chris Sibley and Fiona Barlow. Cambridge: Cambridge University Press, 2017, 267–294

Doyle, Kerrie, Catherine Hungerford, and Mary Cruickshank. "Reviewing Tribunal Cases and Nurse Behaviour: Putting Empathy Back into Nurse Education with Bloom's Taxonomy." *Nurse Education Today* 34 (2014): 1069–1073.

Duckitt, John. *The Social Psychology of Prejudice*. New York: Praeger, 1992.

Dunning, David. "Judgment and Decision Making." In *The SAGE Handbook of Social Cognition*. Ed. Susan Fiske and C. Neil Macrae. London: Sage, 2012, 251–272.

Echols, Stephanie, and Joshua Correll. "It's More Than Skin Deep: Empathy and Helping Behavior across Social Groups." In *Empathy: From Bench to Bedside*. Ed. Jean Decety. Cambridge, MA: MIT Press, 2012, 55–71.

Eisenberg, Nancy, Snjezana Huerta, and Alison Edwards. "Relations of Empathy-Related Responding to Children's and Adolescents' Social Competence." In *Empathy: From Bench to Bedside*. Ed. Jean Decety. Cambridge, MA: MIT Press, 2012, 147–163.

Feagin, Susan. "Empathizing as Simulating." In *Empathy*. Ed. Amy Coplan and Peter Goldie. Oxford: Oxford University Press, 2011, 149–161.

Feather, Jennifer. "To 'Tempt the Rheumy and Unpurged Air': Contagion and Agency in Julius Caesar." In *Shakespeare and Moral Agency*. Ed. Michael Bristol. London: Continuum, 2010, 86–98.

Feshbach, Norma Deitch, and Seymour Feshbach. "Empathy and Education." In *The Social Neuroscience of Empathy*. Ed. Jean Decety and William Ickes. Cambridge, MA: MIT Press, 2009, 85–98.

Florescu, Radu, and Raymond McNally. *Dracula*. New York: Hawthorn, 1973.

Fontaine, Johnny. "Dimensional Emotion Models." In *The Oxford Companion to Emotion and the Affective Sciences*. Ed. David Sander and Klaus Scherer. Oxford: Oxford University Press, 2009, 119–120.

Forgas, Joseph. "Introduction: The Role of Affect in Social Cognition." In *Feeling and Thinking: The Role of Affect in Social Cognition*. Ed. Joseph Forgas. Cambridge: Cambridge University Press, 2000, 1–28.

Foucault, Michel. *The Archaeology of Knowledge and the Discourse on Language*. Trans. A. M. Sheridan Smith. New York: Harper and Row, 1972.

*Ethics: Subjectivity and Truth*. Ed. Paul Rabinow. New York: The New Press, 1997.

*The History of Sexuality, Vol. 3: The Care of the Self*. Trans. Robert Hurley. New York: Vintage, 1988.

Frijda, Nico. *The Emotions*. Cambridge: Cambridge University Press, 1986.
Frijda, Nico, and Klaus Scherer. "Affect (Psychological Perspectives)." In *The Oxford Companion to Emotion and the Affective Sciences*. Ed. David Sander and Klaus Scherer. Oxford: Oxford University Press, 2009, 10.
Fu, Yu-wen. "Breaking through the *Rabbit-Proof Fence*: Colonial Displacement and Aboriginal Resistance in Doris Pilkington Garimara's Storytelling." *Concentric: Literary and Cultural Studies* 45.1 (2019): 167–188.
Gallese, Vittorio, and Michele Guerra. *The Empathic Screen: Cinema and Neuroscience*. Trans. Frances Anderson. Oxford: Oxford University Press, 2019.
Gardner, Dan. *The Science of Fear*. New York: Dutton, 2008.
Garimara, Nugi. (Doris Pilkington.) *Follow the Rabbit-Proof Fence*. Queensland, Australia: University of Queensland Press, 2002.
Gazzaniga, Michael. *Who's in Charge? Free Will and the Science of the Brain*. New York: Ecco, 2011.
Geertz, Clifford. *The Interpretation of Cultures: Selected Essays*. New York: Basic Books, 1973.
Gilbert, Daniel, and Patrick Malone. "The Correspondence Bias." *Psychological Bulletin* 117.1 (1995): 21–38.
Gill, Michael, and Stephanie Cerce. "He Never Willed to Have the Will He Has: Narratives, 'Civilized' Blame, and the Need to Distinguish Two Notions of Free Will." *Journal of Personality and Social Psychology* 112 (2017): 361–382.
Gilman, Sander. *The Jew's Body*. New York: Routledge, 1991.
Gilovich, Thomas, Dale Griffin, and Daniel Kahneman, eds. *Heuristics and Biases: The Psychology of Intuitive Judgment*. Cambridge: Cambridge University Press, 2002.
Gohlke, Madelon. "'I Wooed Thee with My Sword': Shakespeare's Tragic Paradigms." In *Representing Shakespeare: New Psychoanalytic Essays*. Ed. Murray Schwartz and Coppélia Kahn. Baltimore, MD: Johns Hopkins University Press, 1980, 170–187.
Goldie, Peter. "Anti-Empathy." In *Empathy*. Ed. Amy Coplan and Peter Goldie. Oxford: Oxford University Press, 2011, 302–317.
Goldie, Peter, ed. *The Oxford Handbook of Philosophy of Emotion*. Oxford: Oxford University Press, 2010.
Goldman, Alvin. "Two Routes to Empathy: Insights from Cognitive Neuroscience." In *Empathy*. Ed. Amy Coplan and Peter Goldie. Oxford: Oxford University Press, 2011, 31–44.
Grady, Hugh. "Moral Agency and Its Problems in *Julius Caesar*: Political Power, Choice, and History." In *Shakespeare and Moral Agency*. Ed. Michael Bristol. London: Continuum, 2010, 15–28.
"Great Learning, The" (Dà Xué, 大學). Trans. James Legge. In *Liji*. Chinese Text Project. Ed. Donald Sturgeon. https://ctext.org (accessed September 2, 2020).
Greenblatt, Stephen, ed. *The Norton Shakespeare*. New York: Norton, 1997.
Greenblatt, Stephen. *Will in the World: How Shakespeare Became Shakespeare*. New York: Norton, 2004.

Greenfeld, Liah. *Nationalism: Five Roads to Modernity*. Cambridge, MA: Harvard University Press, 1992.

Greenspan, Patricia. "Learning Emotion and Ethics." In *The Oxford Handbook of Philosophy of Emotion*. Ed. Peter Goldie. Oxford: Oxford University Press, 2010, 539–559.

Guan Hanqing. "Rescuing a Sister." Trans. George Kao and Wai-Yee Li. In *The Columbia Anthology of Yuan Drama*. Ed. C. Hsia, Wai-Yee Li, and George Kao. New York: Columbia University Press, 2014, 272–329.

Guo, Christine. "The Neuroscience of Empathy." In *The Routledge Handbook of Philosophy of Empathy*. Ed. Heidi Maibom. New York: Routledge, 2017, 44–53.

Hadfield, Andrew David, ed. *Julius Caesar*. New York: Barnes and Noble, 2007.

Haidt, Jonathan. *The Righteous Mind: Why Good People Are Divided by Politics and Religion*. New York: Pantheon, 2012.

Haji, Ishtiyaque. "Empathy and Legal Responsibility." In *The Routledge Handbook of Philosophy of Empathy*. Ed. Heidi Maibom. New York: Routledge, 2017, 253–263.

Hakemulder, Frank. *The Moral Laboratory: Experiments Examining the Effects of Reading Literature on Social Perception and Moral Self-Concept*. Amsterdam, the Netherlands: John Benjamins, 2000.

Halpern, Jodi. "Clinical Empathy in Medical Care." In *Empathy: From Bench to Bedside*. Ed. Jean Decety. Cambridge, MA: MIT Press, 2012, 229–244.

Hamington, Maurice. "Empathy and Care Ethics." In *The Routledge Handbook of Philosophy of Empathy*. Ed. Heidi Maibom. New York: Routledge, 2017, 264–272.

Hardy, Sam, and Gustavo Carlo. 2011. "Moral Identity." In *Handbook of Identity Theory and Research*. Ed. Seth Schwartz, Koen Luycks, and Vivian Vignoles. New York: Springer, 2011, 495–513.

Hauser, Marc. *Moral Minds: How Nature Designed Our Universal Sense of Right and Wrong*. New York: Ecco Press, 2006.

Hawley, William. "*A Midsummer Night's Dream*: Relating Ethics to Mutuality." *The European Legacy* 15.2 (2010): 159–169.

Hein, Grit, Giorgia Silani, Kerstin Preuschoff, C. Daniel Batson, and Tania Singer. "Neural Responses to Ingroup and Outgroup Members' Suffering Predict Individual Differences in Costly Helping." *Neuron* 68.1 (2010): 149–160.

Hellman, Lillian. *The Children's Hour*. New York: Dramatists Play Service, 1934.

Henrich, Joseph. *The WEIRDest People in the World: How the West Became Psychologically Peculiar and Particularly Prosperous*. New York: Farrar, Straus and Giroux, 2020.

Henry, Devin. "Aristotle on the Mechanism of Inheritance." *Journal of the History of Biology* 39.3 (2006): 425–455.

Hess, Ursula. "Mimicry (Psychological Perspectives)." In *The Oxford Companion to Emotion and the Affective Sciences*. Ed. David Sander and Klaus Scherer. Oxford: Oxford University Press, 2009, 253–254.

Hess, Ursula, and Pierre Philippot, eds. *Group Dynamics and Emotional Expression*. Cambridge: Cambridge University Press, 2007.

Hibbing, John, Kevin Smith, and John Alford. "Differences in Negativity Bias Underlie Variations in Political Ideology." *Behavioral and Brain Sciences* 37.3 (2014): 297–307.

Hinton, Perry. "Implicit Stereotypes and the Predictive Brain: Cognition and Culture in 'Biased' Person Perception." *Palgrave Communications* 3 (2017). www.nature.com/articles/palcomms201786 (accessed September 14, 2020).

Hirsh, Jacob B., Colin G. DeYoung, Xiaowen Xu, and Jordan B. Peterson. "Compassionate Liberals and Polite Conservatives: Associations of Agreeableness with Political Ideology and Moral Values." *Personality and Social Psychology Bulletin* 36.5 (2010): 655–664.

Hirstein, William, Katrina Sifferd, and Tyler Fagan. *Responsible Brains: Neuroscience, Law, and Human Culpability*. Cambridge, MA: MIT Press, 2018.

Hitler, Adolf. *Mein Kampf*. München, Germany: NSDAP, 1943.

*Mein Kampf*. Ed. and trans. John Chamberlain et al. New York: Reynal and Hitchcock, 1940.

Hobsbawm, Eric. "Mass-Producing Traditions: Europe, 1870–1914." In *The Invention of Tradition*. Ed. Eric Hobsbawm and Terence Ranger. Cambridge: Cambridge University Press, 1983, 263–307.

Hoffman, Martin. *Empathy and Moral Development: Implications for Caring and Justice*. Cambridge: Cambridge University Press, 2000.

"Empathy, Justice, and the Law." In *Empathy*. Ed. Amy Coplan and Peter Goldie. Oxford: Oxford University Press, 2011, 230–254.

Hogan, Patrick Colm. *Affective Narratology: The Emotional Structure of Stories*. Lincoln: University of Nebraska Press, 2011a.

*American Literature and American Identity: A Cognitive Cultural Study from the Revolution through the Civil War*. New York: Routledge, 2020.

*Beauty and Sublimity: A Cognitive Aesthetics of Literature and the Arts*. Cambridge: Cambridge University Press, 2016.

"*The Butterfly Lovers*: Sex, Gender, and Emotion-Based Story Prototypes." In *Emotion in Animated Films*. Ed. Meike Uhrig. New York: Routledge, 2018, 60–82.

*The Culture of Conformism*. Durham, NC: Duke University Press, 2001.

*How Authors' Minds Make Stories*. Cambridge: Cambridge University Press, 2013.

*Imagining Kashmir: Emplotment and Colonialism*. Lincoln: University of Nebraska Press, 2016.

*The Mind and Its Stories: Narrative Universals and Human Emotion*. Cambridge: Cambridge University Press, 2003.

"The Paradox of Tragedy and Emotional Response to Simulation." *Behavioral and Brain Sciences* 40 (2017): 31–32.

"Paradoxes of Literary Emotion: Simulation and The Zhào Orphan." In *The Routledge Companion to Literature and Emotion*. Ed. Patrick Colm Hogan, Bradley Irish, and Lalita Pandit Hogan. New York: Routledge, 2022a.

*Personal Identity and Literature*. New York: Routledge, 2019.

*Sexual Identities: A Cognitive Literary Study*. New York: Oxford University Press, 2018.

"Stories: Particular Causes and Universal Genres." In *The Routledge Companion to Literature and Emotion.* Ed. Patrick Colm Hogan, Bradley Irish, and Lalita Pandit Hogan. New York: Routledge, 2022b.
  *Understanding Nationalism: On Narrative, Cognitive Science, and Identity.* Columbus: Ohio State University Press, 2009.
  *What Literature Teaches Us about Emotion.* Cambridge: Cambridge University Press, 2011b.
Hogan, Patrick Colm, Bradley Irish, and Lalita Pandit Hogan, eds. *The Routledge Companion to Literature and Emotion.* New York: Routledge, 2020.
Holland, Ashley, and Glenn Roisman. "Adult Attachment Security and Young Adults' Dating Relationships over Time: Self-Reported, Observational, and Physiological Evidence." *Developmental Psychology* 46.2 (2010): 552–557.
Holland, John, Keith Holyoak, Richard Nisbett, and Paul Thagard. *Induction: Processes of Inference, Learning, and Discovery.* Cambridge, MA: MIT Press, 1986.
Hsia, C., Wai-Yee Li, and George Kao, eds. *The Columbia Anthology of Yuan Drama.* New York: Columbia University Press, 2014.
Ibn Rushd (Averroes). *Averroes' Commentary on Plato's Republic.* Ed. and trans. E. Rosenthal. Cambridge: Cambridge University Press, 1966.
  *Averroes' Middle Commentary on Aristotle's Poetics.* Ed. and trans. Charles Butterworth. Princeton, NJ: Princeton University Press, 1986.
Ibn Sinā (Avicenna). *Avicenna's Commentary on the Poetics of Aristotle.* Ed. and trans. Ismail Dahiyat. Leiden, the Netherlands: Brill, 1974.
Ickes, William. "Empathic Accuracy: Its Links to Clinical, Cognitive, Developmental, Social, and Physiological Psychology." In *The Social Neuroscience of Empathy.* Ed. Jean Decety and William Ickes. Cambridge, MA: MIT Press, 2009.
Idema, Wilt. "Traditional Dramatic Literature." In *The Columbia History of Chinese Literature.* Ed. Victor Mair. New York: Columbia University Press, 2001, 785–847.
Ingalls, Daniel, ed. The *Dhvanyāloka* of Ānandavardhana with the *Locana* of Abhinavagupta. Trans. Daniel Ingalls, Jeffrey Masson, and Madhava Patwardhan. Cambridge, MA: Harvard University Press, 1990.
Jackson, Liz. *Beyond Virtue: The Politics of Educating Emotions.* Oxford: Oxford University Press, 2021.
Jayánta, Bhatta. *Much Ado about Religion.* Ed. and trans. Csaba Dezső. New York: New York University Press, 2005.
Ji Junxiang. *The Zhao Orphan.* Trans. Pi-Twan Huang and Wai-Yee Li. In *The Columbia Anthology of Yuan Drama.* Ed. C. Hsia, Wai-Yee Li, and George Kao. New York: Columbia University Press, 2014, 20–55.
Kahneman, Daniel. *Thinking, Fast and Slow.* New York: Farrar, Straus and Giroux, 2011.
Kahneman, Daniel, and Dale T. Miller. "Norm Theory: Comparing Reality to Its Alternatives." *Psychological Review* 93.2 (1986): 136–153.
Kālidāsa. *The Abhijñānaśākuntalam of Kālidāsa.* Ed. M. R. Kale. 10th ed. Delhi: Motilal Banarsidass, 1969.

Kant, Immanuel. *Grounding for the Metaphysics of Morals and "On a Supposed Right to Lie Because of Philanthropic Concerns."* Trans. James Ellington. Indianapolis: Hackett, 1981.

Kaplan, E. Ann. "Empathy and Trauma Culture: Imagining Catastrophe." In *Empathy*. Ed. Amy Coplan and Peter Goldie. Oxford: Oxford University Press, 2011 255–276.

Kauppinen, Antti. "Empathy and Moral Judgment." In *The Routledge Handbook of Philosophy of Empathy*. Ed. Heidi Maibom. New York: Routledge, 2017, 215–226.

Keen, Suzanne. "Colonialism and Postcolonialism." In *The Routledge Companion to Literature and Emotion*. Ed. Patrick Colm Hogan, Bradley Irish, and Lalita Pandit Hogan. New York: Routledge, 2022.

*Empathy and the Novel*. New York: Oxford University Press, 2010.

Kelly, Daniel. *Yuck! The Nature and Moral Significance of Disgust*. Cambridge, MA: MIT Press, 2011.

Keown, Damien. *Buddhist Ethics: A Very Short Introduction*. Oxford: Oxford University Press, 2005.

Kidd, David, and Emanuele Costano "Reading Literary Fiction Improves Theory of Mind." *Science* 342 (2013): 377–380.

Kidd, David, Martino Ongis, and Emanuele Castano. "On Literary Fiction and Its Effects on Theory of Mind." *Scientific Study of Literature* 6.1 (2016): 42–58.

Kim, Ji-Woong, S.-E. Kim, J.-J. Kim, B. Jeong, C.-H. Park, A. Son, J. Song, and S. Ki. "Compassionate Attitude toward Others' Suffering Activates the Mesolimbic Neural System." *Neuropsychologia* 47 (2009): 2073–2081.

Kim, Sue. *On Anger: Race, Cognition, Narrative*. Austin: University of Texas Press, 2013.

Kitcher, Philip. "Ethics and Evolution: How to Get Here from There." In *Primates and Philosophers: How Morality Evolved*. By Frans de Waal. Ed. Stephen Macedo and Josiah Ober. Princeton, NJ: Princeton University Press, 120–140.

Klein, Dorothee. "Narrating a Different (Hi)Story: The Affective Work of Counter-Discourse in Doris Pilkington's *Follow the Rabbit-Proof Fence*." *Interventions* 18.4 (2016): 588–604.

Kling, Blair. "Gandhi, Nonviolence, and the Holocaust." *Peace & Change* 16.2 (1991): 176–196.

Knight, Sabina. *Chinese Literature: A Very Short Introduction*. Oxford: Oxford University Press, 2012.

Kǒngzǐ (Confucius). *Analects* (*Lún Yǔ*, 論語). Trans. James Legge. *Chinese Text Project*. Ed. Donald Sturgeon. https://ctext.org (accessed September 2, 2020).

Kosslyn, Stephen. "Foreword." In *Mind Time: The Temporal Factor in Consciousness*. By Benjamin Libet. Cambridge, MA: Harvard University Press, ix–xvi.

*Image and Brain: The Resolution of the Imagery Debate*. Cambridge, MA: MIT Press, 1994.

Kringelbach, Morten, and Helen Phillips. *Emotion: Pleasure and Pain in the Brain.* Oxford: Oxford University Press, 2014.
Kunda, Ziva. *Social Cognition: Making Sense of People.* Cambridge, MA: MIT Press, 1999.
Kushner, Tony. *Angels in America: A Gay Fantasia on National Themes.* Revised ed. New York: Theatre Communications Group, 2013.
Lamb, Sarah. "Aging, Gender and Widowhood: Perspectives from Rural West Bengal." *Contributions to Indian Sociology* 33 (1999): 541–570.
Landy, Joshua. "Fiction, Politics, and the Limits of Empathy." Paper delivered at the annual convention of the Modern Language Association of America, New York City, January 6, 2018.
Laplanche, Jean, and Jean-Bertrand Pontalis. *The Language of Psychoanalysis.* Trans. Donald Nicholson-Smith. New York: Norton, 1973.
Leary, Mark, and June Tangney, eds. *Handbook of Self and Identity.* 2nd ed. New York: Guilford Press, 2012.
LeDoux, Joseph. *Anxious: Using the Brain to Understand and Treat Fear and Anxiety.* New York: Penguin, 2015.
 *The Emotional Brain: The Mysterious Underpinnings of Emotional Life.* New York: Touchstone, 1996.
 *Synaptic Self: How Our Brains Become Who We Are.* New York: Penguin, 2002.
Leiser, Erwin, dir. and screenplay. *Germany, Awake!* Zürich: Erwin Leiser Filmproduktion, 1968.
Lepore, Jill. *These Truths: A History of the United States.* New York: Norton, 2019.
Levy, Neil. *Neuroethics.* Cambridge: Cambridge University Press, 2007.
Lewis, Mark. *The Early Chinese Empires: Qin and Han.* Cambridge, MA: Belknap Press, 2007.
Li, Wai-Yee. "Introduction [to Rescuing a Sister by Guan Hanqing]." In *The Columbia Anthology of Yuan Drama.* Ed. C. Hsia, Wai-Yee Li, and George Kao. New York: Columbia University Press, 2014, 269–272.
Liu Jung-en. "Introduction." In *Six Yuän Plays.* Ed. and trans. Liu Jung-en. New York: Penguin, 1972, 7–35.
Lovrod, Marie. "Narrow Escapes: Gendered Adolescent Resistance to Intergenerational Neo/Colonial Violence across Time and Space." *Rocky Mountain Review* 69.1 (2015): 68–86.
Lueders, Bill. "Let's Overthrow the Government." *The Progressive* (October–November 2019): 6–7.
Lukianoff, Greg, and Jonathan Haidt. *The Coddling of the American Mind.* New York: Penguin, 2018.
MacIntyre, Alasdair. *A Short History of Ethics: A History of Moral Philosophy from the Homeric Age to the Twentieth Century.* 2nd ed. London: Routledge, 1998.
Macintyre, Stuart. *A Concise History of Australia.* 2nd ed. Cambridge: Cambridge University Press, 2004.
Maibom, Heidi. "Affective Empathy." In *The Routledge Handbook of Philosophy of Empathy.* Ed. Heidi Maibom. New York: Routledge, 2017, 22–32.
Maibom, Heidi, ed. *The Routledge Handbook of Philosophy of Empathy.* New York: Routledge, 2017.

Maitner, Angela, Eliot Smith, and Diane Mackie. "Intergroup Emotions Theory: Prejudice and Differentiated Emotional Reactions Toward Outgroups." In *The Cambridge Handbook of the Psychology of Prejudice*. Ed. Chris Sibley and Fiona Barlow. Cambridge: Cambridge University Press, 2017, 111–130.

Manvell, Roger. "Introduction." *Masterworks of the German Cinema*. London: Lorrimer, 1973.

Mar, Raymond, Keith Oatley, and Jordan Peterson. "Exploring the Link between Reading Fiction and Empathy: Ruling Out Individual Differences and Examining Outcomes." *Communications: The European Journal of Communication* 34 (2009): 407–428.

Marcus, Ruth Barcan. "Moral Dilemmas and Consistency." *Journal of Philosophy* 77.3 (1980): 121–136.

Markandaya, Kamala. *Nectar in a Sieve*. New York: Signet, 2002.

Marsh, Abigail. "Empathy and Compassion: A Cognitive Neuroscience Perspective." In *Empathy: From Bench to Bedside*. Ed. Jean Decety. Cambridge, MA: MIT Press, 2012, 191–205.

Masters, Anthony. *The Natural History of the Vampire*. New York: Putnam's Sons, 1972.

Matravers, Derek. *Empathy*. Cambridge: Polity Press, 2017.

McEachern, Claire, ed. *The Cambridge Companion to Shakespearean Tragedy*. Cambridge: Cambridge University Press, 2002.

McFarland, Sam. "Identification with All Humanity: The Antithesis of Prejudice, and More." In *The Cambridge Handbook of the Psychology of Prejudice*. Ed. Chris Sibley and Fiona Barlow. Cambridge: Cambridge University Press, 2017, 632–654.

McRae, Emily. "Empathy, Compassion, and 'Exchanging Self and Other' in Indo-Tibetan Buddhism." In *The Routledge Handbook of Philosophy of Empathy*. Ed. Heidi Maibom. New York: Routledge, 2017, 123–133.

Mèngzǐ. *Mengzi* (孟子). Trans. James Legge. *Chinese Text Project*. Ed. Donald Sturgeon. https://ctext.org (accessed September 2, 2020).

Miller, Barbara Stoler, ed. and trans. *The Bhagavad Gita: Krishna's Counsel in Time of War*. New York: Bantam, 1986.

Morton, Adam. "Empathy for the Devil." In *Empathy*. Ed. Amy Coplan and Peter Goldie. Oxford: Oxford University Press, 2011, 318–330.

Murnau, Friedrich Wilhelm, dir. *Nosferatu, eine Symphonie des Grauens*. Written by Henrik Galeen (from a novel by Bram Stoker). Berlin: Jofa-Atelier, 1922.

Murphy, Gregory, and Aaron Hoffman. "Concepts." In *The Cambridge Handbook of Cognitive Science*. Ed. Keith Frankish and William Ramsey. Cambridge: Cambridge University Press, 2012, 151–170.

Mussolini, Benito (and Giovanni Gentile). *The Doctrine of Fascism*. New York: Aristeus Books, 2012.

*La Dottrina del Fascismo*. Roma: Istituto della Enciclopedia Italiana, 1935. www.geocities.ws/fransavari/DottrinaFasc.pdf (accessed October 11, 2020).

Nagel, Thomas. *Mind and Cosmos: Why the Materialist, Neo-Darwinian Conception of Nature Is Almost Certainly False*. Oxford: Oxford University Press, 2012.

*Mortal Questions*. Cambridge: Cambridge University Press, 1979.

*Nāṭya Śāstra*. Delhi, India: Sri Satguru, n.d.

Nell, Onora. *Acting on Principle: An Essay on Kantian Ethics*. New York: Columbia University Press, 1975.

Nickerson, Raymond, Susan Butler, and Michael Carlin. "Empathy and Knowledge Projection." In *The Social Neuroscience of Empathy*. Ed. Jean Decety and William Ickes. Cambridge, MA: MIT Press, 2009, 43–56.

Nielsen, Ken. *Tony Kushner's* Angels in America. New York: Continuum, 2008.

Nienhauser, William. "Tetrasyllabic *Shi* Poetry: *The Book of Poetry* (*Shijing*)." In *How to Read Chinese Poetry: A Guided Anthology*. Ed. Zong-Qi Cai. New York: Columbia University Press, 2008, 13–35.

Noë, Alva. *Varieties of Presence*. Cambridge, MA: Harvard University Press, 2012.

Nortvedt, Per. "Empathy and Medical Therapy." In *The Routledge Handbook of Philosophy of Empathy*. Ed. Heidi Maibom. New York: Routledge, 2017, 273–282.

Nussbaum, Martha. *Anger and Forgiveness: Resentment, Generosity, Justice*. Oxford: Oxford University Press, 2016.

*From Disgust to Humanity*. New York: Oxford University Press, 2010.

*Hiding from Humanity: Disgust, Shame, and the Law*. Princeton, NJ: Princeton University Press, 2009.

*The Monarchy of Fear: A Philosopher Looks at Our Political Crisis*. New York: Simon & Schuster, 2019.

*Upheavals of Thought: On the Intelligence of Emotions*. Cambridge: Cambridge University Press, 2003.

Oatley, Keith. *Best Laid Schemes: The Psychology of Emotions*. Cambridge: Cambridge University Press, 1992.

O'Flaherty, Wendy. "The Clash between Relative and Absolute Duty: The Dharma of Demons." In *The Concept of Duty in South Asia*. Ed. Wendy O'Flaherty and J. Duncan M. Derrett. London: South Asia Books/School of Oriental and African Studies, 1978, 96–106.

Ortony, Andrew, Gerald Clore, and Allan Collins. *The Cognitive Structure of Emotions*. New York: Cambridge University Press, 1988.

Paluck, Elizabeth. 2009. "Reducing Intergroup Prejudice and Conflict Using the Media: A Field Experiment in Rwanda." *Journal of Personality and Social Psychology* 96 (2009): 574–587.

Parekh, Bhikhu. *Colonialism, Tradition, and Reform: An Analysis of Gandhi's Political Discourse*. New Delhi, India: Sage, 1989.

Parkinson, Brian. *Heart to Heart: How Your Emotions Affect Other People*. Oxford: Oxford University Press, 2019.

Parvini, Neema. *Shakespeare's Moral Compass*. Edinburgh: Edinburgh University Press, 2018.

Paxton, Robert. *The Anatomy of Fascism*. New York: Vintage, 2005. Unpaginated Kindle edition.

Pestana, Mark. "Complexity Theory, Quantum Mechanics and Radically Free Self Determination." *Journal of Mind and Behavior* 22.4 (2001): 365–388.

Piaget, Jean. *Biology and Knowledge: An Essay on the Relations between Organic Regulations and Cognitive Processes*. Trans. Beatrix Walsh. Chicago: University of Chicago Press, 1971.

Pilkington, Doris. (Nugi Garimara.) *Follow the Rabbit-Proof Fence*. Queensland, Australia: University of Queensland Press, 2002.

Pinker, Steven. *The Better Angels of Our Nature: Why Violence Has Declined*. New York: Penguin, 2011.

*How the Mind Works*. New York: Norton, 1997.

Plutarch. *Lives of the Noble Romans*. Ed. Edmund Fuller. New York: Dell, 1959.

Preston, Stephanie D., and Frans de Waal. "Empathy: Its Ultimate and Proximate Bases." *Behavioral and Brain Sciences* 25.1 (2002): 1–72.

Prinz, Jesse. "The Moral Emotions." In *The Oxford Handbook of Philosophy of Emotion*. Ed. Peter Goldie. Oxford: Oxford University Press, 2010, 519–538.

Pulvermüller, Friedemann. *The Neuroscience of Language: On Brain Circuits of Words and Serial Order*. Cambridge: Cambridge University Press, 2002.

Putnam, Hilary. "Quantum Mechanics and the Observer." *Realism and Reason: Philosophical Papers*, Vol. 3. Cambridge: Cambridge University Press, 1983, 248–270.

Ray, Larry, David Smith, and Liz Wastell. "Shame, Rage and Racist Violence." *British Journal of Criminology* 44 (2004): 350–368.

Reisenzein, Rainer. "The Schachter Theory of Emotion: Two Decades Later." *Psychological Bulletin* 94.2 (1983): 239–264.

Ridley, Aaron. "Tragedy." In *The Oxford Handbook of Aesthetics*. Ed. Jerrold Levinson. Oxford: Oxford University Press, 2005, 408–420.

Richeson, Jennifer, John Dovidio, J. Nicole Shelton, and Michelle Hebl. "Implications of Ingroup-Outgroup Membership for Interpersonal Perceptions: Faces and Emotion." In *Group Dynamics and Emotional Expression*. Ed. Ursula Hess and Pierre Philippot. Cambridge: Cambridge University Press, 2007, 7–32.

Ricoeur, Paul. *Freud and Philosophy: An Essay on Interpretation*. Trans. Denis Savage. New Haven, CT: Yale University Press, 1977.

Riefenstahl, Leni, dir. *Triumph of the Will*. Berlin, Germany: Leni Riefenstahl-Produktion and Reichspropagandaleitung der NSDAP, 1935.

Robbins, Philip, and Murat Aydede, eds. *The Cambridge Handbook of Situated Cognition*. Cambridge: Cambridge University Press, 2009.

Rogoff, Barbara. *The Cultural Nature of Human Development*. Oxford: Oxford University Press, 2003.

Rosch, Eleanor. "Prototypes." In *The Cambridge Encyclopedia of the Language Sciences*. Ed. Patrick Colm Hogan. Cambridge: Cambridge University Press, 2011, 680–682.

Ross, Lee. "The Intuitive Psychologist and His Shortcomings: Distortions in the Attribution Process." In *Advances in Experimental Social Psychology*, Vol. 10. Ed. Leonard Berkowitz. New York: Academic Press, 1977, 174–221.

Rottschaefer, William. *The Biology and Psychology of Moral Agency*. Cambridge: Cambridge University Press, 1998.

Roughley, Neil, and Thomas Schramme. "Empathy, Sympathy, Concern and Moral Agency." In *Forms of Fellow Feeling: Empathy, Sympathy, Concern and Moral Agency*. Ed. Neil Roughley and Thomas Schramme. Cambridge: Cambridge University Press, 2018, 3–55.

Royzman, Edward B., and Paul Rozin. "Limits of Symhedonia: The Differential Role of Prior Emotional Attachment in Sympathy and Sympathetic Joy." *Emotion* 6.1 (2006): 82–93.

Ryff, Carol, and Burton Singer. "The Role of Emotion on Pathways to Positive Health." In *Handbook of Affective Sciences*. Ed. Richard Davidson, Klaus Scherer, and H. Hill Goldsmith. Oxford: Oxford University Press, 2009, 1083–1104.

Sander, David, and Klaus Scherer, eds. *The Oxford Companion to Emotion and the Affective Sciences*. Oxford: Oxford University Press, 2009.

Sapolsky, Robert. *Behave: The Biology of Humans at Our Best and Worst*. New York: Penguin, 2017.

Sargeant, Winthrop, ed. and trans. *The Bhagavad Gītā*. Albany: State University of New York Press, 1994.

Sathyu, M. S., dir. *Garam Hawa*. Written by Kaifi Azmi and Shama Zaidi. New Delhi: Film Finance Corporation, 1974.

Scarry, Elaine. *Dreaming by the Book*. New York: Farrar, Straus and Giroux, 1999.

Schachter, Stanley, and Jerome Singer. "Cognitive, Social and Physiological Determinants of Emotional State." *Psychological Review* 69 (1962): 379–399.

Scheff, Thomas. "Social-Emotional Origins of Violence: A Theory of Multiple Killing." *Aggression and Violent Behavior* 16 (2011): 453–460.

Schivelbusch, Wolfgang. *The Culture of Defeat*. Trans. Jefferson Chase. New York: Metropolitan, 2003.

Schramme, Thomas. "Empathy and Altruism." In *The Routledge Handbook of Philosophy of Empathy*. Ed. Heidi Maibom. New York: Routledge, 2017, 203–214.

Schulz, Armin. "The Evolution of Empathy." In *The Routledge Handbook of Philosophy of Empathy*. Ed. Heidi Maibom. New York: Routledge, 2017, 64–73.

Schwartz, Seth, Koen Luycks, and Vivian Vignoles, eds. *Handbook of Identity Theory and Research*. New York: Springer, 2011.

Sen, Ranjit. "The West and the Metropolitan Indian Mind: A Case Study of Calcutta in the Nineteenth Century." *Proceedings of the Indian History Congress* 52 (1991): 725–731.

Shakespeare, William. *All's Well That Ends Well*. In *The Norton Shakespeare*. Ed. Stephen Greenblatt. New York: Norton, 1997, 2183–2243.

*Julius Caesar*. In *Julius Caesar*. Ed. Andrew David Hadfield. New York: Barnes and Noble, 2007, 39–281.

*Romeo and Juliet*. Ed. Brian Gibbons. London: Methuen, 1980.

*The Tragedy of Hamlet, Prince of Denmark*. In *The Norton Shakespeare*. Ed. Stephen Greenblatt. New York: Norton, 1997, 1668–1756.

Shoemaker, David. "Empathy and Moral Responsibility." In *The Routledge Handbook of Philosophy of Empathy*. Ed. Heidi Maibom. New York: Routledge, 2017, 242–252.

Sinclair, Ian. "Resisting the Nazis in Numerous Ways: Nonviolence in Occupied Europe." (An interview with George Paxton.) *Open Democracy* (July 19, 2017). www.opendemocracy.net/en/non-violence-against-nazis-interview-with-george-paxton/ (accessed September 6, 2020).

Slovic, Paul, Melissa Finucane, Ellen Peters, and Donald MacGregor. "The Affect Heuristic." In *Heuristics and Biases: The Psychology of Intuitive Judgment*. Ed. Thomas Gilovich, Dale Griffin, and Daniel Kahneman. Cambridge: Cambridge University Press, 2002, 397–420.

Slovic, Paul, and Daniel Västfjäll. "The More Who Die, the Less We Care: Psychic Numbing and Genocide." In *Numbers and Nerves*. Ed. Scott Slovic and Paul Slovic. Corvallis: Oregon State University Press, 2015, 27–41.

Soutschek, Alexander, Christian Ruff, Tina Strombach, Tobias Kalenscher, and Philippe Tobler. "Brain Stimulation Reveals Crucial Role of Overcoming Self-Centeredness in Self-Control." *Science Advances* 2.10 (2016). https://advances.sciencemag.org/content/2/10/e1600992 (accessed September 5, 2020).

Spaulding, Shannon. "Cognitive Empathy." In *The Routledge Handbook of Philosophy of Empathy*. Ed. Heidi Maibom. New York: Routledge, 2017, 13–21.

Stern, Jessica, and Jude Cassidy. "Empathy from Infancy to Adolescence: An Attachment Perspective on the Development of Individual Differences." *Developmental Review* 47 (2017): 1–22.

Ta, Vivian, and William Ickes. "Empathic Accuracy." In *The Routledge Handbook of Philosophy of Empathy*. Ed. Heidi Maibom. New York: Routledge, 2017, 353–363.

Tagore, Rabindranath. *Selected Short Stories*. Trans. William Radice. New York: Penguin, 1991.

Tāng Xianzu. *The Peony Pavilion (Mudan Ting)*. Trans. Cyril Birch. Boston: Cheng & Tsui, 1980.

Tangney, June, and Jessica Tracy. "Self-Conscious Emotions." In *Handbook of Self and Identity*. 2nd ed. Ed. Mark Leary and June Tangney. New York: Guilford Press, 2012, 446–478.

Taylor, Ella. "In a Better World: Oscar-Feted Compassion Porn." *The Village Voice* (March 30, 2011). www.villagevoice.com/2011/03/30/in-a-better-world-oscar-feted-compassion-porn/ (accessed September 1, 2020).

Thaler, Richard, and Cass Sunstein. *Nudge: Improving Decisions about Health, Wealth, and Happiness*. New York: Penguin, 2009.

"Three Strikes Basics." *Three Strikes Project*. Stanford Law School. https://law.stanford.edu/stanford-justice-advocacy-project/three-strikes-basics/ (accessed September 8, 2020), n.d.

Toates, Frederick. *How Sexual Desire Works: The Enigmatic Urge*. Cambridge: Cambridge University Press, 2014.

Tomasello, Michael. *A Natural History of Human Morality*. Cambridge, MA: Harvard University Press, 2016.

Tsai, Ming Chin, dir. *The Butterfly Lovers*. Written by Ming Chin Tsai and Ya-Ya Teng. Taipei, Taiwan: Central Motion Pictures, 2004.

Van Gulik, Robert, ed. and trans. *Celebrated Cases of Judge Dee*. New York: Dover, 1976.

Varden, Helga. "Kant and Lying to the Murderer at the Door ... One More Time: Kant's Legal Philosophy and Lies to Murderers and Nazis." *Journal of Social Philosophy* 41.4 (2010): 403–421.

Västfjäll, Daniel, Paul Slovic, and Marcus Mayorga. "Pseudoinefficacy and the Arithmetic of Compassion." In *Numbers and Nerves*. Ed. Scott Slovic and Paul Slovic. Corvallis: Oregon State University Press, 2015, 42–52.

Vitale, Alex. *The End of Policing*. New York: Verso, 2017. (Unpaginated Kindle edition.)

Von Trotta, Margarethe, dir. *Rosenstrasse*. Written by Pamela Katz and Margarethe von Trotta. Hamburg, Germany: Studio Hamburg Letterbox Filmproduktion, 2003.

Vorauer, Jacquie. *Empathy and Concern with Negative Evaluation in Intergroup Relations: Implications for Designing Effective Interventions*. Cambridge: Cambridge University Press, 2019.

Vyasa, Krishna-Dwaipayana. *The Mahabharata*. Trans. Kisari Mohan Ganguli. 4 vols. New Delhi, India: Munshiram Manoharlal, 1993.

Waller, Bruce. *Against Moral Responsibility*. Cambridge, MA: MIT Press, 2011.

Waller, Gregory. *The Living and the Undead*. Urbana: University of Illinois Press, 1986.

Walsh, Alistair. "Iran Defends Execution of Gay People." *DW.com* (June 12, 2019). www.dw.com/en/iran-defends-execution-of-gay-people/a-49144899 (accessed May 24, 2021).

Waters, Everett, Nancy Weinfield, and Claire Hamilton. "The Stability of Attachment Security from Infancy to Adolescence and Early Adulthood: General Discussion." *Child Development* 71.3 (2000): 703–706.

Watson, Burton. "Mozi: Utility, Uniformity, and Universal Love." In *Sources of Chinese Tradition: From Earliest Times to 1600*. 2nd ed. Ed. Theodore de Bary and Irene Bloom. New York: Columbia University Press, 1999, 64–76.

Watson, Robert. "Tragedies of Revenge and Ambition." In *The Cambridge Companion to Shakespearean Tragedy*. Ed. Claire McEachern. Cambridge: Cambridge University Press, 2002, 160–181.

Wegener, Paul and Carl Boese, dirs. *The Golem*. Written by Paul Wegener and Henrik Galeen. Berlin: Projektions–AG Union, 1920.

Weinmeyer, Richard. "The Decriminalization of Sodomy in the United States." *AMA Journal of Ethics* (November 2014). https://journalofethics.ama-assn.org/article/decriminalization-sodomy-united-states/2014-11 (accessed October 10, 2020).

Weinreich, Max. *Hitler's Professors*. 2nd ed. New Haven, CT: Yale University Press, 1999.

Wheatley, Thalia, and Jonathan Haidt. "Hypnotic Disgust Makes Moral Judgments More Severe." *Psychological Science* 16 (2005): 780–784.
Wills, Thomas. "Downward Comparison Principles in Social Psychology." *Psychological Bulletin* 90 (1981): 245–271.
Wong, David. "Moral Sentimentalism in Early Confucian Thought." In *Ethical Sentimentalism: New Perspectives*. Ed. Remy Debes and Karsten R. Stueber. Cambridge: Cambridge University Press, 2017, 230–249.
Wong, Roderick. *Motivation: A Biobehavioural Approach*. Cambridge: Cambridge University Press, 2000.
Xunzi. *Xunzi: The Complete Text*. Trans. Eric Hutton. Princeton, NJ: Princeton University Press, 2014.
Yong, Ed. "Self-Control Is Just Empathy with Your Future Self." *The Atlantic* (December 6, 2016). www.theatlantic.com/science/archive/2016/12/self-control-is-just-empathy-with-a-future-you/509726/ (accessed September 5, 2020).
Zaki, Jamil, and Kevin Ochsner. "The Cognitive Neuroscience of Sharing and Understanding Others' Emotions." In *Empathy: From Bench to Bedside*. Ed. Jean Decety. Cambridge, MA: MIT Press, 2012, 207–226.
Zamir, Tzachi. *Double Vision: Moral Philosophy and Shakespearean Drama*. Princeton, NJ: Princeton University Press, 2006.
Zeami Motokiyo. *Atsumori*. Trans. Karen Brazell. In *Traditional Japanese Theater: An Anthology of Plays*. Ed. Karen Brazell. New York: Columbia University Press, 1998, 128–142.
Zembylas, Michalinos. "Pedagogies of Strategic Empathy: Navigating through the Complexities of Anti-Racism in Higher Education." *Teaching in Higher Education* 17.2 (2012): 113–125.
*The Politics of Trauma in Education*. New York: Palgrave, 2008.
Zhang, Dainian. *Key Concepts in Chinese Philosophy*. Trans. Edmund Ryden. New Haven, CT: Yale University Press, 2003.
Zong-Qi Cai. "Introduction." In *How to Read Chinese Poetry in Context: Poetic Culture from Antiquity through the Tang*. Ed. Zong-Qi Cai. New York: Columbia University Press, 2018, 1–10.

# Index

abandonment, in family separation and reunion genre, 124
action
 emotions and outcomes, 66–67
 empathy and outcomes, 226–227
 ethical orientation and, 38–39, 64–69
 readiness in emotion systems and, 155
 self-interest and, 19
 traumatic memories and, 153–154
activation of emotions, 151–152
adaptation. *See also* evolution
 of ethics, 81–86
Aeschylus, 73–74, 104
aesthetic norms, ethics and, 16
affect as information thesis, 155–157
*Affective Narratology: The Emotional Structure of Stories* (Hogan), 69, 71–72
affective science
 ethics and, 64–69
 interpersonal stance and, 165
 reason *vs.* emotion in, 155–158
affect theory
 emotion and, 151–152
 empathy and, 160–162
 ethics and, 64–69
African Americans
 in *Angels in America* (Kushner), 252–254
 empathy blocking and, 203–204
*Against Empathy* (Bloom), 211–219
agency
 ethical orientation and, 38–39
AIDS crisis, empathy and, 243–244
Alford, John, 56
allegory, in *The Zhao Orphan*, 103

All-India Progressive Writers Association (AIPWA), 56, 129–131
allocentrism
 in *Angels in America* (Kushner), 254–257
 emotion contagion and, 169–170
 empathy and, 6
 Golden Rule and, 19–20
 out-group dynamics and, 19n.7
 self-interest and, 18–19
 in Shakespeare's *Julius Caesar*, 45–46
 valence parameter and, 27–29
*All's Well That Ends Well* (Shakespeare), as seduction/sexual violation genre, 75, 119–124
altruism
 biological definition of, 19n.6
 empathy and, 171–172
 self-interest and, 18–19
*American Literature* (Hogan), 125
*Analects (Lún Yǔ)* (Confucius)
 governance in, 106
 moral theory in, 63–64
 shù (Confucian empathy) in, 19–20
*Angels in America* (Kushner)
 attachment betrayal and trust in, 249–252
 critical empathy in, 7, 242–259
 endogenous and exogenous empathy in, 245–248
 guilt and shame in, 254–257
 out-grouping in, 252–254
anger
 empathy and, 168–169, 210–211, 236
 moral out-grouping and, 262–263

## Index

animals, emotions in, 166–168
anti-Semitism
   in *Angels in America*, 252–254
   moral out-grouping and, 260–261
   *Nosferatu* and, 134–146
*Antony and Cleopatra* (Shakespeare), 40–43
appraisal, emotion elicitation and, 152–155
Arendt, Hannah, 173
arousal
   emotion and, 150–158
   of emotions, 151–152
*Atsumori* (Zeam), 147–148
attachment
   betrayal of, critical empathy and, 249–252, 257–259
   in criminal investigation genre, 104
   in family separation and reunion genre, 124–131
   to non-kin, 83
   in revenge genre, 99–103
   in romantic genre, 74–75, 115–119
   in sacrificial genre, 132
attention orientation, emotion systems and, 155
Atwood, Margaret, 124
audience, empathy and, 199–200
Australian Aborigines, family separation and reunion literature and, 126–129
autonomy, free will and, 265–266
availability heuristic, false empathy and, 229
aversion, simulation and, 200–202
AZT (AIDS drug), in *Angels in America*, 257–259

Baker, Robert, 4–5
Banks, Antoine, 210–211
Barrett, Justin, 16–17
Batson, C. Daniel, 125–126, 171–172, 197–198
Bechara, Antoine, 155–157
behavior, free will and, 265n.2
Berkowitz, Leonard, 262–263

*Bhagavad Gītā* (Song of God)
   ethics in, 95–98
   heroic genre and, 94–99
bias
   critical empathy and, 257–259
   empathy and, 207–211
Black Lives Matter (BLM), 227–228n.8
Blair, Karina, 221–222
Blair, Robert, 221–222
blame, limits of ethics and, 260–270
Bloom, Paul
   on blocking empathy, 203–204
   on compassion and care *vs.* empathy, 222–228
   critique of empathy by, 7, 211–219
   on disgust and empathy, 197–198
   failed empathy and, 232–235
bodily experience, emotional elicitation and, 154
*Book of Lord Shang*, 111–112
*The Book of Vampires*, 138–139
Boyer, Pascal, 166–168
bravery, in revenge genre, 100
Brecht, Bertolt, 202–204
Breithaupt, Fritz, 237–240
Brewer, Marilynn, 20–21
Brinton, Howard, 19–20
Brontë, Charlotte, 183
Buchanan, Allen, 85
Buddhism
   Chinese Legalism and, 111–112
   empathy, 226
   spiritual realization genre and, 146–148
Buonomano, Dean, 264–265
Butler, Susan, 20n.9

cancel culture, politics and, 80–81
Caracciolo, Marco, 154
care, ethics of, 30
   empathy and, 222–228
   family separation and reunion genre, 76–77, 124–131
   Haidt's foundation of, 78–80
Carlin, Michael, 20n.9

caste dharma (varṇadharma), 53–54, 95–98
categorization
  ethics and, 4–5
  narrative and, 70
  research on, 9–11
  varieties of, 4–5
celebrity, Breithaupt on empathy and, 240
Cerce, Stephanie, 270
character development, ethics in literature and, 13–17
Cheng, Anne, 101
children, obligatory and non-obligatory benefits for, 26–27
*The Children's Hour* (Hellman), 199–200
China
  criminal investigation narratives in, 73–74, 105
  moral theory in, 63–64
Chinese Legalism, 63–64, 106–115
Chomsky, Noam, 9–10n.1, 32, 86n.14
Christian theology, despair in, 232–233
Christov-Moore, Leonardo, 223
Churchland, Patricia, 52n.1, 56, 83, 151–152
*Classic of Poetry (Shījīng)* (Confucius), 1
*The Classic of Rites* (Lǐjì), 101–103
cognition
  emotions and, 67, 89–92
  empathy and, 207–219
  simulation and, 184–186
cognitive empathy, 159–160, 180
cognitive motivations, reason and emotions, 157n.1
Cohn, Roy, 243–244, 249
collateral damage, in criminal investigation genre, 104
colonialism, in family separation and reunion genre, 126–131
*A Comedy of Errors* (Shakespeare), 124–125
communality, cultural perspectives on, 58–64
comparative literature, narrative and, 71–72

compassion, empathy and, 172–173, 222–228
compassionate helping, group selection and, 83
compassion porn, empathy and, 198–199
concept, ethics and, 4–5
concern, ethics and, 221
Confucianism (Rú Xué), 63–64, 105–107
  in *Selling Rice in Chenzhou*, 107–115
Confucius (Kǒngzǐ)
  on empathy, 6–7
  on ethics, 1, 19–20
  filial piety in philosophy of, 101–103
  on governance, 106
  on moral theory, 63–64
conscience, ambiguity of terminology on, 52n.1
consequentialism, method parameter and, 31–33, 38–39
conservatism
  anti-change *vs.* right-wing conservatism, 57–58
  heroic genre and, 80–81
  liberal/conservative opposition and, 55–58
  moral foundations in, 58–64
  narrative prototypes and, 81
  vindictive protectiveness in, 227–228n.8
corrective inferences, false empathy and, 229–231
criminal investigation genre, 73–74
  Chinese legalism and, 107–115
  in Chinese literature, 104–115
  cross-cultural perspectives and, 91
  role of state in, 76–77
critical empathy, 7
  in *Angels in America* (Kushner), 242–259
  attachment betrayal and trust and, 249–252
critical ethics, in Shakespeare's *Julius Caesar*, 43–50
critical period experiences, elicitation of emotions and, 153

# Index

cross-cultural perspectives
  cognition and emotions and, 89–92
  correspondence bias in, 60–61
  dominant precepts and, 54–55
  ethics and literature and, 3–5
  evolution of ethics and, 84–85
  Haidt's moral foundations and, 86–88
  moral thought and action, 16–17
Cruikshank, Mary, 218–219
cultural clichés, consequences of, 61n.4
cultural differences
  empathy and, 178–180
  views of war and peace and, 53–54
*The Culture of Conformism* (Hogan), 138–139, 260–261

Damasio, Antonio, 155–157
*Dark Sides of Empathy* (Breithaupt), 237–240
Debes, Remy, 161
Dehaene, Stanislas, 264–265
Delgado, Richard, 205–207
deontological evaluation
  ethics in literature and, 13–17
  method parameter and, 30–35
descriptive ethics
  complications of, 11–12
  definitions of, 9–11
  focus of, 36–39
  literature and, 2
despair
  empty empathy and, 234–235
  failed empathy and, 232–235
deterrence, free will and, 266n.3
deviance of homosexuality, empathy and, 243–244
de Waal, Frans, 19n.6, 82
dharma (ethical duty)
  categories of, 95–98
  varṇadharma (caste dharma), 53–54
disgust
  in *All's Well That Ends Well* (Shakespeare), 119–124
  in *Angels in America* (Kushner), 254–257
  emotion systems and, 69–70, 76–77, 151–153
  empathy and, 197–198, 213n.5, 243
  ethics and, 43–50, 85
  fear and, 47–48, 57
  hedonic restriction and, 27–29
  hypnotic suggestion and, 65–66
  in *Midsummer Night's Dream*, 194–195
  morality and, 14–15
  in *Nectar in a Sieve*, 129–131
  neurological specificity of, 150–151
  in *Nosferatu*, 131–145
  toward out-groups, 167–168
  politics and, 81
  purity as response to, 79
  in sacrificial narratives, 132
  self-disgust, 132
  in *Selling Rice in Chenzhou*, 104–115
*The Doctrine of Fascism* (Mussolini and Gentile), 25
*Do the Right Thing* (Lee), 203–204
Douglass, Frederick, 125
Dovidio, John, 72–73, 166–168, 232
downward comparisons, well-being and, 22–23
Doyle, Kerrie, 218–219
Durkheim, Emile, 19–20
dynastic political structure, in *The Zhao Orphan*, 103

ecology, ethics of, 220n.7
Edwards, Alison, 169–170
egocentric self-interest
  emotion contagion and, 169–170
  empathy and, 224
  morality and, 262
  normative ethics and, 6
  in Shakespeare's *Julius Caesar*, 16–17
Eisenberg, Nancy, 169–170
eliciting conditions
  emotions and, 66–67, 152–155
  empathy and, 180
embodied theory of emotion, 154
emotional empathy, 160
emotion contagion, empathy and, 169–170

emotions
- cognition and, 67, 89–92
- components of, 152–155
- in criminal investigation genre, 104–105
- eliciting conditions, 152–155
- ethics and, 69–70, 86–88, 211–219
- genres and, 69–78
- liberal/conservative opposition and systems of, 57
- literature and, 6–7
- motivation and, 36–39
- normative ethics and, 150–158
- reason and, 155–158
- shame and, 257–259
- stories and, 64–69
- systems approach to, 150–158
- valence and, 27–29

empathetic perspective shifting (Goldie), 174–178
empathic accuracy, 162
empathic concern and understanding, 169n.8, 195–196
empathy
- action outcomes and, 226–227
- advocacy of, 212–214
- alienation/estrangement effect and, 202–204
- altruism and, 171–172
- attachment and, 74–75
- blocking of, 203–204
- Bloom's critique of, 211–219
- Breithaupt's critique of, 237–240
- care ethics and, 222–228
- cognitive science and, 207–219
- compassion and, 172–173, 198–199, 222–228
- critical empathy, 7, 242–259
- critiques of, 7
- defined, 159
- emotion contagion and, 169–170
- empty empathy, 234–235
- endogenous empathy, 245–248
- ethical motivation and, 219–222
- ethics in literature and, 2–3, 6–7
- evolution and, 37n.15, 82–83, 170n.9
- exogenous empathy, 245–248
- failed empathy, 232–237
- false empathy, 205–207, 228–237
- in family separation and reunion genre, 127–128
- Goldie's discussion of, 174–178
- guilt and, 221–222
- humanists vs., 198–204
- identity and, 165–169
- innumeracy in, 33–34, 217–218
- in *A Midsummer Night's Dream* (Shakespeare), 183, 186–195
- misguided advocacy for, 33–34
- normative ethics and, 159–180
- paradox of tragedy and, 200–202
- paternalism and, 127–128
- personal distress and, 170–171
- physicians and, 217–218
- as political good, 197–198
- practice of, 163–164
- Prinz's critique of, 207–211
- promiscuity of, 84–85
- proneness to, 56–57
- scope of, political morality and, 58
- shù (Confucian empathy), 19–20
- in "Táo Yāo" (poem), 178–180
- Vorauer's perspective on, 176–177
- voyeurism and, 199–200

empathy–altruism hypothesis, 197–198
*Empathy and the Novel* (Keen), 3n.1
emplotment, narrative structure and, 87–88
empowerment, family separation and reunion literature and, 126–129
empty empathy, 234–235
enactivism, 182–184
endogenous empathy, defined, 245–248
epic theater, empathy and, 202–204
epilogue of suffering
- heroic genre and, 92–99
- in heroic narrative, 78–80
- story universals and, 72–73, 78

ethics. *See also* morality
- academic/nonacademic perspectives on, 14–15
- affects and stories and, 64–69

## Index

in *Bhagavad Gītā*, 95–98
of care, 30
character development and, 13–17
comparative literature contributions to, 71–72
definitions of, 4–5, 9–11, 17–21
emotions and, 69–70, 76–77, 86–88
empathy and, 86–88, 207–219
evolution of, 81–86
fundamental ethical orientation, 21–36
limits of, 260–270
literature and, 1–8, 216–217
method parameter and, 23, 29–35, 38–39
in *A Midsummer Night's Dream* (Shakespeare), 187n.1
motivation and empathy, 219–222
as prototype concept, 17–21
prototypes of, 5
revolution and, 40–43
scope parameter of, 22–23
spontaneous response and, 13–14
story universals and, 77
valence parameter and, 23, 27–29, 37–38
virtue signaling and, 262
ethnicity, in *Angels in America* (Kushner), 252–254
Euripides, 97–98
evolution. *See also* adaptation
ethics and, 81–88
mechanisms of emotion and, 154–155
exemplar-defined categorization
defined, 9–11
ethics and, 4–5
exogenous empathy, defined, 245–248
expressive-communicative outcomes, emotion systems and, 155

Fagan, Tyler, 266n.3
failed empathy, 232–237
despair and, 232–235
habituation and, 235–237
fairness, in narrative prototypes, 79–80
false empathy, 205–207, 228–237

availability heuristic, 229
Breithaupt on, 239–240
false premises, empathy and, 229–231
family separation and reunion genre, 75
care ethics and, 76–77
parent–child separation and, 124
Fascism
ethics and, 21–22
scope parameter and, 25
Feather, Jennifer, 49n.1
Feshbach, Norma Deitch, 198n.2
Feshbach, Seymour, 198n.2
fiction, paradox of, 200–202
filial piety, in romantic genre, 115–119
Florescu, Radu, 135–136
folk physics, biology and psychology, 184–186
*Follow the Rabbit-Proof Fence* (Garimara), 126–129
forgiveness, in *Angels in America* (Kushner), 257–259
Foucault, Michel, 86n.14
on ethics, 13–14
foundationalism
ethics and, 15
fairness and, 79–80
free will
limits of ethics and, 260–270
moral blame and, 263–264
quantum indeterminacy and, 264–265
Fried, Paul, 189n.3
Frijda, Niko, 235–236
Fu, Yu-Wen, 126n.6
fundamental ethical orientation, 9–11, 21–36
scope parameter, 22–23
in Shakespeare's *Julius Caesar*, 43–50
future discounting, reason and emotion and, 157–158

Gaertner, Samuel, 232
Galeen, Henrik, 134–146
Gallese, Vittorio, 154, 160
Gandhi, Mahatma, 31–32
*Garam Hawa* (film), 234
Garimara, Nugi, 126–129

Geertz, Clifford, 174
gender norms
  in *A Midsummer Night's Dream* (Shakespeare), 186–195
  in sexual violation genre, 75
  in Shakespeare's *Julius Caesar*, 48
genetics, group selection and, 83–84n.12
genres. *See also* specific genres (e.g., romantic genre)
  cross-cultural perspectives and, 89–92
  emotions and, 69–78
  individual preferences in, 78
  norms and, 72
  as story structures, 67–69
Gentile, Giovanni, 25, 260–261
German nationalism, *Nosferatu* and, 136–146
Gill, Michael, 270
Golden Rule, ethics and, 19–20
Goldie, Peter, 20n.9, 174–178
*The Golem*, 137
Grady, Hugh, 49n.1
grand narratives (Haidt), 67–69
*The Great Revenge of the Zhao Orphan*, 101–103, 111–112
Greenspan, Patricia, 20–21, 53, 82
group polarization, empathy and, 239–240
Guan Hanqing, 118–119
*Guanzi*, 111–112
Guerra, Michele, 154
guilt
  in *Angels in America* (Kushner), 254–257
  empathy and, 221–222
  ethics and, 221
  as moral adaptation, 82–84
  in sacrificial narrative, 132
Guo, Christine, 162n.4

habituation, failed empathy and, 235–237
Hadfield, Andrew David, 42
Haidt, Jonathan
  on cross-cultural precepts, 16–17, 52–53, 86
  on emotions, 64–69
  empathy research, 212
  on ethics, 14–15, 19–20
  on evolution of ethics, 82
  on hypnotic suggestion, 65–66
  on moral foundations and limits of liberalism, 58–64, 86
  narrative prototypes and morality of, 78–80, 147–148
  on political morality, 55, 80–86
  on reasoning, 84–85
  vindictive protectiveness of, 227–228
  on virtue signaling, 262–263
Hakemulder, Frank, 216–217
Halpern, Jodi, 218–219
Hamington, Maurice, 30n.23
*Hamlet* (Shakespeare)
  as revenge narrative, 99–103
  as seduction/sexual violation genre, 122–124
*The Handmaid's Tale* (Atwood), 62, 124
Hán Fēizǐ, 106, 108
harm
  in criminal investigation genre, 104
  in narrative prototypes, 78–80
  purity concerns and, 58–64
  in revenge genre, 102
Hauser, Marc, 9–10n.1
Hebl, Michelle, 72–73, 166–168
hedonic restriction
  asymmetry in habituation, 235–236
  valence and, 27–29
Hellman, Lillian, 199–200
Henrich, Joseph, 61n.4
heroic genre
  cross-cultural perspectives and, 91
  epilogue of suffering in, 78–80
  ethical orientation in, 51
  identity group and, 72–73
  in-group dynamics and, 76–77
  *Mahābhārata* as, 94–99
  9/11 attacks and, 86–87
  politics and, 80–81
  revenge genre compared with, 99–100, 103
  revolution and ethics and, 40–43

## Index

threat-defense sequence in, 92–99
usurpation-restoration sequence in, 92–99
Hibbing, John, 55–58
hierarchical organization of groups, in heroic genre, 72–73
Hindu ethical theory, scope parameter in, 27
Hirstein, William, 266n.3
historical events, parametric categorization of, 40–43
Hoffman, Aaron, 4–5
Hoffman, Martin, 171–172, 207–211
homosexuality
  in *Angels in America* (Kushner), 254–257
  deviant characterization of, 243–244
honor cultures, 62
hostility attribution bias, 168–169
  in *Angels in America*, 252–254
*The Hound of the Baskervilles* (Doyle), 105
Huerta, Snjezana, 169–170
humanism, empathy *vs.*, 198–204
humanitarian (military) intervention, consequentialist perspective on, 32
human nature
  in Chinese philosophy, 106
  emotions and, 166–168
Hume, David, 212–214
humor, in *Angels in America*, 244
Hungerford, Catherine, 218–219
hypnotic suggestion, Haidt's study of, 65–66
hypocrisy, in Shakespeare's *Julius Caesar*, 46–47, 51

Iacoboni, Marco, 223
Ickes, William, 168n.7, 228–229
ideals
  emotion systems and, 86–88
  ethics and, 76–77
identity
  empathy and, 165–169
  group polarization and, 239–240
  moralization of, 261
  moral out-grouping and, 261

*Imagining Kashmir* (Hogan), 153–154
implicit bias, reduction of, 232
incomplete material reductionism, free will and, 264, 266–267
India
  concepts of war and peace in, 53–54
  cultural identity, 61–62
  family ethics in, 64
  family separation and reunion genre in, 129–131
  liberal/conservative opposition in, 56, 60–61
  marriage customs and, 115–119
  moral theory in, 63–64
  Muslim plight in, 234
individualistic cultures, moral values in, 61–62
individual revenge, in revenge genre, 102
inference
  empathy and, 163–164
  failed empathy and, 232–237
  false empathy and, 229–231
information
  emotion and, 155–158
  reason and, 157–158
in-group
  in criminal investigation genre, 105–106
  empathy and, 165–166, 207–211
  family separation and reunion genre, 125
  in heroic genre, 72–73, 76–77, 92–99
  in *Mahābhārata*, 94–99
  scope parameter and, 22–23
  universalism and, 20–21
in-group/out-group divisions, proneness to empathy and, 56–57
inhibition of emotions, 151–152
in-his-shoes perspective shifting (Goldie), 174–178
intensity, empathy and, 162–163
interpersonal stance
  in *Angels in America* (Kushner), 244–245, 257–259

interpersonal stance (cont.)
   empathy and, 165–168, 202
   failed empathy and, 232–237
   racism and, 168–169
interracial understanding, false
   empathy and, 205–207

Jackson, Liz, 211n.4
*Jane Eyre* (Brontë), 183
Jewish identity, in *Nosferatu*, 134–146
Judeo-Christian fall narrative, 132
*Jud Süß* (film), 144–146
*Julius Caesar* (Shakespeare)
   ambiguity of legitimacy in, 40–43
   critical ethics in, 43–50
   ethical analysis of, 5, 49n.1, 51
   as heroic story, 93–94
   revenge in, 73n.5
   revolution and ethics in, 40–43
   tacit ethical concerns in, 40
justice
   Foucault on, 86n.14
   pro-violence approach to, 74n.7

Kahneman, Daniel, 229
Kant, Immanuel, 4–5
   empathy and works of, 227–228
   on ethics, 15, 19–20
   method parameter and deontology of, 30–31, 33–35
   on morality, 63
Kaplan, Ann, 234–237
karmic retribution, Chinese Legalism and, 111–112
*karuṇarasa*, 129–131
Kauppinen, Antti, 212–214
Keen, Suzanne, 3n.1, 205–207
Kelly, Daniel, 161–162, 213n.5
kin selection, empathy and, 83
Klein, Dorothee, 126n.6
Kosslyn, Stephen, 264–265
kṣatriyadharma (warrior/ruler), heroic genre and, 95–98
Kushner, Tony, 7, 242–259

Landy, Joshua, 203–204, 216–217
laws and institutions
   cultural clichés and, 61n.4
   free will and, 266n.3
Lee, Spike, 203–204
Legge, James, 180
legitimacy, ambiguity of, in *Julius Caesar* (Shakespeare), 40–43
Levy, Neil, 155–157
liberal/conservative opposition, analysis of, 55–58
liberalism
   moral foundations and limits of, 58–64
   narrative prototypes and, 81
   as obstacle to unity, 61–62
   romantic genre and, 80–81
   universalism and, 67–69
libertarian paternalism, 209–211
liberty
   in narrative prototypes, 79
   in seduction/sexual violation genre, 119–124
Lǐ Sī, 106
literature
   ethics and, 1–8, 216–217
   politics and progressive literature, 233–234
   tacit ethical concerns in, 40
Liu, Jung-en, 103
Lovrod, Marie, 129n.17
loyalty
   in narrative prototypes, 79
   in revenge genre, 100
Lueders, Bill, 236
Lukianoff, Greg, 227–228, 262–263

MacIntyre, Alasdair, 54n.2
Macintyre, Stuart, 127–128
Mackie, Diane, 270
*Mahābhārata*, heroic emplotment in, 94–99
Maitner, Angela, 167–168
mānavdharma (human dharma), 95–98
Manvell, Roger, 136–137

Markandaya, Kamala, 125–126, 129–131, 234
marriage customs
  in China, 178–180
  in India, 115–119
  in *A Midsummer Night's Dream* (Shakespeare), 186–195
  in seduction/sexual violation genre, 119–124
Marsh, Abigail, 161–162
Masters, Anthony, 135–136
material reductionism, 264
  subjectivity and, 267–268
Matravers, Derek, 6–7, 159n.2, 160, 175, 231
McFarland, Sam, 232
McNally, Raymond, 135–136
McRae, Emily, 226
*Measure for Measure* (Shakespeare), 193
mechanisms of emotion, adaptive function of, 154–155
medicine, empathy and, 217–218, 224–225
medieval Muslim literary theory, ethics in, 1
*Mein Kampf* (Hitler), 136–138
memes, ethics and, 84–85n.13
memories, emotions and, 153–154
Mencius (Mèngzǐ)
  Chinese Legalism and, 106–107
  on empathy, 113
  on governance, 108
  on human goodness, 106
  on morality, 63–64
mental illness, in *Nosferatu*, 141
mental state attribution system, empathy and, 164–165n.5
metaethics, narrative genres and, 86–87
method parameter, ethical orientation and, 23, 29–35, 38–39
#MeToo movement, proportionality and, 58–64
*A Midsummer Night's Dream* (Shakespeare), 6–7
  empathy in, 183, 186–195
  romantic genre and, 115–119

Milgram, Stanley, 173
Mill, John Stuart, on morality, 63
Miller, Barbara Stoler, 94
*The Mind and Its Stories: Narrative Universals and Human Emotion* (Hogan), 3–5, 69, 71–72, 216–217
mirror neuron theory, empathy and, 160–162
misinformation, failed empathy and, 232–237
modulation of emotions, 151–152
morality. *See also* ethics
  empathy and, 209–211
  limits of ethics and, 260–270
  limits of liberalism and, 58–64
  method parameter and, 29–35
  in seduction/sexual violation genre, 119–124
Morton, Adam, 173, 261
*The Mother-in-Law* (Terence), 75
motivation
  action and, 66–67
  emotion and, 36–39, 150–158
  empathy and, 207–211, 219–222
  ethics and, 69–70
  liberal/conservative opposition and, 58
Mòzǐ, 63–64
"Murders in the Rue Morgue" (Poe), 105
Murnau, Friedrich Wilhelm, 5, 133
Murphy, Gregory, 4–5
Muslim literature, ethics in, 4–5
Mussolini, Benito, 25, 260–261

Nagel, Thomas, 267n.5
narrative prototypes, 64–69, 71, 78–80. *See also* genres *and* prototypical stories
  comparative literature and, 71–72
  emotions and, 67–69
  ethics in literature and, 2–3, 5
  fairness in prototypes of, 79–80
  goals in, 69–70
  morality and, 133–134
  particularity and generality, 70
  politics and evolution and, 80–86

## Index

narrative prototypes (cont.)
  prototypes of, 71, 78–80
  stories and, 69
nationalism, in *Nosferatu*, 136–146
national literature, ethics and, 71–72
*Native Son* (Wright), 203–204
*Nāṭya Śāstra* (Treatise on Drama), 1
Naziism
  consequentialist perspective on, 31, 217–218
  nonviolent response to, 31–32
  *Nosferatu* in context of, 133–146
  Nuremburg rallies, 62
*Nectar in a Sieve* (Markandaya), 129–131, 234
negativity bias in right-wing politics, analysis of, 55–58
neo-group selection, compassionate helping and, 83
neurological specificity, emotions and, 150–151
neutrality, ethics and, 84–85, 89–92
Nickerson, Raymond, 20n.9
Nienhauser, William, 180
9/11 attacks, moral adaptation, 86–87
non-obligatory benefits, scope of ethics and, 26–27
nontraumatic experiences, emotions and, 153–154
normative ethics
  in *Angels in America* (Kushner), 257–259
  criteria for, 6
  emotions and, 150–158
  empathy and, 159–180
  focus of, 36–39
  free will and, 268–270
  fundamental orientation and, 25n.11
  literature and, 2
  moral out-grouping and, 263–264
normative outcomes, empathy and, 209–211
norms, genres and, 72
*Nosferatu, a Symphony of Horror* (film), 5
  as sacrificial narrative, 131–145
Nussbaum, Martha

on disgust, 197
on ethical rights, 13–17, 30
on honor cultures, 62
literature and ethics and, 1
on punishment and incarceration, 269–270

Occam's razor, 84–85n.13
Ochsner, Kevin, 37n.15, 164–165n.5
*Oresteia* (Aeschylus), 73–74, 104
outcomes, method parameter and, 30
out-groups
  allocentrism and, 19n.7
  in *Angels in America* (Kushner), 252–254
  in criminal investigation genre, 105–106
  empathy and, 56–57, 166–168, 207–211, 216–217, 227–228
  ethics and, 260–261
  failed empathy and, 232
  in heroic genre, 92–99
  in *Mahābhārata*, 94–99
  moral out-grouping and, 260–270

pain, empathy and, 225–226
Paluck, Elizabeth, 216–217
paradox of fiction, 200–202
paradox of tragedy, empathy and, 200–202
parameter setting
  deliberative decision making and, 52–55
  ethics and, 40–43
  genre preferences and, 78
  in *Julius Caesar* (Shakespeare), 43–50
  method parameter, 23, 29–35, 38–39
  scope parameter, 22–27, 37
  simulation, 184–186
  valence parameter, 23, 27–29, 37–38
Parkinson, Brian, 165n.6, 224–225
paternalism, in family separation and reunion genre, 127–128
patriarchy, in *A Midsummer Night's Dream* (Shakespeare), 186–195
Paxton, Robert, 31

Pearson, Adam, 232
*The Peony Pavilion* (Tang), 115–119
personal distress, empathy and, 170–171
*Personal Identity and Literature* (Hogan), 264, 266–267
phenomenological tone/feeling, emotion systems and, 155
physicians, empathy and, 217–218, 224–225
physiological outcomes, emotion systems and, 155
Pinker, Steven, 84–85, 221–222, 260
pity, empathy and, 173
plague, in *Nosferatu*, 136–146
Plato, on ethics and literature, 1, 3
Poe, Edgar Allan, 105
police dramas, in comparative literature, 73–74
policy preferences, of liberals and conservatives, 58–64
politics
 emotions and, 55–64
 empathy and, 197–198, 203–204
 family separation and reunion genre and, 129–131
 narrative and, 55–64, 80–86
 negativity bias of right-wing views, 55–58
 progressive literature and, 233–234
poststructuralist theory, racism and, 126n.6
pride, in heroic genre, 92–99
Prinz, Jesse, 7, 207–211, 221–222, 236
problem comedies, 75
processing strategies
 emotion systems and, 155
 empathy and errors in, 229–231
prodigal son parable (Luke 15:11–32), 124–125
proportionality, conservatives linked to, 58–64
pro-social intentions, altruism and, 18n.5
prototypical stories. *See also* narrative prototypes *and* genres
 critical versions, 118
 cross-cultural perspectives and, 89–92
 emotions and cognition and, 89–92
 ethics and, 4–5, 17–21, 24
 heroic story prototype, 40–43
prudence
 empathy and, 239
 ethics and, 21
punishment
 Chinese Legalism and, 106–107
 crime drama rationalization of, 73–74
 in criminal investigation genre, 104
 deterrence and, 74n.8
 empathy and, 210–211
 moral responsibility and, 269–270
 in sacrificial genre, 75–76
purity
 harm and impact of, 58–64
 in narrative prototypes, 79
 in seduction/sexual violation genre, 119–124
"Purloined Letter" (Poe), 105
putative altruism, 171–172

quantum indeterminacy, free will and, 264–265

racism
 in *Angels in America* (Kushner), 252–254
 empathy blocking and, 203–204
 failed empathy and, 232
 false empathy and, 205–207
 in family separation and reunion genre, 127–128
 interpersonal stance attribution, 168–169
reason, emotions and, 155–158
 ignoring evidence and, 158
*The Recognition of Śakuntalā* (*Abhijñānaśākuntalam*), 115–119
relativism, ethics and, 15
religion, in *Angels in America* (Kushner), 252–254
responsibility
 critique of, 266n.4
 free will and, 266n.3

restoration sequence
  in criminal investigation genre, 104
  in heroic genre, 92–99
  in *Julius Caesar* (Shakespeare), 93–94
  in *Mahābhārata*, 94–99
revenge genre
  cross-cultural perspectives and, 91
  *Hamlet* and, 99–103
  heroic genre compared with, 99–100, 103
  loyalty and social authority in, 76–77
  story universals and, 72–73
  *The Zhao Orphan* and, 101–103
revolution, ethics and, 40–43
reward dependency, romantic genre and, 115–119
Rhys, Jean, 183
Richeson, Jennifer, 72–73, 166–168
Ricoeur, Paul, 85
Riefenstahl, Leni, 62
right-wing political views
  negativity bias in, 55–58
  sanctity/purity linked to, 79n.9
Rogoff, Barbara, 53–54
Roman Republic, in Shakespeare's *Julius Caesar*, 42
romantic genre, 74–75
  care ethics and, 115–119
  cross-cultural perspectives and, 91
  loyalty in, 79
  *A Midsummer Night's Dream* (Shakespeare) as, 183, 186–195
  politics and, 80–81
*Romeo and Juliet* (Shakespeare), 40–43, 67–69
  family dynamics and, 115–119
Rosaldo, Renato, 60–61
Rosch, Eleanor, 24
Rosenberg, Ethel, 247–249
Rottschaefer, William, 18n.5, 82n.11
Rousselin, Alexandre, 73
rule-based categorization
  defined, 9–11
  ethics and, 4–5
Rú Xué. *See* Confucianism (Rú Xué)

sacrificial genre, 75–76
  cross-cultural perspectives and, 91
  group opposition in, 76–77
  liberalism and, 80–81
  *Nosferatu* as, 131–145
  sanctity/purity in, 79
sādhāraṇadharma (universal dharma), 95–98
sadism, Breithaupt on empathy and, 240
salience, empathy and, 207–211
sanctity, in narrative prototypes, 79
Sanskrit aesthetic theory, in *Nectar in a Sieve*, 129–131
Sapolsky, Robert
  on compassion, 83
  on ethics and spontaneous response, 13–14
  on failed empathy, 232–235
  on free will, 265, 269
  on in-group dynamics and empathy, 165–166
  on pain and empathy, 225–226
Scarry, Elaine, 237
Schachter, Stanley, 65–66
schadenfreude
  empathy and, 165–169
  sadism and, 240
Schivelbusch, Wolfgang, 136–137
Schramme, Thomas, 18
Schulz, Armin, 170n.9
scope parameter
  ethical orientation and, 22–27, 37
  ethics of ecology and, 220n.7
  in Shakespeare's *Julius Caesar*, 43–50
seduction/sexual violation genre, 75
  in *All's Well That Ends Well*, 119–124
  cross-cultural perspectives and, 91
  in *Hamlet*, 122–124
  sanctity/purity in, 79
  virtue and responsibility in, 76–77
self-care, Foucault's concept of, 86n.14
self-interest, ethics and, 17–21
self-loss, Breithaupt's concept of, 239
self-sacrifice, in *Nosferatu*, 143–144
*Selling Rice in Chenzhou*, 104–115
Serbia, NATO attack on, 32

# Index

sexual desire
  empathy and, 199–200
  in romantic genre, 74–75
  sadism and, 240
  in seduction/sexual violation genre, 119–124
Shakespeare, William
  ethics and literature and, 5
  tacit ethical concerns in work of, 40
shame
  in *Angels in America* (Kushner), 254–257
  in heroic genre, 92–99
  in sacrificial genre, 132
  vindictive protectiveness and, 227–228
Shang Yang, 111
shared representations system, empathy and, 164–165n.5
Shelton, J. Nicole, 72–73, 166–168
Shoemaker, David, 209, 228–229
shù (Confucian empathy), 19–20
Sifferd, Katrina, 266n.3
simulation
  Breithaupt's critique of empathy and, 237–240
  cognition and, 184–186
  empathizer–target relation and, 231
  false empathy and, 231
  fiction as, 200–202
simulation theory, empathy and, 164, 195–196
sin, sacrificial genre and purging of, 75–76
Singer, Jerome, 65–66
situated cognition, 182–184
Smith, Adam, 212–214
Smith, Eliot, 270
Smith, Kevin, 56
social appraisal, emotions and, 170n.10
social dynamics, liberal/conservative opposition and, 58
social obligations, scope of ethics and, 26
social revenge, in heroic genre, 102
sociocentric cultures, community concerns in, 61–62

socioeconomic class, in romantic genre, 74–75
spiritual realization genre
  characteristics of, 146–148
  *Mahābhārata* and, 95–98
spontaneous ethical response, deliberative ethics and, 52–55
*Stella Dallas* (film), 124
stereotypes
  empathy and, 166–168
  false empathy and, 229–231
  of liberals and conservatives, 58–64
  in *Nosferatu*, 134–146
stories
  emotions and, 67–69
  ethics and, 64–69, 77
  triggering of prototypes and, 133–134
Stowe, Harriet Beecher, 75, 125, 203–204
suffering, empathy and, 166–168
Sunstein, Cass, 209–211
swadharma (self/particular dharma), 27, 95–98
symhedonia, empathy and, 172, 178–180
sympathy, empathy and, 169n.8, 172, 178–180

Ta, Vivian, 228–229
Tagore, Rabindranath, 61–62, 75, 125–126
Tangney, June, 221–222
"Táo Yāo" (poem), empathy in, 178–180
Terence, 75
Thaler, Richard, 209–211
theory of mind (ToM), 9–10n.1
  celebrity empathy and, 240
  empathy and, 159, 180
  evolution of ethics and, 81–86
  false empathy and, 228–229
  romantic genre and, 186–195
theory theory, empathy and, 164
thought experiments, method parameter and, 34
three strikes laws, proportionality in, 58–64
TimesUp, proportionality and, 58–64
Tomasello, Michael, 37n.15

Tracy, Jessica, 221–222
tragedy, paradox of, 200–202
transcendental freedom, free will and, 266–267
trauma culture
  empty empathy and, 234–235
  habituation and, 236
traumatic experiences
  emotions and, 153–154
  simulation and, 200–202
*Triumph of the Will* (documentary), 62
*Trojan Women* (Euripides), 97–98
trolley dilemma, 9–10n.1, 34
Trump, Donald, 262–263
trust, critical empathy and, 249–252

*Uncle Tom's Cabin* (Stowe), 75, 203–204
*Understanding Nationalism* (Hogan), 69, 80, 95, 117–118
United States, cross-cultural perspectives and morality in, 63–64
universalism
  in dominant precepts, 53–54
  ethics and, 20–21
usurpation sequence
  in heroic genre, 92–99
  in *Julius Caesar* (Shakespeare), 93–94
  in *Mahābhārata*, 94–99

valence parameter
  emotion and, 150–158
  empathy and, 161–162
  ethical orientation and, 23, 27–29, 37–38
  negative and positive emotions and, 172
vampire legends, sacrifice genre and, 135–136
varṇadharma (caste dharma), 53–54
*Verfremdunseffekt* (alienation/estrangement), 202–204
victims
  anger and seeking of, 262–263
  trauma culture representation of, 234–235
Vidyasagar, Chandra, 61–62

vindictive protectiveness
  empathy and, 227–228
  moral out-grouping and, 262–264
*vīrarasa* (heroic engagement), 93
virtue signaling
  moral out-grouping and, 263–264
  in political and ethical discourse, 262
Vitale, Alex, 73–74
voluntarism, family separation and reunion genre and, 126–129
Vorauer, Jacquie, 176–177, 197–198
voyeurism, empathy and, 199–200

Waller, Bruce, 265n.2, 269–270
Walton, Kendall, 231
war
  consequentialist perspective on, 31
  cultural differences in views of, 53–54
  in *Hamlet*, 100
  in *Mahābhārata*, 92–99
well-being, ethics and, 22–23
*What Literature Teaches Us about Emotion* (Hogan), 125–126
Wheatley, Thalia, 212
*Wide Sargasso Sea* (Rhys), 183
widowhood practices, cross-cultural perspectives on, 61–62
Wilde, Oscar, 260
witnessing to suffering, habituation and, 236–237
women, emotions of (in seduction/sexual violation genre), 119–124
Wright, Richard, 203–204

*Xiàojīng (Classic of Filial Piety)*, 25
Xúnzǐ, 106

Yama (mythic deity), 111–112

Zaki, Jamil, 37n.15, 164–165n.5
Zeami Motokiyo, 147–148
Zembylas, Michalinos, 198–199
*Zhao Pan'er Uses Seductive Wiles to Rescue a Sister Courtesan*, 118–119
*zhōng* (loyalty), 101–102

# STUDIES IN EMOTION AND SOCIAL INTERACTION

*Titles Published in the Second Series (continued from page ii)*

*Speaking from the Heart: Gender and the Social Meaning of Emotion,* by Stephanie A. Shields

*The Hidden Genius of Emotion: Lifespan Transformations of Personality,* by Carol Magai and Jeannette Haviland-Jones

*The Mind and Its Stories: Narrative Universals and Human Emotion,* by Patrick Colm Hogan

*Feelings and Emotions: The Amsterdam Symposium,* edited by Antony S. R. Manstead, Nico H. Frijda, and Agneta H. Fischer

*Collective Guilt: International Perspectives,* edited by Nyla R. Branscombe and Bertjan Doosje

*The Social Life of Emotions,* edited by Larissa Z. Tiedens and Colin Wayne Leach

*Emotions and Multilingualism,* by Aneta Pavlenko

*Group Dynamics and Emotional Expression,* edited by Ursula Hess and Pierre Philippot

*Stigmatization, Tolerance and Repair: An Integrative Psychological Analysis of Responses to Deviance,* by Anton J. M. Dijker and Willem Koomen

*The Self and Its Emotions,* by Kristján Kristjánsson

*Face-to-Face Communication over the Internet: Emotions in a Web of Culture, Language and Technology,* edited by Arvid Kappas and Nicole C. Krämer

*What Literature Teaches Us about Emotion,* by Patrick Colm Hogan

*Emotion: A Biosocial Synthesis,* by Ross Buck

*Emotional Mimicry in Social Context,* edited by Ursula Hess and Agneta Fischer

*The Interpersonal Dynamics of Emotion: Towards an Integrative Theory of Emotions as Social Information,* by Gerban A. van Kleef

*From Self to Social Relationships: An Essentially Relational Perspective on Social Motivation,* by Martijn van Zomeren

*The Aesthetics of Emotion: Up the Down Staircase of the Mind-Body,* by Gerald C. Cupchik

*The Expression of Emotion: Philosophical, Psychological and Legal Perspectives,* edited by Catharine Abell and Joel Smith

*Emotional Lives: Dramas of Identity in an Age of Mass Media*, by E. Doyle McCarthy

*Interpersonal Emotion Dynamics in Close Relationships*, edited by Ashley K. Randall and Dominik Schoebi

*Emotion and Narrative: Perspectives in Autobiographical Storytelling*, by Tilmann Habermas

*Foundations of Affective Social Learning: Conceptualizing the Social Transmission of Value*, edited by Daniel Dukes and Fabrice Clément

*Heart to Heart: How Your Emotions Affect Other People*, by Brian Parkinson

*Beyond Virtue: The Politics of Educating Emotions*, by Liz Jackson

*Literature and Moral Feeling: A Cognitive Poetics of Ethics, Narrative, and Empathy*, by Patrick Colm Hogan

Milton Keynes UK
Ingram Content Group UK Ltd.
UKHW020627081223
434004UK00008B/70